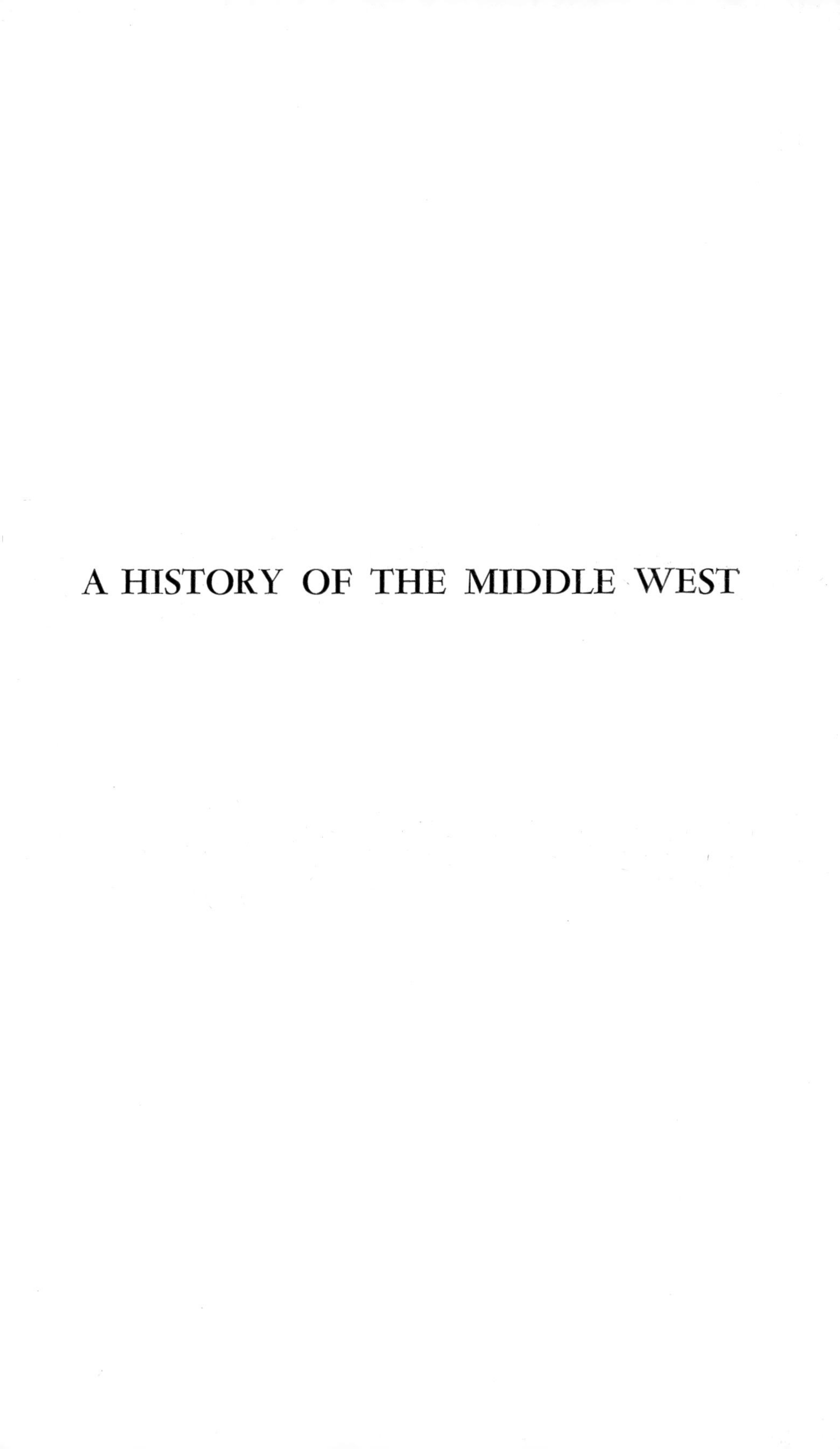

A HISTORY OF THE MIDDLE WEST

A HISTORY OF THE MIDDLE WEST

From the Beginning to 1970

by

KENNETH R. WALKER
Professor of History
Arkansas Polytechnic College

Library of Congress Catalog No. 72-84804

Book Design by
C. ARMITAGE HARPER
Printed in U.S.A.

Dedicated to Marylou, Elizabeth, and Mary and others who played a part in the preparation of this book.

PREFACE

The Midwest as described in the following pages includes the twelve North Central states. This group of states is one of the geographical groupings of the United States used by the national census bureau in its statistical publications. The state which is most questionable as to its being a part of this region is Missouri. Although there is little question as to Missouri's inclusion geographically, there is question historically because of the Compromise of 1820 and its accompanying slavery code which gave Missouri a more southern orientation than the other eleven states at least up to the Civil War.

The Midwest is also difficult to set off as a region. Nothing in its geography or history has ever uniquely isolated it, as was the case, for instance, with the South. It tends to merge into the surrounding states on the west, the south, the east, and the north. The people of the inner Midwest are somewhat distinctive, but their identities, too, seem to blend in with the characteristics of the people of the surrounding states as one approaches the boundaries of the North Central states. Even this distinctiveness in the inner core has become less pronounced as the United States has become increasingly tied together by transportation, communication, and mobility of population.

Although it is virtually impossible to generalize about a region or the attitudes and nature of its population, one can suggest a few tentative observations. Because of its inner location, its people have tended to be isolationist in foreign affairs. Its climate and soil have made the Midwest the breadbasket of the United States. Because of this agricultural dominance, the Midwest has played a major role in most of the major American agrarian movements as diverse as the Populists, the Grange, and the Farm Bureau. Because of its tremendous resources, its people are generally prosperous and optimistic. Although the climate is variable and at times uncomfortable, the area is healthful, invigorating, and vibrant.

While the Midwest has been extremely productive in many areas, it reached its peak influence in the pattern of national development during the period 1860 to 1900. This was certainly the heyday of its political power. As the United States filled out its boundaries, the Midwest became relatively less significant in its relationship to the ever-enlarging nation.

The bibliography which is consolidated at the end of the book is broken down into general works, books and articles that are related to each of the six chronological sections, and works that cover the major topics discussed throughout the book. To determine the total number of bibliographical sources relating to any particular topic, one needs to consult all three of these areas within the bibliography.

The time period and geographical area covered by this work are extensive. To write a definitive, comprehensive history of the Midwest would take thousands of pages and many volumes (*The History of the South* series, for example). Perhaps this volume on the history of the Midwest may serve as a small beginning toward that eventual goal. Hopefully, out of the unlimited facts and statistics that could be included in this work, the author has made representative choices of material that could be covered.

CONTENTS

ILLUSTRATIONS

PART I

SETTING, EXPLORATION, AND SETTLEMENT TO 1801

—1—

The Middle West as a Region

Topography

Few regions of the world, great or small, possess the excellent combination of physical and natural conditions found in the North Central portion of the United States.* The central part of the region had at one time in its geological history lain beneath the ocean, gradually lifting to form a level lowland comparable to the coastal plain of Virginia and the Carolinas. Over this area in a later period the great glaciers moved, leveling the land and leaving behind moraines to mark temporary or permanent stopping places.

Thus was created a central lowland or prairie plain which varies in elevation from a few hundred feet to over a thousand feet above sea level. Although essentially flat, this lowland has some areas that are definitely rolling.

Stretching out in all directions from this central lowland of the Middle West are transition zones which in general are less advantageous. In the north the outer margins fade away into the lake-studded, glaciated lowland of the upper Great Lakes with its sand dunes, moraines, swamps, lake plains, beach lines, and wandering boulders. The last ice cap began its retreat from this area about 35,000 years ago.

To the more romantic, the physical features of Wisconsin and Minnesota have been attributed to the exploits of that mythical woodsman, Paul Bunyan, who has been credited with scooping out Lake Superior with one hand in order to slake his thirst. Similarly,

*For purposes of this study, the North Central United States or the Midwest includes: Illinois, Indiana, Iowa, Kansas, Michigan, Minnesota, Missouri, Nebraska, North Dakota, Ohio, South Dakota, and Wisconsin.

Minnesota's thousands of lakes were allegedly made by the footsteps of Bunyan's choreboy as he lugged water to his master in the north country.

On the western edge of the Middle West are the Great Plains which slowly rise in elevation to 5,000 feet at their western extremity. Apparently formed by water erosion of the Rockies, they were built up by deposition to form a high-tilted, rolling plain. Colorful areas of this plain are the Bad Lands, once the site of a great lignite bed which burned, leaving the mounds and colors which have been improved with time and nature's help; and the Black Hills, a region of black-granite slopes containing some of the highest mountains east of the Rockies.*

In the southern Middle West, there is a transition from the plains to the unglaciated periphery of the hills of southern Ohio, Indiana, and Illinois and the Ozark Plateau south of the Missouri River. Eastward the transition zone terminates in the maturely-dissected terrain of the Appalachian Plateau. Breaking this boundary are the lacustrine plain of Lake Erie and the course of the Ohio River which flows westward into the Mississippi.

Soils

The Midwest exceeds any area of comparable size in the world in the areal extent of its highly productive soils. The superiority of these soils, especially in the western and central portions, has been due to several causes, of which one of the most important was glaciation in the pre-historic period. Not only did the ice, which advanced and retreated several times, cover the original eroded surface with a deep layer of rock waste and glacial debris, but it also imported and deposited excellent soil-building materials such as limestone, sandstone, and shale. The southernmost limit of the deposition of beneficial materials is marked by the Shelbyville moraine which runs through southern Illinois, Indiana, and Ohio and along the Missouri River. Varying deposits of loess added

*The highest point in the Black Hills is Harney Peak which extends 7,242 feet above sea level.

another mantle of good soil material from Illinois westward as did old lake beds of glacially impounded water south and west of Lakes Michigan and Erie.

In the eastern part of the Midwest, the soils have developed under hardwood-forest conditions and are catagorized as gray-brown, podzolic soils. Of all soils developed in the Western Hemisphere, these are the most productive. Southward from Lake Michigan into Illinois and westward into Iowa extend the black-prairie soils which have developed under deep-rooted, tall grasses that have deposited a tremendous amount of organic material in the soil. In western Iowa and eastern Nebraska are the chernozems or blackearths, with their rich store of humus and plant food, which have developed under a short grass cover. According to the U. S. Soil Conservation Service, the inner Midwest has a higher percentage of lands that call for a minimum of conservation practices than any other major agricultural section in the United States.

In all directions from this peak of productivity in the inner Midwest, the soil quality declines. Northward in the upper sections of Michigan, Wisconsin, and Minnesota, soils of lesser depth and quality, interspersed with stony and sandy areas, have developed on the uneven terrain. Southward in the lower portions of Ohio, Indiana, Illinois, and Missouri, the soil becomes less fertile partly because of lack of glaciation. Brown forest soils to the east terminate in the mature, dissected Appalachian highlands. At approximately the 99th meridian, drought reduces the productivity of the chernozem soils to the west.

Climate

Contributing to the soil-making process and to the overall fertility of the region is the variable moderate climate of the Middle West. A majority of the region enjoys 30 to 40 inches of precipitation annually; in the north it tapers off to 20 to 30 inches and in the western section it decreases to an inadequate 10 to 20 inches.

The majority of the Midwest is located in a moderate, humid-continental climate. On the west this humid-continental climate gives way to the semi-arid and on the south to the humid-subtropical. The frost-free season extends from 120 to 160 days in the north and west to 150 to 200 days in the south and east. Temperatures vary from an average of about 20 degrees in January to an average of around 70 degrees in July.

But more important the area is characterized by extremes. In the summer there are torrential thunderstorms, accompanied by vivid displays of lightning, blazing sunshine and humid heat. The climate varies from season to season and from year to year. The year 1816 was described as having no summer. In 1819 the winter was so mild that boats could reach Detroit in January. In Illinois in the winter of 1830-1831, the snow was six feet deep and the weather was so cold that stock died for lack of food, deer stood in their tracks and froze to death, and prairie chickens and quail, having alighted in the snow, could not fly out. In contrast in January of 1833, frogs were singing along the Sangamon River in Illinois.

Some springs have brought floods and others droughts. Droughts have been a perennial threat, especially on the drier, western margin of the Middle West where every decade brings new suffering and privation. South Dakota, for example, reported droughts in the 1860's, 1880's, the decade after 1910, and the 1930's. Icy winds in winter, steaming, clammy heat in summer, frost in May, and temperatures of 100 degrees in July leave much to be desired for the most comfortable living, but this kind of weather does produce bumper crops in large sections of the Midwest.

Vegetation

In addition to parent material and climate, the third factor which has contributed to the development of rich soils in the Middle West is vegetation. Actually many of the earlier visitors to the Middle West did not feel that the vegetation, or the land either, would ever be valuable for anyone or anything. In 1783 when Edward Tiffin was sent to the area to survey two-million acres of congressional military lands, he reported that the whole of Michigan Territory did not contain 1/100 of that amount in tillable land. He said that the land was low and wet and that it was covered with swamp grass, bush, and slime. James Monroe, three years later, described the Michigan and Wisconsin areas as being miserably poor. He viewed the land along the Mississippi and Illinois rivers as extensive plains which did not have, and probably never would have, a single living bush. In the period between 1800 and 1825, the part of the North Central region west of the Missouri River was labeled a barren land by explorers such as Meriwether Lewis and William Clark, Zebulon M. Pike, and Stephen H. Long. In his *Tours of the Prairies,* Washington Irving wrote: "It could be well named the Great American Desert. It spreads forth in undulating and treeless plains and desolate sandy wastes, wearisome to the eye from their extent and monotony." The label, the "Great American Desert," was utilized on the maps of the period to describe the area that became Kansas and Nebraska. The people of the East, having been convinced of its worthlessness, were willing in the 1820's and 30's to set this area aside as Indian land.

In reality the Middle West has lush and varied vegetation. Originally, with the exception of some small prairies and openings in the forests (apparently burned-over areas), broadleaf-deciduous trees prevailed in the eastern portion. In the area south of the Great Lakes, hardwoods such as elm, beech, hickory, oak, walnut, maple, and poplar are plentiful. To the north in the less hospitable sandy soils of northern Michigan, Wisconsin, and Minnesota grow broadleaf deciduous and needleleaf evergreen (pine, fir, spruce, and other conifers). To the west stretch treeless prairies, broken only by scattered forest growth along streams and on such isolated elevations as the Black Hills. Western Illinois, Iowa, northern Missouri, southern Minnesota, eastern Kansas, and eastern Nebraska are tall-grass country. Here much of the area was originally covered with wild flowers and grass six feet in height. Beyond the Missouri River the grass is shorter, dwindling to sage brush on the western fringe of the Midwest. Just as the vegetation has helped to determine the depth and richness of the soil in the North Central region, the soil and climate in turn have helped to determine whether conifer or deciduous forests or tall or short grass would prevail in a given area.

Water Resources

Of special importance to the Midwest is the drainage system which initially tied the region together and served as a potential water-transportation system. The Mississippi, Missouri, and Ohio rivers with their tributaries and the Great Lakes with their vast supply of fresh water have been of inestimable value to the region. Other major rivers of the Midwest include the Wabash, the Illinois, the Arkansas, the Platte, the Iowa, the Des Moines, the Red, the Minnesota, and the Wisconsin. But none of these waterways compares with the meandering Missouri whose course crosses or touches five states in the Midwest; or the Mississippi, the father of waters, which forms the boundary between the eastern and western sections of the North Central states; or the historic Ohio which serves as the southern boundary of the eastern Middle West.

However, this water resource has not been an unmixed blessing. The City of Marietta, for example, has had floodwater damage upon 40 occasions since 1873. Many other river cities in the Middle West could cite similar statistics.

Animal Life

With its abundant vegetable and water resources, the Middle West was initially a natural haven for wild life. In the eastern Middle West, passenger pigeons were so thick that they darkened the sky for hours as they went to and from feeding grounds. The deer that abounded from Missouri to Minnesota were mercilessly slaughtered by the first settlers. J. E. Scott, an early settler of

Scott City, Iowa, killed 100 deer in less than two months. By 1802 all of the buffalo or bison in Ohio had been killed, and by 1820 they had ceased to range east of the Mississippi River. With the exception of the more populated areas, bears, wolves, deer, geese, and turkeys were still plentiful in Ohio in 1817. The forests and streams on either side of the Mississippi River abounded in fur-bearing animals, especially beaver and fox. The lakes and streams were full of fish including trout, bass, pike, and perch. The forests and streams also contained innumerable insects and reptiles such as flies, mosquitoes, spiders, and snakes. Further west on the grassy plains the prairie chicken, grouse, migratory waterfowl, songbirds, donkey-eared jack-rabbits, coyotes, buffalo, antelope, mule deer, kit foxes, ground squirrels, and prairie dogs were found in abundance. At the same time that some animal life like insects and reptiles were a source of irritation, disease, and death, other animal life furnished much of the food for the Indians and first settlers in the region.

Why the Middle West Became a Region

Partly because of the similarity of its basic physical and cultural features, the Middle West developed as a region. Since 1870 geographers and the census bureau have generally grouped the twelve midwestern states together as the North Central region. The historian, Frederick J. Turner, followed the lead of the geographers and designated the general area of the Middle West as the Prairie Plains. The reason for grouping these states together was primarily geographic. The general topography of the region is similar. The rich soils which cover most of the region make this area an agricultural entity. Because of the relative uniformity of climate and soils, the area produces similar crops. Its rivers and lakes tie the area together both as a drainage system and as an economic unit. The lakes and rivers became routes of immigration as well as routes for commerce.

Basically an area gains significance as a region only from its relation to a nation or the world. The South became a region largely because of its geography, its agriculture, and its slavery system which made it a unit in its relationship to the rest of the United States. The Middle West has never been isolated as a unit against a military foe; however, in addition to its geographical setting, it does have a number of other attitudes, characteristics, and conditions which set it apart as a region in its relation to the United States.

Originally, the Middle West was populated largely by the Algonquin Indians who were surrounded by Iroquois on the east, Muskogians on the south, and Sioux on the west. These Indians have left their influence in the names of rivers, locations, and political divisions, the location of roads, and in the crops produced. Because of the region's common drainage system, it was originally explored and settled largely by the French who were aided in this endeavor on the south by the Spanish. Obtained by the United States within a twenty-year period, its later exploration and settlement were accomplished as a unit by the same explorers and by a similar kind of population. Its people came largely from the same eastern and southern states within the United States and from the same countries in western Europe. Actually the settlement of the trans-Mississippi Midwest was due largely to the westward movement of people from Ohio, Indiana, Michigan, Wisconsin, and Illinois. Hence its population through blending is relatively homogeneous. Because of their inner geographical position, the people of the Midwest have developed historically an isolationistic attitude. And again because of its geographical position, its resources, and the composition of its population, it has developed a society and culture which is probably most characteristic of that called "American." Historically it was anti-slavery although at the same time anti-Negro. Politically it has been pivotal, having never completely settled on either political party. It has seldom united on major issues, but it has developed an economic system, a literature, a society, and a point of view which gives it the status of a region in its relationship to the United States.

—2—

Indians

Origins

There are many theories on how the Indian came to be in America. Some authorities maintain that the American Indian came from northern Europe by way of Greenland. Others believe the Indian either migrated from Atlantis, a legendary continent in the Atlantic, or from an alleged continent in the Pacific that has since disappeared. Still others hold that the Indian originated on this continent and is the only true American. Probably the most logical hypothesis is that Indians are descendants of a people who came to America from Asia by way of the Bering Straits 10,000 to 15,000 years ago.

In addition to the relative ease of crossing from Siberia to Alaska, the latter thesis is also substantiated by the similar physical and psychological characteristics of the Asians and the Indians and the presence of Indian mounds in America which are similar to mounds found in Siberia.

The upper-Mississippi Valley and the Great Lakes region have a large number of Indian mounds and buried artifacts. Wisconsin, alone, has 12,000 mounds. One of these mounds located at Man Mound Park near Baraboo, Wisconsin, represents a man walking toward the west. It is 210 feet long and 47 feet across the shoulders. Another unusual mound in the Midwest is the Great Serpent Mound in Adams City, Ohio. It is 1,330 feet long and averages three feet in height.

The names of the cultures of these pre-historic Americans are derived either from the place where artifacts of their culture were found, from the man who found the artifacts, or from aspects of their culture. The Folsom culture, which apparently existed in the Great Plains sometime before 8,000 B.C., received its name from Folsom, New Mexico, where remains of this culture were first identified. The Folsom culture was associated with large, pre-historic animals such as the mastodon, ground sloth, giant beaver, and giant cat. The Great Plains apparently had much more water and vegetation 10,000 years ago than they do now. The Adena culture, which apparently existed in Ohio about the time of the Christian era, received its name from the estate of Thomas Worthington near Chillicothe, Ohio. The chief centers of this culture in Ohio were the Scioto and Miami valleys. The Hopewell Indians, named for a man in Ross County on whose land their mounds were discovered, probably developed their culture in the Midwest around 900 A.D. Names of other pre-historic Indian cultures located in the Midwest include the Early Woodland, the Ft. Ancient, the Shell Mounds, the Middle Mississippi, the Dismal River, and the Oneato. These cultures were identified largely by their pottery, tools, food, and the way they buried their dead. These pre-historic peoples were undoubtedly the ancestors of the historic and present-day Indians of America.

Indian Life

When the first Europeans arrived in the Middle West, they found the Indians living in a stone-age culture. Their implements were of stone or bone. With the exception of the dog and in some localities the sheep, goat, and turkey, the Indians had no domestic animals. The horse, the wheel, and the axle were foreign to them. Their chief means of transport were boats, canoes, women, and dogs. Their dependence upon the products of nature for food and clothing made it necessary for them to be semi-nomadic. They made periodic journeys to hunt, fish, and gather wild berries and then return to relatively fixed abodes.

Although the teepee, with its tripod support of poles and

covering of skin or bark, has been associated with Indian life in general, only a small portion of the tribes, particularly those of the Great Plains, actually used it to any extent. The wigwam, used by many of the tribes east of the Mississippi, was an oval or dome-shaped, bark-covered dwelling.

Most middle-western Indians engaged in agriculture. Although maize was the principal crop, beans, squash, pumpkins, melons, gourds, and sweet potatoes were also grown. Many Indians were adept in basketry, pottery, and the decoration of leather goods. Their clothing was composed mainly of leather and skins.

In their political life the Indians usually had a division between civil and military authority. The civil rule was ordinarily vested in a hereditary ruler and the military authority in a chief elected for his prowess in war. The shaman or medicine man also had great influence over the tribe because of his supposed other-worldly powers. Blood for blood or tooth for tooth were generally the rule in punishment for crime. Personal effects such as horses, utensils, and food were regarded as private property, but individual ownership of land was almost unknown.

The Indians were fond of dances and games, including lacrosse, hockey, a dice and bowl game, jackstraws, stick dice, football, and all the sports and games associated with hunting and war. Smoking a pipe was common among most tribes, especially as a part of ceremonies.

Before the Indians learned by sad experience that many white men could not be trusted, the majority of Indians kept their pledges and promises. To many settlers, however, the Indians appeared treacherous, cruel, and immoral. An Indian could kill on a moment's notice, or he could offer his wife to a stranger for the night as a gesture of hospitality. The Indian shared his possessions freely; he enjoyed giving, even to the point of poverty. He had great pride, preferring death to slavery. Indians generally led a hard, bare life. Women, charming in their teens, were old hags at the age of thirty. The aged and infirm were often left to die.

Indian Tribes

There were three main Indian cultural groups in the Middle West, the Algonquin, the Siouan, and the Iroquoian. The Erie or Cat nation of northern Ohio belonged to the Iroquoian as did the Hurons who lived between Lakes Erie and Huron. The main group east of the Mississippi River, however, were the Algonquin. In the fertile prairies that now compose Indiana, Illinois, Wisconsin, and Michigan lived the Menominee, Sauk, Fox, Peoria, Potawatomi, Pennashaw, Miami, Kickapoo, Illinois, Chippewa, Mascouten, and Shawnee. The central Wisconsin country was peopled by Winnebago of the Siouan group.

Directly west of the Mississippi River lived the prairie Indians including the Mandan, Iowa, Kansa, Missouria, Omaha, Ponca, Otto, Osage, Pawnee, Wichita, Caddo, Hidesta, eastern Dakota, and Arikara. Although considered a part of the Siouan group, the Pawnee, Wichita, Caddo, and Arikara were actually members of the Caddoan linguistic stock and spoke dialects of that language. The culture of the prairie Indians was more like that of the Algonquins east of the Mississippi than the plains Indians to the west. The prairie Indians planted maize and erected permanent villages of earth or bark lodges to which they returned each fall after summer excursions in pursuit of buffalo. In the northern Great Plains the Blackfeet, Crows, Grosventres, and Teton-Dakota were the dominant groups. In the southern Great Plains, the Arapaho, Cheyenne, Comanche, and Kiowa held sway. Most of the Great Plains Indians were of the Siouan culture, but some like the Arapaho and Cheyenne were of the Algonquin linguistic stock. All of these Indians used stone knives and scrapers, bone awls, bows, and long buffalo lances.

Indian geography was very confusing. First, Indians travelled widely in search of food. Second, they had no specific lands that they claimed as their own. In the seventeenth century Indian geography was drastically changed as a result of the Iroquois being armed by their Dutch neighbors to the east. The Algonquin were pushed west and north, in turn forcing the Siouan tribes further west. When the Iroquois pressure eased, the Algonquin and Sioux returned to their original locations.

When the whites reached Ohio in 1650, there were few Indians there. The Algonquins had moved west and the Erie (an Iroquoian tribe) had been virtually exterminated by the Iroquois confederation. With the relaxation of Iroquois pressure from the east, the Miami returned to northern Indiana and western Ohio in the early 1700's. Shortly after, a Shawnee group came into Ohio from the South. The Illinois tribes that had moved north to escape the Iroquois returned to the Illinois country after 1700.

The Iowa country had at least seventeen different Indian tribes living there between 1763 and 1930. The Iowa Indians were in the area for 150 years; the Illinois, Miami, Winnebago, and Potawatomi among others were there for shorter periods. In Missouri the peaceful Missouri and Osage were the major tribes. On occasion, outside tribes like the Sauk and the Fox would raid into Missouri and cause dislocations and shifts in tribal locations.

Most Kansas Indians belonged to the Siouan linguistic stock and included the Osage, Quapaw, Omaha, and Ponca. During much of the 18th and 19th centuries, the Osage were at war with the plains' Indians to the west and the woods' Indians to the east. The Wichita Indians of the Caddoan linguistic stock were forced south into Oklahoma after 1720. The Kiowa, Comanche, Arapaho, and Cheyenne also ranged through Kansas hunting buffalo.

The Pawnee, also of the Caddoan stock, were in Kansas and Nebraska. They were probably in that area in 1541 when Francisco V. de Coronado came through and were definitely there in 1673 when they were put on Jacques Marquette's map. The Pawnee lived in semi-permanent earth lodges. As in many other Indian tribes, the women did most of the work and owned the personal property. The men hunted and the women grew corn. pumpkins, beans, and squash.

Next in importance to the Pawnee in Nebraska were the sedentary Siouan tribes such as the Omaha, Ponca, Oto, and Iowa that lived along the Missouri River. These latter four tribes were relative late comers to Nebraska. The Omahas probably moved up the Mississippi from the mouth of the Ohio into Iowa, crossed southeastern Minnesota, and then proceeded southwestward into Nebraska where they arrived sometime after 1650. The Poncas reached Nebraska about fifty years later. The Oto, the Iowas, and the Missouria were all of Winnebago stock and probably came to Nebraska from Green Bay. Roaming bands of Dakota, Cheyenne, Arapahoe, Comanche, Kiowa, Teton, and Yankton were also in Nebraska.

Around 1600 the Arikaras or Rees, related to the Pawnee, wandered into the South Dakota area from Nebraska. The Arikaras traded with the Spanish and brought some of the first horses into South Dakota. The Sioux reached the Missouri River shorty before 1750 and drove the Arikaras further north. Fleeing from the encroaching whites, the Arikaras left South Dakota in 1832 and joined the Mandan (originally from the Atlantic Coast) at the present site of Mandan, North Dakota.

The leading group in the Dakotas was the Dakota, a Siouan tribe from Minnesota, that came into the states that bear their name between 1725 and 1775. The Dakota or Sioux changed from a more sedentary agricultural life to a nomadic one (following the buffalo herds) when they moved into the Dakota country. For the Sioux the dog served as food and a beast of burden until the horse took over the latter function in about 1760.

Other Indians in the Dakotas for long or short periods of time included the Cheyenne, the Assiniboin, the Grosventres, and the Chippewa. Although other tribes wandered through, Minnesota was basically the home of the Dakota and the Chippewa. Henry W. Longfellow immortalized these tribes in the personalities of Hiawatha and Minnehaha in *Hiawatha*.

Indian Policy, 1600-1763

From the outset the white policy toward the Indians consisted of exploitation, conversion, removal, concentration, and degradation. The Indians were viewed by the Europeans as heathen who had no right to the land that they hunted and farmed and were treated accordingly.

Under the French the midwestern Indians probably received the best treatment that they were accorded during the period 1600 to 1900. The French devoted their efforts among the Indians to missionary work and fur trading. These early French Catholic missionaries included Father Rene Menard, Father Claude J. Allouez, and Father Jacques Marquette. The Jesuit missionaries even persuaded King Louis XIV to stop the fur trade because they thought it was corrupting the souls of the Indians. This victory, however, was of very short duration, and the overall benefit of the missionary effort to the Indians was negligible. The missionaries not only had to struggle against the superstitions and customs of the Indians but also against the vices and liquor brought to the Indians by Europeans.

The French fur trade in itself was probably not detrimental to the Indian, but its accouterments were. Worst of these were the wars that could be traced largely to the struggle over the fur trade. The Iroquois wars of the 17th century against the Erie, Huron, Ottawa, and other Algonquin tribes could be traced primarily to this cause. The Dutch and later the English supplied the Iroquois with firearms so that the latter could subdue the tribes friendly to the French and secure the fur trade for the Dutch and English. As a result of this power struggle over furs, the Erie and Ottawa were nearly annihilated, and thousands of other Algonquin Indians were killed and forced to flee to the West. This flight, in turn, resulted in more wars among the Indians unnaturally forced together.

Similarly the Sioux, armed by the French, became dominant in the upper Great Plains and brought death and destruction to neighboring Indians. During the 1690's the French rallied the Algonquins against the Iroquois and the English. The Iroquois who bore the brunt of the fighting on the English side were weakened and diminished by this affray. This campaign was the beginning of a series of battles known in Europe as the Second Hundred Years War (1689 to 1763). In its counterpart in America, the Indians allied with the French and the English and served as arrow and musket fodder. The first and second Fox wars, occurring in the first quarter of the 18th century, were due primarily to the French desire to maintain trade relations with the Ottawa and the Huron and to open the Fox-Wisconsin waterway, a route needed by the French in order to trade with the Sioux, a Fox enemy.

In addition to the devastation wreaked on the midwestern Indians by the wars, the Indians were further degraded by the liquor, diseases, and vices of the whites. Although the French were not the only offenders in this degradation of the Indians, they did play their part.

—3—

The Spanish and French Arrive

The Spanish Explorers

After the mound builders and their Indian descendants, the next people to arrive in what was to become the Midwest may have been the Scandinavians. Although there is some doubt as to its authenticity, the Kensington Rune stone, bearing a Scandinavian inscription found in Minnesota, could possibly indicate that Norsemen were in that area sometime during the thirteenth or fourteenth centuries.

The first major white exploration of the Middle West, however, came from the south. The Spanish explorer Francisco V. de Coronado, accompanied by about 1,000 friendly Indians and 300 Spaniards, was sent north in 1540 by the Mexican viceroy to find the mythological golden cities and treasures of Cibola reported by the priest Fray Marcos. Instead of gold, all they found were the mud-walled pueblos and maize fields of the Zuni Indians. An Indian slave of the Pueblo tribe then told Coronado of gold to the east in a Wichita Indian village called Quivira. Their hopes revived, Coronado and his men traveled north and east to Quivira, which turned out to be a collection of grass huts somewhere in central Kansas or Nebraska. Many historians believe that Coronado's party crossed the Arkansas River near present day Dodge City, Kansas, and proceeded some distance further in a northeasterly direction. Coronado, in writing of the Kansas area, said: "The earth is the best possible. The country itself is the best I have ever seen for producing all the fruits of Spain; for, besides the land itself being flat and black and being well watered by rivulets, springs, and rivers, I found prunes like those in Spain and nuts and very sweet grapes and mulberries." He described the prairies as "mighty plains and sandy heaths, smooth and wearisome and bare of wood." He said that "the plains are as full of crooked-back oxen as the mountain Serena in Spain is full of sheep." Discouraged by not finding gold, Coronado returned to Mexico; but before his departure he put up a marker, claiming the land for Spain.

However since they found no gold, Spanish interest in the lands north of Mexico languished. The Spaniards did carry on a little trade with the Algonquin and Siouan Indians, exchanging horses and trinkets for Indian women and furs. Later, relations between the Spaniards and the Indians worsened, partly because the Indians learned that their women were being sold into slavery in Mexico. In 1593 an expedition of thirty Spaniards was wiped out by a group of plains Indians in the Kansas area. Fifty years later Juan de Archuleta, sent north to capture a group of Pueblos who had fled from the Spanish at Taos, learned that the Pawnee were trading with the French. But the Spanish took little action to stop this illicit trade, because it would divert them from their main interest of finding gold. Their failure to find gold after extensive explorations in this area caused them to turn south to exploit the mineral riches of Central and South America, leaving the bulk of North America to be explored and settled by people of French and English descent.

The French Explorers

The next white explorers in the Middle West were the French who came in through Canada. The French claim to North America was established by the voyage in 1524 of Giovanni da Verrazano, a native of Florence. Commissioned by Francis I to find a waterway across North America to the Far East, Verrazano was stymied by the new continent. He sailed along the coast, probably from about present-day Cape Fear (in the Carolinas) to Newfoundland. Ten years later Francis I sent out Jacques Cartier to search for the elusive waterway to China. In all Cartier made three voyages to America between 1534 and 1541. He explored the St. Lawrence River, attempted to make a settlement at Quebec, and reached the height that still bears the name he gave it, "Mont Real."

The first permanent French settlement in Canada was made by Samuel de Champlain at Quebec in 1608. Champlain had been a seaman and soldier for Henry IV of France prior to his first voyage to Canada in 1603 on a trading venture. After settling Quebec, Champlain turned his attention to the interior. He explored the Ottawa River and discovered Lakes Huron, Ontario, and Champlain. Champlain not only made expeditions himself but also selected young men of promise like Jean Nicolet to go into the Indian country and establish a fur trade. In 1634 Nicolet pushed far westward to Green Bay on the western edge of Lake Michigan. Nicolet made this trip to the Wisconsin area in order to pacify the Ottawa and Winnebago Indians, whose war was hurting the French fur trade. To impress the Indians on visits of this nature, Nicolet would put on his robe of China damask, with its colorful flower and bird design, and carry his two pistols. Because the name of the Winnebago Indians was interpreted as "people of the sea," Nicolet erroneously believed that he was close to the Pacific Ocean when he arrived at Green Bay. Although Nicolet was far from the Pacific on his Green Bay junket, he did discover Lake Michigan and he was the forerunner of the French in the Mississippi Valley.

Champlain's siding with the Algonquins against the Iroquois proved disastrous for both the French and their Indian allies in the 1640's. In 1614 the Dutch had founded New Amsterdam. The Iroquois received guns from the Dutch and began to drive the Algonquins west. The Dutch also threatened Montreal and on occasion even forced the French to retrench and discontinue their fur trading in the West. The only notable French exploit in the West in the two decades after Nicolet's expedition was the journey of two Jesuits, Fathers Charles Raymbault and Isaac Jacques, from their Huron mission to Sault Ste. Marie in 1641.

The year after this notable journey by Raymbault and Jacques, the Iroquois attacked and killed several hundred Huron.

In 1648 the Iroquois destroyed the remainder of Huronia and the French missionaries who were with them. The Iroquois did not wage this merciless war against the French and Algonquin only because of Champlain's action in 1609. The Iroquois wanted to be the middlemen in the fur trade between the Dutch and the western Indians, and they did not want the French and their Indian allies encroaching on this profitable business.

As a result of the Iroquois raids, the Algonquin Indians fled to the area west of Lake Michigan. The Iroquois, overconfident, pursued the Algonquin into Wisconsin and there met a crushing defeat in the early 1650's. This defeat curbed the warlike activity of the Iroquois for a time, and the French once more expanded their fur trade and exploration.

The fur trade was developed largely by picturesque French adventurers known as *coureurs de bois,* generally unlicensed traders. Many of these men evaded regulations, lived among the Indians, and had a squaw in each village and a wife in Canada. Others like Medart Chouart, Sieur des Groseilliers, and his brother-in-law, Pierre Esprit, Sieur de Radisson, were more respectable. Between 1655 and 1660, these two men made two trips to the Lake Superior country. They penetrated deeply into Wisconsin, discovered the Wisconsin River, explored the southern shore of Lake Superior, and visited the Sioux Indians in eastern Minnesota. Irritated by the confiscation of their furs by the French authorities, they allied with the English and helped establish the Hudson's Bay Company in 1670.

Another group that traded with the Indians were the *bourgeois* or licensed traders. A noted *bourgeois* in the region was Nicolas Perrot. Born in Canada in 1644, he first ventured into the West in about 1665. In 1667 he reached Chequamegon Bay in western Lake Superior. The next year he was with the Potawatomi near Green Bay. He was the first European to visit the Fox Indians on the Wolf River in Wisconsin. He helped to keep the Indian tribes loyal to France and led them against the English and Iroquois in the 1680's. Overall, Perrot was one of France's best representatives to the Indians. He told them of his "Great Spirit," loaned his gun to young braves for hunting and his kettle to old men for cooking meat, and delighted the women and children with awls, knives, and bright beads.

The high point in French exploration of the upper-Mississippi Valley was attained during the decade 1669-1679. Louis Joliet, Father Marquette, and Rene R. Cavalier, Sieur de La Salle, the most famous of the French explorers in America, were active during this decade. Joliet, not yet 30 when he undertook his explorations with Marquette, had already been on Green Bay, had skirted the northern shore of Lake Erie, and had attended the elaborate pageant at Sault Ste. Marie in 1671 where Simon F. Daumont, Sieur de St. Lusson, had assumed sovereignty over the surrounding area in the name of the French king.

Marquette had begun his missionary service at Sault Ste. Marie in 1668. The following year he went to the mission at St. Esprit on Chequamegon Bay. In 1671 he returned with his Huron charges (the Iroquois pressure had declined) to the northern side of the Strait of Michilimackinac and erected the mission of St. Ignace. It was here that Joliet found Marquette when they began their long journey of exploration in 1673. Marquette was interested in this trip primarily as an opportunity to contact and convert more Indians.

Setting out from St. Ignace with five other Frenchmen in two bark canoes, they had only some Indian corn and smoked meat for food. They traversed Green Bay, the Fox River, and the Wisconsin River to the Mississippi. Marquette wrote of the Wisconsin River: "It is very wide; it has a sandy bottom which forms various shoals that render its navigation very difficult. It is full of islands covered with vines. On the bank one sees fertile land, diversified with woods, prairies, and hills . . ." Proceeding down the Mississippi, they saw Indians and strange fish and animals, the strangest of which to them was the bison which they described in detail. Continuing downstream, they passed through the turbulence where the Missouri River pours its muddy flow into the Mississippi. Passing the mouth of the Ohio River, they eventually reached an Indian village called Akamsea at the mouth of the Arkansas River. Having established the fact that the Mississippi flowed into the Gulf of Mexico, they turned back because they did not wish to fall into the hands of the Spanish.

On their return trip, Marquette and Joliet altered their original course and traversed the Illinois River to Lake Michigan. It was during this time that Joliet conceived the idea of constructing a string of posts from the Great Lakes to the mouth of the Mississippi. Near the end of the voyage, Joliet lost his maps and records in the La Chine Rapids when his canoe upset. Therefore, the only records left were Marquette's journals which were later published. After a year of recuperation, Marquette set out again and traveled to a large Indian village (near present day Peoria) on the Illinois River. He ministered to these Indians during the Easter season and died on the return trip at the mouth of the Marquette River (near present day Ludington, Michigan) in 1675.

La Salle, the third of these famous French explorers, was born of a wealthy family in Rouen in 1643 and arrived in Canada in 1666. His first exploration was in the Ohio River area in 1669. Two Sulpitian missionaries accompanied him. Although this trip is shrouded in mystery, La Salle apparently went down the Ohio as far as the falls (near present day Louisville).

La Salle originally planned to explore the Mississippi, because he believed it was the long sought route to China. When Marquette and Joliet proved that the Mississippi flowed into the Gulf of Mexico, La Salle changed his plans and decided to establish a fur trading empire in the Mississippi Valley. To bring his plans to fruition, La Salle worked long years and made several trips to France for money, men, and the authority to build posts. Despite the able assistance of Henry de Tonti, an ex-officer in the Italian Army, most of La Salle's projects ended in disaster. In 1679 La Salle started west with a sailing vessel, *The Griffin.* At Green Bay *The Griffin* was loaded with furs and started back to Ft. Frontenac. Meanwhile, La Salle proceeded to the mouth of the St. Joseph River in Lake Michigan where he built Ft. Miami. Henry de Tonti joined him there and they used the Kankakee portage to reach the Illinois River, where they erected Ft. Crevecoeur (near the present site of Peoria). When *The Griffin* failed to return to Ft. Miami, La Salle proceeded to Ft. Frontenac. There he was told that *The Griffin* had been lost, that most of Tonti's men had deserted from Ft. Crevecoeur, and that the Iroquois were raiding in the Illinois country. After a fruitless trip back to the Illinois country, La Salle eventually found Tonti safe at Michilimackinac.

After journeying back to Montreal for more supplies, La Salle and Tonti returned to Illinois and followed the Mississippi River down to the Gulf of Mexico. They claimed the Louisiana country for King Louis XIV and then retraced their steps up river. In 1682 they arrived back in the Illinois country and built Ft. St. Louis on Starved Rock (near present day Ottawa) on the Illinois River in the midst of a large Indian village. La Salle organized the Illinois tribes against the Iroquois, and the Illinois began to return.

But fate struck again. La Salle's ally, Count de Frontenac, was replaced as governor by Le Febvre de la Barre, an enemy of La Salle. Leaving Tonti in charge at Ft. St. Louis, La Salle once more journeyed to France, where he obtained men and money to found a colony at the mouth of the Mississippi River. Leaving Rochelle, France, in 1684, La Salle sailed directly for the Gulf of Mexico. But he missed the mouth of the Mississippi and landed at Matagorda Bay in Texas. After two starving years, La Salle and a few followers set out overland for the Illinois country. They had gone only a short distance when La Salle was ambushed and slain by his men in 1687.

After La Salle's death, Tonti became commander at Ft. St. Louis and built an Illinois Indian confederacy to fight the Iroquois. But in 1696 most of the fur traders were pulled out of the outlying region and within a few years Tonti had to give up Ft. St. Louis. In 1704 Tonti went to Louisiana to aid Pierre Le Moyne de Iberville with his post at Mobile; soon after Tonti died of fever.

Another of LaSalle's associates was Father Louis Hennepin, who was commissioned by La Salle in 1680 to explore the upper-Mississippi Valley. Shortly after reaching the Mississippi, Hennepin and his companions were captured by a band of Sioux Indians. The Indians conducted the Frenchmen up the Mississippi past Lake Pepin to the vicinity of the Falls of St. Anthony (present site of St. Paul). There they abandoned their canoes and went overland to the Sioux villages of Mille Lacs in central Minnesota.

Eventually, Hennepin and his men were rescued by Daniel Greysolon, Sieur du Luth, a contemporary of La Salle, who was active in the West between 1678 and 1689. On his first expedition

Robert Cavelier, Sieur de
LaSalle (1643-1687)
French explorer in North America
From *Dictionary of American Portraits* by Hayward and Blanche Cirker, Dover Publications, Inc., New York, 1967. *Reprinted through permission of the publisher.*

Anthony Wayne (1745-1796)
General in Revolutionary and
Federalist periods
Painting attributed to James Sharples, Sr., Courtesy Independence National Historical Park. From *Dictionary of American Portraits* by Hayward and Blanche Cirker, Dover Publications, Inc., New York, 1967. *Reprinted through permission of the publisher.*

George R. Clark (1752-1818)
Revolutionary officer in the Old Northwest
Engraved by Thomas B. Welch from a painting by James B. Longacre after a painting by John W. Jarvis. From *Dictionary of American Portraits* by Hayward and Blanche Cirker, Dover Publications, Inc., New York, 1967. *Reprinted through permission of the publisher.*

Arthur St. Clair (1736-1818)
Revolutionary general, first governor of
Northwest Territory
Painting by Charles W. Peale, Courtesy Independence National Historical Park. From *Dictionary of American Portraits* by Hayward and Blanche Cirker, Dover Publications, Inc., New York, 1967. *Reprinted through permission of the publisher.*

to Lake Superior, du Luth arranged a peace treaty between the Sioux and the Chippewa and between the Sioux and the Assiniboin. These peace treaties opened the area west and north of Superior to French traders. In July 1679 du Luth took possession of all the Sioux country in a ceremony at Mille Lacs in the name of Louis XIV. Du Luth also explored the St. Croix River down to the Mississippi River.

The Catholic Missionaries to the Indians

Protestantism and the discovery of America were almost contemporaneous events. In commenting on this, William W. Sweet, in his *Story of Religion in America,* observed that the timing looked as if God had saved American for Protestantism.

In the early Midwest, however, it looked as if the Catholics would win the region. Priests of the Jesuit, Recollect, and Sulpitian orders were extremely active in carrying Christianity to the Indians of the Midwest. This activity is attested to by the 73 printed volumes of *Jesuit Relations and Allied Documents* describing the Catholic missionary effort among the Indians. To win souls these priests forsook ease and comfort and bore filth, loneliness, privations, and fiendish tortures. Unfortunately, some of the later French missionaries became more concerned about France than the kingdom of heaven and stirred the Indians to cruel raids on the French enemies whether red or white.

Jesuit missionaries were with the Ottawa in the Great Lakes region as early as 1645. The first missionary in Wisconsin was Jesuit René Menard. He established a mission for remnants of the fugitive Ottawa at La Pointe du St. Esprit on Chequamegon Bay in 1660. The next year he disappeared on a journey of mercy.

In 1665 Father Menard's work was continued by Father Claude Allouez. Allouez worked in the western missions until his death in 1689. He was first at St. Esprit. In 1669 he went to the Fox River where he founded four missions. The most important of these was the St. Francis Xavier Mission at Green Bay which served the Potawatomi, Sauk, Menominee, and Fox. At the time of his death he was working with the Miami and Potawatomi in southern Michigan. As noted above, Father Marquette was also very active in this period.

Generally, this missionary work was not very successful. The Indians seemed more susceptible to debauchery by the traders than to receiving Christianity through the priests. To improve this situation the Jesuits brought pressure to bear on King Louis XIV to order all traders and forts out of the Indian country. Since the French fur market was glutted, Louis acceded to this request in 1696. But within a few years the fur trade declined, the English and Spanish began to move in, and the French king decided to rescind his trader-evacuation order. The traders returned and the missionaries were again faced by the vice and corruption of their own race among the Indians.

In 1699 a group of priests from the Seminary of Foreign Missions built a chapel at Cahokia in Illinois. The Jesuits, resenting the action of this rival order, then built a mission station at Kaskaskia. St. Anne's Chapel was built at Detroit by a Recollect priest in 1701. By 1754 Catholic missions, largely Jesuit, dotted the Old Northwest with the exception of the Ohio region. French settlements like Green Bay, Prairie du Chien, Mackinac, Vincennes, and Kaskaskia were all Catholic. The French-Canadian phase of Catholicism in the area ended in 1789. At that time the region was put under the control of Bishop John Carroll of the Baltimore diocese.

With the transfer of the Old Northwest from France to England and later to the United States, the strength of Catholicism began to fade. When the English in 1774 proclaimed the Quebec Act, which protected the French Catholics of the eastern Midwest and put them under the jurisdiction of Quebec, the American colonists were incensed. They believed England was trying to keep American Protestants out of the Midwest. When the Old Northwest became a part of the United States after 1783, American Protestants began to pour in and the French Catholics were swamped.

French Indian Relations and Colonialism

As the preceding accounts have suggested, the two main purposes of the French in exploring and building posts in the upper-Mississippi Valley were to obtain furs and to convert the Indians to Christianity. The first of these two goals, which received the greater emphasis, inevitably led to wars with the Indians (especially the Iroquois) and finally the English. The Iroquois would probably have soon forgotten Champlain's aid to their enemies if their economic interests had not tied them to the Dutch and later the English. The Iroquois preferred the Dutch and English as allies for two reasons. First, the Dutch and English paid about twice as much for furs as the French; and second, the Dutch and English allowed the Iroquois to serve as middlemen in the trade with the western Indians, whereas the French explorers and traders often dealt directly with the western Indian tribes. As a result the Iroquois proved to be very valuable to the English in crushing the western tribes, in acting as a buffer against the French, and in helping England acquire the eastern portion of the Middle West.

The Iroquois threat to the French was particularly severe in the 1630's and 40's and in the 1670's and 80's. The Algonquin allies of the French were driven to the western bank of the Mississippi River several times during these periods. The French had to abandon their outlying posts and on occasion even draw back to Montreal in the face of determined Iroquois attacks. In 1689 the English joined the Iroquois in their battle with the French, partly as a result of competition over the fur trade but more as a result of an English-French war (War of English Succession) in Europe.

By the middle of the 1690's, the Iroquois threat had waned and great quantities of furs were glutting the Montreal market. At this time the Jesuits and other missionary groups obtained the ear of the king through Madame de Maintenon, a former mistress whom Louis XIV had recently married. They convinced him that the fur trade was corrupting the souls of the Indians. As noted earlier, the upshot of this was an edict issued in 1696 calling for the evacuation of the far western posts and the revocation of all licenses to trade. As a result the French fur trade declined and the English gained firmer control of the fur trade in the area.

Partly because of the weaknesses of the withdrawal policy of 1696 and partly because of the persuasions of Antoine de la Mothe Cadillac, a protege of Governor Frontenac and a former commandant at Michilimackinac, a new Indian policy was developed in 1701. This plan consisted of gathering the Indians around such posts as Detroit, Ft. St. Louis (on the Illinois River), and New Orleans, where the Indians could be more easily supervised.

As a result of this policy, the Huron, Ottawa, Chippewa, Mississaugua, and Potawatomi began moving back to the Detroit area (partly because the power of the Iroquois had diminished and partly because of Cadillac's invitation to them to return). As early as 1706 this proximity of Indian tribes plus the presence of some unscrupulous white agents led to trouble, and the Ottawa and Miami began a war among themselves. Cadillac mediated the controversy. In 1710, the same year that Cadillac was convicted of alleged wrong-doing, divested of his property, and banished to Mobile, a group of Fox Indians came to Detroit. The French were already angry at the Fox because the latter seemed overly friendly with the English and because the Fox had also closed the Fox-Wisconsin waterway in order to keep French goods from reaching the Sioux, a Fox enemy. Therefore, since the restraining influence of Cadillac was gone and since the French believed it was to their advantage to weaken the Fox, the French joined with the Ottawa, Huron, and a few other tribes in attacking the Fox around Detroit in 1712. About 1,000 Fox were killed in the slaughter.

As a result of this massacre, the remaining Fox stepped up their raids against the Ottawa and Huron Indians and the French. These raids came at a bad time for the French. Not only were they fighting the British in the War of Spanish Succession, but they also had to be prepared to defend themselves against the Indian tribes of the lower-Mississippi Valley who appeared sympathetic to the British. As a result the French had neither the resources nor the men to fight the Fox. With the Treaty of Utrecht signed in 1715, the French sent out an army to punish the Fox. The French did find a main Fox encampment in Wisconsin; but after a three day seige, they negotiated a peace with the Fox which stipulated that the Fox would trap furs for the French. This was the end of the first Fox war.

The concentration program was also accompanied by a new policy toward the *coureurs de bois.* On earlier occasions and especially from 1691 to 1701, these unlicensed traders had been outlawed. After 1701, however, the King of France granted them a general amnesty. They now became heroes because they were needed to lead the French-Indian allies against the Iroquois and the British.

Upon the death of Louis XIV in 1715, the Canadian officials, convinced that the West could not be safely left to priests and unregulated traders, again changed the Indian policy. All the important western posts were occupied and new ones were built. The post at Nitchitoches on the Red River, established by Louis Juchereau de St. Denis in 1713, served as a base for later explorations of the Red, Missouri, Osage, and other western rivers as well as a post for trading with Indian tribes such as the Pawnee, Oto, Osage, Iowa, and Missouri. In 1717 Ft. La Baye was erected at Green Bay. The commandant there was a judge who had absolute authority. La Baye generally had peaceful relations with the surrounding Indians who were mostly of the Menominee tribe. On one occasion, however, in 1758, white dishonesty resulted in the murder of eleven Frenchmen before the Menominee could be calmed.

Minnesota was the site of considerable French activity. In 1718 Ft. La Pointe was constructed on Chequamegon Bay. Nine years later Rene Boucher, Sieur de la Pevriere, took an expedition to Minnesota and built a post on the Minnesota bank of Lake Pepin (near present day Frontenac). In 1731 during the second Fox war, Pierre Gaultier de Varrennes, Sieur de la Verendrye, commandant of a small post on Lake Nipigon, became obsessed with the idea of finding a river that would open up the fur trade further west. Within ten years he had built a chain of six forts known as the "Post of the Western Sea" stretching from Rainy Lake to the mouth of the Saskatchewan. In 1738 he visited the

Mandan Indians on the upper-Missouri River. Four years later his son Pierre led a trading party westward to the Bighorn Mountains.

Jean Baptiste de Vincennes and his son Francois Marie were closely associated with the reoccupied posts on the Maumee-Wabash route in Indiana. The elder Vincennes, who was in command of the post at the mouth of the St. Joseph River on Lake Michigan in 1696-97, was put in charge of the post at the Miami Village (near present day Ft. Wayne). The younger Vincennes, who had been at Ouiatanon (near present day Lafayette) prior to 1720, was made commandant of the new post at Vincennes in 1731.

In southern Illinois the Jesuit mission of Kaskaskia was established in 1700, and the posts of Cahokia and Kaskaskia were garrisoned at about the same time. In 1720 the French established a third fort in the region at Ft. de Chartres.

At approximately the same time that Ft. de Chartres was founded, Charles Claude du Tisne, a resident of Kaskaskia, ascended the Missouri River to the Osage villages and then went overland to the Pawnee villages on a trading mission. While Tisne was moving south, the Spanish explorer Pedro de Villasur set out from Santa Fe with 45 Spaniards and 60 Indians to stop French inroads into the lower Middle West. He got as far north as the South Platte River where his party was apparently wiped out by Pawnees.

Shortly after, the French sent Etienne Veniard de Bourgment up the Missouri to check on Spanish activities in that area. He found no Spanish but he did establish Ft. Orleans (near present day Brunswick, Missouri) which was manned for four years. In 1724 another French reconnaissance party went up to the site of present-day Kansas City. They found no spanish either. Although there were some Spanish in the plains of the Middle West in the seventeenth century, they were nearly non-existent there after 1720.

Partly as a result of the renewed activity of the French in the West, the French colonies of Canada and Louisiana had a jurisdictional dispute over the boundaries of their respective territories. In 1718 Terre Haute became the approximate dividing line. Vincennes and the southern Illinois country were included in Louisiana.

But despite France's renewed vigor in the West, the Fox Indians and the English continued to trouble the French. The Fox controlled the Fox-Wisconsin route, waged war against the Illinois Indians, and scalped an occasional Frenchman. Full scale war, however, did not break out until after a Fox leader, Kiala of the Wisconsin country, formed a confederacy composed of the Fox, the Sioux, the Iowa, the Missouri, the Iroquois on Lake Ontario, and the Oto of the Southwest. In 1728 the second Fox war had its official beginning when Sieur de Legnery challenged the Fox confederacy by leading 400 French and 1,200 Indians to the Green Bay area to crush the Fox. But finding no Indians, Legnery returned after destroying the French post at Ft. La Baye. In 1729 Indians allied with the French attacked the Fox, and the Fox sued for peace. A group of Fox tried to go east and join the Iroquois, but they were caught south of present day Chicago and around 300 were massacred by the French and their Indian allies. Kiala and some other Fox leaders, who later surrendered to the commandant of the reconstructed La Baye, were treacherously taken to Montreal and deported. Kiala ended his days as a slave in the French West Indies.

Events seemed to be going well for the French until 1731 when the French got into a dispute with the Sauk Indians over some Fox prisoners that the French wanted turned over to them. There was a skirmish, some French and Indians were killed, and the Sauk and Fox became allies. The war flared again. The Sauk and Fox moved to central Iowa where the French led an unsuccessful attack against them in the winter of 1734-35. To make matters worse, the Sioux and Chickasaw became hostile to the French. Therefore, in 1740 the French ended their policy of trying to crush the Fox Indians and began a general conciliation of the western tribes. As a result of all these Indian wars, French resources were depleted trying to save their western empire, the battles caused a shift of the western fur-trade routes to the east making them more accessible to the English, and many of the Indians were left sullen, ready to cooperate with the British against the French in the ensuing battles. If the Fox Indians in the West had remained peaceful, French sovereignty in the Midwest might never have been shaken.

In addition to building forts and fighting the Fox, the French also took other steps to consolidate their position in the West. The French government acquiesced in a scheme promoted by John Law to sell stock to the French people and use the proceeds to develop and exploit the Mississippi Valley. The project, known as the "Mississippi Bubble," burst in 1720 after six years of high-pressure advertisement. Although very few people settled in America as the result of this promotion, many Frenchmen lost money on it.

Also in an attempt to hold the region, the French government allowed some small French settlements to develop in the West. La Baye was the center of the chief French community in Wisconsin after 1717. Following the Canadian custom, the farms in the community were long and narrow, with one end on the river, the highway of the day.

In the Illinois country, there were between 1,500 and 2,000 French and Negroes scattered in the southern Illinois villages of Kaskaskia, Prairie de Rocher, St. Philips, Ft. de Chartres, and Cahokia. Phillippe F. Renault was instrumental in importing Negro slaves in 1719 to work in the mines.

Practically all of the French settlers in Missouri in 1750 were kinfolk or descendants of the French in the southern Illinois villages. As early as 1732 a few French people from Illinois built cabins at a location that became Ste. Genevieve, Missouri.

Generally, however, French influence and settlements in the Middle West were concentrated in four main areas: St. Louis; the southern Illinois country, clustered around Cahokia and Kaskaskia; the Wabash Valley, centering on Vincennes; and the Detroit region. But in comparison to the English settlements on the coast, the French settlements were insignificant. The English population in America in 1760 numbered 1,300,000 compared to a population of 80,000 for the French.

The French attempted to keep the English out of the Midwest with ever decreasing success. As early as 1685 Captain Johannes Rosebloom, an English trader, led a trading expedition of eleven canoes to Mackinac and got back to Albany safely. When in 1686 he tried this again, he was captured by the French and his furs were confiscated. Governor Frontenac launched a vigorous campaign during King William's War to keep Albany traders out of the West.

After 1700 this became even more difficult as the western fur routes shifted to the east, and the Miami Indians settled at the British trading post of Pickawillany (near present day Piqua, Ohio). In 1749 Celeron de Blainville with 180 soldiers and Indians made a trip into the Ohio Valley to push the British out. He accomplished little beyond burying some lead plates, claiming the area for France, at the mouths of the tributaries of the Ohio. He did tell the Miami to leave Pickawillany and return to the French post (near present-day Ft. Wayne). Old Britain, chief of the Miami tribe, refused. Three years later the French leader, Charles de Langlade, with 250 Ottawa braves swept down on Pickawillany and destroyed the village. The English traders at Pickawillany were killed or captured, and Old Britain, who had dared to defy the French, was boiled and partly eaten.

In 1753 Governor Marquis Duquesne followed up Langlade's action by creating a force of 1,500 troops to protect the region and by constructing new forts at Presque Isle, Le Boeuf, and Venango. This then was the setting in 1754 for the French and Indian War, the seven-year conflict that resulted in the French loss of the Old Northwest to the English.

—4—

The English Arrive

English Activity to 1754

England's claim to America rested on the explorations of John Cabot. Commissioned by Henry VIII, Cabot in 1497-98 explored the eastern coast of America from Cape Breton Island to the Carolinas. After several false starts, England began her successful colonization in 1606, when King James I granted the land between the 34th and 45th parallels to the London and Plymouth companies. The next year the London Company was successful in founding Jamestown, the first permanent English settlement in America. From this small beginning the whole eastern seaboard from Georgia to Maine was settled by 1733. In the charters of several of these colonies, it was stipulated that their western boundaries were the Pacific Ocean. Such extensive grants necessarily included parts of the Middle West within the English colonies.

In the actual movement to the Middle West, the commercially-minded Dutch at Albany (who settled on the east coast simultaneously with the British) took the lead. Through their allies the Iroquois, they began to receive furs from the West prior to 1620. In 1643 the Dutch made a formal trading agreement with the Iroquois. When the English gained control of New York in 1664, they inherited the friendship of the Iroquois from the Dutch. The Iroquois played an important role in reducing French trade in the West and in extending English trade into that area.

English efforts in the West were also aided by the two Frenchmen, Groseilliers and Radisson, discussed above, who helped the British establish the Hudson Bay Company in Canada in 1670. Although the Hudson Bay posts were held for a time by the French during King William's and Queen Anne's wars, the British were relatively successful in using them to obtain a large part of the fur trade in the upper Midwest.

During King William's War the French almost stopped the Albany trade with the West. But during the course of the war, the trade took a new direction. Instead of going through the Great Lakes, the English crossed Pennsylvania and went down the Ohio to trade with the Miami Indians, among others, who were filtering back from Wisconsin. The English trader, Arnaut Viele, followed this route in 1692. On paper the English position was further strengthened in 1701 when the English governor of New York secured from the Iroquois a deed to their beaver lands, an immense area thought to extend as far west as present day Chicago.

During King George's War in the 1740's, Pennsylvania frontiersmen moved into the Ohio Valley. In the forefront of this aggressive advance was George Croghan, a trader of Irish descent, who arrived in Pennsylvania in 1741. Within a few years he had posts and warehouses at Pine Creek, Logstown, and Beaver Creek on the upper-Ohio River. In 1748 he climaxed his expansion by building a palisaded fort at the Miami village of Pickawillany in the heart of the French territory. His success was largely the result of his knowledge of the Indian, his marriage to an Indian woman, and the fact that he offered more and better goods in exchange for furs than his French rivals.

The three English colonies taking the lead in westward expansion were Virginia, Pennsylvania, and New York. Virginia and Pennsylvania claimed the Ohio Valley through charter, and New York claimed it through cessions from the Iroquois. Each was represented in the Midwest by traders like Conrad Weiser, Thomas Cresap, and Croghan. In 1747 a group of Virginians (Thomas Lee, Lawrence and Augustine Washington, George Fairfax, and others) went even further than trade and established the speculative Ohio Company. In 1748 this company obtained from the English Board of Trade a grant of 200,000 acres on the eastern bank of the upper-Ohio River. The company was to receive 300,000 more acres if it could bring in 100 families within seven years. Although its efforts to secure immigrants failed, the Ohio Company did begin extensive trading and exploring operations under the direction of the frontier surveyor, Christopher Gist. Gist established a storehouse at Wills Creek, laid out a crude trail to Redstone Creek, and explored much of the upper-Ohio River region.

As noted above, the French, disturbed by this activity, sent Celeron de Blainville with 200 soldiers to the Ohio country to dislocate the English. Blainville's mission a failure, Marquis Duquesne, governor of New France, sent down Charles de Langlade in 1752 with a band of French and Indians. They attacked Pickawillany, killed its defenders, and carried large quantities of English trading goods back to Detroit. As a result the Miami, Huron, and many Shawnee deserted the English, and British prestige sank to a low ebb. Duquesne decided this was an opportune time to ride the crest and build a chain of forts from Lake Erie to the forks of the Ohio to fence the English out of the Ohio Valley. Early in 1753 a French construction party set out from Ft. Niagara. It stopped first at the Lake Erie entrance to the French Creek portage and built Ft. Presque Isle. Moving inland they built Ft. Le Boeuf at the junction of French Creek and the Alleghany River. An early winter prevented them from building a fourth fort at the forks of the Ohio.

Alarmed by these French moves, Virginia's vigorous governor, Robert Dinwiddie, decided to act on his own. In December 1753 he sent a small party under the twenty-one-year-old George Washington to warn the French at Forts Venango and Le Boeuf that they were on Virginian soil. The French ignored this notice. Meanwhile, Dinwiddie sent Captain William Trent with a work party to erect an English fort at the forks of the Ohio. Upon Washington's return to Williamsburg, he was commissioned to raise troops to occupy the fort on the Ohio. When Washington reached Will's Creek on his way west, he met the returning work party which reported that the French were in control of the forks and were building Ft. Duquesne. Washington, outnumbered ten to one, marched on Ft. Duquesne with more valor than judgment. Having defeated a small French scouting party at Great Meadows near the French fort, he was attacked by a large French force. After fighting all day in a crudely constructed fort, appropriately named Ft. Necessity, he had to surrender. The English were thus driven from the Ohio country and the French and Indian War had begun.

The French and Indian War

At first this war went badly for the English. General Edward Braddock and his regulars landed in the colonies in early 1755. He divided his forces in four parts for attacks on Ft. Duquesne, Ft. Niagara, Ft. Crown Point, and Ft. Beausejour. He took personal command of the 1,900 regulars and colonials that moved west toward Ft. Duquesne in June 1755. Seven miles from Duquesne on an open plain, Braddock's advance detachment of 1,200 men was attacked by a French force of 800. Using the European tactics of open-field fighting, his army was decimated by the French and Indians firing from cover. Braddock was killed; of the original 1,900-man force, Washington, who was also present, was able to get only 500 uninjured back to Ft. Cumberland. As for the other three prongs of Braddock's campaign, the British captured only one objective, Ft. Beausejour. Impressed by the military successes of the French, the Indians flocked to the French. The back country of Pennsylvania, Maryland, and Virginia became "dark and bloody ground."

After many desperate petitions for help, the western frontiersmen finally stirred the eastern-controlled. colonial assemblies into building and garrisoning a series of 200 forts to guard the western mountain passes. This brought a measure of protection to the back country. In 1756 and 1757 the depredations of the victorious French and Indians shifted to the north with the fall of Ft. Oswego on Lake Ontario and the overrunning of Ft. William Henry on Lake Champlain.

But in 1757 the English position began to improve after the rise of William Pitt to the office of prime minister. He obtained huge sums of money for the war effort, promoted young officers on the basis of merit, poured more men and supplies into America, and began building a powerful navy. Despite the heroic efforts of the Marquis de Montcalm, the tide began to turn in 1758. Louisbourg and Frontenac fell to the larger British forces in the summer of 1758 and New France was cut in two. In the fall of 1758 General John Forbes cut a new road across Pennsylvania to

Ft. Duquesne. Upon his arrival the French, realizing the futility of resistance, burned the fort and fled. With the fall of Ft. Duquesne and the construction of Ft. Pitt, the western Indians, realizing that French power was fading, began to aid the English in the task of driving the French from the Great Lakes area in the winter of 1758-59. The Indians were so effective in their campaign that by 1759 only Ft. La Baye, Detroit, Michilimackinac, and the Illinois villages were still in the hands of New France.

But all other battles in the area were dwarfed by the struggle for Quebec between General James Wolfe and General Montcalm, both of whom were killed in the epic battle. The British, victorious in this contest, acquired the mighty French citadel. A year later Montreal surrendered to the British and the war in America was ended. Although the war lasted three more years in Europe, the die was cast. In the Peace of Paris of 1763, England obtained all French territory east of the Mississippi River with the exception of two small islands in St. Lawrence Bay and the city of New Orleans. Spain gave up the Floridas to England, and France compensated its ally for this loss by ceding Spain the Louisiana Territory. The French thus left the Middle West in the hands of the Spanish and the British.

British Administrative Policy in the Middle West, 1763-1774

Establishment of a western policy for that portion of the English empire lying in an irregular triangle formed by the Ohio and Mississippi rivers proved extremely difficult. First the French posts had to be taken over by the British. In 1760 Major Robert Rogers and 200 Rangers were sent out to occupy these midwestern posts. He obtained the surrender of Detroit, Ft. Miami (Ft. Wayne), and Ft. Ouiatanon almost immediately. Mackinac, La Baye, and St. Joseph were not turned over to the English until the following year, and Ft. Chartres in the Illinois country was not relinquished by the French until 1765.

After acquiring the area there was a dispute between the

British government and the American colonies over who was going to administer it. In 1748 Virginia had objected to the English Board of Trade granting a land charter to the Ohio Company. Virginia claimed that this was a violation of her original charter and that she should issue the land grants. Acting upon this principle, Virginia in 1748 granted land to the Loyal Land Company headed by John Robinson, speaker of the House of Burgesses. When peace broke out, these two companies along with dozens of others attempted to acquire or renew western land grants in England and in the colonies.

In addition to the land companies, there were also large numbers of settlers who wanted to obtain tracts of rich land across the Ohio River. After 1758 these squatters began to rush in, even though the region west of the Ohio had been guaranteed to the Indians as a hunting ground by treaty in 1758. Although the English commandant at Ft. Pitt tried to check these white encroachments by herding settlers eastward and by burning cabins, they still came.

The presence of several thousand French in the region further complicated the situation. What was to become of them? The English administration was also besieged by fur traders who petitioned that the Old Northwest be left as Indian country in order that their trade would not be impaired.

Uninformed English ministers with no precedents to build upon were unable to devise a system that would satisfy jealous colonials, individualistic frontiersmen, sentimental humanitarians, rabid imperialists, greedy traders, English merchants, land-hungry speculators, and nomadic Indians. The problem was made even more difficult to resolve by unregulated British traders who were cheating and corrupting the Indians, by English settlers who were moving into the Indian lands, and by British officials like Jeffrey Amherst who treated the Indians like beasts of the forest. Amherst favored exterminating the Indians with smallpox and hunting them down with dogs. In the winter of 1762-63 the Indians were informed that their accustomed gifts would not be distributed. Under these conditions it was natural that the Indians listened to French traders who told them that the French government was now ready to help them drive the hated redcoats into the sea.

The Indian chieftain who took it upon himself to accomplish

this task was an Ottawa named Pontiac. Working quietly during the winter of 1762-63, he developed a plan and organized a confederation of Algonquin Indians to attack the British forces and drive out the English settlers.

In May of 1763 the Indians made a surprise attack on Detroit and Ft. Pitt. Although these garrisons beat off the attack, many other western posts did not. Mackinac fell on June 2 when a band of Chippewa playing lacrosse in front of the fort rushed into the stockade under the ruse of recovering their ball and then suddenly attacked the defending soldiers. Forts Miami and Ouiatanon were also taken by trickery; others simply fell to fierce Indian onslaughts. St. Joseph, Green Bay, Sandusky, Presque Isle, Le Boeuf, and Venango were all captured or evacuated. There were no survivors at some of the forts. In the Middle West only Detroit and Ft. Pitt remained intact, and they underwent long sieges. Whether it was a planned, simultaneous uprising as Francis Parkman suggested or an unplanned, spasmodic affair as Howard H. Peckham maintained, the conspiracy was successful in its initial stages.

After the Indians had destroyed the forts, they attacked the frontier cabins on the western side of the Appalachians. The fall of the forts and the raids in the back country finally convinced Amherst, commander-in-chief in America, that something must be done. On June 12, 1763, he sent two expeditions west; one to relieve the besieged Detroit and the other to raise the siege at Ft. Pitt. Both were relatively successful. In October Pontiac, discouraged by his inability to take Ft. Pitt and Detroit and the failure of the French to help him, arranged a temporary truce and slipped away to the Illinois country to recruit more tribes for the campaign. But his confederacy disintegrated, and in the early summer of 1764 when William Johnson, Indian superintendent for the Northern Department, invited the Indians to a peace conference at Niagara, most of the western tribes accepted.

To punish those who did not, notably the Shawnee and the Delaware, Amherst sent forth in the summer of 1764 military forces under Colonels Henry Bouquet and John Bradstreet. Bouquet's troops marched across western Pennsylvania and eastern Ohio to terrorize into submission the Delaware along the Muskingum River. Bradstreet's force marched along the southern edge of Lake Erie and up to Detroit to overawe the Indians in those areas. With these campaigns, a precarious peace was again restored to the West.

But General Thomas Gage, who had replaced Amherst as American military commander, was still concerned about the actions of Pontiac who was lurking in the Illinois country. To accomplish the delicate task of stalemating Pontiac and of extending English jurisdiction over the French villages in southern Illinois, Gage sent George Croghan west in May 1765. Leaving Ft. Pitt with two boatloads of presents, Croghan's party reached the mouth of the Wabash without incident. There his party was captured by a band of Kickapoo and Mascoutin Indians and taken to the vicinity of Ft. Ouiatanon. Yielding to the protests of the neighboring Indians, the Kickapoo and Mascoutin released Croghan and his men. Shortly after they had a conclave with Pontiac at Ouiatanon and signed a peace treaty with him. When news of the treaty reached Ft. Pitt, the commandant sent 100 troops under Captain Thomas Starling to join Croghan and go with him to Ft. Chartres to regarrison the fort. On October 10, 1765, the Union Jack was raised at Chartres and the West was secured for the British.

As for Pontiac his influence waned. In 1766 he made a dreary journey to Oswego on Lake Ontario to smoke the pipe of peace with William Johnson. Three years later the great Indian leader was murdered in an Indian village in the Illinois country. One story is that Pontiac got drunk and was killed in a brawl by an Indian assassin, hired by a British trader. Another version is that after Pontiac signed a final peace with the British, he moved to the junction of the Kankakee and Des Plaines rivers with the Ottawas. Kineboo, an Illinois chieftain who lived there, did not like this intrusion and at a peace conference murdered Pontiac.

In the meantime the British decided to shift American colonial affairs from the secretary of state for the Southern Department to the president of the Board of Trade. In order to give himself more time to determine what would be the best policy for the American Midwest, the president of the Board of Trade, acting upon the findings of his predecessor, issued as a stopgap measure the Proclamation of 1763.

This proclamation, which had as its purpose the quieting of

the fears of the Indians and the aiding of the fur traders, proved unsatisfactory to all parties. Illegal traders and settlers continued to filter in to cheat and inflame the Indians. Indian uneasiness was further increased by the Treaty of Ft. Stanwix in 1768 by which the Iroquois conveyed to the British a shadowy claim to Kentucky. The Cherokee, Shawnee, and Delaware tribes protested that this was their hunting land and the Iroquois had no right to cede it.

The frontiersmen were angry, first because they could not legally go into this fertile land, and second because the fur traders were selling firearms to the Indians with which the latter could better raid the frontier settlements.

The land speculators were disgruntled and frustrated because they could not obtain western lands. Prior to 1768 the Military Associates, the Illinois Company, and the Indiana Company were all unsuccessfully petitioning the crown for tracts of land in the Middle West. When the Earl of Shelburne took over colonial administration in 1766, he advocated a western policy favoring the speculators, but it was not put into effect. In 1768 when William Johnson began to shift the Proclamation line west with the Treaty of Ft. Stanwix, he gave the speculators new hope. Although Stanwix opened only a small part of the western land along the Susquehanna, Allegheny, and Ohio rivers, the speculators felt this was the beginning of a new era, but again they were disappointed. Their petitions for grants of land from the English government and their schemes to buy land directly from the Indians came to naught. Then with the passage of the Quebec Act of 1774 which reinstated French law and Catholicism down to the Ohio River, the speculators felt that all was lost.

The French, who comprised the majority of the white population in the Middle West, also felt mistreated. Left with no civil government by the Proclamation of 1763, they were placed under military rule with no recourse to the courts. The fate of the French in Quebec where English law was enforced was even more tragic. This system, which extended anti-papal decrees against a Catholic province, in effect deprived these people of nearly all their political and civil rights and left them at the mercy of unscrupulous Englishmen who during the next decade systematically stripped them of their property. Thus the Quebec Act, viewed so harshly by American colonists, was actually a belated attempt by the English government to provide fairer treatment for the French.

But even the fur traders, who along with the Indians were to be the favored parties under the provisions of the Proclamation, were dissatisfied with its administration. The eastern Midwest was placed under the supervision of William Johnson, superintendent of Indian affairs for the Northern Department. This department was to be redivided into two or three sub-districts under deputy superintendents; these, in turn, were divided into 26 smaller areas, each embracing one tribe. Each of these tribal districts was to be served by a post where Indians could trade without the danger of being cheated by dishonest traders.

The British government was slow in implementing this system and the administration in practice proved somewhat different. Johnson ruled that all trade must be conducted at Mackinac and Detroit and no traders were to go out to the Indians. The Indians, used to being served at home, refused to come in to the honest traders. Therefore, trade was taken over by the unlicensed traders from Montreal and Albany who furtively went into the Indian villages to barter and by the illegal French *voyageurs* who swarmed over the Northwest from the Spanish posts of Ste. Genevieve and St. Louis (founded in 1764). Both sent their furs down the Mississippi to New Orleans where they received cash, supplies, and more trading goods. Both England and the American colonies were highly disturbed by these illegal Mississippi traders who were making such large inroads into the English peltry trade.

The English officials agreed that something must be done. The commandant at Mackinac believed that traders should again be sent out to divert the furs back into English channels. He tried this in 1767 and paid for his folly with a court martial. On the other hand Johnson felt the system of regulated trading would work if new posts were established at La Baye, Sault Ste. Marie, Sandusky, St. Joseph, Ouiatanon, and Ft. Miami; but the cost of this plan was prohibitive. After considering several alternatives, the newly appointed English secretary of state for the Colonies (which took over the colonial function from the Southern Department in January 1768) settled on a plan for the West. The Indian superintendents were retained, but their powers were restricted to imperial functions, diplomatic questions, land purchases from the

Indians, and readjustments of boundary lines. Thus, the clock was turned backward, and the responsibility for defending the frontiers and for regulating the fur trade was returned to the colonies. Garrisons were withdrawn from all western posts except Mackinac, Detroit, Ft. Pitt, and Ft. Chartres; in 1771 the latter two were also evacuated. The traders were delighted. They swept into the wilderness. In 1769 alone, 77 licenses were issued. Peltry again moved toward Montreal, but at a price. The Indians soon began to complain and grumble about the bad conduct and dishonesty of the unregulated traders.

Just as 1763 marked the beginning of British policy in the West, 1774 marked the end. After that year the British had to concentrate on holding the American colonies rather than on developing western-land and Indian policy. When the revolutionary contest was over, the British no longer had a western problem because they no longer held the West.

The two main events of 1774, the Quebec Act and Lord Dunmore's War, were interesting because of their commentary on things past and their portent for things to come. They demonstrated the weakness in British administration and they also proved an incentive and aid to the Americans in the Revolutionary War.

The Quebec Act, passed in June of 1774, extended the jurisdiction of the Quebec Province south to the Ohio River and west to the Mississippi River. Its main purpose was to return to the French in the Middle West civil rights and religious toleration; rights the French had been wrongly deprived of by the Proclamation of 1763. Whereas the British intended this as a rectification of policy toward the French settlers, the American colonists viewed this as one of the intolerable acts leading to their bid for independence. They felt England was stopping their westward expansion, cancelling their western-land charters, and putting the Catholic church and French law in the Ohio region.

The basic cause of Lord Dunmore's War was a struggle over Kentucky. The Indians wanted it as a hunting ground and the whites wanted it for homes and farms. From 1770-73 the Indians, especially the Shawnee, occasionally raided the white settlements, but the whites were generally the aggressors. In spite of the white attacks, the Indians displayed great restraint until the spring of

1774. Then two events occurred. The Virginians seized the disputed area around the forks of the Ohio from Pennsylvania. The Shawnee had hoped that the Pennsylvania Quakers would find a peaceful solution; but with the coming of the Virginians to Pittsburgh under Dr. John Connolly, they decided peace was impossible. In April 1774 Connolly, using a minor attack on a surveying party as an excuse, urged the frontiersmen to defend themselves. This was tantamount to declaring open season on Indians. A group of frontiersmen under Captain Michael Cresap gathered at the mouth of Wheeling Creek and set out to kill all the Indians they could find. The final breaking point came in late April when a group of Shawnee and Mingo went to trade at a minor post, 15 miles above present-day Steubenville. When the Indians fell into a drunken sleep, a white named Greathouse and a couple of his cohorts proceeded to murder nine of them. Among those killed was a sister of the Mingo chief Logan. The Indians still sought peace, but when their overtures were rebuffed and some Indians killed in the process, the young braves retailiated by killing thirteen frontiersmen.

Since he felt there was no longer a chance of averting war, Governor Dunmore warned the frontier settlements that war had begun and sent out military forces to engage the Indians. In July he sent Major Angus McDonald and 400 men up the Muskingum Valley with orders to destroy any Indian villages they found. McDonald's route of march was to throw a screen between the Ohio tribes and the upper-Ohio settlements. Dunmore also planned two expeditions into Shawnee country, one from Pittsburgh and one from upper Virginia. Changing his original plans, Dunmore, commanding the Pittsburgh force of 1,100 men, decided to drift down the Ohio and strike overland at the Shawnee villages via the Hocking River. The 1,000 Virginians under Colonel Andrew Lewis were to move down the Great Kanawha, cross the Ohio, and ascend the Scioto.

Chief Cornstalk, overjoyed that the Virginians were divided, decided to crush the armies separately. Gathering 1,000 Indians, Cornstalk moved south and intercepted Lewis at Point Pleasant, near the mouth of the Great Kanawha. An all day battle ensued on October 9, 1774. Although the contest was a draw, Cornstalk, believing Virginian reinforcements had arrived, retreated during the night. When Dunmore, marching up the Hocking Valley, received the news, he decided to march right on to the Shawnee villages without waiting for Lewis. He felt the Indians, dispirited by their recent defeat, would surrender in the face of another sudden attack. He was correct. The Indians sued for peace and agreed to the Treaty of Camp Charlotte, which gave the whites the right to occupy Kentucky and to ply their trade on the Ohio River without molestation from the Indians. Thus, this miniature war, waged by the Loyalist Dunmore, helped to keep the western tribes quiet during the years 1775-77, an event which proved very helpful to the Americans in their winning of the West, as well as the East, in the Revolution.

—5—

The Middle West in the Revolution

Actually the coming of the Americans was primarily a continuation of the British and American colonial activity in the Middle West. However, there was a difference in that the Americans were now operating under the auspices of a new independent American government rather than the British government.

Many reasons have been given for the creation of this new independent America during the period 1775-83. They include such causes as British mercantilism, failure to solve the imperial-colonial relationship, social and religious differences, taxation, geographical location, and the desire of Americans to rule the area that they had settled. In a sense the Middle West contributed to these causes of the revolution by inflaming and bringing them to a head. A major reason for the British government instituting new and higher taxes on the colonies was to help pay for the management of its newly acquired empire of which the Middle West was a part. Moreover, the Quebec Act of 1774, which extended Catholicism and French law down to the Ohio River, was viewed by the colonials as one of the intolerable acts. The colonials also believed that the cause of the Indian raids on the frontier was due to the British administrators and traders in the Midwest furnishing the Indians with guns and inciting them to drive the American land companies and settlers out of the area.

The Middle West both influenced the outcome and in turn was also affected by the Revolutionary War. The main military factor in the West was Indians, and the English had more to offer the Indians than the Americans. The English could provide protection for the Indians at Detroit, Mackinac, Oswego, and Niagara and also furnish them with better trading goods and higher prices. In addition, the English promised assistance to the Indians in keeping settlers out of the Indian territory and in retaining the Middle West as a fur country.

Despite their poorer bargaining position, the Americans still tried to neutralize the Indian threat through peaceful means. In 1775 the Continental Congress appointed Indian commissioners who attempted to keep the Indians neutral. The Shawnee and the Delaware responded favorably in 1775 and 1776 to these neutrality overtures largely because of the smarting memories of Lord Dunmore's War. In 1775 the colonists also captured Dunmore's agent who was trying to stir up the western Indians against the Americans. Another reason for America's success in restraining the western Indians was the fact that Henry Hamilton, lieutenant governor of England's western territories, had very few troops. He had only 120 men to protect his own post at Detroit and even smaller garrisons at Mackinac, St. Joseph, Ouiatanon, Vincennes, and Kaskaskia.

The American position in the West, however, worsened in 1777. In the spring of that year, the Shawnee chief, Cornstalk, of Dunmore War fame, came to Fort Randolph (Point Pleasant) to warn the American commander of an imminent Shawnee attack. He and his son and their companions were murdered in cold blood by trigger-happy militiamen who were avenging a Virginia volunteer killed by Indians. This helped cause the Ohio Indians to increase the tempo of their attacks.

Indian raids were particularly severe in Kentucky in 1777. The Kentuckians had to abandon their outlying posts and take shelter at Boonesborough, Harrodsburg, and St. Asaphs. The Kentuckians, however, were not even safe at these larger posts. For example, Chief Blackfish with 300 Shawnee besieged Boonesborough, and the white inhabitants there nearly starved before Blackfish finally left.

In an attempt to protect the western boundary from Indian attacks led by Alexander McKee, Matthew Elliott, Simon Girty, and Charles de Langlade, Virginia built Fort Kittanning, Fort Pitt, Fort Henry, and Fort Randolph; but these forts had little effect. In February 1778 the Continental Congress ordered General Edward Hand to invade the Indian country as far as Sandusky, Ohio, and destroy crops and villages as he went. He returned in disgrace after killing a few friendly Delawares.

The most successful American campaigner in the West during these bleak years was the Virginian, George Rogers Clark, who was responsible for the defense of Kentucky. To stop the English and their Indian allies from harrassing Kentucky, Clark felt it was necessary to capture the English forts in the Middle West. First, he sent out men to determine how the French villagers felt about the American-British conflict. When Clark's spies reported that they thought the French could be won over to the American side, Clark hastened to Williamsburg where he got the aid and backing of Governor Patrick Henry to capture these western posts. After obtaining supplies and men, Clark returned to Fort Massac (10 miles below the Falls of the Ohio). On June 26, 1778, he set out from Fort Massac with 175 seasoned Indian fighters. They reached Kaskaskia after a cross-country march on July 4, 1778. The Illinois posts capitulated without a shot, and soon after Vincennes and Ouiatanon also surrendered to Clark, partly as a result of the persuasive assistance of the French priest, Father Gibault.

This was the high point in American conquests in the West during the Revolutionary War. From this time forward, the Americans managed only to fight a holding action. In October 1778 a force of 1,000 men under the American General Lachlan McIntosh set out from Fort Pitt for an attack on Detroit. He built Fort McIntosh on Big Beaver Creek and left a garrison temporarily at Fort Laurens on the Tuscarawas; but overall his campaign accomplished little.

At the same time that McIntosh began his campaign, Henry Hamilton set out from Detroit with a combined force of 500 Indians and British troops to regain the territory captured by Clark. Hamilton quickly recaptured Ouiatanon and Vincennes and then went into winter quarters to wait for spring. But Clark, with his famous march across icy, swollen streams to Vincennes in February 1779, surprised and tricked Hamilton into surrendering.

But the British and their Indian allies, far from being discouraged by these minor setbacks, continued their forays. In 1780 Emanuel Hesse with a mixed force of 1,000 British and Indians moved south from Mackinac to overwhelm the Illinois villages and to attack forces of America's new ally, Spain. When Hesse reached Cahokia in May 1780, he was met by Clark, whose mere presence scared Hesse's Indians so much that they fled after a few half-hearted sorties. Hesse next went to St. Louis where the Spanish met him with cannon, and he retreated to Mackinac. At about the same time, Captain Henry Bird with 1,150 British troops and Indians was dispatched from Detroit to harass Kentucky and to divert Clark. Bird was more successful. He captured and looted Riddle's and Martin's stations in Kentucky before returning to Detroit.

Nettled by Bird's raid, Clark travelled to Harrodsburg in June 1780, recruited a force of 1,000 men, and moved north. After burning Old Chillicothe, Clark marched on the Indian village of Piqua on the Big Miami River where Simon Girty and several hundred Indians were assembled. Clark forced Girty to flee after several hours of fierce fighting. Clark's vigorous campaigning freed Kentucky from attack for the remainder of the year.

Despite Clark's efforts, the American position in the Middle West in 1780 was precarious. The Indians remained friendly to the British, and the French villagers began to defect to the English because they did not like America's strict rules, traders, and land speculators. The American position did improve slightly in 1781. Colonel Andrew Brodhead led 300 troops against the Delaware in 1781, captured their village, and executed several as a lesson to the others. The Delaware heeded the warning and moved west. In the same year Captain Eugene Pouree led a band of Spaniards and Indians from St. Louis, captured St. Joseph (Niles, Michigan) from the English, held the post 24 hours, and then retreated.

But defeats in the west remained more common than victories. Clark could not get Kentuckians or Virginians to help him attack Detroit, so in the fall of 1781 he began to construct a new fort, Ft. Nelson, at Louisville. Meanwhile, Indian raids continued, and Virginia, engaged in fighting at home, allowed the chain of forts on the upper Ohio to fall into decay.

Also in 1781 the British moved a group of Christian Delawares along with their mentors (Moravian missionaries) to "Captives Town." Facing starvation, 150 of them returned to their former village to gather their crops for winter. Shortly after, a group of hot-headed Pennsylvanians, ousted from their homes by the settlement of the Virginia-Pennsylvania boundary, crossed the Ohio to seize land. They arrived at Gnadenhatten and were given food and lodging by the friendly Delawares. On the fourth day the whites fell on their hymn-singing hosts in the Moravian church and slaughtered them all—men, women, and children. This wanton brutality gave the Ohio Indians a new reason for war. The Delaware, Shawnee, and Wyandot made the whole borderland unsafe.

To meet this threat, Colonel William Crawford marched out from Ft. Pitt into the Ohio country. On the upper reaches of the Sandusky River, the Americans engaged a band of Shawnee and Delaware. After a bitter battle Crawford began a retreat on June 4, 1782, that turned into a rout. Fifty Americans were killed and nine were carried away to Delaware villages to be tortured to death.

Taking advantage of the favorable situation created by the Indian raids against the Americans, two British expeditions set out from Detroit in 1782. The one led by Joseph Brant attacked Ft. Henry and raided as far east as Hannastown, Pennsylvania. The other under Captain William Caldwell and Alexander McKee went to Kentucky and stormed and burned Bryant's station. A hastily formed group of Kentuckians followed them and fell into an ambush at Licking River in the Battle of Blue Licks. Sixty Americans were killed. Not even Clark's successful march against the Shawnee at Chillicothe and Piqua in November of 1782 could wipe out the sting of Blue Licks. Clark's march proved to be the last campaign of the Revolution. When Clark returned, the preliminary Peace of Paris had been signed.

The Americans received in peace what they could not accomplish by war. Although Kentucky was still in American hands, Detroit, Mackinac, and even the Illinois country were British held. Despite this the United States received that part of the Middle West east of the Mississippi River. Why England was this generous is difficult to say. Perhaps it was England's desire to give a generous peace and by so doing improve relations with America; or perhaps Clark's campaign entered into the decision. All that is certain in this matter, however, is that Europe was aware of Clark's campaign. Joseph Mathias Gerard de Rayneval, secretary to the Comte de Vergennes, noted it in a memorandum during the peace negotiations.

With the cession of the eastern Middle West to the United States in 1783, the Americans appeared to have a firm hold in the area. However, with the opposition of the Indians and English in the eastern Midwest and the entrenched position of the Spanish in the western Midwest, the American position in the area was still extremely tenuous.

—6—

The Decade of Indian Wars, 1785-1795

To open the land and facilitate the entrance of American squatters into the Middle West, land commissioners made a series of treaties with the Indian tribes in the area. At Ft. Stanwix in 1784, land commissioners pressured the Iroquois into surrendering all claims to the Old Northwest in exchange for a few small presents. Shortly after in January 1785 the Chippewa, Ottawa, Delaware, and Wyandot were summoned to Ft. McIntosh and forced to give up all their Ohio lands except for a reservation between the Cuyahoga-Tuscarawas portage and the Maumee River. These treaties only made the Indians angrier, because they maintained that the tribes who surrendered these lands did not even own them.

Meanwhile the Americans continued to pour in. Colonel Josiah Harmar, who commanded the federal troops, tried to restrain and drive out the Americans illegally settling on the land, but he had little success.

Especially embarrassed were the land commissioners who were trying to obtain Shawnee consent to the cession of land. The commissioners used threats of war to bring Wyandot, Delaware, and Shawnee tribesmen to a conference at the mouth of the Great Miami in January 1786. The Shawnee reluctantly signed the Treaty of Ft. Finney, which reaffirmed the Ft. McIntosh cession and extended the boundary westward along the White River to the mouth of the Wabash. As soon as the Shawnee were safely back in their villages, however, they repudiated the Finney agreement. Under Shawnee leadership Indian dissatisfaction reached a boiling point in the spring of 1786. Throughout the Ohio country, bands of Indians fell on traders and raided settlements. These attacks were climaxed in July 1786, when 500 Miami warriors temporarily laid siege to Vincennes.

Since the few soldiers stationed at Forts Harmar and Finney were unable to afford protection to the trespassing Americans, the latter took matters into their own hands. They fitted out two expeditions. One under the command of an overaged and somewhat alcoholic George R. Clark marched north from Ft. Steuben, a new federal outpost across the river from Louisville, to crush the Miami Indians on the upper-Wabash and Miami rivers. But Clark's 1,200 militiamen mutinied at the mouth of Vermillion Creek and returned in disorder without sighting a single foe. The second expedition led by Colonel Benjamin Logan destroyed ten towns and 15,000 bushels of corn. The Indians, unimpressed by these two campaigns, continued their attempt to drive the "Big Knives" completely out of the Ohio country.

Despite the disturbed state of Indian affairs, the federal government in an effort to reduce its indebtedness decided that it would sell land in the Ohio country. Between 1785 and 1787 the United States began a survey of the first seven ranges in Ohio and put them up for sale. Even though land speculators were active during this period, land sales proved very disappointing.

Acquisition of Indian lands by the whites continued and relations grew more tense. The Indians were in agreement that they should keep the Americans out, but for a time they could not agree on where the boundary should be drawn. Whereas the Shawnee, Kickapoo, and Miami insisted on the Ohio River boundary, the Wyandot, Delaware, and Seneca refused to endorse this plan because they believed it would lead to war. When the Indians met with the U. S. commissioners at Ft. Harmar in January 1789, they were so torn with dissension that Arthur St. Clair, governor of the newly created Northwest Territory, was able to dictate a treaty reaffirming the treaties of Ft. McIntosh and Ft. Finney. The Indians drifted back into the wilderness, angered and disgruntled. To make matters worse the Kentucky frontiersmen, fearing the Indian confederation would cause a new war, began sending small raiding parties against the Indians in the summer of 1788. These actions by the whites united the Indians into a common cause, and the United States found itself involved in a new Indian war.

The first two U. S. expeditions sent out to crush the militant red men were failures. General Josiah Harmar, commander of the western army, led 1,400 troops northward from Ft. Washington in September 1790. He moved so slowly that the Indians had time to disappear into the forests along the Maumee River. In all he killed a few Indians, burned a few villages, and lost 183 men. The Indians continued to raid and kill, supplied and equipped by the English at Detroit and by other traders who wanted Indian furs.

Accompanied by several village-burning detachments, Arthur St. Clair in the summer of 1791 led 3,000 troops against the Indians. Plagued by desertions, he frittered away the summer moving slowly toward Maumee. He built three log forts, Ft. Hamilton, Ft. St. Clair, and Ft. Jefferson. On arrival at the Maumee in November 1791, he failed to take a defensible position or to post adequate guards. His decimated command was surrounded and 630 were killed and 238 were wounded. The Indians, jubilant over this victory, carried the war to every settlement north of the Ohio River during the winter of 1791-92. The British took advantage of this situation to urge the Americans to set up an Indian buffer state in the Old Northwest with which England could continue to trade. Thomas Jefferson, American secretary of state, rejected this proposal and demanded that the British withdraw their garrisons from American soil as provided in the Treaty of Paris of 1783. The British, realizing that further negotiations on this subject were futile, broke off talks in December 1792. They realized that only further victories by their Indian allies would force the United States into creating a buffer state.

In the spring of 1793 American commissioners were selected to confer with the Indians at Sandusky. Upon arrival in Ohio, the commissioners learned that the Indians would accept only the Ohio River as a boundary and so they retraced their steps to inform President George Washington of their findings. Washington, anticipating such a report, sent word to his new military commander in the West, General Anthony Wayne, to begin a new campaign. Wayne proceeded slowly. He built a new outpost, Ft. Greenville, six miles beyond Ft. Jefferson and spent the winter of 1793-94 drilling his 1,000 seasoned troops. In the spring of

1794 Wayne moved his force northward. He stopped at the site of St. Clair's defeat, built Ft. Recovery, and beat off a sizable Indian attack. This defeat disheartened the Indians. Pushing on along the Au Glaize River, Wayne reached the Maumee in August 1794.

Meanwhile 2,000 Indians had gathered at Ft. Miami. This fort had been constructed by the British in the spring of 1794 to defend Detroit against a possible attack by Wayne. England, at war with France and on bad terms with the United States, had promised the Indians that England would aid them against the Americans. The Indians, assured of English aid, were confidently awaiting Wayne's arrival.

After throwing up a rude fortification on the Maumee, Wayne sent out word to the Indians that he would march against the position they had selected (a tangle of fallen trees) near Ft. Miami on August 17, 1794. On the appointed day he moved forward, but instead of attacking he camped 10 miles away. He had sent out false information on the time of his attack on purpose, because he knew the Indian habit of fasting before battle. For three days he remained immobile. Then on August 20 when 500 warriors wandered away to gorge food at Ft. Miami, he attacked. For a few minutes the Indians stood their ground and then they retreated. The Battle of Fallen Timbers, which had taken months of preparation, was over in less than two hours. Wayne's victory was not decisive because of the number of Indian casualties (only 50 were killed), but because their spirit was broken when the English failed to come to their aid. Wayne destroyed the Indian villages up to the gates of Ft. Miami while the British commandant fumed and did nothing. After building Ft. Wayne to guard his conquest, Wayne summoned the dejected, deserted, scattered chiefs together and dictated the Treaty of Greenville in 1795. By this treaty the Indians surrendered all of Ohio, except a strip along Lake Erie, a triangle of land in Indiana, and 16 small, fur-trading areas. From 1795 until 1810 the western Indians were relatively quiet and Americans poured into the area.

The fate of the British posts in America (Dutchman's Point and Point-Aufer on Lake Champlain, Oswegatchie on the St. Lawrence, and Oswego, Niagara, Miami, Detroit, and Mackinac on the Great Lakes) was also affected by the Battle of Fallen

Timbers. The British had agreed to pull out of these posts in 1783, but the Northwest Company convinced the British government that to pull out would result in the loss of a fur business valued at one-half million dollars. The English, using the failure of the Americans to pay their debts to the English as an excuse, kept the posts and encouraged the Indians to fight the United States.

For a time the Indians, as noted above, were relatively successful, but Fallen Timbers was a bad omen for both the Indians and the British. In addition, the British had European troubles. The first coalition against Napoleon was collapsing, and the countries of northern Europe were uniting in the League of Armed Neutrality to protest England's high-handed interference with their shipping. Rumors were rife that the United States would join this League and England wished to prevent this. England decided it was wiser to back down on the border posts, especially since fur trade south of the Great Lakes had declined and since it would take large sums of money and thousands of men to repair and garrison the posts. As in 1783 Europe's distress proved to be America's success (as the noted historian, Thomas A. Bailey, expressed it).

In 1794 John Jay began negotiating with Baron Grenville, English secretary of state for Foreign Affairs, on the removal of the English from the western posts. Grenville was very conciliatory until he learned from George Hammond, English minister to the United States, that the United States' threat to join the League of Armed Neutrality was only a bluff. In his attempt to stay on good terms with England, Alexander Hamilton had passed this information along to Hammond and actually undercut Jay. Despite this, Jay's Treaty did provide for English removal from the disputed posts by June 1, 1796. The United States, however, had to guarantee Canadian traders indefinite passage over portages along the border, allow them to operate south of the boundary, promise not to tax the furs they carried back to Montreal, and agree to levy the same tax on English trading goods as on American trading goods. But despite these latter provisions, the Jay Treaty went a long way toward making the eastern section of the Midwest truly a part of the United States.

—7—

The First American Settlers in the Eastern Middle West

In the period after the Revolutionary War, the removal of the Indians and English from the eastern Middle West was accompanied by the arrival of American settlers who began to populate the region. These settlers generally came in three waves. First came the hunter who trapped, hunted, dared the wilderness, and often married a squaw. Next came the farmer-hunter who purchased the hunter's site, cleared more land, pastured his stock on the wild range, but still lived largely by his rifle. His squalid cabin often did not have even the most rudimentary comforts. He was adventurous, restless, and shiftless and felt cramped by the presence of close neighbors. When neighbors pressed about him, he would sell his claim, gather together his cattle and few possessions, and wander forth again to seek uncleared land. The third group consisted of men who were thrifty as well as adventurous, but more industrious than restless. These men brought more luxuries to the backwoods, held the land, and passed it on to their children.

As conditions became more settled, villages and towns developed. After a few lots were sold and a few houses built, a storekeeper would come who in turn would be followed by a saloon keeper, a doctor, a lawyer, a blacksmith, and a schoolmaster who was also usually the minister. Then whether the town grew or remained a village depended on the natural resources of the community and the availability of transportation facilities.

The chief topics of thought and conversation of the settlers were land and Indians. On one occasion George R. Clark could raise no men for an Indian expedition until he closed the local land offices. Nearly every hunter and Indian fighter kept watch for some fertile bottom on which to build a cabin. Occasionally more than one man would claim the same land by squatter's rights or prior settlement and this could lead to lawsuits or bloody affrays.

This desire for land inevitably led to conflict with Indians as well as whites. The Indians viewed this land as their hunting grounds; when the whites took it, the Indians often resisted. Indian-white relations were made still worse by the dual set of standards that frontiersmen had for Indians and whites. A frontiersman would usually treat another white fairly, but he had no respect for an Indian's rights, privileges, property, or even his life. In his *Winning of the West,* Theodore Roosevelt glossed over and rationalized this questionable set of values by saying that it made little difference whether this land was won by treaty or murder, because Americans had been ordained to possess and utilize this land for the benefit of civilization and mankind.

To facilitate the populating of the Middle West, the federal government, beginning in about 1785, made treaties with the Indians to open the land and also provided a system of land survey to regulate settlement and sales. This survey system, which was innaugurated by the Land Ordinance of 1785, initially applied to the southeast corner of Ohio. It provided for the division of the area into ranges of townships six miles square surveyed on a given base line. These townships were in turn subdivided into thirty-six sections of 640 acres each. The minimum acreage that could be purchased was a section and the price was set at one dollar an acre.

Although this seemed a reasonable price, land sales were slow during the decade after 1787. There were several reasons for this. First, land was plentiful and $640 was a lot of money to most settlers. Consequently many frontiersmen, instead of buying, squatted on a piece of land outside the survey area. Second, Indians were on the warpath in the Midwest during this period, and many settlers did not wish to risk being separated from his scalp.

With land selling slowly, Congress was willing to listen to a scheme put forth by the Ohio Company, established by Brigadier

Generals Rufus Putnam and Benjamin Tupper in 1786. The Ohio Company spokesman was Reverend Manasseh Cutler who through manipulation and collusion managed to buy 1,500,000 acres of land at about eight cents an acre. Another part of this venture, the Scioto Association scheme, which involved the purchase of 3,500,000 acres, was to reward the cooperative government officials who aided in the Ohio Company purchase.

While in Washington Manasseh Cutler also worked for the passage of the Ordinance of 1787, which set up a system whereby portions of the Old Northwest could be admitted as equal states in the United States. This act served as a stimulus to the westward movement because settlers were now more certain of having more control in their local governments.

During the winter of 1787 and 1788, a group of settlers led by Rufus Putnam of the Ohio Company proceeded down the Ohio River to the Ohio country and built a village. First called Adelphia, it was later renamed Marietta in honor of Marie Antoinette, the French queen, as an expression of thanks for French aid during the Revolution.

Following the lead of the Ohio Company, John C. Symmes, a New Jersey politician, purchased a large tract of land along the Great Miami River in the Ohio region. Major Benjamin Sites brought the first boatload of pioneers down the Ohio River to the Symmes Purchase around 1788. Within the first two or three years, the Indians killed 20 of these settlers. This tended to discourage additional settlement.

Although Symmes thought he had purchased one-million acres of land in Ohio, Congress actually allotted him only 248,500 acres. As a result he granted land that he did not own. Among those so victimized were the groups that laid out Columbia (1788) near the mouth of the Little Miami; Losantiville (1788), rechristened Cincinnati by Arthur St. Clair; and Dayton (1795). This confusion discouraged settlement still more.

The Scioto Company proved to be a much greater scandal. The company sent the dreamy poet, Joel Barlow, to France to sell land. Barlow got involved with a corrupt Englishman named William Playfair. The upshot was that 600 Frenchmen were sold land that the Scioto Company did not own and Playfair kept the proceeds. The French were told they had been duped when they arrived at Alexandria, but a number of them went west to the rude cabins at Gallipolis anyway. Of these, some stayed at Gallipolis and others moved to a 24,000-acre grant that a sympathetic Congress gave to them in 1795.

Other settlements in Ohio prior to 1800 included Chillicothe, which was established in 1796, and Cleveland, founded in 1798 by Oliver Phelps and Moses Cleaveland of the Connecticut Land Company. Cleveland was one of the first towns laid out in the Connecticut Reserve of northern Ohio.

Since Ohio was a buffer area between the French and English, French settlements in Ohio were almost nonexistant and the American settlers there had to start from scratch. However, in many parts of the Middle West the American settlers in the 1780's and 1790's simply moved in and transformed the sparsely populated French villages into American outposts. The estimated 1,040 French adult males in the Old Northwest in 1787, widely scattered at such settlements as Vincennes, Ft. Wayne, Detroit, Cahokia, Kaskaskia, Prairie du Chien, Dubuque, Mackinac, Green Bay, St. Louis, and Duluth, were quickly inundated by Americans.

Vincennes was an excellent example of this process. At the time of the coming of the Americans to Vincennes, the French there were easy-going and fun-loving. To American money-making, improvements, and politics, they were indifferent. A fiddle, some wine, some dancing, and conversation were the wellsprings of their existance. Inter-marriage with the Indians was even accepted. Against the ambition and drive of the Americans, their culture could not long endure and they were soon absorbed in the American stream.

Other examples of this transformation were observable at villages in Iowa, Illinois, and Missouri. Julien Dubuque had been the first man to become a permanent settler in the state of Iowa. He obtained permission from the Sauk and Fox Indians to work the lead mines of the area around 1788. His miners roamed unmolested among the Indians on both sides of the Mississippi. It was not long, however, before he had trouble with the Indians, lost his mining concession to the United States government, and was deluged by a flood of Americans who moved into the region.

Within a year after the departure of George R. Clark from Kaskasia in 1780, John Dodge of Connecticut moved into this southern Illinois community and practically took over its political administration. This situation continued until about 1790 when Arthur St. Clair, governor of the Northwest Territory, finally put an end to Dodge's tyranny.

The first settlement in Missouri was in the St. Louis area. Forty Spanish and French families had moved there in 1764. By 1772 there were 1,288 (803 white and 485 Negro) people in Missouri of which nearly half were in St. Louis. The Americans did not begin to pour in until after 1795, when Spain, fearing loss of the Louisiana Territory to England, threw open the gates for Americans to come into Missouri to serve as a buffer against England. Moses Austin came to St. Louis in 1798. He sank the first lead shaft and built a shot tower on a cliff at Herculaneum. Daniel Boone joined his sons at La Charette, Missouri, in 1799. On his arrival Boone was given command of the district where he settled and a land grant of 8,500 acres on the Missouri River. Boone and his sons began making salt at Boone's lick and were soon supplying the residents of St. Louis with salt.

—8—

The Admission of Ohio as a State

In 1779 that portion of the Midwest north of the Ohio River and east of the Mississippi River began its governmental existence as Illinois County in the state of Virginia. At that time a system of elected judges was established. These judges acted officially until 1782 and unofficially until 1787. Under the Articles of Confederation, the Old Northwest led a harried existance. There were Revolutionary War battles, Indian raids, and struggles between various eastern states for control of the region. However, amidst this turmoil the Articles Congress did lay the foundation for a settlement of the political problems of the Midwest.

The landed eastern states were eventually persuaded to turn over their western claims to the federal government. Once under federal control, the Articles Congress passed legislation for the regulation of the Old Northwest. The most important of these laws was the Land Ordinance of 1785, which established a system of land survey for the Middle West, and the Ordinance of 1787. The latter ordinance laid the political basis for the eastern Midwest. It established the Northwest Territory, bordered by the Ohio River on the south and the Mississippi River on the west. This territory was to be divided into not less than three nor more than five states. The greatest contribution of this Ordinance to the theory of government was its provision which allowed the admission of colonies to the union as states on an equal footing with the older states.

This statehood came in three stages. The first stage was an autocracy in which the federal government appointed the territorial officials. The second stage began when the population reached 5,000. At that time the people could elect one of the two territorial legislative bodies. When the population reached

60,000, the territory could be admitted as a state by Congress. This equality principle, admitting new states on an equal basis with the old which was incorporated in the United States Constitution in 1787, began a new epoch in the history of colonization. In addition, the Ordinance of 1787 had a bill of rights, clauses prohibiting slavery and aiding education, and a democratic inheritance clause which provided an even distribution of property to the heirs in case a person died without leaving a will.

With the Northwest Ordinance as its basis, the government of the Northwest Territory went into operation in July 1788. Originally at Marietta, the seat of government was soon moved to Cincinnati. During its first eleven years, the Northwest Territory did not have a legislature and was under the control of an appointed oligarchy. Governor Arthur St. Clair and Judges Samuel H. Parsons, John M. Varnum, and John C. Symmes were the first officials in charge of the territory. Despite its undemocratic form, the government was relatively efficient and just because the officials were relatively honest and fair.

The pioneers in the Northwest, however, did not like the undemocratic nature of the first territorial stage. In addition, they did not like St. Clair because he was an autocrat and a Federalist and they were Republicans. His defeat by the Indians in 1791 further lowered his prestige. In 1798 St. Clair was finally goaded into ordering a census, which showed that there were more than 5,000 adult males in the area. Therefore despite his coolness to the idea, the Northwest Territory went into the second territorial stage and St. Clair called an election to select a legislature. This newly elected legislature, dominated by Republicans, chose William H. Harrison as delegate from the Northwest Territory to Congress. This action was also displeasing to the governor and his friends because they wanted the governor's son, Arthur St. Clair, Jr., to receive the post.

The following year St. Clair began his campaign to keep the Northwest Territory Federalist and to prevent any part of it from becoming a state. His scheme was to gerrymander the Northwest Territory into three territories, divided by boundaries running north from the mouths of the Scioto and Kentucky rivers. By doing this he felt that he could reduce the population below statehood level in all three areas and split the Republican strength in the Scioto Valley, so as to allow the Federalist machine at Marietta to dominate the eastern territory and his machine at Cincinnati to dominate the western section.

The Republicans countered with a plan to divide the area into two parts with the boundary running north from the mouth of the Miami River. This not only would keep the Republicans united in the Scioto Valley but would also retain over 60,000 people in the eastern portion so that immediate statehood would be possible. Harrison sided with the Republican plan and helped to push through Congress a modified version which divided the Northwest Territory into two parts on a line running north from the mouth of the Kentucky River. The western portion of the Old Northwest Territory thus established was renamed the Indiana Territory with its capital at Vincennes. For his efforts in its creation, Harrison was rewarded with the governorship.

St. Clair still opposed statehood for the eastern part of the Northwest Territory. He believed that it would become a Republican state, that it was too far from Washington, and that the people were too ignorant for self-government. But the power of St. Clair was on the wane. Thomas Jefferson and the Republicans had become dominant in Washington, and a group of Ohions led by Thomas Worthington were working to make Ohio a state. In November of 1802 a convention met at Chillicothe, listened to an anti-Republican tirade by St. Clair, and then voted for immediate admission to the Union. Although they modeled their constitution after Tennessee's, they went further in liberalizing its provisions. The people of Ohio gave suffrage to all citizens who were white, male, tax paying, and over 21, increased the power of the legislature, took the veto and appointive powers away from the governor, and provided that the state judges be elected by the legislature. Ohio also agreed not to tax public lands for five years in return for federal public lands to be given the state for education and road building. Congress accepted both the constitution and the other provisions, and in 1803 Ohio became the first state of the Middle West to be admitted to the United States.

—9—

Spanish Interlude, 1763-1800

At the same time that England acquired from France that portion of the Midwest east of the Mississippi River, Spain obtained that portion west of the Mississippi River. The main center of Spanish activity in the Middle West after 1763 was at St. Louis. In 1763 Pierre L. Liguest (Laclede) came up to the St. Louis area from New Orleans and established a trading post for the purpose of exploiting the Missouri fur trade. His stepson, Auguste Chouteau, began construction on a site in February 1764 which became the future city of St. Louis. In 1769 Alexander O'Reilly took over the administration and exploration of the upper-Louisiana Territory for the Spanish. His Spanish-Missouri Fur Company, established on the French trading-post system, began the exploration of Nebraska and the Dakotas.

Despite their activity, the Spanish had moved only a short distance out of St. Louis by 1785. After 1785 the Spanish began to travel the upper-Missouri River more to protect their land and keep out the British and Americans than to obtain trade. In 1789 Juan Munier discovered the Poncas living near the mouth of the Niobrara River and started trading with them. Jacques D'Eglise made expeditions up the Missouri to the Mandans in 1790 and 1793. In the latter year the Company of Explorers of the Upper Missouri, established by Jacques Clamorgan, also began trading with the Mandan. In all, this company made two or three expeditions into the Dakota area. The main French and Spanish settlement in Kansas at this time was in the Kansas City area.

PART II

THE YOUNG MIDDLE WEST
1801-1841

—10—

Acquisition and Exploration of The Western Middle West

The American conquest of the western portion of the Middle West took place largely after 1803. The assault against Spanish control in the West in the 1780's was led by England's Hudson Bay and Northwest companies. Operating out of Mackinac and Prairie du Chien, these traders went as far west as the Mandan villages on the upper-Missouri River. By 1791 Spain, fearing the loss of northern-Louisiana Territory, took steps to retain control of the area. Auguste Chouteau, a French woodsman, was dispatched to build Ft. Carondelet among the Osage villages in 1794. At the same time French traders were authorized to form a trading company at St. Louis.

The Spanish also invited American settlers in to serve as a bulwark against the English. Immigrants could obtain land for the cost of the filing fee. They were supposed to be Catholic and loyal to the Spanish king, but these provisions were not rigidly enforced. The leading Spanish towns in the Missouri country in the 1790's were St. Louis, Ste. Genevieve, New Madrid, St. Charles, Cape Girardeau, and La Charette. Despite their efforts Spanish influence in the Middle West was weak outside of the Missouri country. As late as 1803 the Chippewa and Sioux Indians in Minnesota and Dakota were still controlled more by British trading companies than by the Spanish.

The Americans in the Middle West first came in conflict with the Spanish over the navigation of the Mississippi River. In 1783 the British turned their right to navigate the Mississippi over to the Americans. The Spanish, however, opposed the transfer of this navigation right to the United States. After twelve years of squabbles, negotiations, and threats, the Spanish finally agreed to a place of deposit for Amercan goods at New Orleans by the Thomas Pinckney Treaty of 1795. But within a few years the Spanish were again threatening to close the Mississippi to the transit of American goods.

At this juncture Napoleon Bonaparte conceived a scheme for a world empire. By the Treaty of San Ildefonso in 1800, Napoleon acquired the Louisiana Territory in exchange for the small northern Italian kingdom of Tuscany. But Napoleon's scheme for a colonial empire with France, Santo Domingo, and Louisiana as its focal points broke down. Just as yellow fever and the defeat of the French army in Santo Domingo by Toussaint l' Ouverture caused French withdrawal from that island, the European war caused Napoleon to relinquish Louisiana.

Just as circumstances were conspiring to cause Napoleon to favor selling Louisiana, events were occurring in the United States to make President Thomas Jefferson want to buy it. In October 1802 the Spanish intendant closed the Mississippi River to the Americans and immediately the West was up in arms. The West was also afraid of the consequences if the powerful France took over this area lying so close to America's western boundary. Jefferson, realizing that something must be done, obtained approval from Congress to purchase the New Orleans area. When Jefferson's representative, Robert R. Livingston, reached Paris, Napoleon shocked him by offering to sell the whole Louisiana area for $15,000,000 (four cents an acre). Although Jefferson was a strict constructionist and Congress had not given him the authority to spend this much money or to buy this much land, he instructed Livingston and James Monroe to make the purchase.

Actually Louisiana was not Napoleon's to sell; he had an agreement with Spain that he would not sell it to a third party. This fact caused Professor Edward Channing to conclude that the United States acted as "the accomplice of the greatest highwayman in modern history, and the goods which we received were those which he compelled his unwilling victim to disgorge."

Theodore Roosevelt took quite another approach to the purchase. He said that the United States would have acquired the Louisiana Territory even if Jefferson had not bought it. The American frontiersmen swarming into the valleys of the Ten-

Meriwether Lewis (1774-1809)
Explorer of American Northwest

Painting by Charles W. Peale. From *Dictionary of American Portraits* by Hayward and Blanche Cirker, Dover Publications, Inc., New York, 1967. *Reprinted through permission of the publisher.*

William Clark (1770-1838)
Explorer of American Northwest

Painting by Charles W. Peale. From *Dictionary of American Portraits* by Hayward and Blanche Cirker, Dover Publications, Inc., New York, 1967. *Reprinted through permission of the publisher.*

Daniel Boone (1734-1820)
Pioneer

Engraved by James B. Longacre from a painting by Chester Harding. From *Dictionary of American Portraits* by Hayward and Blanche Cirker, Dover Publications, Inc., New York, 1967. *Reprinted through permission of the publisher.*

Zebulon M. Pike (1779-1813)
Western explorer and discoverer of
Pike's Peak

Painting by Charles W. Peale, Courtesy Independence National Historical Park. From *Dictionary of American Portraits* by Hayward and Blanche Cirker, Dover Publications, Inc., New York, 1967. *Reprinted through permission of the publisher.*

nessee, the Cumberland, and the Ohio would have flowed on across the Mississippi to acquire the area by occupation. Be this as it may, the United States obtained a bargain in the Louisiana Purchase of 1803. It not only gave the United States navigation of the Mississippi, but also added the future states of Louisiana and Arkansas and all or part of the midwestern states of Minnesota, North Dakota, South Dakota, Nebraska, Iowa, Missouri, and Kansas.

After purchasing the Louisiana Territory in 1803, Jefferson decided that he should have this unknown area explored. He selected Meriweather Lewis and William Clark for the mission. In May 1804 they set out from St. Louis with a party of 45 men in three boats. Ascending the Missouri River, they passed a few Creole and American villages in Missouri. They made their first Kansas landfall at the present site of Kansas City. As they proceeded up the Missouri, they saw large numbers of buffalo, elk, antelope, deer, coyotes, wolves, and wild turkeys. Late in October 1804 they reached the villages of the friendly Mandan Indians north of present-day Bismarck, North Dakota. Here they built Ft. Mandan and spent the winter. It was here that they secured the services of Toussaint Charbonneau, valuable mainly because of his Indian wife, Sacajawea (bird woman), who served as a guide to the Lewis and Clark party on its journey to the Pacific Coast. In April 1805 the expedition left Ft. Mandan; after a successful trip to the Far West, it retraced its steps and arrived back at St. Louis in September 1806.

A second famous American explorer in the Middle West in this period was Lieutenant Zebulon M. Pike. In August 1805 Jefferson sent the 26-year-old Pike with 20 men to find the headwaters of the Mississippi River. Pike spent the winter in Minnesota where he held councils with the Sioux and the Chippewa. He obtained some land from the Indians for military posts and warned the British not to fly the British flag over their fur-trading posts in Minnesota. Although successful in his English and Indian parleys, he failed in his original mission. He mistook Leech Lake for the source of the Mississippi. He returned to St. Louis in April 1806.

Upon his return Pike was sent west in July 1806 with a party of 23 men to make peace with the Pawnee Indians and to explore the area drained by the Arkansas and Red rivers. In spite of a larger Spanish force in the area, Pike was able to persuade the Pawnee to take down the Spanish flag and run up the Stars and Stripes. Pike then proceeded west to Colorado where he set up a camp. Venturing too far south, he was captured by the Spanish and taken first to Santa Fe and then to Chihuahua. After questioning Pike and the men with him, the Spanish finally delivered them to United States authorities at Natchitoches, Louisiana, in July 1807.

Later expeditions included Henry R. Schoolcraft's exploration into the Ozark Mountains of Missouri and Arkansas in 1818 and Colonel Henry Atkinson's "Yellowstone Expedition" in 1819. Atkinson's group went up the Missouri to Council Bluffs where they built Ft. Atkinson to serve as winter quarters. The scientific portion of this expedition was commanded by Major Stephen H. Long. Long reached Denver but failed in his objectives of finding the sources of the Platte and Red rivers. He did aid in building the image of the western Midwest as the "Great American Desert."

In 1820 Governor Lewis Cass of Michigan Territory traveled through the upper Midwest and into Minnesota to negotiate with the Indians and survey the area. Henry R. Schoolcraft, who accompanied him, kept a journal of the trip.

Three years later Stephen H. Long commanded an exploring party which ascended the Minnesota River and visited the Pembina settlement on the Red River of the North. Long ascertained the location of the 49th parallel in the Pembina region and proved that Pembina was located on territory belonging to the United States. After visiting Lake Winnipeg, Long's party journeyed eastward to the north shore of Lake Superior and returned to the East by way of the Great Lakes.

In 1832 Henry S. Schoolcraft again returned to Minnesota seeking the source of the Mississippi. Schoolcraft discovered that Pike had been in error and that Lake Itasca rather than Leech Lake was the true source of the Mississippi River. Schoolcraft derived the name Itasca for the lake from a combination of *caput* (head) and *veritas* (true). Joseph N. Nicollet, exploring in the

Minnesota area in 1833, confirmed Schoolcraft's findings as to the source of the Mississippi.

In addition to the legal settlers and the authorized explorers, other informal explorers in the Middle West were the squatters and fur traders who traversed the rivers and streams of the area.

—11—

Indian Policy and Administration

Indian Policy, 1783-1815

With the coming of the Americans in 1783, the Indians began a 100-year period of wars, treaties, and removals that was to end their culture as they knew it and to place many of them in premature graves. From 1783 to 1815 the Americans contended that the Indians were allies of the British and as such were enemies to be despoiled of their land. This acquisition of Indian land by the Americans was accomplished through a series of treaties and Indian wars. For a decade the Indians almost fought the Americans to a standstill; then in August 1794 General Anthony Wayne decisively crushed them at Fallen Timbers and the Indians were forced to sign the Treaty of Ft. Greenville in 1795. By this battle and this treaty, Wayne not only obtained for the United States most of Ohio and the southeastern corner of Indiana but also relative peace in the Midwest for the next fifteen years.

The Indian war that began in 1810 was due largely to the land-grabbing tactics of William H. Harrison, governor of Indiana Territory. He began this land-acquisition program in 1802 when he called representatives of the Delaware, Kickapoo, and Wea tribes together at Vincennes to adjust disputes growing out of the Greenville Treaty. At this meeting he not only adjusted the outstanding disputes in favor of the United States, but also coerced and bribed the Indians into ceding territory allegedly purchased by the Wabash Land Company 25 years earlier.

Harrison regularly made similar treaties with the Indian tribes for the next seven years. In 1803 he persuaded the weakened Kaskaskia to surrender their flimsy title to the Illinois country

Tecumseh (1768-1813)
Shawnee Indian chief

Courtesy Bureau of American Ethnology, Smithsonian Institution. From *Dictionary of American Portraits* by Hayward and Blanche Cirker, Dover Publications, Inc., New York, 1967. *Reprinted through permission of the publisher.*

William H. Harrison (1773-1841)
President of the United States

John J. Astor (1763-1848)
Fur trader and financier

Painting by Gilbert Stuart. From *Dictionary of American Portraits* by Hayward and Blanche Cirker, Dover Publications, Inc., New York, 1967. *Reprinted through permission of the publisher.*

Peter Cartwright (1785-1872)
Methodist frontier circuit rider

Engraving by John C. Buttre. From *Dictionary of American Portraits* by Hayward and Blanche Cirker, Dover Publications, Inc., New York, 1967. *Reprinted through permission of the publisher.*

in return for aid in a threatened war against the Potawatomi. A year later the Sauk and Fox ceded 15,000,000 acres south of the Wisconsin River in return for annuities. When Harrison was informed of Indian objections to his tactics, he called another conference at Vincennes, pitted the tribes against one another, and extracted another two-million acres from them. These grants, along with smaller cessions from the Delaware and Piankashaw and a large grant arranged by Governor William Hull of Michigan Territory, gave the United States control of eastern Michigan, southern Indiana, and most of Illinois by 1807.

Indian resentment against these land cessions might have subsided except for the leadership provided by Tecumseh and The Prophet. Two brothers born to a Creek squaw and a Shawnee warrior in the 1760's, Tecumseh and The Prophet began in the years after 1805 to line up resistance against Harrison's land policy. Squeezed between the Sioux and Chippewa, who had moved into the Wisconsin country, and the Americans, the Great Lakes tribes began to rally under Tecumseh and The Prophet to drive out the whites. The brothers founded a village at Prophetstown, at the junction of the Wabash River and Tippecanoe Creek, in order to have a central position from which to extend their influence over the Indians. In 1808 they visited Ft. Malden, the British post across the river from Detroit. The commandant there gave them encouragement, because he expected a war to occur between England and the United States over the blockade and other controversies.

In 1809 Harrison proceeded with his land acquisition. At a conference held at Ft. Wayne, he acquired from the Indians three-million acres of Indiana land for which he paid $7,000 in cash and an annuity of $1,750. For Tecumseh this was the last straw. He went to Vincennes and told Harrison that he would resist white attempts to occupy the Ft. Wayne treaty lands. Harrison responded that force would be met by force.

Indian attacks against outlying settlements began in the spring of 1810, and by the fall of that year a full-scale border war was in progress. Despite the worsening of the situation, Tecumseh tried to restrain his overeager braves as long as the disputed land was not occupied. In 1811 Tecumseh went south to meet the Creeks, Cherokees, and Choctaws to arrange an alliance. Recognizing that Tecumseh's absence was a golden opportunity, Harrison with 1,000 troops marched up to Prophetstown and won an indecisive battle against The Prophet and his followers at Tippecanoe. Upon Tecumseh's return he stepped up the raids against the outlying American settlers.

Although American seizures of Indian lands were probably the primary cause of these Indian uprisings, the United States preferred to blame the British for instigating them. Thus these midwestern Indian raids along with the English seizure of American ships and seamen and the United States' desire to acquire Canadian territory were the major reasons for the United States declaring war on England in 1812. Although the United States won few battles in the War of 1812, one of the few it did win, the Battle of Thames in 1813, resulted in the death of Tecumseh and the reduction of Indian power in the Ohio and Wabash areas. When the Treaty of Ghent was finally signed in 1815, the United States actually obtained little for their dead except a promise from the English to stop trading south of the American line and more complete control over the Indians.

Indian Policy, 1815-1840

From 1815 to 1825 the basic United States policy toward the Indians in the eastern Midwest was to resettle them in less accessible areas and make more land available for white settlement. In July 1815 President James Madison sent commissioners to the village of Portage des Sioux to inform the Fox, Sauk, Kickapoo, Winnebago, and other tribes as to which lands they had already surrendered. In 1816 the Chippewa and Potawatomi ceded two-million acres of land between the Illinois and Mississippi rivers. A treaty with the Wyandots, Senecas, Ottawas, Potawatomi, and Chippewas in 1817 opened northwestern Ohio and northeastern Indiana to white penetration. In July 1819 the Kickapoo ceded their claims south and east of the Illinois and Kankakee rivers. These treaties along with many others opened a large part of

Indiana, Illinois, Michigan, and Ohio to white settlement, but many whites still felt that more needed to be done. After all in 1825 the Indians still claimed 5,000,000 acres in Illinois alone.

This removal policy generally did not work for the best interest of the Indians. For example, Isaac McCoy, a Baptist missionary to the Miami and Potawatomi, reported that the period between 1815 and 1825 was a time of terrible privation for the Indians.

To stem the Indian restlessness and raids that grew out of this resettlement and to protect the white inhabitants, the national government began to build and man forts on a large scale after 1815. Ft. Wayne and Ft. Harrison in Indiana were rebuilt, Ft. Shelby (Detroit), Ft. Gratiot, and Ft. Mackinac in Michigan were regarrisoned, and Ft. Dearborn and Ft. Clark were re-established in Illinois. Ft. Edward in western Illinois, Ft. Armstrong on Rock Island, Ft. Crawford at Prairie du Chien, and Ft. Howard near the mouth of the Fox River were all built in 1816. Each fort consisted of a stoutly built stone or timber palisade and enough blockhouses and barracks to garrison 100 or more troops. Ft. Snelling on the upper Mississippi, Ft. Saginaw in Michigan, and Ft. Brady at Sault Ste. Marie were added between 1819 and 1822. Colonel Henry M. Atkinson and Major Stephen H. Long were in charge of the fort-building expedition up the Missouri River around 1820. This irregular line of garrisoned forts swept 1,500 miles across Michigan, Wisconsin, Illinois, Iowa, and Missouri to the Missouri River.

In 1823 Secretary of War John C. Calhoun suggested that the approximately 15,000 Indians left in the Old Northwest in 1825 should either be removed to northern Wisconsin or Minnesota or to the plains region west of the Missouri River to get them out of the white-men's way. This new phase of the removal program was begun in 1825 by Governor Lewis Cass of Michigan Territory and General William Clark, superintendent of Indian affairs at St. Louis, who called the western tribes together at Prairie du Chien. Ostensibly the federal government gathered the Indians together for the purpose of determining the Indian boundaries to make it easier to keep the peace, but actually the government wanted to determine these boundaries in order to more easily acquire the Indian lands. In 1826 the Potawatomi and Miami ceded enormous slices of territory in Indiana for a nominal amount of money and annuities. During the next few years Indians were forced to surrender land in Ohio, Indiana, Illinois, Michigan, and Wisconsin.

In 1831 the Shawnee of Ohio were relieved of all their remaining possessions in that state by the Treaty of Wapakonetta. The United States official who negotiated the transaction told them that they would have to get off the land or be killed. He also told them that they would receive $115,000 more than the treaty actually provided and that the additional 100,000 acres they were to receive was in a land grant which they had already obtained.

After waiting for a time the Shawnee sent a delegation to Washington, D. C., to obtain the money promised them. They received nothing. In 1832 they were informed that they were going to be moved and so they planted no crops. The move was delayed and the Indians nearly starved. Provisions furnished by the War Department saved them. In the winter of 1832-33 they were finally moved. No shelter or food was provided for them on this 800-mile trek. The promised mills and blacksmith shops which were to be constructed for them at their destination never materialized. Even the promised annual payments were held up for several years, and when it was paid a large portion of this money was diverted into the hands of fraudulent traders.

The realization that the whites were continuing to take over their lands caused the last two uprisings in the eastern Midwest. The first began in 1827 when the Winnebago chief, Red Bird, alarmed by the steady encroachment on his tribal lands at Fever River, led some of his braves against the farmers around Prairie du Chien. Red Bird and his followers killed a family or two and attacked two keelboats. Troops dispatched from St. Louis, Galena, and Green Bay forced Red Bird to surrender. This campaign had the usual sequel. United States officials met the Chippewa, Ottawa, Potawatomi, and Winnebago at Prairie du Chien in the summer of 1829. The first three tribes had to agree to cede land between the Illinois and Wisconsin rivers, and the fourth had to give up their western lands south of the Wisconsin River.

The second uprising occurred in 1832. The conflict had its beginning in a treaty made by a few representatives of the Sauk and Fox Indians at St. Louis in 1823. In return for an annuity of $1,000, they had ceded to the United States their claims to fifty-million acres of land bounded by the Wisconsin, Mississippi, Fox (of Illinois), and Illinois rivers. Although Chief Black Hawk denounced this treaty as illegal, settlers moved into western Illinois, put up fences, burned Black Hawk's summer village, and plowed up the Indian burying grounds. In 1829 when a mob of whites drove the Sauk and Fox from their fertile lands near the Rock River-Mississippi River junction, Keokuk, a peace-loving chief, moved across the Mississippi with his people. But Black Hawk, a rival of Keokuk and much more warlike, refused to leave Illinois with his Sauk and Fox tribe. In 1831 the white citizenry called on Governor John Reynolds to dispossess Black Hawk's band. A force of 500 to 1,500 militia moved against Black Hawk, and he slipped across the Mississippi ahead of them in June 1831. The militia fired Black Hawk's village and went home.

About a year later Black Hawk and his people, who were starving in Iowa, returned across the Mississippi to their original homes. This put the frontiersmen in a frenzy. In May 1,300 militia under General Henry Atkinson moved against Black Hawk. An advance party of 340 militia caught up with Black Hawk and 40 of his braves. When Black Hawk tried to surrender, the militia fired on him. The Indians then returned the fire and drove off the larger force.

With this the Black Hawk War, as it was called, began in earnest, and between May and July 200 whites and an equal number of Indians were killed. Atkinson with 4,500 troops finally caught up with Black Hawk's starving people at the Mississippi. In the affray that followed, known as the Bad Axe Massacre, the whites slaughtered about 300 men, women, and children. With the tacit approval of the United States government, a party of Sioux then followed the Sauk and Fox who escaped the massacre and killed a large number of them. Of the 1,000 Indians who had crossed over into Illinois three months earlier, only 150 were left alive.

In addition to the Indian slaughter, the Black Hawk War

also resulted in the opening up of more Indian lands for white settlement. By a treaty signed in 1832, the Sauk and Fox gave up a 50-mile strip of land along the west bank of the Mississippi in the area that became the territory of Iowa. The Winnebago also, partly because of their assistance to Black Hawk, were forced to surrender the remainder of their lands south and east of the Wisconsin-Fox rivers. The only people who actually gained fame or land from the Black Hawk affair were some white settlers and a few militia and army officers like Captain Abraham Lincoln, Colonel Zachary Taylor, and Lieutenants Jefferson Davis, Albert S. Johnson, and Robert Anderson (of Ft. Sumter fame). Black Hawk spent much of the remainder of his life in federal prison and traveling in the eastern United States.

The Red Bird and Black Hawk uprisings convinced the midwestern tribes that they must either move or be annihilated. During the five year period from 1832 to 1837, the Indians sold to the federal government 190,879,937 acres of land for a total of $70,059,505 in gifts and annuities and moved west.

In most of these transactions, the Indians were subjected to untold physical suffering and monetary exploitation. In 1833 when 5,000-8,000 Chippewa, Ottawa, and Potawatomi gathered in Chicago to collect the one-million dollars in money and goods for land ceded along the western shore of Lake Michigan, they were met by traders with fraudulent claims and whisky who obtained the largest share of the money.

This chicanery was a common occurrence. Traders were often unscrupulous in their dealings with the Indians. Books were kept dishonestly, the Indians were overcharged, Indian goods were purchased at a fraction of their value, and whisky was used to facilitate these illegal practices. Whites would get an individual Indian deeply in debt and then force the whole tribe to pay. In 1836 near Logansport, Indiana, a group of Potawatomi were paid $63,000 for lands they had ceded to the federal government. White traders successfully put in their claims (many of them unsupported) for the money. By 1840 the Miami of Indiana were in debt to the traders for $300,000. The Miami had to sell their land in order to pay. The traders even got a clause inserted in the sales agreement that the money obtained must be used by the

Indians to pay their debts to the traders. The federal government bought millions of acres of land from the Indians at about four cents an acre, and the Indians did not even obtain value received from this small amount of money.

Sometimes poor government planning also contributed to Indian suffering in their removal to the West. An outstanding example of this occurred in Indiana with the Potawatomi. In September 1838 Governor David Wallace sent General John Tipton with 100 soldiers to move the Potawatomi in the Lafayette-Peru area out of the state. Tipton rounded up the 859 Indian men, women, and children and started them on their trek west. Because of lack of provisions and equipment, this march resulted in the death of an estimated 30 to 100 Indians.

By 1842 this land-cession and removal policy had nearly cleared the Old Northwest of Indians. It was in this year that the Indians ceded the last strip of any size still owned by Indians in the area. The federal government contended the reasons for moving the Indians were that they were indolent, murderous, and corrupted by the white men. But probably the most important reason for their removal was that the white men wanted the Indian lands for settlement.

The western Midwest was also affected by the removal of the Indians, but it had more moved in than moved out during this period. As early as 1825 Superintendent of Indian Affairs William Clark got the Kansas and Osage Indians to cede much of their land in Kansas to make it available for the eastern Indians coming west. During the decade of the 1830's, some 10,000 uprooted eastern Indians were transplanted in Kansas. Some of the eastern Indians did well farming in Kansas. The Shawnee of Ohio, who emigrated to a Kansas reservation in 1834, tended to be fairly successful in agriculture. Some of the Wyandots became wealthy. Of all the immigrant Indians in Kansas, only the Ottawas and the Wyandots formulated a system of government.

Another problem of the U. S. authorities in the western Midwest was keeping these compressed Indian tribes from killing each other. Soon after the arrival of the eastern tribes, conflicts began between the western and eastern Indians. The United States had to build forts to keep them apart. Ft. Towson on the Red

River (1824) and Ft. Leavenworth on the Missouri River (1827) were both built for this purpose. The Comanche and Kiowa attacked the eastern Indians in 1834. Stopped temporarily in 1837 by treaty, skirmishes soon began again. The government supported the eastern Indians, but the latter usually got the worst end of the battle anyway. Whisky vendors, predatory rascals, and later the Civil War worked to the disadvantage of the transplanted Indians. The Miamis were debauched by liquor, and the Wyandots also succumbed to corrupting and degrading influences. Although conceived as the red-man's sancutary, Kansas and the rest of the Middle West lying west of the 95th meridian rapidly became his mortuary.

Supervision and Administration of the Indians

The procedures for the supervison and administration of the Indians by the federal government changed gradually in the years after 1789. In the earlier years the factory system overshadowed the Indian service. These government trading factories, which offered goods at cost to the Indians, were originally established in 1796 to break the Indian-British alliance by underselling the Canadian traders. The law of 1796 established two factories and subsequent laws provided for six more. They were relatively effective and efficient. They not only took trade away from the Canadian companies but also from private American firms. These private American companies objected so strenuously that Congress discontinued the factory system in 1822 and left the Indians to the "mercies" of the private traders.

The overall supervision for Indians in the territories was vested in a superintendent of Indian affairs who was also usually a territorial governor. Examples of persons with this combination of authority were William H. Harrison of Indiana Territory (1800-13), Lewis Cass of Michigan Territory (1830-31), and William Clark of Missouri Territory (1807-38). These superintendents worked under the direction of the secretary of war. In the chain of command under the superintendent were the agents and subagents who lived among the tribes. These agents were supposed to be the ears and eyes of the government and keep the government informed on the conditions and attitudes of their charges. They were also to keep peace, dispense justice, distribute government annuities, pass out patriotic medals, help bury the Indian chiefs, impress the Indians with white power and prestige, and keep white poachers and squatters off the Indian land. They were probably least successful in the last-named duty for any attempt to keep out settlers usually brought political repercussions. The Indian-agency plant consisted of warehouses, a blacksmith shop, farm buildings, a council house, a school house, and homes for the agent, interpreter, teacher, farmer, and blacksmith.

The Indian agent had a difficult task. He was harassed by unscrupulous traders and encroaching settlers who stirred up the Indians. In 1822 when Congress passed a law forbidding the transport of liquor into Indian country, the law was flaunted. In 1832 Congress made this law even more stringent but with little noticeable effect. The American Fur Company distributed 8,776 gallons of whisky to its traders in 1832 and 5,573 gallons in 1833. The American Fur Company said it did not favor selling liquor to the Indians, but its competitors did and it felt it must in order to stay in business. Even with the Indian Intercourse Act of 1834, which allowed only licensed traders on reservations, the liquor traffic did not cease. Smuggling liquor into the Indians past the authorities became a game for unscrupulous traders.

The situation was further disturbed by settlers who wanted the Indian lands. Partly because of the encroachments and provocations of these whites, the Indians went on the warpath against settlers, trains, stage coaches, and Indian agents. The whites also brought diseases to the Indians. The most dread disease was smallpox and the Indians feared vaccination. A scourge in 1837 wiped out thousands.

Moreover, a number of Indian agents were corrupt. There was ample room for graft in the Indian agency system. In addition to the government subsidies which could be misappropriated, there were always bribes available for the agent who was willing to allow dishonest and fraudulent practices. When Horace

Greeley was asked how an Indian agent receiving $1,500 a year could save up $40,000 in four years, he answered that it was beyond his arithmetic.

In an effort to improve Indian administration, Congress created the commissioner of Indian affairs in July 1832 and placed the office under the secretary of war. In March 1849 when Congress created the Department of the Interior, they transferred the Indian commissioner to this newly created department. This action, however, did not seem to greatly improve Indian administration. Two departments of the national government were now charged with the responsibility for Indian affairs. Under the War Department the army had the function of garrisoning and patrolling the Indian country. The Interior Department had the actual Indian-administration responsibility and supervised the Indian commissioners, superintendents, and agents. This meant that there was now a possible source of conflict in function and authority between the army officers and the civilian officials. This conflict was demonstrated in the extreme when Indian agents in the performance of their duties issued guns and ammunition to their charges which made the latter more formidable in their battles with the army.

— 12 —

War and Foreign Affairs

Navigation of the Mississippi River

In the period prior to 1800, the Midwest had an influence on foreign relations not because it was powerful, but because it was a vacuum. The Spanish, French, and English, and especially the latter two, had a vigorous contest over who would obtain the region. By 1800 this contest had been virtually settled and none of these powers was successful. Americans were in control of the Midwest east of the Mississippi and the Spanish were on the decline in the area west and south of the Midwest.

Since this was the situation in 1800, it was not surprising that the Midwest had a foreign-relations problem with Spain which soon expanded to include France. Spain owned the Louisiana Territory which controlled the mouth of the Mississippi River. The midwesterners converted their corn into liquor and their hogs into bacon and shipped them down the Mississippi River. When the Spanish closed the mouth of the Mississippi to American commerce, the West became very agitated. The westerners considered declaring independence or joining the Spanish or French empires in order to obtain navigation of the Mississippi. In 1794 Citizen Edmond C. E. Genet, French minister to the United States, even proposed an expedition to capture Louisiana from Spain. The hero of Vincennes, George R. Clark, was to lead this expedition, but it fell apart for lack of funds. The navigation problem was solved temporarily in 1795 by the Pinckney Treaty which provided for American navigation of the Mississippi and a place of deposit for American goods at New Orleans. The Midwest heartily approved of this treaty. The navigation issue, however, would not remain settled.

To the dismay of the Midwest, the war went badly in that region. Several factors contributed to this situation. The army was rundown, volunteer, poorly paid, and badly led. In 1790 the pay of soldiers in St. Clair's army per month was $3 for privates, $4 for sergeants, $22 for lieutenants, $30 for captains, and $60 for colonels. Pay had increased very little by 1812. Presidents Thomas Jefferson and James Madison had both neglected the army.

Even though Congress declared war in 1812, the United States was not ready for war and the succeeding engagements demonstrated it. Ft. Mackinac fell to the British without a shot being fired in July 1812. During the same month General William Hull, sixty-year-old governor of Michigan Territory, was dispatched to capture Ft. Malden across from Detroit. He reached Detroit with 2,000 men on July 7, 1812. The Canadian General Isaac Brock frightened Hull by sending a small force to capture the village of Brownstone, a link in the American supply line lying on the lower Detroit River. When Hull sent one fourth of his troops down to reopen the supply lines, Brock attacked Detroit and bluffed Hull into surrendering in August 1812. At almost the same time the garrison at Ft. Dearborn was massacred and the fort captured by Winnebago, Menominee, and Potawatomi Indians when the troops there attempted to go to the aid of Hull at Detroit.

William H. Harrison was now put in charge of the western troops. He spent the summer of 1812 repulsing British attacks from Ft. Wayne and Ft. Harrison. In the winter of 1812 and 1813, 1,000 of Harrison's men under James Winchester set out to capture Frenchtown. Disobeying Harrison's orders Winchester was surprised on the River Raisin by a British and Indian war party and lost 250 dead and 500 captured. This massacre stopped any hope of invading Canada and Harrison concentrated on defending Ohio and strengthening Ft. Meigs. General Brock, having been killed at the battle of Queenston, was succeeded in command of the Canadian force by Colonel Henry Proctor, who continued to carry the war to the Americans. In April 1813 Proctor unsuccessfully laid seige to Ft. Meigs with 1,000 men. Three months later Proctor attacked Ft. Stephenson. However, when the com-

In 1800 the French repossessed Louisiana from Spain and the United States feared this strong power on her western border. Two years later the Spanish intendent at New Orleans closed the Mississippi. President Thomas Jefferson sent Robert Livingston to France to purchase the New Orleans area, but Napolean Bonaparte wanted to sell the whole of Louisiana. Despite certain qualms Jefferson decided to accept Napolean's offer. Thus at one stroke Jefferson not only solved the Mississippi navigation problem but also acquired a large tract of real estate which included the rest of the Midwest.

War of 1812

After 1800 the Midwest began to fill wtih people; and as the population increased, the influence of the region in foreign affairs similarly increased. The Midwest played a prominent role in the causes leading up to the War of 1812. The settlers of the Middle West not only desired to acquire Canada, but they also mistreated Indians in their land-grabbing practices. Rather than take any of the blame for the Indian uprisings under The Prophet and Tecumseh in 1810, however, the Midwest preferred to blame the disturbances on the British, who the Americans accused with some justification of inciting the Indians to attack the American frontiersmen. Even the preliminary battle of the war was fought at Tippecanoe in Indiana in 1811. General William H. Harrison, governor of the Indiana Territory, launched the campaign against Tippecanoe primarily to stop minor Indian raids and to crush Indian opposition to his land-acquisition policies. Because they felt they could profit by a war, the midwestern congressmen and delegates joined Henry Clay and the other War Hawks in wringing a war message out of President James Madison. Although the Midwest maintained that England caused the war through impressment of American seamen, violation of neutral trading rights, and inciting the Indians to violence, the West went to war primarily in an attempt to gain more land in Canada and to crush the Indians.

mander there, Major George Croghan, raked Proctor's force with grapeshot and Harrison counter-attacked with a large force, Proctor fled to Ft. Malden.

Harrison now went on the offensive. In order to protect western supply lines, Oliver H. Perry was given the task of building a fleet to defeat the British gunboats on Lake Erie. In August 1813 Commander Perry set out to engage the British fleet. In September he fought the British fleet in Put-in-Bay near South Bass Island. After a furious three-hour battle, he emerged victorious. Harrison, with supply lines secure, now crossed over below Ft. Malden with 3,000 men. With only 400 regulars and 600 Indians, Proctor made his stand along the Thames River on September 27, 1813. After a short engagement the English force collapsed, Tecumseh was killed, and Proctor fled. This Battle of the Thames was very important to the Midwest; it broke the Indian power in the Ohio and Wabash country and disrupted Tecumseh's federation.

To complete the disintegration of Indian power, 1,400 Illinois and Missouri militia under General Benjamin Howard cut a wide path of destruction across Illinois in the winter of 1813 and 1814. In June of 1814 William Clark, superintendent of Indian affairs for the upper Mississippi, led a force of 200 men to Prairie du Chien and captured this portage point. Although he left 60 men to guard the area, it fell a month later to an English force of 600 whites and Indians. The English continued to hold Prairie du Chien for the rest of the war. In August 1814 a United States force attacked Mackinac but was driven off. The Midwest actually lost ground during the war and was fortunate to emerge with boundaries status quo ante bellum. The West gained nothing from the Treaty of Ghent except a promise from the British to stop their fur trade south of the Canadian border and a free hand to do with the Indians as it pleased.

Expansion of the United States

After the War of 1812 the people of the Midwest maintained a nationalistic and aggressive spirit in foreign affairs, somewhat modified by isolationism. On the leading foreign relations issue, expansion on the North American continent, the West was generally favorable. This attitude was displayed in such events as the purchase of Louisiana Territory, the War of 1812, and the purchase of Florida.

The Middle West displayed a similar attitude toward the Oregon Territory. By the Convention of 1818, renewed in 1827, the United States and England agreed to joint occupation of the Oregon Territory which lay between 42° and 54° 40′. In 1825 Senator Thomas H. Benton of Missouri, in commenting on Oregon, stated that he hoped the Rocky Mountains would be the ever-lasting boundary of the republic. This probably expressed the midwestern view until 1840, when settlers began to pour in to Oregon especially from Iowa and Missouri. Victims of the Oregon fever, the 500 in Oregon in 1841 had grown to 5,000 by 1845. One Indiana representative felt the United States would win the Oregon area by virtue of the American multiplication table. He explained that the ingredients for this multiplication were a young man and his wife of eighteen and a lapse of thirty years by which time the original two would have increased to 22. Although many people in the Middle West would have favored the boundary at 54° 40′, their desire for expansion was at least partially satisfied by the acquisition of Oregon up to the 49th parallel.

—13—

Settlement of the Middle West

Reasons for the Expanding Westward Migration

The nineteenth century was the boom period for migration to the Middle West. The reasons for this mass movement were legion. First the Indians were continuously and resolutely forced on to smaller and smaller reservations in desolate, isolated regions during this period. Low-priced land was another important inducement for the westward movement. At first the price was one dollar an acre for a minimum acreage of 640 acres. Then in 1796 Alexander Hamilton persuaded Congress to double the price of land in order to keep laborers in the East and build up manufacturing. This policy, however, was of short duration. Four years later William H. Harrison came to Washington as a representative of the Old Northwest with the primary goal of liberalizing the land policy. Under his goading Congress reduced the minimum tract of land from 640 to 320 acres. Although the price remained at two dollars an acre, credit was extended by the government; one fourth down and four years to pay the balance. In 1804 the price was dropped to $1.64 an acre, and the minimum acreage was reduced to 160 acres. This act aided the rapid population growth of Ohio which had been admitted to statehood in 1803. The Land Act of 1805 extended the survey to the newly acquired Louisiana Purchase. In 1820 Congress, suspecting that credit on land had contributed to the panic, abolished the credit system, lowered the price to $1.25 an acre, and reduced the minimum size tract to 80 acres.

Liberalization of land laws in other ways also encouraged the westward migration. The West had long favored pre-emption (the squatter on a piece of land had the first chance to buy it when it was put up for sale). Before pre-emption became legal, settlers formed claims associations, gathered at the land offices, and saw to it, with force if necessary, that the man obtained the land where he lived. In 1830 Congress partially legalized pre-emption with a law that stated that a settler could occupy 160 acres and buy the land later at the minimum price free of competitive bids. Eleven years later Congress finally agreed that a settler could legally pre-empt land even before the government surveyors laid it out.

Increasing publicity about the attractiveness of the West also encouraged migration westward. Soldiers returning from the wars, whether the War of 1812, the Black Hawk affair, or other Indian wars, told of the rich western land and instilled in people a desire to move west. Each state, territory, and land speculator early developed an effective publicity system. Among these western publicists in the period 1778 to 1812 were Thomas Hutchins, Gilbert Imlay, and John Melish.

Between 1815 and 1825 more than a dozen travel books on the region north of the Ohio were published in England and America. Morris Birkbeck wrote a glowing account of the Midwest in *Notes on a Journey in America* published in 1817. Birkbeck, financially interested in the Illinois country, emphasized the opportunites for material gain, independence, and happiness in that area. Rufus Easton, a representative from the Missouri Territory, wrote in 1816 that in this fine country, destined to become the foothold of the genius of American liberty, every man would become a prosperous landholder with enterprizing children.

Western newspapers continuously helped this campaign by printing land sales, commodity trade lists, trade opportunities, and the need for artisans and professional people. When in August 1817 President James Monroe visited Detroit, the newspapers utilized the event to advertise Michigan Territory. The eastern papers became concerned enough about the westward migration that they published a variety of disparaging remarks about the West; but to no avail, the people continued to move west.

Still another factor favoring westward migration was the improvement of transportation facilities. At first the favorite route to the Old Northwest was down the Ohio River into southern Ohio, Indiana, Illinois, and Missouri. Later the National Road and the Erie Canal (1825) became extremely important. After 1833 a regular packet line from Buffalo to Detroit moved the migrants west. In the 1830's and 1840's the steamboats on the Ohio, Mississippi, and Missouri rivers further implemented the westward march. Throughout, however, wagons and stagecoaches played an important role in the westward movement of peoples.

Other reasons for the western migration included the failure of the back country of the eastern states to get their political rights, the spread of slavery into the piedmont area which forced out free labor, the exhaustion of the eastern soil, an increasing population, and the desire for adventure and greener pastures.

Settlement, 1790-1820

Since the Ohio River was the primary route for settlement of the Midwest up to 1820, the central and southern portions of Ohio, Indiana, and Illinois were first to be settled. Since there was a tendency in the United States for migration to follow a parallel west, the largest number of settlers in the southern Midwest came from Virginia, Pennsylvania, the Carolinas, and Kentucky.

Among the early settlements in southern Ohio, Cincinnati was one of the most prosperous. By 1820 it had surpassed Pittsburgh in population and contained about 1,100 buildings of which 60 were business establishments. There were blacksmiths, coopers, glassmakers, stone cutters, cabinet makers, a cotton mill, and a steam mill. Among its cultural attractions were a library, a seminary, a theater, a college, a museum, and two newspapers.

Indiana was the second state in the Midwest to receive a heavy migration of settlers. When Indiana Territory was organized, the nearest land office was in Cincinnati. Land offices, however, were soon opened further west. Indiana land sales annually averaged 45,000 acres from 1807 to 1811 and soared to 166,000 acres in 1814. Between 1807 and 1820, 2,490,736 acres of land were sold in Indiana at a total price of $5,137,350.

With this influx of people, villages early began to grow in Indiana. One of the largest, early villages was Vincennes which in 1816 had a population of 1,000 to 1,500. Populated largely by French-Americans, Vincennes had 250 houses, 18 stores, 6 taverns, 24 shops, 2 newspaper-and-printing offices, a Catholic Church, and an academy.

Twenty-five miles to the southwest was the New Harmony settlement with 125 families, established by George Rapp in 1815. On their 20,000 acres, the Rappites had grain, orchards, vinyards, a silk plant, a distillery, a woolen mill, a brick yard, an oil well, and an inn.

In contrast with southern Ohio, southern Indiana had few streams of navigable size which reached back more than 40 miles from the Ohio River. Early settlement in Indiana therefore tended to form a crescent with the Whitewater and Wabash valleys as its tips. In the years following the War of 1812, however, the interior of this crescent began to fill. A high point in this settlement was 1816, the year Indiana became a state. An estimated 42,000 persons arrived during this one year. As a result of this continuing influx, Indiana increased in population from 5,641 in 1800 to 147,178 in 1820.

The third of this tier of states to be settled by southern settlers following the Ohio River route was Illinois. Like Indiana the population in Illinois by 1815 formed a crescent. Starting above Vincennes the semi-circle of population ran along the Ohio and the Mississippi rivers to the mouth of the Illinois. The region lying between the Kaskaskia and Mississippi rivers was most thickly populated.

Illinois' main settlements during this period were the old French villages. Kaskaskia, for example, which had lost many of its original inhabitants after 1765, was made a land office in 1804 and the capital of Illinois Territory in 1809. In 1817 the town contained about 160 houses of French design. Most of them had large, picketed gardens in the rear. Besides the land office, there was a post office, a printing office, nine general stores, a hat shop, three tailor shops and a tavern.

Nearly all of the early pioneers avoided the prairies and stayed in the wooded lowlands of Illinois. The exception to this rule was a group of English immigrants under the leadership of Morris Birkbeck and George Flower. Arriving in 1818 without the prejudices of forest-trained frontiersmen, they made their homes in the grasslands around Albion and Wanborough, Illinois. Outside of southern Illinois there were only two other main areas of settlement. One was in the lead mining region around Galena and the other was Chicago.

In the three years following the War of 1812, the population of Illinois nearly doubled. When Illinois became a state in 1818, it had a population of 35,000. By 1820 its population had jumped to 55,211.

Missouri, the fourth state from the Midwest to be admitted into the Union (1821), had also profited by the Ohio River migration. Theoretically, Missouri had an advantage over its three sister states in attracting settlers from the South. The Land Ordinance of 1785 and the provisions of the Northwest Ordinance (1787) both applied to Missouri with the exception of the slavery clause. It did not apply to Missouri because the United States had accepted the Spanish property law allowing slaves which was in force when the U. S. purchased the Louisiana Territory in 1803. Thus, a number of southerners did cross Indiana and Illinois into Missouri because only the latter allowed slaves. Some Illinoians referred to the Missourians as pukes, because they said Illinois regurgitated them.

Settlement in Missouri up to 1815 was slow. One reason for this was the fact that Missouri had a land-title problem. Few people had received good titles from the Spanish government. It took a congressional commission thirty years to get the titles straightened out. Land offices were not even opened to sell land in the area until 1818, and as a result Missouri had many squatters.

In 1812 the Missouri settlement was confined to a cluster of French towns (New Madrid, St. Charles, Cape Girardeau, Ste. Genevieve, and St. Louis) in the eastern part. But people slowly pushed west, and a group of settlers formed a village at Franklin on the Missouri River. After this town was established, the settlers decided that a road was needed to connect St. Charles to Franklin. Daniel Boone's sons helped in this road-building project in 1815. This road, sometimes referred to as the "Boone's Lick Road," was used heavily by the farmers who came into the Missouri area with a rush between 1815 and 1819.

With this influx of settlers, Missouri's population expanded by leaps and bounds. From 19,783 in 1810, Missouri's population grew to 66,586 by 1820. Seven eighth's of these people were farmers, and most of them lived in the Missouri River-Boonville-Franklin area. The slaves present were used as servants or in general farming; there were few staple crops or plantations.

Thus, these three midwestern states, Indiana, Illinois, and Missouri, reached statehood and received a large number of their early inhabitants in the period from 1816 to 1821, the period Frederick J. Turner termed the great migration.

In contrast with the relatively rapid settlement of the southern portions of Ohio, Indiana, Illinois, and Missouri, the influx of people into the upper Middle West prior to 1825 was extremely slow. Michigan had only 8,896 people in 1820. Surveyors sent to the interior of that state in 1815 found the Indians hostile and returned without doing any surveying. Northern Michigan had the small trading villages of Mackinac and Sault Ste. Marie. The leading settlement in Michigan, however, was Detroit, founded by Cadillac in 1701. Although burned to the ground in June 1805, it was rebuilt and incorporated as a city in 1815. Although it had 800 people in 1810, its population dropped during the War of 1812, because of its proximity to the battle front. At that time the town was garrisoned with troops. After the war Detroit rapidly gained population and by 1818 was up to 1,100 people.

The leading settlement in 1815 in what later became Wisconsin was the French village at Green Bay. Here the population was still largely Indian, French, and Canadian. The genial, easy-going life of the French set the tone of society. The French at Green Bay managed to eke out an existence by raising some livestock and vegetables and by hunting and trapping wild animals. In 1812 Green Bay had 250 people, 2 trading stores, 3 blacksmiths, a tailor, and a carpenter. In 1816 Fort Howard was established there and garrisoned by Americans.

One of the first settlements in the adjoining state of Minnesota occurred during the years 1812 to 1814. At that time a group of Scotch and Irish arrived in northern Minnesota and settled on land acquired by the Scottish Earl of Selkirk, who had a controlling interest in the Hudson's Bay Company. They were later joined by a group of Swiss who came in 1820. These unfortunate settlers ended up in the middle of a struggle between the Hudson's Bay and the Northwest Fur companies. The Northwest Company lured some away and murdered others. The battle between these two companies continued until 1821 when they merged.

Outside of these few isolated villages, the settlement of the eight northern and western North Central states was virtually nil up to 1820. The census of that year recorded no population in any of these states except Michigan which at that time had 8,896 residents. The total population of the Midwest in 1820 was 859,305, less than one fifth of the United States population.

Settlement, 1820-1840

With the completion of the Erie Canal in 1825, the immigration route to the Middle West began to shift from the Ohio River to the Great Lakes. After 1830 settlers coming from the South declined and the majority of people migrating into the Midwest came from the northeastern states or from Europe. This meant that settlers after 1830 tended to move into northern Ohio, Indiana, and Illinois, southern Michigan and Wisconsin, and central Iowa.

In Ohio this shifting migration route was reflected in the establishment and growth of northern towns. In 1826, 40 new houses were begun in Cleveland. By 1840 its population had risen to 6,000. Port Lawrence, renamed Toledo in 1834, was a flourishing village by the late 1820's. The two leading towns, however, were still in southern Ohio. In 1830 Zanesville had 3,000 people, and was second only to Cincinnati, "Queen City of the West," which had a population of 25,000. Enlarged by the Jacksonian migration in the 1830's, Ohio's total population had increased to 1,519,467 by 1840.

The laying out and populating of villages in northern Indiana proceeded slowly even after 1820. In 1821 Ft. Wayne had 32 houses, a barracks occupied by an Indian agent, a mission station, and a school for Indians. South Bend, which lay within the tract ceded by the Indians at Chicago in 1821 became a trading-post annex to Fort Wayne. Further south Indianapolis, which had been chosen as the site of the new capital in 1821, had 1,000 people in 1827. Indiana's total population in 1840 was 685,866.

The settlement of southern Michigan like that of northern Indiana was directly affected by the opening of the new Erie Canal-Great Lakes route to the West. Roads from Detroit to Saginaw and Detroit to Chicago were built and improved during the 1820's and 1830's and these aided settlement. By 1838, the year after Michigan became a state, almost half of the state had been surveyed and a total of 39 counties were mapped. Approximately two thirds of Michigan's settlers came from New England and New York. This fact was most clearly demonstrated in the 10,000 people of Detroit who had a distinctly eastern flavor. Over all, Michigan had a total population of 12,267 in 1840.

The settlement of Illinois from 1820 to 1840 was closely associated with that of Indiana. After 1820 the band of settlements along the Wabash, Ohio, and Mississippi rivers began to widen at its western end to include the area east of the lower Illinois River.

To the north Chicago in 1820 consisted of a hotel, six houses, and a number of Indian wigwams. After the gorvernment trading factory was closed there in 1822 and the garrison at Ft. Dearborn evacuated in 1823, Chicago declined still more. In 1825 it had 14 taxpayers. But the soldiers returned in 1828 and with the projection of the Illinois-Lake Michigan Canal and the influx of settlers coming in over the Great Lakes route, the settlement returned to life. When the town was platted in 1830, it had a population of about 50 persons. Within three years the population had increased to 1,000. After 1837 when Chicago was incorporated, its population mushroomed.

Far more populous in 1830 than Chicago was the Fever River district centered around Galena in northwestern Illinois. Although Dubuque had begun mining operations there in the 1780's,

Cincinnati (1835)

St. Louis (1847)

the area did not really develop until after 1822 when the Kentucky promoter, James A. Johnson, arrived. He moved in with supplies, miners, and 150 slaves. His success inspired one of the first mineral rushes in the Midwest. By 1830, 10,000 prospectors had staked out claims in the area, built the bustling town of Galena, and were shipping fifteen-million pounds of lead annually to New Orleans. The Fever River district had also acquired the usual mining town accouterments, saloons, gambling halls, knife fights, and lawlessness. By 1840 Galena had a population of 3,000.

This lead rush was partially responsible for the Red Bird and Black Hawk uprisings in the 1820's and early 1830's. It was Fever River settlers encroaching on Indian lands that alarmed both Red Bird and Black Hawk and started them on the warpath. Moreover, it was Major Henry Dodge, leader of the Fever River mining district after 1827, who commanded a group of militia that helped defeat both Red Bird and Black Hawk. Although harmful to the Indians, these campaigns benefited both Henry Dodge and the frontiersmen. Dodge later became territorial governor and United States senator from Wisconsin, and the settlers got more land at the expense of the Indians. The influx of whites also increased, and by 1840 had 476,183 inhabitants.

In addition to Illinois, the settlement of Wisconsin and Iowa was also implemented by cessions resulting from the Red Bird and Black Hawk wars. Although Wisconsin originally was to be set aside as an Indian reservation, the government reversed its stand in 1832 and used the Red Bird and Black Hawk affairs as a lever to pry eastern Wisconsin loose from the Indians. Continuing in 1836 the authorities began a systematic program of extinguishing the Indian title in Wisconsin, and within twelve years the expulsion of Indians from Wisconsin was nearly completed. They were being rapidly replaced by whites of whom 30,945 were already there in 1840.

Another land cession, extracted from the Indians because of the Black Hawk War, similarly opened up Iowa to white settlement in 1833. From the small lead-mining area around Dubuque, the settlers spread out into the fifty-mile strip which was acquired along the western bank of the Mississippi. From this beginning Iowa was quickly cleared of its remaining Indians. By 1841 Iowa had 18 organized counties and eight principal towns. The capital, Iowa City, had four lawyers, three physicians, two blacksmiths, one gunsmith, one saddlery, a hotel, a church, a primary school, nineteen other places of business, and 100 buildings rising. The population of this expanding territory was 43,112 in 1840.

With the shift of the immigration route to the north after

1825, migration to Missouri slowed down. Despite this decline in the rapidity of settlement, Missouri's population still increased to 383,702 by 1840.

On the whole the Middle West had tremendously increased in population by 1840 even though five states (Minnesota, North Dakota, South Dakota, Nebraska, and Kansas) still had no recorded population. The fast rate of increase was demonstrated by the fact that the total population of the Midwest had more than tripled during the 1820's and 1830's and the number of inhabitants in 1840 stood at 3,351,542.

—14—

Admission of Middle Western States

Admission of Indiana

Upon its creation in 1800 Indiana Territory was bounded on the east by a line that ran from the mouth of the Kentucky River to Ft. Recovery and thence north to Canada. Two years later Indiana Territory acquired more land when Ohio reduced its boundaries preparatory to statehood. Indiana obtained the "gore," a triangle of land in the southeast corner of Indiana, and all land north of a line running east from the southern tip to Lake Michigan.

Indiana Territory continued under the oligarchical system that had formerly existed in the Northwest Territory. The ruling triumverate was composed of Harrison, William Clarke, and Henry Vander Burgh. Indiana had earlier received an exemption from the provision of the Ordinance of 1787 which required 5,000 adult males for advancement to second-class status. Many persons, including office seekers, abolitionists, and others opposed to Harrison's rule, wished to use this exemption to increase their representation in government. Harrison opposed advance to second-grade status and emphasized the higher taxes that would result. In 1804 he reluctantly agreed to put the issue before the voters; of the 400 who voted, 269 favored the advance. Harrison proclaimed the entrance of Indiana Territory into the second stage in December 1804 and called for an election to choose the nine members for the state house of representatives in January 1805,

In the meantime Indiana had again undergone boundary changes. In 1804 all of the recently acquired territory of Louisiana lying north of the thirty-third parallel was temporarily attached to Indiana under the name of the District of Louisiana. But this arrangement lasted only about a year. In 1805 Louisiana Territory was given a separate government. In the same year the area north and east of a line running through the center of Lake Michigan was separated from Indiana as Michigan Territory.

Even after attaining the second stage of territorial government, the people of Indiana were still dissatisfied. As early as July 1805 the council (upper legislative house) stated that it felt the governor had too much power. Three years later the Indiana lower house passed resolutions requesting Congress to allow the people of Indiana Territory to elect the members of the territorial council and the territorial delegate to Congress, to abolish the absolute veto of the territorial governor, and to repeal the power of the governor to dismiss and dissolve the general assembly. In 1809 Congress granted those requests concerning the election of the territorial delegate and the legislative council. In addition, Congress also extended the suffrage to all adult, white, male taxpayers.

Before attaining statehood, Indiana had two more boundary changes. In 1809 Illinois Territory was created with its eastern boundary on the Wabash up to about forty degrees and then due north from that point. Until admission as a state in 1816, Indiana's boundaries were the same as today, except that the northern line was ten miles further south, and the territory included the tip of the Green Bay peninsula and a portion of the upper peninsula of Michigan lying directly north of Indiana. Upon attaining statehood, Indiana was awarded a ten-mile strip of its northern boundary in order to have access to Lake Michigan.

The War of 1812 and the Indian menace increased the desire for statehood. The people felt that a state government would be better able to handle the Indian problem, would be more democratic, and would provide more political offices with higher salaries. Even though Congress had put the elections under the control of the judges rather than the sheriffs and replaced voice voting with written ballots in 1811, the residents of the territory wanted still more democracy. The Indiana house of representatives passed a resolution favoring statehood in December 1811, and a group of Indiana citizens sent a similar petition to Congress in February 1815. The general assembly asked for statehood again in December 1815, and this time the federal government approved the request. With statehood Indiana was granted five per cent of the proceeds from the sale of its public lands, one township for the use of a seminary, and four sections of land for a permanent seat of government.

The Indiana constitutional convention met at Corydon in June 1816 with Jonathan Jennings as president. A majority of the delegates were both rural and southern in origin. Some of Indiana's major constitutional provisions were as follows: 1) the governor was elected for three years and his veto could be overridden by a majority vote of both houses; 2) representatives were chosen annually and senators every three years; 3) suffrage was given to white, male, adult citizens over twenty one; 4) the militia was to consist of able-bodied, white males between the ages of eighteen and forty five (Negroes, Indians, and mulattoes were exempt, along with conscientious objectors who were fined but not forced to bear arms); and 5) it contained an education article, a penal code, and an anti-slavery provision.

In 1816 Indiana demonstrated in politics its faith in the common man and began its statehood under the leadership of Governor Jonathan Jennings. To keep the slave-free state ratio in balance, Indiana was paired off with Mississippi which was admitted in 1817.

Admission of Illinois

Illinois Territory had stable boundaries after its creation in 1809. It included the land west of Indiana Territory and east of the Mississippi up to the Canadian border. The capital selected for this new territory was Kaskaskia, and its governor was Ninian Edwards of Kentucky.

Illinois moved even more rapidly toward democracy and statehood than Indiana. In 1812 Illinois entered second-grade territorial status with 13,000 population. In this second stage,

Congress allowed all white, adult taxpayers in Illinois to vote and to choose their legislative council members and territorial delegate to Congress. Six years later Illinois' petition for statehood was received favorably by Congress, even though Illinois was 25,000 short of the required 60,000 population. Illinois promptly convened a constitutional convention at Kaskaskia under the presidency of Jesse B. Thomas. By the provisions of the constitution, the governor was to be elected for a four-year term. A Council of Revision (composed of the governor and state supreme court judges) could veto bills, but the legislature could pass it over the council's veto by a majority vote. The right to vote was given to all white males over 21. The militia act was the same as Indiana's. Slavery was illegal, but if people already owned slaves they could keep them under the indenture clause. The children of slaves, however, were free.

Shadrach Bond, Jr., was chosen the first governor of this free state, which was balanced off in 1819 with the admittance of Alabama as a slave state. At its inception Illinois received three per cent of the government land sales in Illinois for education, two per cent for roads, section 16 of each township for schools, a township for a seminary, and the salt licks.

Admission of Missouri

In 1803 the United States purchased the Louisiana Territory, which contained the fourth midwestern state admitted to the Union. Three months after its purchase, the newly acquired Louisiana Territory was divided by Congress at the thirty-third parallel. The enormous area north of this line was named the District of Louisiana and for a short period was attached to the Indiana Territory for administration. During this period, U. S. institutions and laws were introduced into Missouri by William H. Harrison in a fifty-five page volume of statutes. But the attempt to govern St. Louis and the other Missouri settlements from Vincennes proved unsuccessful, and Congress in 1805 formed the Territory of Louisiana with its capital at St. Louis.

The scheming James Wilkinson was appointed governor of Louisiana Territory. After a stormy term of less than two years, he was replaced in 1807 by Meriwether Lewis, who had just returned from his expedition with Clark. Lewis died two years later, apparently by suicide, and he in turn was succeeded by William Clark.

In 1812 Louisiana Territory was renamed Missouri Territory to avoid confusion with the newly admitted state of Louisiana. At the same time Missouri went into the second territorial stage and was allowed to elect its legislature.

Missouri applied for admission to the Union in 1818. A controversy arose when Representative James Talmadge of New Jersey proposed an amendment to the enabling act prohibiting further importation of slaves into Missouri and providing for gradual emancipation of those already there. Thomas Jefferson described the furor as "an alarm bell in the night." Missouri was really the first state to pose the problem of slavery. Kentucky and Tennessee came in before it was an issue, the Northwest Ordinance barred it north of the Ohio, and Alabama, Mississippi, and Louisiana were southern by location. The slavery line had been drawn along the Mason-Dixon line and the Ohio River. But now the question arose as to where the line went from the mouth of the Ohio.

The issue was further inflamed by the South's desire to retain numerical equality with the North in the Senate. Since House equality was impossible because of the rapidly growing northern population, the South felt its last line of defense was equality in the Senate. With the relinquishment of claims by the United States to the area south and west of the Sabine-Red River-and-forty-second parallel line in 1819, the South was left with only Florida, Arkansas, the Indian Territory, and Missouri as possible slave states. The South had to have Missouri if it hoped to retain a slave-free state balance.

Meanwhile in 1819 Missouri's boundaries were drawn along their present lines. The area to the south became Arkansas Territory and that to the west and north remained unorganized. The parallel of 36° 30′ was the southern boundary with the exception of the New Madrid region. There the boundary dipped to 36 degrees in order to include the New Madrid settlements in Missouri.

After considerable rancor and debate, Missouri was finally admitted as a state in 1820 under the provisions of the Missouri Compromise. This provided that Missouri would be admitted as a slave state paired off with Maine as a free state. Moreover, no slavery was to be allowed in any other portion of the Louisiana Purchase north of 36° 30′. The actual admittance of Missouri into the Union was held up for another year due to a provision in its constitution which in effect barred free Negroes from the state. This brought on a new debate in Congress over whether or not this abridged the privileges and immunities of citizens as stated in the Constitution of the United States. The so called second compromise provided that the president of the United States would proclaim Missouri a state if the Missouri legislature would promise not to pass a law abridging the privileges and immunities of citizens of other states. The Missouri legislature agreed to this arrangement, and Missouri was officially declared a state in August 1821.

Missouri thus began its statehood with St. Charles as its temporary capital and Alexander McNair as its first governor. In 1826 the capital was moved to its permanent location at Jefferson City.

Admission of Michigan

A period of sixteen years was to elapse before another midwestern state entered the Union. Michigan had begun its territorial period in 1805. It had become a separate territory early because the 4,000 Detroit inhabitants, 300 miles from Vincennes and in jeopardy from the Indians and English, wanted a closer territorial capital.

The first governor of the territory was General William Hull, noted for his defeat at Detroit by the British in 1812. Consequently during the War of 1812, Michigan had its main populated areas occupied by the British; at the end of the war, the boundaries were returned to their pre-war locations. In 1813 Lewis Cass became the second governor at the territorial capital of Detroit and he served until 1831. When Illinois acquired statehood in 1818, Michigan was given additional territory. Wisconsin and the portion of Minnesota east of the Mississippi were put under the jurisdiction of Michigan. The resulting increase in population made Michigan eligible for the second territorial stage. The people of Michigan, however, put off the advancement five years until 1823 because of the additional expense that would ensue.

In 1834 Michigan's jurisdiction was extended over the vast unorganized area west of the Mississippi, north of the state of Missouri, and east of the Missouri River. At this time Michigan Territory included the future states of Michigan, Wisconsin, Iowa, Minnesota, and part of the Dakotas.

Although agitation for statehood in Michigan began in 1832, the Black Hawk War and a cholera epidemic temporarily sidetracked the movement. By 1834 Michigan with 87,000 people was fully eligible for statehood. A year later Michigan, fearing that it would lose Sault Ste. Marie to Wisconsin if it delayed longer, established a constitution and drew its boundaries even before Congress passed an enabling act. Michigan drew its Ohio boundary along the parallel touching the southern tip of Lake Michigan.

This action precipitated a boundary dispute with Ohio, which claimed the Toledo area. Michigan was in the right on this issue, because it was following the line originally drawn. Ohio,however, fearing that the parallel touching the tip of Lake Michigan might cut it off from Lake Erie, had specified in its constitution that its boundary should touch Lake Erie no further south than Toledo. Ohio had never obtained congressional sanction for this action, and consequently Michigan's act caused the Ohio authorities to take vigorous action. Governor Robert Lucas of Ohio persuaded his legislature to pass an act in 1835 extending Ohio's jurisdiction into the disputed tract and providing for the election of local officials. Governor Stevens T. Mason of Michigan took similar action. The militias of both states were moved into the area, where they glared at one another. This was the bloodless "Toledo War." Michigan had the survey lines in its favor, but Ohio had electoral votes and President Andrew Jackson did not want to jeopardize Martin Van Buren's chances of winning the 1836 election. Congress passed a law authorizing the president to admit Michigan when it accepted the boundary desired by Ohio. Michigan was to be compensated for its loss by receiving the upper penninsula lying between Lake Michigan and Lake Superior.

For a time Michigan rejected this compromise and remained officially a territory, even though it had elected Mason governor. President Jackson responded to this situation by sending a territorial governor, John S. Horner, to Michigan. Ignored, Horner soon left. Partly because Michigan wanted to share in the treasury surplus, it agreed to the prescribed boundaries in December 1836 after having turned them down in convention twice before. Michigan was officially admitted to the Union in January 1837. Michigan's entrance again made the number of slave and free states even since Arkansas had been admitted as a slave state in 1836.

Michigan's constitution was very similar to its sister states of the Old Northwest Territory. Michigan, too, had the word white in its suffrage clause. Its greatest contribution was in education, which was quite far reaching for the time. The capital which was still at Detroit in 1837 was moved to Lansing a decade later.

— 15 —

Political Issues and Personalities

Minorities

The midwestern area had domestic, political problems from the outset. One of the first of these was Indian removal. The politicians who were successful in defeating or removing the Indians were popular on the frontier and those who failed were unpopular. Governor St. Clair's ill-fated expedition to the Maumee River in 1791 caused his political stock to fall. In contrast William H. Harrison, who helped bury the dead from St. Clair's defeated army, built a political career out of his Indian dealings. As territorial governor of Indiana, he acquired the bulk of Indiana by forcing the Indians to cede their land. When the Indians objected too strenously, he attacked Prophetstown near Lafayette, Indiana, and won lasting fame at the battle of Tippecanoe. The settlers looked upon the Indians as a furtive, thieving lot and could hardly wait to move them out. In 1825 Secretary of War John C. Calhoun outlined an Indian policy that was faithfully carried out with midwestern support for twenty years. The Indians were moved to the Great Plains which were considered too poor for white settlement. When Indian chiefs such as Red Bird and Black Hawk refused to yield their lands, they were mercilessly crushed. Thomas H. Benton expressed the feeling of the West when he stated that the Indians should be replaced by white men.

A second issue which was politically significant in the early Midwest concerned a people of a yet darker race, the Negro. Although the Northwest Ordinance of 1787 prohibited slavery, that provision did not end the dispute over the existence of the "peculiar institution" in the Middle West. Up through 1820 a majority of the people in Ohio, Indiana, and Illinois were from the South and many of them favored slavery. Although Ohio had virtually disposed of the issue by 1803, it dragged on in Indiana and Illinois. The Indiana constitution of 1816 left the issue slightly in doubt by the retention of the indenture clause under which slaves might conceivably be held.

Illinois' fight over slavery was similar to Indiana's. Although the dispute over slavery hastened Illinois into statehood, the Illinois constitution of 1818 which was to settle the issue still left it cloudy. Not until 1824 was the question firmly decided in Illinois when the anti-slavery group won out.

In Missouri the issue turned out differently. Since Missouri was exempted from the slavery clause of the Northwest Ordinance and since it had a larger influx of southerners with slaves, Missouri maintained slavery as an active institution during its territorial period and came into the Union as a slave state under the famous Missouri Compromise. That the rest of the Midwest was still divided and somewhat objective on the subject of slavery in 1820 was demonstrated by the fact that the region as a whole supported the Missouri Compromise.

Land, Money, and Tariff

An issue of paramount importance to the Midwest during these formative years was the price and terms offered in the sale of public lands. Whereas the East was interested in raising the price of western land in order to raise revenue and keep the people near the seaboard, the West wanted the price low so that settlers could buy land cheaply and thus would be attracted to the sparsely settled region. Many political campaigns in the Midwest had cheap land as a major issue.

With the large amount of land for sale in the Midwest, it was natural that land speculation and chicanery would result. The large tracts of land for sale favored speculators. At the outset in the Ohio and Scioto company projects, speculators had greatly influenced politics and this trend continued. The political factions in Illinois, Indiana, and Ohio were based partly on land manipulation. Even the delegates of the Illinois constitutional convention, influenced by land speculation, imposed the obligation upon the legislature of moving the capital as soon as it could obtain a land grant from Congress.

Since money tends to gravitate toward developed areas, scarcity of money and hard times were the rule during the early development of the Middle West. This factor had considerable influence on the shaping of the political and economic views of the midwesterner. The West tried to blame its depression during the period of 1808 to 1812 on English interference with American trade. During the three years after the end of the War of 1812, prosperity and speculation were rampant. The Midwest reaped the whirlwind of its actions in the Panic of 1819. Prices dropped to half of their former value, and 153,000 acres of land reverted to the United States in 1819. Instead of blaming the downward spiral on their own mistakes, however, the westerners blamed it on the United States Bank which was drawing in currency and tightening credit. Ohio, following the lead of Maryland, decided to place a high tax on the U. S. branch bank in Ohio in 1819 and thus destroy this "blood-sucking monster." Ignoring the *McCullock v. Maryland* decision, Ohio persisted in its course until 1824, when its bank-taxing law was similarly destroyed by *Osborn v. The Bank of the United States.*

When midwestern banks collapsed in the 1820's and 1830's, the westerners again blamed the United States Bank for the West's financial ills and supported President Jackson wholeheartedly in his battle against that "un-American monopoly," the national bank. The West, however, turned on Jackson when he issued the deflationary Specie Circular, which stated that land had to be paid for in hard money. And then when the Panic of 1837 struck the Midwest and unstable banks fell like ten pins, the West (for this and other reasons) showed its spite by voting out Jackson's hand-picked successor, Martin Van Buren, in 1840. Actually, speculation, over-investment in internal improvements, and lax banking practices had largely caused the panic, but the people preferred to blame the administration at Washington rather than themselves.

To relieve the shortage of money, Congress considered the issuance of treasury notes. In the Midwest as well as elsewhere in the nation, the Whigs favored it and the Democrats opposed it. The Whigs maintained that this extra currency was just what the economy needed. The Democrats maintained that this bill was simply a ruse to enable the federal government to charter another national bank and increase federal control. Thomas H. Benton said that paper money would act as a seditive to put people to sleep as to the true economic facts. The bill did not pass.

Whether to its interest or not, the Midwest favored moderate to high tariffs. The agrarians of the North Central states believed that a protective tariff would protect and promote American industry which in turn would process their agricultural goods into finished products. They also believed that a tariff would protect the market for their produce. They did not seem to realize that other countries could pass retaliatory tariffs to keep out American farm products, or that tariffs on industrial goods coming in would raise the prices on the manufactured products which they had to buy. Despite the pros and cons of the subject, a majority of the westerners supported a protective tariff. Ohio voted for protective tariff in 1816 and it was joined by Indiana and Illinois in voting for protective tariffs in 1820, 1824, 1828, and 1832. At the same time the Midwest favored Andrew Jackson, not for his low tariff or internal improvements view, but because he favored Indian removal and abolition of the national bank and was a nationalistic westerner. About the only time in this period that the West really supported a lower tariff was in 1846 when it joined the South in passing the Walker Tariff. The Middle West agreed to this lower tariff because England reciprocated by repealing its corn laws and allowing American farm products to enter England with less duty.

Internal Improvements

Since the Middle West was a new area, it was understandable why it would support internal-improvement schemes to develop the region. In Ohio in 1824 the three big political topics were canals, schools, and tax reform. Midwestern congressmen backed 34 successive appropriations proposed for internal improvements, such as the Cumberland Road, the Survey of 1824, and the Maysville Road of 1830. Henry Clay's popularity in the West lay partly in his proposal for nationally financed internal improvements in his "American System." Clay's party, the Whigs, even grew in strength in the Midwest in the 1830's despite Andrew Jackson's popularity, because the latter vetoed appropriations for the Maysville Road, the National Road, and the Wabash and Michigan City harbor.

The midwestern states began building internal improvements (especially canals) in the 1820's, and their efforts led several of them to bankruptcy after the Panic of 1837. These bankruptcies cost English investors about $100,000,000. The states were led to the brink of disaster by their own optimism and by the prospect of getting money through the Distribution Act of 1836, which provided that excess federal government funds would go to states to aid them in their internal improvements.

Illinois was a good example of a state that had over-extended in 1841 and repudiated its debts. Abraham Lincoln, who lived at Springfield, was a member of the state assembly that had helped place Illinois in a ruinous financial condition. Although Lincoln had not favored the enormous internal improvements project for Illinois, he did want Springfield as the capital. Therefore he and his colleagues from Sangamon County voted for the internal improvements in 1837 in order to obtain votes for their desired project. When Governor Joseph Duncan and his Council of Revision disapproved the reckless internal improvements measure, the legislature contemptously passed it over his veto. Log-rolling tactics, such as the ones engaged in by Lincoln, helped to put other western states in similar financial difficulties.

Elections

Although the states of the Old Northwest started voting Democratic-Republican upon admittance to the Union, they were really not much concerned with national politics between 1812 and 1824. Campaigns were fought on more local issues. However, because of their moving from state to state and their dependence on the federal government, the Midwest tended to be nationalistic rather than sectionalistic. At the same time, however, many objected to John Marshall's use of judicial review in knocking down state laws, such as the one taxing the United States branch bank in Ohio. Consequently there was enough division of opinion that these states could not even agree on Jackson in 1824. Although these states did take the lead in the democritization of suffrage upon their admission to the Union, basically they tended to be economically and politically conservative.

Although elections were not necessarily a valid index of how people felt about political issues, they did reveal trends. The unanimous backing of Andrew Jackson in 1832 by the Midwest indicated its support of his battle against the national bank. In 1836, however, two of the five midwestern states registered a protest against Jackson's stand against federally financed internal improvements and easy credit (Specie Circular) by voting for their home-grown candidate, William H. Harrison, and against Jackson's hand-picked successor, Martin Van Buren. The reverse occurred in 1840 when three midwestern states voted for Harrison and only two, Missouri and Illinois, remained true to Van Buren and the Democratic Party. This shift on the part of the Midwest probably revealed its dislike of the Panic of 1837 and its approval of its home-grown, frontier candidate.

—16—

The Fur Trade

The fur trade continued to be a point of contention between England and the United States for some time after 1800. In 1796 England finally pulled out of Detroit and Mackinac, as well as several other posts, in accord with the provisions of the Jay Treaty. General Anthony Wayne's victory against the Indians at Fallen Timbers in August 1794 had apparently convinced the English that it was time to leave. Besides they felt they could carry on their trade almost as well from the Canadian side of the line; Malden across from Detroit and St. Joseph Island near Mackinac Island.

British withdrawal from these posts, however, did not keep the fur trade from being a contributing factor to yet another war. The Americans felt the English were supplying the Indians with weapons in return for furs and encouraging them to use the weapons against the frontiersmen. This idea was a factor in the American decision to declare war on England in 1812. Even with the war, however, England continued to trade with the Indians of the Midwest; but after the war, England's trade with the Indians began to decline.

Two main events contributed to this. The first was the action taken by the United States government. The Confederation Congress, fully appreciating the importance of the fur trade in the Ohio Valley, created in 1786 northern and southern Indian departments, each with a superintendent. About a decade later Congress set aside money to establish government trading posts or factories in the Indian country. Under this act posts were established at Detroit, Ft. Wayne, Chicago, Sandusky, Mackinac, and elsewhere. The purposes of these factories were to assure the Indians fair dealing, to check the evil practices of private traders, and to keep out the British. Although these factories were not too effective, they won some customers and helped Indian relations. Their greatest critics were the private American traders who did not want honest competitors who would give the Indians a fair deal. After weathering many attacks, the government factory system was finally abolished in 1822 when both Lewis Cass and Thomas H. Benton joined in advocating its dissolution. If given more support the factory system might have been of great value to the Indians. Even so it was helpful in winning some of them away from the British and setting a standard for American traders.

But probably the most important factor in the winning of the American fur trade by Americans was the entrance of dynamic, unscrupulous American trading companies on the scene. Among the first important American trading concerns was the Missouri Fur Company under the direction of Manuel Lisa. Lisa had obtained an exclusive right to trade with the Osage Indians before 1800. With the transfer of Louisiana to the United States in 1803 and the resulting Lewis and Clark Expedition, Manuel Lisa became increasingly active. In 1807 Lisa and 42 trappers went up the Missouri and Yellowstone rivers to the mouth of the Big Horn in pursuit of furs. When Lisa returned to St. Louis in 1808, he had plans for establishing an extensive fur company. A year later his plans came to fruition and the Missouri Fur Company was formed.

Lisa had originally built a fort at the mouth of the Big Horn River in Crow Indian country; but since he had trouble with the Blackfeet, he decided to establish Ft. Lisa near the present site of Omaha and Council Bluffs in 1812. Concentrating his company's activities at this post, he controlled the trade with the Omaha, Pawnee, and Oto. Lisa took a beautiful Omaha Indian girl as a wife and had two children by her. She did prove a source of embarrassment to him in 1819 when the original Mrs. Lisa accompanied her husband to the post. Lisa died in 1820.

Joshua Pilcher took over the company on Lisa's death. From 1812 to 1823, when Astor's American Fur Company forced it out, the Missouri Fur Company was the most important trading company on the Missouri River.

The fur company, however, that did most to force English traders, as well as other American traders, out of the Indian country was the American Fur Company established by John J. Astor in 1808. Born in Waldorf, Germany, in 1763, he landed in the United States with twenty-five dollars and seven flutes. By 1800 he was one of the largest fur merchants in the United States. The American Fur Company was actually just a holding company to facilitate his far-flung operations. The actual field work of his company was done by Ramsey Crooks, a Scotchman, and by traders, many of whom were French-Canadians. When the actions of his company were hampered by the Mackinac Company in 1815, Astor bought it out. In 1816 he pressured Congress into excluding foreign fur companies from the United States. A year later he set up the headquarters of his company at Mackinac Island. Spreading into Wisconsin, Minnesota, and the Dakotas, he crushed his competitors by using political influence, superior trading posts, lower prices, liquor, and traders who often went native and married Indian wives. By 1828 the American Fur Company was buying 95 per cent of the $250,000 to $300,000 worth of furs handled annually at Mackinac.

In 1822 Astor moved into the Missouri River area and soon after absorbed the Missouri Fur Company. He also went into competition with the Rocky Mountain Fur Company which had been recently established by General William H. Ashley and Major Andrew Henry. These were the days of Jim Bridger, Kit Carson, and Jedediah S. Smith. In 1822 there were an established 1,000 fur traders on the upper Missouri and 500 on the upper Mississippi. In June 1827 Ft. Atkinson was abandoned and the Sixth Infantry was transferred to Jefferson Barracks near St. Louis. Bellevue, a post a few miles south of Ft. Atkinson, was then established by the American Fur Company as the center of the fur trade on the Missouri River.

The western division of the American Fur Company established its headquarters at Ft. Union in 1829. Located on the Missouri River near the mouth of the Yellowstone River, this headquarters was housed in a typical stockade. Two-hundred feet square, it was constructed of logs 12 inches in diameter and 12 feet long. The pallisades were further reinforced by cross-beam supports. On the corners were block houses, 12 feet square and 20 feet high, pierced with loopholes. Several houses were built inside the inclosure.

In the late 1820's and early 1830's, the American Fur Company continued its policy of breaking its competitors. In 1827 it absorbed the Columbia Fur Company which controlled a large share of the trade with the Sioux and Omaha Indians. The American Fur Company had to wage an all out campaign to defeat the Rocky Mountain Fur Company. In 1830 both companies replaced their keelboats on the upper Missouri with steamboats to speed up their trade. Each side debauched the Indians with liquor and encouraged them to attack parties of rival traders. Finally in 1834 the Rocky Mountain Company was dissolved and the American Fur Company reigned supreme.

The American Fur Company, however, was no longer under John J. Astor. Astor, at age 72, chose 1834 as the year to sell out to Ramsey Crooks and associates.

Astor picked a good time to retire. The fur trade was beginning to decline as settlers poured into the Middle West. Even the taking of liquor into the Indian country, which had been declared illegal by Congress in 1822, could not stop the decline. It seemed that as the furs became more scarce, the liquor became more plentiful. At Mackinac alone, the American Fur Company distributed 8,776 gallons to ten outfits in 1832 and 5,573 gallons in 1833. The Indian Intercourse Act of 1834 again forbade liquor sales to the Indians but again with little result. The American Fur Company, among others, figured out all kinds of dodges to get liquor past the inspectors. By 1840 the American Fur Company favored the stoppage of liquor to the Indians because the smaller companies were using it too well.

This cutthroat competition among the fur companies was one of the reasons that the American Fur Company went broke in 1841. Probably a more important reason was the fact that the romantic period of the beaver was drawing to a close. Although the millions of beaver, mink, muskrat, otter, and fox had made an industry in the early years of American history, they had been greatly depleted and settlers were moving into put the land and the resources to more productive use. Fur trapping and trading were a remnant of a hunting, fishing, collecting economy that rapidly disappeared from the Midwest after 1845.

— 17 —

Agriculture

The second economy to come to the Midwest and one that has remained important was agriculture. The Indians had done a little farming in the Midwest prior to the coming of the white man. The first settlers to the Ohio Valley found corn fields extending for miles along the Ohio River bank. General Anthony Wayne wrote in 1794 that he had never before seen such immense fields of corn. The Indians produced an estimated one-million bushels of corn annually. Although the Indian understood the domestication of wild plants, the breeding of plants, fertilization, and the tilling of the soil, his methods were very primitive. He killed the trees and farmed around them. With a stick or other crude tool, he made shallow holes three to four feet apart, put in a fish for fertilizer, and then planted a few grains of corn or beans. Between these hills he planted pumpkin and squash.

As a result of the limited farming of the Indians, the soils of the Midwest were probably at their peak of fertility when they were first broken by the white man. The earliest pioneers were only a little ahead of the Indians in their use of the land. In selecting a site they wanted running water, good drainage, rich soil, cleared land, and access to markets. Although some pioneers grouped together near a post for protection from the Indians, most of them were individualistic and built their cabins far apart on a corner of their land. They thus differed from their European ancestors who lived in agricultural villages. There were a few rural villages in the early and later periods of Midwest history such as the Rappite Colony at New Harmony, Indiana, the Amana Society of Iowa, and the Hutterian Brethren in Bon Homme County, South Dakota. But these were the exception to the rural dissemination pattern. Moreover, because of the land ordinances of 1785 and 1787, most of the farms in the Midwest were laid out in a rectangular pattern.

The agricultural implements of the early pioneers in the Midlands were primitive and simple. The long rifle and woodsman's axe were the most important tools. The rifle not only afforded protection but also furnished the settler with meat, such as bear, deer, partridge, turkey, pigeon, duck, geese, quail, and squirrel. Wild honey was also plentiful in the woods, and fish were present in large numbers in the streams. Hook and line were considered too slow for fishing by many, and the gig and seine were often used.

With an axe a man could cut down a tree up to ten feet in diameter. Usually, however, farmers would only cut down trees up to 20 inches in diameter and girdle the larger ones. Timber was used for rails, buildings, and furniture. An average man could split 100 rails a day. The worm fences constructed of these rails were 7 to 10 rails high and lasted 15 to 20 years. Broad axes were used to dress the wood and frows to split the timber into clapboards. Drawing knives, augers, saws, and reaming tools were later added. At first crosscut saws were rare on the frontier.

Since much of the early agriculture was of the subsistence variety, many of the crops grown were for home consumption. A small orchard of apple, cherry, plum, peach, and pear trees was set out for fruit, cider, vinegar, and fruit butters. Farmers had one to a dozen cows to furnish the milk. The women and children usually did the milking. Butter was churned and some German and Swiss families made cheese and cottage cheese. Corn, barley, buckwheat, pumpkins, beans, and potatoes served as the staple foods and were supplemented by cabbages, cucumbers, asparagus, rhubarb, radishes, lettuce, peas, turnips, melons, grapes, strawberries, blackberries, gooseberries, peppers, mints, mustard, horse-radish, and tomatoes. Originally considered poisonous, tomatoes were seldom eaten until after 1830. Paw paws, persimmons, walnuts, hickory nuts, pecans, chestnuts, and mushrooms were also gathered. Beverages were made from sassafras roots, herbs, fruit, parched corn, and barley. Corn meal was pounded in a burned-out log, and johnny cake, mush, and hominy were made from it. Maple sugar was made in the spring when the sap came up in the maple trees.

Forested regions were developed for agriculture first. Later the clearings and prairies of northern Indiana and Illinois and southern Michigan and Wisconsin were farmed when the people lost their fear of treeless areas. At first when land wore out, the settlers just moved, but by 1800 they began to practice rotation of crops. The new land often produced a lot of straw but not much wheat. Hessian fly and army worms were present at the outset; thistles, pigweed, wild oats, cheat, sandburs, and quack grass did not come until later. Farmers used wooden plows. Although cast-iron plows were patented by Charles Newbold and Jethro Wood around 1800, these iron plows did not become plentiful until 1825. Plowing new ground with its trees, roots, and stumps was a hard job. It often required 3 or 4 yoke of oxen for the first plowing. Prairie sod with its tall grasses was even more difficult. Little could be done with it until John Deere developed a successful prairie plow in 1837. Just as the plow, at first, was the main tool in planting, the scythe was the tool most used in harvesting.

Among the field crops raised were corn, wheat, rye, oats, hay, and grasses. Although the average was far less, some rich soils produced 100 to 120 bushels of corn per acre. A good yield of wheat was 25 to 40 bushels per acre.

With the exception of Missouri, most of the farming in the Midwest up to 1830 was east of the Mississippi. And in Missouri the agricultural pattern was similar to the rest of the Midlands. Although the Missouri farmers had some slaves, they used them in general, diversified farming. There were few staple crops or plantations.

Farm labor generally was scarce in the West. The Midwest was also short on markets for its agricultural produce. The Ohio Valley began to ship flour, pork, whisky, and tobacco to New Orleans before 1800. Many farm products were shipped south especially after 1820. By 1835 wheat and flour were beginning to go east, but most of the corn was still going south.

To get their animals to market in these early days, the farmers often had animal drives. These drover routes led to eastern cities, southern plantations, Chicago, or Cincinnati (Porkopolis). Horses could average better than 20 miles per day, cattle 7-9 miles per day, and hogs less. In a mixed drive of cattle, horses, and hogs, hogs could subsist on the undigested corn left by cattle. There were several men in a drover crew of which the boss and perhaps one other were mounted. The drovers usually did not stay at taverns but at drove stands (farms with adequate pens and supplies for drovers and animals). Drovers were paid about $15 a month and on the return trip were required to walk 33 miles a day.

Harriet Martineau, in commenting on American agriculture in the mid-1830's, said that the American farmer ploughed around the stumps of the trees he had cut and was not careful to measure the area he ploughed or the seed he sowed. In contrast, she noted that the Englishman cleared half as much land thoroughly, ploughed deep, sowed his seed thick, and raised more per acre. Even though she favored the English procedure, she did admit that the American seemed to be more prosperous than his English cousin.

—18—

Money and Banking

Money and banking, which were necessary adjuncts to the economic development of the region, were a special problem in the Middle West up to 1840. During this period the West was a debtor region, and money had to come from the East to finance land purchases and internal improvements. Therefore this frontier area generally favored paper money and extensive credit because specie was scarce.

Among the earliest banks in the Midwest were the Miami Exporting Company and the Bank of Marietta. In 1803 a group of Cincinnati merchants incorporated the Miami Exporting Company with a capital of $500,000. Four years later it became a regular bank. The Bank of Marietta was doing business in 1807. In 1808 the Bank of Chillicothe was chartered; followed the next year by the Bank of Steubenville.

Up to 1811 the Bank of the United States exercised some restraint on state banks and their issue of paper money. But when the United States Bank expired, the number of state banks in the Midwest increased by leaps and bounds. In 1814 The Indiana territorial legislature chartered two banks. The Illinois territorial legislature incorporated four banks between 1816 and 1818. The Bank of Michigan was chartered in 1817 with a capital of $100,000. In 1818 there were 392 private banks in the United States of which the Midwest had about a third.

This meant an enormous expansion of credit and currency and neither speculators nor settlers checked to see if the inflated currency had a sound basis. The years 1815 and 1816 were the heyday of swindlers and amateurs. Virtually no capital was needed to start a bank. At Zanesville, Ohio, in 1816, thirty kinds of paper money were in circulation. This money bore the names of institutions such as the Canton Bank, the Owl Creek Bank, the Virginia Saline Bank, the Perryopolis Bank, the New Philadelphia Bank, and the Saddlebag Bank. Although Ohio attempted to curb this unbacked paper, it had very little success. After 1816 the newly chartered United States Bank began again to tighten down on paper money. The western states did not appreciate the Second Bank of United States' concern about sound money. Ohio, Indiana, and Illinois sought, without success, to prohibit the establishment of branches of this bank in their states.

The Panic of 1819, which resulted from inflation and speculation, was blamed on the United States Bank by the Midwest. When the Bank of the United States began to ask for specie in payment for paper money, only two or three Ohio banks could produce it. The national government in 1818 said that the treasury would accept only specie, U. S. Bank notes, and Pittsburgh notes for land payments. This meant the end of paper currency. Almost immediately, 153,000 acres of land in the Old Northwest reverted to the government. Congress passed relief acts to aid the defaulting settlers. In the 1820's prosperity began to return, but many banks did not weather the economic storm. The Indiana state treasurer reported that of the 85 banks established in Ohio, Indiana, Illinois, Kentucky, and Tennessee prior to 1830, 76 of them failed during the 1830's.

Money and banking remained at a fairly low level in the decade after 1825. Money was scarce and interest rates of 10 to 36 per cent were not uncomon. The volume of money being circulated by the Ohio banks in 1831 was not much greater than in 1819 and the business needs were far larger. The impending end of the United States Bank reduced the money in circulation in the Midwest still more. To counteract this, new banks were chartered. Ohio chartered ten new banks which brought the total of authorized banks up to 27 in 1835. Indiana also chartered a new state bank in 1834 with a capital stock of $600,000. Although its head office was at Indianapolis, it had ten branches in central and southern Indiana. In the seven years after 1829, Michigan established ten new banks. This brought its total of chartered banks up to 14 in 1837. Wisconsin Territory chartered the Bank of Wisconsin with its offices at Green Bay in 1835. In all, state banks in the United States increased from 329 in 1830 to 800 in 1837 and the Midwest again had at least a third.

Then in 1837 a panic again broke on the country. In the Midwest the underlying causes were wild speculation, reckless banking, over-extension of credit, over-investment in internal improvements, and crop failures. These conditions were brought to a head by Andrew Jackson's actions. First, he undermined the financial structure by crushing the Bank of the United States. Not only did this action remove a regulator from the economy, but it also necessitated the drawing in of U. S. Bank loans in order to make this money available to the national government.

Next Jackson became concerned about the value of bank notes being received by the national government for public lands. In July 1836 he issued the Specie Circular which stated that after August 15, 1836, land offices generally could receive only gold or silver in payment for land. Furthermore, in accord with the Distribution Bill of 1836, national money was drawn out of the "pet state banks" for distribution to the states. This reduced to a fraction the sound money left in circulation and pricked the bubble of prosperity.

As a result banks crashed, prices dropped, real estate sales declined, and even states defaulted on their debts. In May 1837 the New York banks suspended specie payments and the western banks soon followed suit. The second bank of Indiana survived. Many other midwestern banks were less fortunate. The Bank of Mineral Point (Wisconsin) went bankrupt in 1841 and the Bank of Wisconsin in 1846. Most of Michigan's banks went under in 1839 and the Bank of Illinois collapsed a year later. Land sales in 1837 were 33 per cent of those in 1836 and in 1838 they were 17 per cent of those in 1836. Construction of internal improvements stopped. States were left with heavy debts and half-completed transportation facilities. Thus as a result of overspending and undertaxing, Indiana went bankrupt in 1839, Illinois in 1840, and Ohio in 1841. They later repudiated a large amount of this indebtedness.

Finances continued to be hectic in the years directly following 1837. Midwesterners still engaged in extensive land speculation and overbuilding of railroads and other internal improvements. Some midwestern states like Indiana and Illinois did put in pay-as-you-go provisions in their new constitutions adopted around 1850 to prevent another default on debts. Iowa and Wisconsin, among others, also passed laws to regulate state banks more closely. But still the state banks increased in the United States from 307 in 1820 to 1,601 in 1860 and their note circulation from $16,600,000 to $207,000,000. Chief Justice John Marshall had tried to restrict state bank-note circulation under the clause in the U. S. Constitution forbidding states the right to print money. But Chief Justice Roger B. Taney, using a very strict interpretation, made a distinction in 1837 between bills issued on the credit of a state and those issued by a bank chartered by the state. The latter Supreme Court decision, allowing state banks to issue notes, opened the flood gates to paper money. It was soon true again that counterfeit money was sometimes worth more than genuine currency in the Midwest.

On the other hand specie remained scarce. Only small amounts were coined, and gold and silver tended to drive each other out of circulation. Between 1792 and 1834 the relation of silver to gold was 15 to 1. This overvalued silver, and under Gresham's law gold disappeared from circulation. In 1834 the ratio was changed to approximately 16 to 1. Under this new ratio gold, which was overvalued, came back into circulation and silver became scarce. The overvaluation of gold became even more evident after 1849 when California discoveries reduced the price. To keep subsidiary silver in circulation, the national government even had to debase fractional silver in 1853.

When the panic of 1857 broke on the country, the reasons for its occurrence in the Midwest were similar to those of former panics. Banks had been reckless, speculation had been rampant, and there had been an overbuilding of roads and railroads. The failure of the Ohio Life Insurance and Trust Company in August 1857 precipitated the crisis. Primarily financial, the panic affected largely the financial centers and speculative western railway interests. Recovery was rapid and by the time of the Civil War, the Midwest was on the road to a new cycle of prosperity.

With the end of the national bank in 1836, the national government had deposited its money in special state-chartered banks. Later it established an Independent Treasury system through which it collected money and paid its bills. With the restraining hand of the national bank gone, state banks and bank notes flourished. In 1862 there were in circulation an estimated 7,000 kinds of genuine notes plus 4,000 altered and counterfeit varieties. In order to eliminate this chaotic paper currency, as well as to create a market for government bonds and tie financial interests more closely to the Union cause, a new national banking system was established in 1863. The National Bank Act, as amended in 1864, allowed charters to be granted to groups of not less than five stockholders who had to deposit with the federal government federal bonds equal to one third of the bank's capital. The amount of capital stock varied, depending on the size of the city. In return for the bonds on deposit, the banks might issue bank notes up to 90 per cent of the current market value of the bonds (not to exceed par value). These notes were legal tender for all financial transactions except for payment of import duties and for payment of interest or principal on the national debt. There were many provisions protecting the depositor and making bank practices safe. The requirements were strict enough that stockholders continued to obtain charters for state banks rather than take out national bank charters. In 1865 national banks received a boost when a ten per-cent federal tax was levied on state bank notes. This drove state bank notes out of circulation and made national banks the chief creators of currency.

—19—

Land and Water Transportation

Trails and Roads

Trails and waterways were the earliest routes of transportation in the Midwest. One of the earliest important migration trails to the West was Boone's Road which wandered through Cumberland Gap up the Wilderness Road to Louisville, Kentucky. Braddock and Forbes' roads to the West were the result of military expeditions during the French and Indian Wars. Braddock's Trace (1755) ran from Ft. Cumberland on the Potomac River to near the Forks of Ohio. Forbes' Road (1758) connected Philadelphia to Ft. Pitt. A more northern route lay along the Mohawk and Genesee trails to Lake Erie. This route was continued on through Erie, Cleveland, Sandusky, and Maumee to Detroit before the War of 1812. The first significant road in the southern Midwest was Zane's Trace, built by Ebenezer Zane around 1796. It connected Wheeling, Virginia, and Maysville, Kentucky. Before 1812 another road from Marietta through Chillicothe to Cincinnati intersected it. As these roads came into general use, they were choked with mud in spring, thick with dust in summer, and heavy with snow in the winter. Sometimes they developed ruts nearly deep enough to lose a horse in.

Thus the years from 1760 to 1790 were the age of pack-horse travel, because vehicles with wheels usually could not get through. In 1783 the Conestoga wagon first came into general use on the overland routes across the Alleghanies. Its bed was higher at the ends than in the middle so as to keep the goods in. Drawn by four to six horses, it was painted blue and red with broad-rimmed wheels and a dull-white cloth top.

In 1806 Congress took the first step toward connecting the Atlantic coast and the Mississippi by a national highway. Delayed at first by sectionalism and politics, the Cumberland or Old National Road was not begun until 1811. By 1817 it was open to traffic from Washington, D. C., to Wheeling, Virginia. President James Monroe approved a measure to repair the road in 1824; the states were to be responsible for further maintenance. In 1833 the road reached Columbus, Ohio; 1850, Indianapolis, Indiana; and 1852, Vandalia, Illinois. In its finished section in 1850 it was 80 feet wide and had a 30-feet center of crushed stone, one foot deep. After the road was turned over to the states, they posted toll gates to collect money to repair it. In all some 34 federal appropriations were made to complete this road at a total cost of $6,821,000. It became a bond of unity between the Midwest and the East.

In its earlier days the conditions and travellers on the National Road were primitive and picturesque. When built across Ohio and Indiana initially, the only provision was that the trees be cut. Trees one foot in diameter were to be cut even with the ground: one foot to eighteen inches, nine inches from the ground; and over eighteen inches, fifteen inches from the ground. The stumps in the thirty-feet center had to be rounded off so as not to "obstruct" traffic. As could be expected upsets were common and the road was rough and muddy.

The services and equipment of the road were colorful. Stage coaches, trains of Conestoga freight wagons, and pack trains of either mules or horses were plentiful. Two great stage rivals on the National Road were the National Road Stage Company and the Good Intent Line. Meals, at wagon stands, were twelve cents, and a glass of whisky cost three cents. "Stogies," an abbreviation of Conestoga cigars, were developed for use on the National Road and sold four for a penny. The wagoners and stage drivers were a rough and ready group. Although their wages were only $12 to $20 a month, they seemed to enjoy their jobs. When they danced at taverns, they resembled a large den of good-natured, grizzly bears. Boys along the National Road dreamed of being stage-coach drivers rather than river-boat pilots or railroad engineers as boys of these latter eras did.

The newcomers to the Midwest at first used Indian trails. In most states these paths converged at certain points. In Indiana paths led from Vincennes, Louisville, and northern Indiana to a point on the White River where it was joined by Fall Creek. A second converging area was near the site of Ft. Wayne (a Miami village). In Illinois, Kaskaskia and Ft. Massac (on the Ohio River opposite the mouth of the Tennessee River) were trail terminals. Other junctions for trails were the Black Hawk village (on Rock River, three miles above its junction with the Mississippi), Chicago, and Galena. Other states had similar patterns of trails.

Oliver H. Smith, who came to Indiana in 1817, commented on the transportation facilities in the early days. He said that bridges were almost non-existant and travelling overland was done mostly by horseback. When a large family travelled, the man rode in the saddle holding one or two children, and the wife rode behind holding the children that could not walk. Smith noted in travelling through Indiana that bear, deer, and wolf sprang up ahead of him continually.

The whites soon enlarged or improved the Indian paths and called them traces. The first roads built by whites in Indiana were Berry and Whetzel traces. Berry Trace ran from the Falls of the Ohio to the White River and Whetzel Trace from the Ohio border to Barry Trace. They were paths chopped through the forest. The earliest road of importance was the one connecting Louisville and Vincennes, constructed on an old buffalo trail after 1805. A trace parallel to the above, called Kibby's Road, was surveyed around 1802. It was 201 miles long and connected Cincinnati, Madison, Salem, French Lick, and Vincennes. The larger settlements along the Whitewater, Ohio, and Wabash rivers were also connected by roads or trails. The Three Notch Trace was an enlargement of an Indian trial that ran from the Falls of the Ohio to the new state capital at Indianapolis. In 1821 the Indiana legislature projected more than two dozen roads, several of which were to connect the new state capital.

Probably the largest road-building project in Indiana was the Michigan Road advocated by Governor James B. Ray of Indiana. In 1826 the United States government obtained a right of way across the Potawatomi lands from Lake Michigan to the Ohio River. Indiana was authorized to build the road, using proceeds obtained from the sale of land contiguous to the road. Begun in 1832 it was to connect Madison, Indianapolis, Logansport, and

South Bend. When completed it was 265 miles long. It was cleared to a width of 100 feet of which 30 feet were grubbed and graded. In some portions it consisted of seasoned oak timbers, 20 feet long and a foot square, covered by eighteen inches of dirt taken from the ditches. By 1835, $200,000 had been spent on it; land sales covered the expenditure. An artery of settlement for the northern Midwest, it was second only to the National Road in the era prior to the coming of the railroads. The first really improved roads, however, were not built until 1835 when the state began its internal improvements program.

In Ohio the earliest traces were built out of Columbus, Springfield, and Dayton to serve the forts in those areas. In 1821 a 109-mile road was laid out to connect Piqua and Ft. Meigs, Ohio. Five years later John Kilbourn promoted the Columbus and Sandusky Turnpike Company to build roads. During the period 1823 to 1840, roads were built to connect Cleveland to the Ohio and the Maumee rivers.

One of the oldest roads in Illinois ran from Ft. Massac on the Ohio River westward to Kaskaskia and St. Louis. The Goshen Road angled northwest from Shawneetown and connected Carlyle, Edwardsville, and Alton. There were also a Vincennes-St. Louis Road and a trace from Chicago to the mouth of the Wabash. The Illinois legislature of 1823 authorized a dozen roads radiating from Vandalia to various towns including Shawneetown, Kaskaskia, Alton, and Palestine. It was not until 1827, however, that a road was built in northern Illinois. Known as Kellogg's trail, it connected Peoria and Galena. The Potawatomi Trace tying Chicago to Ottawa was a reasonably good road by 1834.

The only trace into Michigan in 1815 was the one used by General William Hull in the War of 1812. The Detroit-Pontiac-Saginaw Road was completed by 1826. In a treaty of 1821 with the Chippewa, Ottawa, and Potawatomi, the United States obtained the right to build a road from Detroit to Chicago. Eleven years later the 263-mile road from Detroit to Chicago was completed.

The area that was to become Wisconsin had no roads prior to 1830. In 1838 a military road was completed between Green Bay and Prairie du Chien. Congress had also appropriated money for a survey of a road from Green Bay to Chicago.

Missouri, settled at about the same time as southern Indiana and Illinois, had a few roads soon after 1800. One of the earliest was Boone's Trace built from New Charles to Boonville and New Franklin around 1815.

Demands for internal improvements at national expense increased in the Midwest after the War of 1812. Internal improvements became a part of the National Republican Party platform. However since the Democratic-Republicans were in power during this period, little was done about constructing nationally-financed, internal improvements. Although the Democratic-Republicans allowed appropriations for the National Road under the post-road provision, they would not approve money for the maintenance of it or for the building of intra-state roads. In 1824 the National Road was turned over to the states for maintenance. Six years later Jackson ended the western dream of federally-built, internal improvements by vetoing the Maysville Road Bill.

The precedent for federal aid to states for internal improvements was set in 1826 by the Michigan Road Act. By this act Indiana was to receive one section of land adjacent to the turnpike for each mile of road built. Indiana was then to sell the land to finance the enterprise. This general procedure was followed for roads, canals, and later railroads. Although the national government footed a part of the bill, it left construction and maintenance up to the states. Michigan, for example, received five per cent of the sales of federal public land within its borders for road and canal building. In many local areas states and counties resorted to toll taxes and corvees to build roads. An early act of the Northwest Territory provided that male citizens would contribute two days of labor a year for road building. Indiana Territory upped this to twelve days. A similar provision was carried over into many of the midwestern states.

Travel on the roads in the early Middle West was irritating and exhausting. Harriet Martineau travelled 10,000 miles in America without serious accident, although she was stuck in the mud, badly shaken, and missed meals on numerous occasions. The roads were terrible. Mudholes had proprietors who pulled out unlucky customers for a fee. Some ungracious people even fenced and dug holes in the state turnpikes. Ruts were deep enough in downtown Indianapolis in the late 1830's to upset a stage. Chicago streets were nearly impassable in the spring. On one occasion a stage coach mired in Clark Street opposite the Sherman House where it remained several days. Some humorous person drove a sign post into the mud beside the stalled vehicle bearing the inscription, "no bottom here." The thousands of cattle, hogs, horses, and turkeys that were driven over the roads in the early days also cut up the roads and clogged them, making it difficult for more rapid conveyances to pass. Many roads were also crooked. Although one reason for this was terrain, another was that north-south roads were laid out to follow township boundaries. Since the meridians tend to converge as they approach the north pole, surveyors made corrections by using abrupt turns and curves in their north-south township lines. This hazard has remained in the Midwest. Some of the roads were so bad that people preferred using stream beds for horse-drawn vehicles rather than the roads.

Between 1820 and 1840 stage lines slowly replaced travel by horseback. By 1840 nearly all the Old Northwest and Missouri had a network of stage lines except for Wisconsin Territory and northern Michigan. Leading stage companies included the Pioneer Line, the National Line, the June Bug Line, and the Shake Gut Line.

The accommodations along the routes were poor. The number of alcoholic beverages was legion, ranging from madeira to corn whisky. The landlord generally supplied the hospitality and his wife and children did the work. There was little privacy for sleeping and vermin were prevalent. The price in the rural Midlands was 50 cents for lodging, meals, and horse care for twenty-four hours; in cities the same accommodations were twice to thrice that amount. Some taverns were run by cutthroats and thieves who plundered their guests. Most of the people in the early days were travelling out of necessity rather than for pleasure. Travel was irritating, expensive, and sometimes dangerous.

The first improvement of dirt roads in the Midwest occurred in the 1830's. Logs were split and laid rounded side up. These "corduroy roads" were extremely rough. In the 1840's and 1850's, planks were substituted. The planks were eight feet long and three inches thick, laid across the road bed. Because of their smoothness they were considered wonderful at first, but were discontinued when horses fell through and broke their legs and carriages slid off and upset. Gravel and crushed stone were later used and found to be much more satisfactory.

Land transportation west of the Mississippi River followed a similar pattern to that east of the river. The more western trails and traces, however, often connected more widely-separated places, and horseback remained in vogue longer as the primary means of locomotion.

From 1830 to 1870 the trans-Mississippi region was noted for its long trails which served more to populate the Far West and to facilitate trade than to develop and serve the western portion of the Middle Border. The first of the trails to the Far West was the Santa Fe founded by Captain William H. Becknell of Missouri in 1821. The trail began at St. Louis, Missouri, crossed Kansas and a corner of Colorado and ended at Santa Fe, New Mexico.

Because of the trail's importance, Congress passed an act in 1825 authorizing the survey of the Santa Fe Trail. Permission was obtained for a right of way from the Great and Little Osage and Kansa Indians. The survey was completed in 1826. Six years later troops began to patrol the trail to protect the traders from Indian attacks. After 1827 the main center of the trail was Independence, Missouri. The Mexican War greatly increased its trade and made it a domestic highway.

The other major trace across the West was the Oregon Trail with its cut-off trails to Salt Lake City and California. The main trail began at Independence, Missouri, followed the Platte River to South Pass and then paralleled the Snake River into Oregon. St. Joseph, Missouri, and Council Bluffs, Iowa, were also favorite jumping-off spots. By 1849 even Des Moines, Iowa, had a government fort and a covered-wagon stop for those going to California and Oregon.

Robert Stuart discovered the Oregon Trail in 1813. The first wagons over the trail were those of David Jackson, Jedediah Smith, and William Sublette in 1830. Captain Benjamin L. E. de Bonneville explored the Platte River Trail across South Pass to the Green River. In 1841 the first band of settlers, 80 in number, set out from Missouri with a mountain man, Thomas Fitzpatrick, as guide. A year earlier the U. S. secretary of war suggested construction of a string of forts west from Ft. Leavenworth to protect the travellers on the trail. In 1845 John C. Fremont was chosen to map the area preparatory to selecting the forts. A year later more than 1,000 people went west over the trail. In 1847 and 1848 some 4,500 Mormons went over the trail to Salt Lake City. In 1849 the lure was California and 40,000 made the journey over the trail in that year.

Water Transportation

With its abundance of streams and rivers, the Midwest early developed a system of water transportation. Nearly every state in the Middle West had access to some waterway, either river or lake. Canoes and rafts were the first type of transportation used on the midwestern waters. Because of their size, length, and location, the Great Lakes and the Missouri, Mississippi, and Ohio rivers were used most. The Great Lakes and the Mississippi River were most important in the early exploration and settlement of the interior United States. They later became the most important commercial routes of the Midwest.

The varieties and types of boats on the streams and rivers of the Middle West in the early 1800's were infinite. The canoe was a dugout made out of a log, 15 to 20 feet long and 3 to 4 feet wide. A pirogue was either a canoe or a pair of canoes fastened together with a sharp bow and a square stern. The bull boat, which was used to transport furs downstream, was made of willow poles tied together with rawhide. The bateau or barge was a flat-bottomed boat, 50 to 75 feet in length and constructed in the shape of a huge box. Its square ends were sloped so that it could proceed more easily through the water. The flatboat was similar to the barge except that it had a tent on it. The keelboat was a more elaborate-type flatboat. It was 60 to 75 feet long and 15 to 20 feet wide. It received its name from the fact that it had a beam or keel running from bow to stern. Capable of hauling 15 to 20 tons, it drew 30 inches of water when empty. The keelboat was fitted with a cabin that covered about two thirds of the deck. It was propelled by wind, poling, or pulling. It was probably the most important boat on the rivers prior to the steam boat. Other boats in use included the yawl, a flat-bottomed rowboat; the Durham boat, another type flatboat; a schooner; a broadhorn; and an ark.

Water transportation in the early days was colorful, dangerous, and hard. There were rapids and shoals present which could wreck a craft. Indians killed some 1,500 persons on the Ohio River prior to 1794. Pioneers settling in the southern Midwest would build a flatboat and start down the Ohio from Pittsburgh or Redstone. Men, women, children, horses, pigs, chickens, cows, dogs, dishes, furniture, provisions, and farm implements all floated down river together. These flatboats were a combination of a log cabin, a fort, a barnyard, and a grocery. Dependent on the current and wind, a flatboat could travel from three to fifty miles a day. If all went well, after a period of one to three weeks on the river, the pioneer and his family would arrive at their destination.

Flatboats and keelboats also hauled much of the early commerce. On the Missouri River, keelboats were ordinarily used in the fur trade. In 1811 Manuel Lisa set a record with a keelboat. He travelled 1,200 miles up the Missouri in 61 days. Flatboats were used as floating stores to supply the Ohio River Valley. From 1795 to 1835 flatboats and keelboats carried a majority of the surplus produce from the southern Midwest south. Abraham Lincoln allegedly made a voyage on a flatboat down the Mississippi around 1830.

The boatmen generally were a fighting, boisterous group. They enjoyed fighting one another to prove their strength. The hero of this era was a somewhat mythical character, Mike Fink, "king of the keelboatmen." Supposedly a real person, he was born in Pennsylvania in 1781. After an exciting, fighting life, he was killed after he murdered one of his best friends.

A new era in water transportation in the Midlands came with the first steamboat in 1811. Although John Fitch of Connecticut built the first steamboat, no one paid much attention to him or his ideas. Robert Fulton copied Fitch's steamboat plans after the latter's death and popularized them. In 1807 Fulton made a successful run on the Hudson River in his *Clermont*. Two years later Robert Fulton and associates sent Nicholas J. Roosevelt to the West to investigate the possibilities of steamboats on the western rivers. Having obtained an exclusive 14-year franchise for steamboating from the Louisiana territorial legislature, the Fulton company instructed Roosevelt to have a steamboat constructed at Pittsburgh. The boat, which was 138 feet long, 26 feet wide, and cost $40,000, was launched in 1811. Roosevelt was captain of the vessel on its maiden voyage from Pittsburgh to Louisville.

Almost immediately other persons began building steamboats for the midwestern waters. The *Comet* was built by Samuel Smith in 1812. The Fulton Company built the 340-ton *Vesuvius* in 1814. Independents next built the 75-ton *Enterprise*. This competition between rival companies came to a head in 1817 when the Fulton-Livingston Company of New York seized the steamboat *Washington* owned by Captain Henry Shreve. The Fulton Company maintained it had a monopoly on steamboat travel. The federal courts, however, in the *Washington* Case decided that the Fulton Company did not have a monopoly and as a result the number of steamboats in the West grew rapidly. Before long they could be found on every navigable stream. In 1817 the *Zebulon M. Pike* reached St. Louis. The first steamboat on the Great Lakes was *Walk-in-the-Water,* built in Buffalo at a cost of $50,000. This vessel was a two-masted boat with two paddle wheels, each 16 feet in diameter. Its first voyage was from Buffalo to Detroit in August 1818. The cost of passenger fare for this junket was $18.

In 1819 the *Independence* sailed up the Missouri river to Franklin. During the same year the *Western Engineer* under the command of Major S. H. Long reached Council Bluffs, Iowa. In 1823 the steamboat *Virginia* went up the uncharted Mississippi to the falls of St. Anthony. The same year the *Florence* reached Vincennes on the Wabash River. In 1832 the *Yellowstone* took George Catlin, the painter, up the Missouri River to Ft. Union at the mouth of the Yellowstone River. The first cabin steamer on the Great Lakes was the *Michigan* built by Oliver Newberry in 1833. This boat with a deck of 156 feet, had three masts, two smokestacks, and sleeping accommodations for 108 people. In that year there were 11 steamboats plying the Great Lakes. In 1834 when the total tonnage of the British Empire was 82,696 tons, the tonnage afloat on the Ohio and Mississippi rivers was 126,278 tons.

Canals

The building of the Erie Canal (1817-1825) had a great influence on water transportation and on the Midwest. Sponsored by Governor DeWitt Clinton of New York, this 363-mile "ditch," which was thirty feet wide and four feet deep, cost seven-million dollars. As a result of it, more commerce began to flow east toward New York. This stimulated the growth of the Great Lakes cities of Chicago, Cleveland, and Detroit. The Erie Canal also decreased the cost of shipping bulky goods to market, and as a result wheat production shifted further west. The construction of the Erie Canal also motivated the midwestern states of Ohio, Indiana, Illinois, Michigan, and Wisconsin to build similar canals.

In 1818 Governor Ethan A. Brown of Ohio recommended that a survey be made for a canal to connect the Ohio River and Lake Erie. The Panic of 1819 delayed any action. Surveys were again made between 1822 and 1824; in 1825 the Ohio legislature authorized the building of the Ohio and Erie and Miami canals. The Ohio and Erie was to run from Portsmouth to Cleveland by way of the Scioto-Muskingum route. The Miami Canal was to follow the Miami River from Cincinnati to Dayton. On July 4, 1825, the Ohio Canal was begun and the Miami Canal was started 17 days later. The 66-mile stretch of the Miami Canal was completed from Cincinnati to Middleton in 1830 at a cost of $900,000. The Ohio Canal was not finished over the Scioto, Muskingum, Tuscarawas, and Cuyahoga route until 1832. This canal connecting Portsmouth and Cleveland cost $4,245,000 and was 26 feet wide and four feet deep. Most of the other canals were extensions or links of these two. Altogether Ohio spent some $95,000,000 on 1,000 miles of canals.

Indiana fared even worse. In 1817 Governor Jonathan Jennings of Indiana advocated a canal to connect the Ohio River to the Great Lakes. Five years later as a congressman he pushed the Wabash and Erie Canal. Finally in 1827 Congress granted Indiana land from the mouth of the Tippecanoe River to Lake Erie to help defray the cost of building the canal. Although Indiana accepted, it did not begin to work on the canal until 1832. The first 30-mile section of the Wabash canal from Ft. Wayne to Huntington, Indiana, was opened in 1835. The next section to Peru was completed in 1837; to Logansport in 1838; and to Lafayette in 1841. At that time Indiana had spent around $9,500,000 for canals, had only 200 miles of canals completed, and received $5,000 a year in tolls.

When the panic struck, Indiana abandoned or turned all her unfinished canals (with the exception of the Wabash and Erie) over to anyone who would complete them. Ohio had agreed to construct the eastern end of the Wabash Canal if it could have the lands in that area furnished by the national government. Indiana agreed and Ohio completed it. In 1843 the 187-mile canal from Lafayette, Indiana, to Toledo, Ohio, was opened. Packet boats began to run from Toledo to Lafayette. The trip took over two days. The canal from Terre Haute to Evansville was finally completed in 1853. The Wabash and Erie was then 458 miles long, the longest canal in the United States. Its business grew during the years 1847 to 1855 and then declined. The competition of the railroads and public hostility ruined it.

Although Illinois also went broke building internal improvements, it fared a little better than Indiana because Illinois put more money in railroads and less in canals. The first canal to be considered in Illinois was one to connect the Great Lakes and Mississippi via the Illinois River. In 1827 Congress ceded federal lands to Illinois for the building of the canal. The actual building of the Illinois and Michigan Canal did not begin until 1836. Abraham Lincoln and his colleagues voted for this canal project not because they favored it but because they wanted to obtain support for Springfield as the capital. The Panic of 1837 caused a suspension of the building of the Illinois and Michigan. It was taken over by the state's creditors and finally opened in 1848. It was soon put out of business by the railroads.

Although Michigan concentrated more on railroads during this period, it also ended up with several half-completed canals. Michigan borrowed money from eastern banks to complete these projects, but the banks collapsed in 1841 before the canals were finished. Michigan's (and the Midwest's) most valuable canal, built later, was the one at Sault Ste. Marie, connecting Lakes

Superior and Huron. Constructed by Michigan in 1855, it was later turned over to the United States government. The flow of commerce in ore and agricultural products through this canal has been tremendous.

In Wisconsin the Milwaukee and Rock River Canal was never built. The canal tying the Fox and Wisconsin rivers together was finally finished through the efforts of Morgan L. Martin. Begun in 1839 it was not completed until 27 years later. Railroad competition caused it to fall into disuse.

Generally canals were expensive, inflexible, and furnished very poor service. It cost about five cents a mile to ride on a canal boat. The food was terrible, sleeping accommodations were uncomfortable, and collisions with other boats frequent. Occasional delays occurred because the water had leaked out of sections of the canals. Charles Dickens, who had lost money in canal building and on copyrights in the United States, complained of drawing muddy water from the canal to wash in. He also criticized his travelling companions who he felt were dull and unmannerly. He said they had brown streaks of dried tobacco juice on their chins and blew their noses with their fingers.

On the credit side these canals caused an increase in the prices of agricultural products and the value of lands adjacent to the canals. They also aided the growth of cities like Cleveland, Toledo, Chicago, and Detroit and stimulated trade between the Ohio Valley and the East.

— 20 —

Religion

Denominations and Religious Bodies

Paralleling the nationalizing of the American government in the period 1784 to 1800, the Methodist, Episcopalean, Presbyterian, Roman Catholic, and Reformed churches were also engaged in nationalizing their ecclesiastical organizations. Thus these churches were prepared organizationally to move with the people as they moved into the Middle West. The only problem was that the settlers usually moved faster than the churches. Although most present-day Americans have somehow received the impression that in early America everyone was a church member, such was not the case. There were often no churches or ministers waiting in the forest for the settlers and so the latter got ahead of the church and stayed ahead across the continent to the Pacific coast.

The Presbyterians were in an especially good position to move into the West. The Scotch-Irish came in the last great wave of immigration prior to the revolution, and they had scattered their Presbyterian churches along the western edge of colonial America. In 1801 the Presbyterians and Congregationalists agreed to the Plan of Union by which the Congregational and Presbyterian settlers in a new community might combine to form a single congregation and call a minister of either denomination. If a majority of the church's members were Congregational, the Congregational discipline would be used, and if Presbyterian the Presbyterian discipline would be used.

The Plan of Union usually worked to the advantage of the Presbyterians. An estimated 2,000 churches organized as Congregational churches under this plan became Presbyterian. The

Presbyterians were simply more tenacious. For example, the first Presbyterian church in Chicago originally had a Congregational minister and 26 of the original 27 members were Congregationalists and yet the church became Presbyterian.

Congregationalism early gained a foothold at Marietta, Ohio, and in the Western Reserve. The first Congregational church in the Western Reserve was at Austinburg (Richfield) founded in 1801. Isaac Reed began a church at New Albany, Indiana, in 1818. By 1825 there were 42 Presbyterian and Congregational churches in Ohio, Indiana, and Kentucky. A year later the General Assembly erected the synod of Indiana. A few Congregational churches were also organized in Michigan. Most of the churches soon became Presbyterian in name and polity in Indiana and Illinois.

The Presbyterians, however, did not keep pace numerically with the Baptists and Methodists for several reasons. The Presbyterians emphasized an educated clergy and less circuit riding. Many of the western people felt the Presbyterian and Congregational ministers with their gloomy sermons were too learned for them. Moreover, the presbyterian system of church government was too authoritarian for many of the democratic frontiersmen.

The first Baptist people began moving into the Midwest between 1774 and 1789. The Baptists had certain advantages for winning the West to their faith. The Baptists featured a democratic church government, their preachers came from the people and were self-supporting, and they appealed to the economic class which was most attracted to the lure of cheap land.

The Baptists depended more on local, established preachers than upon circuit riders and were less emotional than Methodists. The typical Baptist preacher worked on his land during the week except when he held a weekday meeting or funeral. These uneducated and unsalaried farmer-preachers generally took the initiative in establishing a church in a new community. Once established the minister and membership spent a lot of time disciplining the flock. Infractions considered included drinking, fighting, lying, stealing, illicit sex, gambling, fraudulent business dealings, and family disputes.

Most of the early frontier Baptist churches were named after creeks, runs, valleys, or rivers. For example, the Illinois Association of 1807 was made up of seven churches among which were

Mississippi Bottom, Silver Creek, Wood River, Kain Spring, and Richland Creek. Other early Baptist associations were the Miami in Ohio organized in 1797 and the Wabash organized in Indiana in 1808. By 1812 Ohio had four associations with some 60 churches and 2,400 members.

The most successful of the American churches in following the population into the Midwest was the Methodist. Both its organization and doctrine were popular in the West. The Methodist's most significant contribution to religion in the Middle West was the circuit-rider system, which had been devised by John Wesley in England and introduced into America by Bishop Francis Asbury. The length of a circuit varied with the number of settlements. If the country was new, the circuits were usually large and it might require a circuit rider about a month to make the rounds. He established "classes" at convenient places over which he appointed "class leaders." There were usually 20 to 30 of these on a circuit. The circuit rider usually preached every day of the week to one of the "classes." He met them in a log cabin, a tavern, or under the trees and was usually one of the first visitors to a new community. In addition to the itinerant minister, the Methodists also used local, lay preachers who greatly aided the spread of the ministry in the new country. Full of zeal and earnestness, these uneducated lay preachers sometimes became regular travelling ministers, but most of them remained in their local areas to aid the building of the kingdom of God.

The gospel of free will and free grace preached by the Methodist circuit riders was usually readily accepted by the frontiersman. It contrasted favorably with the doctrines of limited grace and predestination espoused by the Presbyterians or even the milder Calvinism held by the Baptists. The frontier Methodist ministers emphasized the concept that the pioneers were the masters of their own destiny and equal to all men.

Two personalized examples of the actions and ideas of Methodist circuit riders in the Midwest were William H. Milburn and Peter Cartwright. Milburn's sermons exhibited the frontier morality that appealed to his midwestern listeners. He condemned the young man who became a dandy, who was dismissed from public school as a dunce, and who was expelled from college as a rowdy. This degenerate, he continued, then went to Europe to finish his education and while there spent most of his time and money in Paris, chasing alleged nymphs of the ballet and opera, who in actuality were chamber maids at his lodging houses. Upon his return to America, he folded his arms and said America was a wooden country not fit for a gentleman to live in. He then strove to become a connoisseur of horseflesh, cigars, brandy smashes, and gin cocktails. He ended this story by asking his audience if they called this thing young America?

Obviously, Milburn did not think so and he went on to illustrate what the young American should be. A few years ago, he said, a lad aged 13, sent to the northern border of Kentucky to look for strayed cows, kept his rifle ready for savages. A scout seeing him thought he would scare the boy by jumping up behind him and sounding an Indian war cry. The scout thought the boy would run, but instead, when the scout stuck his head out to see what the boy had done, the boy, also behind a tree, put a bullet into the scout's brain. Milburn concluded that this scout died a sacrifice to the bravery of the true, young American. Milburn's recurring theme that frontier morality was better than Europe's sinks of prostitution was favorably received by the midwestern frontiersmen.

Peter Cartwright likewise spent his life literally wrestling with the devil in the Illinois river towns. From an improvised pulpit, he would demand that some sturdy young man come forward and be saved. If the young sinner refused, Cartwright would walk to the young man, fling him down in front of the congregation, and ask God to save this erring soul. In his duties as a Methodist circuit rider, Cartwright swam rivers, rode hundreds of miles, and preached some 8,000 sermons. He also took time to raise nine children, defeat Abraham Lincoln for the state legislature in 1832, and help cultivate his 600 acres of land. He was the only kind of saint that most of the Midwest would receive; "a sharp-tongued, keen-witted, heavy-fisted fighter for righteousness."

Like the Baptists the Methodist ministers were called by God. The only difficulty in this was that there seemed to be nothing to prevent the call from occasionally descending upon the ignorant and mean as well as upon the intelligent and kind. At first many Methodist ministers as well as lay people used liquor and tobacco, but after 1825 this consumption declined. Peter Cartwright, among others, strenuously opposed their use. The life of the Methodist minister, especially of the itinerant variety, was a hard and lonely one. He had no excuse for being late for a meeting, neither flood, misfortune, nor Indians. He preached eight sermons a week for which the single minister received $64 a year in 1784 and $100 a year in 1816. Young ministers were not to marry during their first four years of circuit duty. When they later did marry, the Methodist church wanted those serving in the West to marry western wives so they would stay in the region.

The overall administration of the Methodist church in every section of the United States up to about 1800 was handled by Francis Asbury. He made numerous trips across the mountains to advise, appoint, and confer in the West. From 1800 to 1808 all the western circuits were gathered into one district and placed under the direction of William McKendree. It was surprising that a church with a somewhat authoritarian episcopal policy could make such inroads into the frontier West. Actually this could be explained by the democratic nature of the Methodist gospel and by the fact that the bishops moved around the frontier, kept in contact with their people, and tempered the arbitrary nature of the Methodist system.

Methodism on a permanent basis came to America in 1768, and by 1800 there were four Methodist circuits of which two were the Scioto and Miami in the Northwest Territory. Four years later the Ohio district with five circuits was created. Benjamin Young was sent to the Illinois country in 1803. In 1812 the Ohio and Tennessee conferences were established. Southern Indiana was in the Ohio Conference and southern Illinois in the Tennessee Conference. Although Methodist circuit riders entered into Michigan in 1804, there was no important work there until the 1820's. Methodist records indicate that there was a circuit rider at Galena, Illinois, in 1824. Although there was a Methodist society at Platteville, Wisconsin, in 1833, Methodism accomplished little in Wisconsin Territory until after 1836. Methodists were across the Mississippi River in Missouri at a relatively early date. The first Methodist church in Iowa was built at Dubuque in 1834. By 1840 there were eight conferences which were completely or partly in the Old Northwest.

Related to the Methodists, the Episcopaleans, strongest in Ohio, were composed mainly of upper middle-class people from the East. In 1818 the Diocese of Ohio was established with Philander Chase as its bishop. Fifteen years later the Diocese of Michigan was created and attached to the Ohio Diocese. As of 1841 there were about 132 Episcopalean ministers in the Midwest of which approximately 54 were in Ohio.

The Lutherans were strongest in the German areas. Their churches developed around Cincinnati, Detroit, Ft. Wayne, Sandusky, and St. Louis. The Scandinavians and Germans moving into Wisconsin and Minnesota took Lutheranism to the rural areas in those states. Their coming, however, occasionally precipitated a disruption in the church. Those coming from Europe were more conservative and wanted to retain their native tongue in church services.

The United Brethren church had its origin in Pennsylvania when Philip W. Otterbein, a German Reformed, and Martin Böhm, a Mennonite, met Francis Asbury, a Methodist. In essence the United Brethren became the Methodist church for people of German origin. In the Midwest they were even referred to as Dutch (Deutsch) Methodists. In 1800 the United Brethren conference met, adopted a name, and elected bishops. To meet the need of United Brethren families moving to Ohio, the Miami Annual Conference was established in the early 1800's. The Indiana Conference was organized in 1830 and the Wabash Conference five years later. The United Brethren, with its Methodist polity and doctrine, emphasized evangelism, simple piety, and stern morals.

Many of the Quakers of the Old Northwest came from the South. They came partly to escape from the slavery problem and partly to obtain better land. By 1826 Belmont, Jefferson, Harrison, and Columbia counties in Ohio were the center of some 8,000 Quakers. Their basic doctrine was the universal inner light, the spirit of Jesus Christ in every person. The coordinating agency was the yearly meeting. The Ohio Meeting was established in 1813 and the Indiana Meeting in 1821. The Friends generally opposed tax-supported schools, military service, and slavery.

Two other small groups, the Unitarians and Universalists, were found only in the larger cities in the West. For example, the

First Congregational (Unitarian) Church of Cincinnati had its beginning in 1824.

Also present were a small number of Roman Catholics. Most of the midwestern Catholics in 1800 were a hangover from the French settlement. One of the most noted priests in the West from 1792 to 1830 was Reverend Benedict J. Flaget who originally came to Indiana to serve the parish at Vincennes. At the time of Flaget's arrival, there were also Catholic congregations at Vincennes, Kaskaskia, Cahokia, and Detroit. By 1808 the Catholic population in the region had increased to the point that the Catholic church created a new diocese at Bardstown, Kentucky. It included Kentucky, Tennessee, Indiana, and Illinois. Flaget became the first bishop. In 1815 he estimated the number of Catholics in Ohio at fifty families; those in Indiana at 130 families; those in Illinois at 120 families; and those in Detroit at 400 families. As the Catholic population increased so did the dioceses. A diocese at Cincinnati was established in 1829, one at Detroit in 1833, and one at Vincennes in 1834.

Overall the fastest growing of the churches in the pioneer period was the Methodist. In Indiana, for example, its membership grew from 10,840 in 1826 to 52,626 in 1840. As of 1850 the Old Northwest had approximately 7,306 churches of which 2,944 were Methodist, 1,378 were Baptist, 1,263 were Presbyterian, 214 Congregational, 397 were Lutheran, 353 were Christian, 196 were Quaker, 174 were Episcopalean, and 360 were Catholic. In addition to the ones mentioned above, the Midwest also had a sprinkling of other Protestant groups including Mennonites, Amish, Church of the Brethern, Moravians, German Reformed, Dutch Reformed, and Eastern Orthodox.

Revivalism and its Affects

Religion was at an especially low ebb in America from the end of the American Revolution up to the War of 1812. The awakening which began in the East around 1800 had strange affects in the Midwest, primarily because of its frontier characteristics. Revivalism, especially, had unusual manifestations. Since people came long distances to revivals in the West, they began to bring provisions to stay a few days. This was the origin of the camp meeting. Camp meetings at night were especially impressive with the glare of the blazing campfire falling on the assembled people, the flashing of torches, the solemn chanting of hymns, the impassioned sermons, the earnest prayers, and the sobs, shrieks, and physical antics of those overcome with the spirit. Manifestations of extreme emotionalism such as falling, screaming, jerking, dancing, barking, and twisting were common. Cartwright related how young ladies dressed in their finery would take the jerks. "The first jerk or so, you would see their fine bonnets, caps, and combs fly; and so sudden would be the jerking of the head that their long loose hair would crack almost as loud as a wagoner's whip." Frances Trollope, an English traveller, commenting on a Methodist camp meeting that she observed on the Ohio, said she felt the ranting preachers and hollaring girls were terribly degrading. A more friendly observer, reporting a revival at Bloomington, Indiana, in 1836, said: "A considerable number have been added to the church, but the crowning feature of the meeting is the number of clear and powerful conversions. . . . The Lord is at work, sinners are shaken, the trembling throne of infidelity is falling, saints are on the wing and children are born to God. Hallelujah, Amen!"

The affects of the western revivals were both good and bad. Freer sexual relations sometimes accompanied the intense emotional experience of the revival and the souls "saved" under revival circumstance often did not stay "saved." Some also felt that the emotionalism cultivated at revivals at other times broke out in waves of prejudice, passion, and even criminality. Some cynical religious leaders even believed that revivals were extravaganzas put on by imposters to attract the rowdy and breed errors in doctrine. On the other hand, ministers reported that communities that had undergone a revival were often more pious and orderly than before.

Whatever the overall affect of revivals, they did tend to create new Protestant sects in the West, as revivalist leaders convinced groups of people that they had a new grasp of the truth in the *Bible*. This tendency was aided on the frontier by the fact that frontiersmen were individualistic and wanted to go their own way. Revivalism, predestination, church organization, missions, and dozens of other reasons were causes of splits.

The Presbyterian church underwent three major schisms on the frontier. The first involved the licensing of ministers in 1802 that did not have the required educational requirements for the ministry. This grew out of the demand for more preachers which the revivals had created. The main body of Presbyterians refused to accept these poorly trained ministers and the Cumberland Presbyterian church was the result. It spread through Kentucky, Tennessee, and Arkansas, and into the southern Midwest.

The second break came out of Barton W. Stone's revival in Bourbon County, Kentucky. Stone and four of his colleagues began to question the Calvinistic doctrine of predestination. For this heresy they were expelled from the Presbyterian church. They promptly adopted the name Christian church. Later in the 1830's Thomas Campbell's (another defecting Presbyterian) "Disciples" met Stone's "Christians" in Ohio, Indiana, and Illinois, and many of them joined together in the Disciples of Christ.

The third split occurred in the middle 1830's when the Presbyterians had a fight between the Old School and the New School groups. The Old School had finally decided that the Plan of Union established with the Congregationalists to win the West was producing churches that were too liberal in doctrine. Also the New School was too anti-slavery for the Old School. As the result the Old School voted the New School out of the church. Although some of the New School group joined the Congregationalists, a majority joined in forming the New School General Assembly in 1838.

The Baptists in the Midwest also split over slavery, education, and missions. Missions were an especially hot issue. In 1830 the Apple Creek Baptist Association of Illinois, for example, declared that they opposed foreign and domestic missions, Sunday schools, and tract societies. Two years later the Sugar Creek Association of Indiana made a similar statement. By 1846 there were some 68,000 Anti-Mission Baptists in the United States of which the great majority were in the West. One of the leading spokesmen of this movement in Indiana and Illinois was Daniel Parker. He opposed missions because he said they led to church centralization and because God did not need any human help to bring his elect to repentance. As for the non-elect he concluded that they were lost anyway.

Revivals also sparked new denominational colleges to train ministers and an increased missionary effort among the Indians. The Congregationalists established an academy at Marietta in 1790 which developed into Marietta College. The period around 1830 was especially productive of denominational colleges. Bishop Philander Chase of the Episcopal church was responsible for the founding of Kenyon College in Ohio in 1824 and for Jubilee College in Illinois in the mid-1830's. The oldest Methodist college in the Midwest was Lebanon Seminary (later renamed McKendree College) in Illinois that opened in 1828. Illinois College at Jacksonville, Illinois, and Wabash College at Crawfordsville, Indiana, were established by Congregationalists in the early 1830's. Oberlin was begun in 1833 by John J. Shipherd, motivated by the revivalist tactics of the unorthodox Presbyterian evangelist, Charles G. Finney. Four years later the Methodist Indiana Conference established Asbury University (later renamed DuPauw) at Greencastle, Indiana. This was only a representative few of the dozens of denominational colleges that grew out of the denominational-revival spirit in the Midwest.

Another activity motivated by revivals was missionary work, especially among the Indians. The French Catholic missionaries had been among the midwestern Indians as early as 1640, but by 1740 their efforts had dwindled to almost nothing. Among the Protestants the Moravian sect was one of the first to have an Indian mission in the Midwest. Having begun working with Indians in New York in 1740, the Moravian mission eventually reached Ohio in about 1770. It had kept moving west to escape white harassment. Despite its moves, however, this Indian mission was still massacred by a group of trigger-happy Pennsylvanians in 1782.

Methodist interest in Indian missions was awakened by the work of John Stewart, a mulatto converted at an Ohio camp meeting. Stewart started his first Indian mission among the Wyandots near Sandusky, Ohio, in 1816. After two years his work was taken under the wing of the Ohio Conference and that body then appointed a regular missionary.

In 1817 a Baptist, Isaac McCoy, began his work among the Miami and Potawatomi in northern Indiana. In 1820 he established a mission at Ft. Wayne and two years later one in southern Michigan. Major S. H. Long, in charge of a United States exploring mission, stopped at McCoy's Michigan mission in 1823 and wrote a complimentary report of McCoy's work.

In 1820 the Indian missionary effort received a great impetus when the federal government announced that it would distribute a subsidy of several thousand dollars to all missionary societies prepared to engage in missionary activity. The American Board of Commissioners for Foreign Missions, which had been established by the Congregationalists, illustrated the tremendous mission growth that took place. By 1830 this board was supporting an Osage mission on the Missouri, a Green Bay mission, a Mackinac mission, and a Maumee mission, in addition to a number of Indian missions outside the Midwest. Similar activity took place among the Presbyterians, Friends, Baptists, Methodists, and Roman Catholics. The Methodists and Baptists especially moved into Kansas in the 1830's to establish missions to save and civilize the red men. William T. Boutwell, who worked with the Ojibways, chose Leech Lake in northern Minnesota as his mission station. The Presbyterians and Congregationalists sent pastors to the Indians in Wisconsin in 1827. The Roman Catholics began their mission again at Green Bay in 1823. Father Frederic Baraga, missionary to the Chippewa from 1828 to 1868, wrote a grammar and dictionary of the Chippewa language.

The main tasks of these missionaries were to convert their charges to Christianity and to educate them. Some tribes followed polygamy and the missionaries tried to stop this practice. From 1819 to 1832 education was largely the responsibility of the missionary societies. To aid the educational and spiritual process, the missionaries often translated the *Bible* and other books into the Indian language.

The problems of the Indian missionary were legion. The worst was probably the trader who sold the Indians whisky. After once tasting whisky many of the Indians would give nearly anything for more. The continual pushing of the Indians west by the whites also ruined growing missions and Indian agriculture. The Indians had difficulty appreciating the generosity of whites who gave them the consolation of religion for their hunting grounds. The missionaries not only had to combat the superstition of the Indians but also the immoral and treacherous practices of the whites. The Indians were also perplexed by the fact that the Christians could not even agree among themselves as to the true faith. More over, the Indians could not understand why the white Christians, who were supposed to love all their neighbors, would selfishly keep their own dwellings and food rather than share them with their fellowmen. Finally, the missionaries found it very difficult to keep their Indian charges from fighting another tribe, an Indian tradition that seemed especially hard to break.

— 21 —

Communal Societies

Yet another development encouraged by the revivalism and individualism of the West was the appearance of unusual sects and utopian groups. Usually established for the purpose of creating a richer, nobler, more equitable social life, they reached their greatest expansion in the Midwest, even though most of them were not indigenous to the Midwest or even to America. The first of these was Shakerism which came to the West in the midst of the great revival in 1800. The sect had been brought to America from England in 1774 by Ann Lee, a woman of Quaker background. In New York her husband had deserted her and this may have contributed to the Shaker belief that marriage was the root of all evil. The name Shaker came from the peculiar jitters, hand clapping, and dancing associated with the worship. They were also known as the United Society of Believers in Christ's Second Appearing. Ann Lee and her followers believed that she was the bride of Christ come to earth and the world was therefore in the millenium. In a redemptive period after death, the Shakers believed they would save all those not saved before death.

The Shaker missionaries who came to the West were successful in establishing seven, communistic Shaker communities in Kentucky, Ohio, and Indiana. The main centers in the Midwest were at Union Village near Lebanon, Ohio; Shaker Heights, Ohio; and Busseron Creek near Vincennes, Indiana. These colonies reached their peak in the period 1830 to 1850 with a total of about 6,000 persons. The Shakers were a hard-working group that introduced new farming methods, helped the needy, and educated the children in their care. People like Horace Greeley, Charles Dickens, Harriet Martineau, James F. Cooper, and Alexis de Tocqueville, who visited them, praised their aims and their actions. Their main problem was their belief in celibacy which made their growth difficult.

A quite different group, composed of German Separatists, settled at Zoar in Tuscarawas County, Ohio, in 1815. Two years later this pacifistic group organized the religious community of Zoar. Under the leadership of Joseph M. Bimeler, a former Wurtemberg school teacher, they farmed and prospered. The community received $20,000 in the 1820's as wages for labor in the construction of the Ohio Canal. One of the longest-lived, communistic societies in the West, it disintegrated in 1898 after being attacked vigorously by Levi Bimeler, a descendent of the founder.

George Rapp, also of German descent, came to America with his flock in 1803. The leader of a group of Pietists, he and his group had fled Germany to escape persecution. They at first settled in Pennsylvania on 2,000 acres where they produced large quantities of corn, wheat, oats, potatoes, flax, and hemp. But because they could not raise fruit, the weather was too cold, a navigable stream was too far away, and they were outgrowing their settlement, they bought a 30,000-acre tract on the lower Wabash which they moved to in 1814 and named Harmony. Here they again prospered under the dictatorial rule of Rapp. They farmed and manufactured to produce the goods they needed. They lived under the principles of simplicity, love, self-sacrifice, worship, and celibacy. Because of the presence of malaria along the Wabash, the Rappites sold their holdings in 1824 to Robert Owen, an English reformer, for $150,000 and moved to a site on the Ohio River below Pittsburgh. There at the community of Economy, they again flourished. In 1827 they had 522 members, but within 75 years their membership had dwindled to almost nothing. Celibacy apparently proved to be their undoing also.

Owen, the man who bought New Harmony from Rapp, arrived at the village with some settlers in 1825. He established a communistic community with little practical planning. In 1826 he brought in more people including reformers like Joseph Neef and Frances Wright. Owen returned to England in 1827 and when he returned two years later, the community was on the verge of collapse. The colony foundered because the people were like "babes lost in the woods of ideas." Owen's mistake was in giving his property away too soon to unprepared beneficiaries.

Across the Wabash River in Henry County, Illinois, a strange communistic society was begun in the 1830's under the leadership of Eric Jansen. Jansen had been persecuted in Norway for attracting large numbers of Lutherans away from the state church. He fled to America where he established Bishop Hill in Illinois. At the outset the Bishop Hill colonists lived in dugouts and had a miserable existence while Jansen lived in luxury and had his own private physician. When his wife accused him of infidelity, he ignored her. Jansen antagonized the men of the community by the demands he made on their wives and daughters. In some aspects, however, Jansen administered his colony well. The farms were prosperous and mechanized and his factories were well managed. In theory all the property was owned in common, but actually the title to the land and buildings was in Jansen's name. Jansen met his end when he tried to interfere in the domestic life of the adventurer, John Root. Root had married Jansen's sister, and Jansen would not let her leave Bishop Hill. Root finally settled the argument by shooting Jansen. When Jansen failed to rise from the dead in three days, the colony disintegrated and numerous lawsuits resulted in a contest over the property.

Probably the most disturbing sect to move across the Midwest was the Mormons. Joseph Smith, originator of this group, came from a superstitious family in the burnt-over area of western New York. Originally a Methodist, Smith in 1827 asserted that he had found inscribed on golden plates the story of a Hebrew prophet who had led his followers in the year 600 B.C. from Jerusalem to the coast of Chile. Descendants of this group had wandered as far northeastward as the present state of New York before becoming extinct around 400 A.D. Mormon and his son Moroni, the last survivors, gathered the records of their people together and buried them in a hill in western New York. Smith said he found the golden records after the Angel Moroni appeared to him and told him where they were hidden. Smith translated and transcribed them. A debunker's explanation of the source of Smith's *Book of Mormon* was that Smith had merely copied a fanciful tale about the origin of the American Indians written by an ex-minister named Solomon Spaulding.

Be this as it may, Smith's revelation was soon accepted as truth by a number of followers and the Church of Jesus Christ of Latter Day Saints was formed at Fayette in Seneca County in 1830. After a number of lawsuits convinced Smith he should move in 1831, he led his group to Kirtland, Ohio, where they stayed six years. Here Brigham Young, a painter from Vermont, joined them. Lawsuits growing out of unchartered Mormon banks caused Smith to move once more. This time they moved to Missouri where they settled near Independence in Jackson, Clay, and Caldwell counties. But the Mormons soon became unpopular. They opposed slavery, were friendly to the Indians, and were clannish, aggressive, and contemptuous of their neighbors. Since the Missourians also wanted the Mormon lands, they began to jail the Mormons and burn them out. When Smith decided to fight, Missouri called out its militia and Smith had to surrender. With no reimbursement for their lands, the Mormons made their exodus to Nauvoo, Illinois, in 1839. The Mormons again prospered at their "New Jerusalem." Then in 1843 Joseph Smith received a new revelation authorizing polygamy. Ugly rumors about the Nauvoo community began to circulate. The Mormons were accused of debauchery, plural marriage, and horse theiving. A group of Mormons also opposed Smith's polygamy revelation and they started the *Nauvoo Expositor* to denounce Smith. Smith suppressed the paper and destroyed the printing office. Illinois called out the militia to preserve order and Smith and his brother, Hyrum, were placed in prison at Carthage. In June of 1844 a mob entered the jail and shot the two brothers. Brigham Young then assumed the leadership and two years later he led them west. The trek across the country to Salt Lake City was accompanied by extreme suffering by many of the 15,000 Mormons who eventually arrived there. Again they built up a properous community. They eventually dropped polygamy in 1896.

Another small band of Mormons that remained in the Midwest was led by James J. Strang of Wisconsin. Baptised by Smith in 1844, he took his followers to Beaver Island in Lake Michigan where he adopted polygamy and ruled like a king. In 1856 he was murdered, and soon afterward the group disbanded.

A short time after the Mormons moved through Iowa, another communistic group settled in that state near Iowa City. It was the Amana society, founded by Eberhard Gruber in Germany in 1714. In 1843 it had left Germany and settled first at Buffalo, New York, before moving on to Iowa eleven years later. The colony was made up of farmers and artisans who cultivated the land and operated bakeries, dye shops, machine shops, printing shops, flour mills, lumber mills, and other establishments. They ate their meals in a communal kitchen, were buried in a common cemetery, and did no work on Sunday. In 1932 the group finally dropped it communalism.

In addition to all the above, there were a number of other religious and communal aberrations in the Midwest. One was the community at Southport, Wisconsin, based on the Charles Fourier and Brook Farm experiments. Established in 1843 it was named Ceresco after Ceres, the goddess of grain. It disbanded in 1849 and the members went their own ways.

The Icarian movement also made itself felt in more than one state in the Midwest. Etienne Cabet, originator of this social-reform group, founded his first communal colony in Texas. When this collapsed he moved his group to the deserted Mormon town of Nauvoo, Illinois. But dissension once more plagued the community, and in 1856 Cabet took a part of his followers and went to St. Louis. The St. Louis and Nauvoo communities fought at a distance for a few years and then the Nauvoo remnant moved to a new location near Corning, Iowa. After more enmity and splits, the whole Icarian movement finally folded in 1895.

—22—

Education in the Academy Period

Common Schools and Academies

The Midwest began its educational development during the academy or private-school period which was at its peak between the years 1787 and 1837. Midwestern education was given an auspicious start by a passage in the Land Ordinance of 1785 which reserved Lot 16 for the maintenance of public schools within the township. Ohio, admitted to statehood in 1803, was the first state to benefit from this provision. Later midwestern states received two and in some cases four sections of land in each township for the support of schools. However, this was not as helpful as had been hoped. The legislature of each state was responsible for managing these school lands. While some were careful in collecting the rents and applying the money to education, others immediately sold the lands at a low price and profited little. Ohio, for example, belonged to the latter group. On the other hand, Michigan profited from the mistakes of its sister states in the management of educational lands. Michigan even appointed a superintendent of schools to care for the school lands and administer them as one property. The income derived was used to aid all the schools in the state.

Whether the lands were administered foolishly or wisely, however, they still did not provide sufficient funds for adequate public-school systems in any of the early midwestern states. Other considerations also posed problems for public education. The population was too sparse to justify or pay the cost of building schools in every district. Also since the pioneers were primarily intersted in making a living, many of them maintained that their children were needed at home to work and education would have to wait. Some opposed public education for still other reasons. The Pennsylvania Germans and Quakers opposed education for philosophical and financial reasons. The wealthy and the childless had no desire to educate other people's children. Generally those sections of the Midwest that had a large influx of people from the Northeast supported public schools because they had developed a liking for them at home. Those from the South, however, were virtually unacquainted with public-school systems and had less interest in them. Since the latter group predominated in the early period and since the region was a frontier and sparsely populated, public education was at a low ebb.

State laws, relating to education up to 1837, were consequently confused and toothless. Although such documents as the Ordinance of 1787 and the constitutions of Indiana and Michigan paid lip service to the value of education, few of the states did much about establishing an adequate public-school system. In 1821 Ohio finally passed a weak law which allowed the division of townships into school districts if the voters were agreeable. Two thirds of the property holders had to approve if a district schoolhouse were to be built. An Ohio legislative committee investigated education in 1822, could not agree, and went home in a huff. Three years later another Ohio law approved in principle statewide taxation for schools and provided that townships would be divided into school districts, but there was no enforcement clause.

In 1818 Indiana passed a law providing for a trustee in each county to collect fines from those who had conscientious scruples against war. This money was to be used for the support of a public county seminary. Between 1825 and 1840 these fines aided in the establishment of 28 county seminaries. An Indiana law passed in 1824 allowed for the collection of school taxes and one in 1833 established the township-school system. Unrestricted localism was carried to its ultimate, however, in 1836 when the state made it possible for the head of a family to hire a teacher for his children and obtain his family's share of the school funds.

In Illinois a law was passed in 1823 providing for a free public school in each county, but it was not implemented. As of

1829 the paying of school taxes was on a voluntary basis and the amount collected was small.

In 1827 Michigan passed an optional law stating that each township with fifty inhabitants should obtain a school teacher to instruct in reading, writing, arithmetic, spelling, grammer, and French. Even when more state supervision was written into the law in Michigan in 1833, schools continued to develop slowly.

As a result of the weakness of the laws and the indifference of the people, facilities, teachers, and attendance were usually poor at the common-school level. Teaching was generally considered as a part-time job or a stepping stone to medicine, law, or business. Teachers who made teaching a lifetime vocation were often viewed as cripples or misfits who taught instead of working. Oftentimes, friends and relatives of the trustees were given the teaching positions which paid about six to ten dollars a month. In the 1830's some of the states provided certification of teachers which was optional with the district trustees.

For textbooks students had a rather limited selection. Noah Webster's *Elementary Spelling Book* was the most widely used of the spellers. Elisha Bates' *Western Preceptor* was one of Webster's main competitors. The *Western Preceptor* was first published at Mt. Pleasant, Ohio, in 1821. Although William H. McGuffey's reader was most popular, there were also Lindley Murray's *English Reader,* James Hall's *Western Reader,* and Rufus W. Adam's *Young Gentleman and Lady's Explanatory Monitor.* Jedediah Morse and John Kilbourn prepared school geographies, and S. G. Goodrich and William Grimshaw produced histories of the United States which stressed the Revolution. For arithmetic the young midwesterner used Nathan Daboll's *Arithmetic* or else one prepared by Smiley, Bennett, Pike, Jess, or Dilworth. Ray's *Arithmetic* did not appear until after 1840.

Most figuring and writing were done on a slate. For writing on paper, goose and turkey quills were used. Quills were not replaced by steel pens until about 1850. Ink was prepared from maple bark, sumac, or oak balls mixed with vinegar. Inkstands consisted of a sawed-off cowhorn or a pewter container.

The number of students attending school was rather low. In Ohio in 1837, for example, out of 492,837 children of school age, 84,296 attended from two to four months and 62,144 attended more than four months. Indiana in 1840 had 273,784 school-age children of whom only 48,180 attended school. The growing cities like Cincinnati, Detroit, St. Louis, and Chicago made the most progress. By 1840 they had public-school systems which took care of the minimum educational needs of at least one third of their school-age children in fairly adequate buildings. In the country towns and rural areas, the children were fortunate if they had a log building with split-log seats and oiled-paper windows, which they could attend a few months a year and learn the fundamentals of reading, writing, and arithmetic. The Bureau of Education estimated that in 1840 the average U.S. citizen had received 10 months and 8 days of education during his lifetime. The average in the Midwest was close to this national figure.

As the name "Academy Period" suggests, most of the elementary and secondary education carried on during the years up to 1837 was in private schools. The academy was a transitional institution. Largely private it gave children of middle-class families, who had the time and money, an opportunity to progress beyond the elementary school. The academy served as a bridge between the Latin school which was college preparatory and the modern public high school which largely replaced it by 1890.

The dividing line, however, between academies and common schools was not hard and fast. Some schools that were established to teach secondary courses opened their doors to elementary students when times were hard. Tuition and board were low and even then were hard to collect. Payment in kind (raccoon skins, a calf, a barrel of whisky, or cured hams) was often accepted in lieu of currency at the schools as well as at the general store. Courses of study at the academies were similar to the common schools. Reading, writing, arithmetic, English grammar, and geography were the usual subjects taught.

Ohio incorporated around 113 academies and institutes between 1801 and 1840. In the middle 1830's the manual-labor, study-type academy appeared and Ohio chartered several of these. In all, Indiana incorporated around 75 sectarian and nonsectarian schools during the 40 years after 1800. Among Indiana's more important non-sectarian schools were Hanover Academy (later Hanover College), Richmond Red-Brick Academy, Vincennes

Academy, and Crawfordsville Female Academy. Among Indiana's numerous sectarian schools were Blue River and Whitewater academies (Quaker) and Haw Creek Academy (Disciples of Christ). Illinois also had a large number of private schools. Many of the later ones in the period were of the study-manual-labor type. A classical academy was opened in Michigan at Detroit in 1818. Michigan had a number of other private schools, some of which were female seminaries. Among Michigan's private schools established during the 1830's were Michigan and Huron Institute at Kalamazoo, Tecumseh Academy, Grass Lake Academy, and Marshall Female Academy.

Colleges

Just as it was difficult to differentiate between academies and common schools, it was equally hard to draw a line between academies, seminaries, and colleges. Although there were some non-sectarian seminaries and colleges founded during the early period, a majority were sectarian. Of the 23 colleges founded during this period that survived, 19 were privately supported and four were state supported. Two of the first colleges in the Midwest were Ohio University at Athens and Miami University at Oxford. The financial beginnings of these institutions were based on three townships of land that Ohio was granted by the federal government for the building of colleges. Ohio University, chartered in 1804, began instruction four years later. It suspended operations temporarily in 1845. Miami University, chartered in 1809, was established at Oxford a year later and graduated over 250 students in its first 30 years. Cincinnati had an intermittent non-sectarian college from 1819 on. Ohio Medical College at Cincinnati graduated its first class in 1821. At Gambier, Ohio, Kenyon College was founded by the Protestant Episcopal church. Chartered in 1824 it began operations two years later. Franklin College was originally chartered as the College of Alma at New Athens, Ohio, in 1825. The following year Western Reserve College was established at Hudson, Ohio. Controlled primarily by the Presbyterian and Congregational churches, it was later moved to Cleveland. Knox College, chartered in 1837, was also of Presbyterian and Congregational descent. Two of Ohio's other early colleges were deeply involved in the abolitionist movement. One was Lane Seminary, established at Cincinnati in 1829, and the other was Oberlin, established near Elyria, Ohio, in 1833.

One of Indiana's earliest colleges, also founded by the Presbyterians, was Vincennes University chartered around 1806. Likewise the Presbyterians were responsible for the creation of Bloomington Seminary. Chartered in 1820 Bloomington Seminary began operation in 1825. In 1828 its name was changed to Indiana College and ten years later to Indiana University. In 1830 it had a faculty fight and in 1833 a cholera epidemic. Baynard R. Hall, equipped with a master's degree, came from the East around 1840 to head the school. His salary was $250 a year. He has left a pungent and somewhat humorous account of the quarrels within the faculty and the controversies between the college and the townspeople in this early college on the edge of of the frontier.

In 1826 the Presbyterian Church arranged with John F. Crowe of South Hanover to turn his institution into a classical preparatory school. From this log-cabin, boarding school, Hanover College emerged. Also founded by the Presbyterians, Wabash College had its beginnings in 1833. As these examples show, the Presbyterian-Princeton and Congregationalist-Yale took the lead in fathering western institutions.

The Methodist and Baptist churches, however, were also active. Asbury College was established at Greencastle by the Methodists in 1837. It later became DePauw University. Other colleges founded by the Methodists included McKendree College at Lebanon, Illinois, established around 1828; Ohio Wesleyan; and Mount Pleasant Literary Institute (later Iowa Wesleyan) in 1842.

Michigan had several seminaries and colleges established by 1837. They included Spring Arbor Seminary, St. Philips College at Detroit, Grass Lake Academy and Teacher's Seminary, and Marshall College. But the most outstanding of Michigan's collegiate endeavors was the University of Michigan. Established initially at Detroit in 1817, it failed to materialize. Not until 1837 when Michigan became a state did it take firm root and grow at Ann Arbor.

Farther west the number of colleges was less. Illinois College was founded by a group of young men from Yale, and Iowa College in Davenport (later moved to Grinnell) was the outgrowth of the efforts of a group of Andover men.

A picture of a typical denominational college was given in James Stuart's and Reverend John M. Peck's description of Illinois College at Jacksonville in the 1830's. The faculty were poorly paid. To earn additional money, students could spend a part of each day working on the farm or in the workshop. The library contained around 1,500 volumes and the college also had some chemical and physics equipment. Tuition ran around $7.50 per semester and $85.00 to $125.00 would cover the ordinary expenses of a nine-month, academic year.

Adjuncts to Education

The Midwest utilized many of the innovations in education during this early period and provided some of its own. The five states of the Midwest that were in the Union by 1837 had laws providing for free, public education, but these laws were not well implemented. Detroit and Cincinnati were the earliest western outposts of the Lancastrian or monitorial instruction system. Cincinnati began a Lancastrian school in 1815 and Detroit in 1818. The essential feature of the system was that the more advanced students would instruct those who knew less. The system was inexpensive because student instructors were used, but many of the students were not good instructors and the knowledge imparted was often rudimentary. When people were willing to provide more money for better instruction, the system fell into disuse.

Three other educational innovations introduced into the Midwest in the 1830's were educational conventions, journals, and school papers. The Midwest's greatest innovation in education, however, was collegiate co-education. Oberlin College in Ohio began this soon after its founding in 1833. With both male and female students attending, Oberlin was very strict in its rules. Women, for example, were forbidden to receive men in their rooms and marriage was a cause for expulsion.

To further aid education the Midwest had, in addition to schools, libraries and lyceum societies. The Midwest's first semi-public library was the Putnam Family Library, a joint-stock enterprise begun near Marietta in 1796. Six years later Cincinnati developed a subscription library in which stock was sold at $10 a share. Dayton obtained a public library in 1805. In 1814 Daniel Drake and his friends opened a circulating library with 300 volumes at Cincinnati. The Vincennes Library was established in 1806 and the Detroit Library in 1818. St. Louis, Dayton, Indianapolis, Milwaukee, and numerous other cities also supported libraries. By 1840 there were around 200 libraries in the Midwest.

Libraries were badly needed in the Midwest, because even literate families had only a few books, such as a *Bible,* an almanac, and perhaps Hervey's *Evening Meditations.* Ordinarily these libraries featured books by English and northeastern writers. The works of Walter Scott and Lord Byron were especially popular in the West. James F. Cooper, Washington Irving, and William C. Bryant were also well known and read. By 1830 some midwestern writers were also producing books for midwestern consumption. These writers tended to gravitate to Cincinnati, the cultural center of the Midwest during the 1830's.

Like the library the lyceum also served the cause of education, especially among the adult population. Originated by Josiah Holbrook of Massachusetts in 1826, this system of education spread from the East to the Midwest. The idea of lectures was not new, but the establishment of permanent local and state organizations to schedule speakers and administer the program was novel. At these lyceum programs, one could hear lectures by such men as Robert Owen, Ralph W. Emerson, Alexander Campbell, and Henry Clay.

Other preservers and promoters of education included newspapers, gazettes, dramatic clubs, debating societies, and historical societies. A total of 354 western newspapers were reported in the census of 1840. One of the first historical societies was established at Vincennes in 1808. Illinois founded a historical society in 1827, Indiana in 1830, Ohio in 1831, and Michigan in 1838.

There were several people and agencies in the Midwest who were especially helpful in introducing the beginnings of education. Abraham Lincoln stimulated the desire for education by his perseverance in acquiring one. In 1832 in commenting on education, he said, "I can only say that I view it as the most important subject that we as a people can be engaged in. That every man may receive at least a moderate education and thereby be enabled to read the histories of his own and other countries, by which he may duly appreciate the value of our free institutions, appears to be an object of vital importance."

Among the groups who supported education in the Midwest, the Ohio Company was one of the first. It conceived a plan for practical free education. Another early midwestern group promoting education was the Western Literary Institute. Meeting in convention at Cincinnati, it helped to secure the passage of the precedent-setting, public school law of Ohio in 1838 and to help prepare the public for the *Western Academician and Journal of Education and Science* (1837-1838).

— 23 —

Literature and the Press

Literature

In the period up to 1860 Cincinnati was the leading center of literature in the Midwest. A large number of authors of the Middle Border writing during this era were especially interested in describing their life and times. Among the early leading novelists were James Hall, Timothy Flint, and Daniel Drake. Judge James Hall was born in Philadelphia in 1793. His period of greatest productiveness was from 1828 to 1844. During this time he wrote such books as *Winter Evenings: A Series of American Tales* (1829) and *Legends of the West* (1832). From 1836 to 1844 he wrote biographical sketches for the *History of Indian Tribes of North America.*

Timothy Flint, born in Salem, Massachusetts, was a Congregational minister. He lived most of his adult life in Ohio and Indiana where he wrote a group of books including *Recollections of the Last Ten Years . . . In the Valley of the Mississippi . . .* (1826), *The Shoshone Valley: A Romance* (1830), and *Indian Wars of the West . . .* (1833). Although his writing was faulty, his descriptions were good.

Daniel Drake, raised on a Kentucky farm, became a doctor and nearly dominated that profession in the Midwest from 1815 to 1850. He was a great western booster and out of this exuberance came a number of books including *Notices Concerning Cincinnati* (1810) and *Discourse on the History, Character, and Prospects of the West* (1834). In discussing the future of midwestern literature, he said that he believed it would have a strong religious and democratic tone. Because of its magnitude, he was convinced that the Mississippi Valley would provide infinite themes for future writers.

One of the early newspapermen and leading poets in the Midwest was William D. Gallagher, who was born in Philadelphia and came west with his family in 1816. His first two volumes of poetry, *Erato No. I* and *No. II,* were published in 1835. *Erato No. III* appeared in 1837. Four years later he published an edited work, entitled *Selections from the Poetical Literature of the West,* which included verse from thirty-eight midwestern poets. Gallagher was a poet, publicist, and promoter of the West.

Other contemporary midwestern poets emphasizing the western motif included Thomas Pierce, Frederick W. Thomas, Charles A. Jones, William R. Wallace, Otway Curry, and Thomas H. Shreve. In 1860 William T. Coggeshell edited *Poets and Poetry of the West,* containing the works of 152 contributors representing nine different midwestern states.

Historians and chroniclers also scanned the Midwest for material. Moses Dawson of the *Cincinnati Advertiser* wrote *A Historical Narrative of the Civil and Military Services of Major General William H. Harrison* (1824). In 1838 John McDonald wrote a series of biographical sketches on General Nathaniel Massie, General Duncan McArthur, Captain William Wells, and General Simon Kenton. In the same year the first of the state histories of the Old Northwest appeared. It was Caleb Atwater's *History of the State of Ohio, Natural and Civil.* It was followed by James H. Louman's *History of Michigan, Civil and Topographical* (1839), John Reynolds' *Pioneer History of Illinois* (1852), and Edward D. Neill's *History of Minnesota* (1858). Out of Henry R. Schoolcraft's investigations in the Middle West came a five volume work in 1853, entitled *Information Respecting the History, Conditions, and Prospects of the Indian Tribes of the United States.* The Pennsylvania painter and writer, George Catlin, also made a study of western Indians in the *Illustrated Manners, Customs, and Condition of the North American Indians* in 1841. As a result of a later visit in North Dakota, he produced in 1867 another volume on Indian culture entitled *Okeepa: A Religious Ceremony and Other Customs of the Mandans.*

Despite the large amount of literary material produced by

midwestern authors, the people who were reading books in the region generally preferred English and eastern writers such as Walter Scott, Charles Dickens, Lord Byron, James F. Cooper, Washington Irving, William C. Bryant, John G. Whittier, and Henry W. Longfellow. Midwestern authors were not known for their literary excellence until at least 1875.

Newspapers

The Midwest's earliest newspapers developed during the period of the partisan press (1783-1830). Many of the newspapers of this period were either the mouthpiece for a political party or a special organization. The first newspaper in the Old Northwest was *The Sentinel of the North Western Territory* begun by William Maxwell at Cincinnati in 1793. In 1799 Cincinnati obtained a second paper, *The Western Spy and Hamilton Gazette.* The father of the Indiana press was Elihu Stout who founded the Indiana *Gazette* (later revived as the *Western Sun*) at Vincennes in 1804. St. Louis along with Vincennes and Cincinnati also had a paper prior to 1810. It was the *Missouri Gazette* established in 1808. Territorial Illinois had only one paper prior to 1818 and that was the *Illinois Herald* (later the *Illinois Intelligencer*), established at Kaskaskia in 1814. Michigan's first important newspaper was the Detroit *Gazette* which appeared in 1817. The earliest paper in Wisconsin was the Green Bay *Intelligencer,* established by Albert G. Ellis at Navarino in 1833. Minnesota's first paper, the *Minnesota Pioneer* (later the *Pioneer Press*), did not make its appearance at St. Paul until 1849. Some other early important midwestern newspapers included the Cincinnati *Gazette* (1815), the Columbus *Statesman* (1816), the Indianapolis *Gazette* (1822), *The Western Censor and Immigrants' Guide* (later the Indiana *Journal*), *Michigan Sentinel* (1825), *Chicago Democrat* (1833), *Detroit Daily Free Press* (1835), *Milwaukee Sentinel* (1837), the *Chicago Tribune* (1847), and the St. Louis *Missouri Democrat* (1852). As of 1826 Ohio had approximately 60 newspapers and

Indiana, 16. Thirteen years later the Alton *Telegraph* listed 36 Illinois papers by their political affiliation.

The early midwestern editors were staunch party men. James Wilson of the *Western Herald and Steubenville Gazette* (1815-38) was a Whig and published the Whig campaign sheet, *The Log Cabin*, in 1840. Charles Hammond, editor of the St. Clairsville, Ohio, *Federalist* (1813-22) and the *Liberty Hall and Cincinnati Gazette* (1825-40), was a Federalist and later a Whig. He was a leading editor of the period. A Quaker and Democrat, Samuel Medary of the *Ohio Statesman* (1837-57), disliked both abolitionists and Whigs. George S. Chapman, Democratic editor of the Terre Haute *Wabash Enquirer* and later the *Indiana Sentinel,* was famous for inaugurating the Democratic rooster emblem. The political fight in the 1840's between the *Sentinel* and the *Journal* was a classic struggle in midwestern journalism.

Of a different stripe was Dr. E. W. H. Ellis of the Goshen *Democrat.* He was respected for his scholarship and widely quoted. In Illinois other editors included Samuel S. Brooks of the *Illinois Herald,* the *Illinois State Gazette,* and Jacksonville *News;* John Calhoun and John Wentworth of the Chicago *Democrat;* and Hooper Warren of the Chicago *Commercial Advertiser.* In early Michigan John P. Sheldon and Ebenezer Reed of the Detroit *Gazette* were noted editors. An editor on the edge of the Midwest who had an important influence on the Whig papers of the region was George D. Prentice, founder of the Louisville *Journal.*

Most of the pioneer newspapers were small, four-page issues, varying in size from 12 to 18 inches in width by 20 to 30 inches in length. Large headlines were seldom used. Subscriptions ran from $1.50 to $4.00 a year. Advertising and job printing were the chief sources of revenue. Most of the papers were weeklies up to 1840. A normal circulation for a country newspaper was 350 to 400. The Cincinnati *Gazette,* the leading paper in the Midwest in 1840, had a subscription list of around 1,000 for the daily and 2,800 for the weekly edition.

Subjects covered by newspapers were endless. In addition to discussing politics and the essentials of representative government, the papers also furnished information on education, manners, literature, and business. Papers had difficulty being current on the news. Due to the slowness of the communication system, Cleveland, Ohio, in 1837 could not publish Washington news in its newspapers that was less than eight-days old.

— 24 —

Culture and Life

Living Conditions

Life on the frontier was rough, hard, and unpretentious. Families usually lived in widely-separated cabins when the Indians were peaceful. If the family was poor, the cabin was usually one room, made of unhewn logs, and had a dirt floor. If the family was more prosperous, the cabin was usually larger with a large living and eating room, a small bedroom and kitchen and a bedroom in the loft. Floors were usually made of split logs laid round side down (a puncheon floor), the roofs of clapboards, and the windows of greased paper or deerskins. Pegs were driven into the sides of the houses to serve as wardrobes, and antlers held the ever-ready rifles. Tables were large clapboards, set on wooden legs. Most families usually had only three-legged stools for chairs, although the better homes had some rocking chairs. The couches or beds were covered with blankets and skins. Chaff beds were often thrown on the floor of the loft. Although there were pewter spoons in use, table service and utensils consisted mainly of an iron or copper kettle, homemade trenchers, platters, and bowls. Almost every cabin had a hand mill, a hominy block, and a loom. Hickory sticks with long shavings cut back and tied served as brooms.

Products such as soap, candles, and maple sugar were produced in the home. Salt had to be imported into the backwoods. A bushel of alum salt was worth a cow and calf. Thus instead of salting or pickling their venison, the frontiersmen often jerked it by drying it in the sun or smoking it over a fire.

Surrounding the cabin was a clearing, dotted with stumps,

in which the family raised fruit, corn, wheat, and potatoes as well as other grains and vegetables. The family usually had a horse or two, a cow, and perhaps hogs or sheep. Land was plentiful. Settlers blazed trees around their land to show the extent of their holdings. The greatest limiting factor on the size of their acreage initially was their ability to farm it.

Except for some differences resulting from more people and more buildings, the people living in the towns had problems and living conditions similar to those of the country. The storekeepers, plagued by a shortage of money, often bartered their goods for agricultural products. There was little sanitation, law, or fire protection. In the 1820's and 1830's Ohio towns began to forbid roaming animals, dead animals, and firing of weapons on the streets. Having acquired street lights in 1839, Louisville was one of the first towns to have them. The larger cities began to buy fire engines in the 1830's. Indianapolis had good water in wells twenty feet deep, while Vincennes was plagued with bad water. Central city-water systems with iron pipes were unknown in the larger, older midwestern towns until the 1840's. The replacement of the night watchman by something akin to the modern police force was just as slow in coming. The fireplace long remained the major means of heating. By the 1850's the furnace had become a practical gadget and a few homes had one in the basement. Candles were the chief method of lighting although kerosene and gas were coming into use. Tinware was slowly replacing heavy iron and copper utensils.

Family Life

Frontier society was simple and the duties and rights of each member of the family were clear. The man was the armed protector and provider and the woman was the housewife and childbearer.

Since women were scarce on the frontier, they did not have to pay a dowry or take the first man that came along. Courtships, however, were usually short and girls often married at 14 or 15.

They had a fear of becoming maiden aunts, a group who were generally neglected in frontier society. Girls usually settled for nothing less than marriage, but occasionally a frontier boy and girl, with no minister or judge nearby, would merely cohabit and raise a family without benefit of clergy. Widows usually remarried; if a husband who was thought dead returned, the wife could choose the one she wanted and the other had to leave the community.

After being joined in wedlock, most couples began the task of having and raising a large family. Since labor was scarce, children were often viewed as economic assets. This mass production of babies was hard on the women who often had little medical care. As a result women often died young, and many men had as many as three wives. Although women on the frontier might have had scarcity value before marriage, once married the woman was expected to put up with almost anything from her husband. As Reverend William H. Milburn stated it, a woman marries, thinking it a bed of roses; then her husband ignores her, motherhood brings its pain and care, and she does a thousand tasks for which there is no praise. They are born for self sacrifice and always to console. Their's is the greatest task.

Life on the frontier was also lonely and frightening. Nature, isolation, monotony, sickness, death, and toil were always present. Literature often presents the pioneer woman as a creature of inextinguishable vitality who never stopped working or defending her little brood against wolves and Indians. Actually some neurotics and many unhappy people lived in the prairie cabins. In Illinois, for example, Mary W. B. Roberts, thinking of her far distant family, wrote in her diary in 1831, "I wished for them in vain but the tender attention of a dear husband in some means consoled me for the loss of those dear companions and reconciled me to my situation."

Clothing

Everyday clothes were simple, distinctive, and homemade. Of the cloth produced in the frontier homes, linsey-woolsey made of flax and wool was the most common. The man wore a fur cap or felt hat, buckskin moccasins, thin trousers, leggings made of skin, and an Indian breechclout. His fringed hunting shirt of homespun or buckskin reached halfway to the knees and was held in at the waist by a broad belt from which hung a knife or tomahawk. The woman's dress consisted of a hat or poke bonnet, a bed gown, a jacket, a white linsey petticoat, and coarse shoepacks or moccasins. To color and enliven their clothes and their drab existence, the settlers used walnut hulls for dark brown, butternuts for red-yellow, sumac berries for red, bark of hickory for yellow, peach leaves for green, maple or oak for purple, pokeberry mixed with alum for crimson, and sorrel mixed with logwood and copperas for black.

On special occasions a woman might wear a long muslin or cotton dress decked out in brightly-colored ribbons and artificial flowers or feathers and topped off with a most fantastic hat. The local dandy was likely to own a long-tailed, double-breasted, blue broad-cloth coat, complete with a double row of gold-plated buttons. To go with his fancy coat, he had a colorful vest, buff or fawn, tight-fitting trousers, and neat tailored boots that reached halfway to the knee. This paraphernalia was likely to be worn with a tall, bell-crowned, stove-pipe hat of white, gray, or brown and a voluminous frock coat of blue, green, brown, or red, with collar and cuffs of velvet in a contrasting color.

Food

Although not always the best kind of food, rural mid-westerners did eat a large amount of food. The British travellers often described the eating habits of Americans in uncomplimentary terms. The English noted the extraordinary amount of wild fowl, venison, pork, beef, salt-fish, cranberry jelly, potatoes, and starchy foods eaten by Americans and were revolted by their peculiar combinations of food. The English could not imagine how anyone could eat eggs with oysters, ham with apple sauce, beef steak with stewed peaches, and salt fish with onions, hominy, other vegetables, and half-baked, hot rolls. Loading the plate with numerous, incongruous kinds of food, eating with a knife, and failing to talk during a meal were mentioned as shortcomings of midwesterners in their table manners.

Diseases and Medicine

During the period before 1850, the West was viewed as an unhealthy area. Sallow and jaundiced complexions were common. Poor sanitation, bad water, improper diet, mosquitoes, and swamps contributed to such maladies as influenza, fevers, malaria, biliousness, agues, dysentery, pneumonia, bronchitis, rheumatism, typhoid, and cholera. Ague was the most prevalent of the diseases, especially in damp areas. Symptoms were blue fingernails, chattering teeth, fever, headache, and back pains. Typhoid epidemics (called typhus fever, nervous fever, or brain fever) were present but were generally ignored by doctors until 1845. Troops coming from Buffalo to take part in the Black Hawk War in 1832 brought a cholera epidemic to Chicago and the West. As a result thousands died of the plague in 1832 and 1833; there were also smaller recurring epidemics in 1834 and 1849. Even injuries such as nail punctures and broken bones often led to lockjaw and blood poisoning.

Although a few doctors were present in the larger communities, most people in the isolated areas had to rely on practical nurses or home remedies. In the 1830's and 1840's women like Granny Spears in Illinois still existed. At ninety she continued to ride about on horseback to every house where birth was expected.

Captured by the Indians in her youth, she had learned their remedies for sickness.

The number and variety of home remedies seemed infinite. A brew of mullen and sassafras roots or three large pills made of cobwebs were considered good for ague. Peppermint oil was used for toothache. Among the first medical books in the West was Peter Smith's *The Indian Doctor's Dispensatory,* published in Cincinnati in 1813. One of Smith's remedies, prescribed for preserving teeth and curing bad breath, specified that a person should rinse his mouth each morning with his own urine.

Superstitious cures also abounded. Kissing a Negro before the age of one would prevent whooping cough. For epilepsy one should eat the heart of a rattlesnake. A toad tied on a snake bite would draw out the poison. Ague was supposedly cured by wearing a spider around the neck.

Patent medicines (which usually were not patented, but were called that in order to convey the idea of government sanction) were also plentiful in the West. Everything from cathartics to hair tonics were advertised as cure alls. Tomatoes, creosote, and petroleum were advertised as great cures.

Although practical nurses, home remedies, and patent medicines were usually ineffective, the available doctors often were not much better. The country doctor was one of the first professional men to establish himself on the frontier. He sometimes rode a circuit like a minister. His equipment was meager; a horse and saddle bags, a mortar and pestle, a pair of balances, some splints and bandages, a few drugs, and possibly a small set of instruments. By the late 1830's a few doctors had added a stethoscope, tooth forceps, and some obstetrical instruments. Doctors came in two types, herb and bleeding. Some physicians recommended bleeding for nearly every disease including cholera and typhoid. Removal of 10 to 12 ounces of blood at a time was the usual treatment. Irons, heated to gray heat, were used to cauterize wounds and stop infection. Although some of the frontier doctors were crude in their methods, others were aware of the latest medical developments and began using the stethoscope, microscope, anesthesia, and vaccination as soon as they came into vogue.

Occasionally these doctors performed amazing operations, but usually a person would die rather than risk an operation.

The Middle Westerner and His Environment

The backwoodsmen as a group were lean and sallow, inquisitive, independent, and as likely to be shiftless as industrious. Physical courage was taken for granted and little respect was held for easterners or those who dressed too fancily. Equality was not a theory or creed; it was a natural circumstance that entered into every phase of life. In this simple, strong, crude society, both the good features and the bad were placed in bold relief. The views of those observing the frontiersman therefore varied greatly, depending upon which set of characteristics they noted. One traveller would describe the frontiersman as little better than an Indian, wild, squalid, and lawless; while another would admire his enterprize, bravery, and hospitality.

The legal system in the early period of the Midwest was often haphazard and arbitrary. Although William A. White, in his *Changing West,* wrote that the people who moved to the West carried with them the writ of habeas corpus and the right of trial by jury, the actual situation was far from ideal. The territorial frontier was noted for lynch law and an inadequate number of judges. The boldest, the weakest, the most vicious, and the noblest men were all drawn to the frontier, and the unsettled conditions lent themselves to lawlessness and mob rule. To prevent mob action, laws in the early days were strict and harsh. Jails were scarce so other means of punishment were often used. Punishment was quick and occasionally wrong. Whipping was the usual punishment for theft; hanging for more serious offenses. The informality of legal processes and the individuality on the frontier tended to make the midwesterner lawless.

The midwestern area had more social and economic democracy than the older settled regions because of the abundance of land and the resulting, greater equality of opportunity. However, wealth and living conditions varied on the frontier even in the early days due to rural-urban divergence and individual differences stemming from health, ability to manage, location, and inheritance. For this reason the wealthy and the poor lived side by side almost from the beginning in all regions of the Middle West.

—25—

Recreation

Recreation Related to Life

Recreation in the Midwest was a personal and individual matter. There were some differences between the pastimes of the midwestern rural and small-town groups, the lower and lower-middle classes of the larger towns, and the upper-middle and upper classes of the cities. The rural and small-town groups, which dominated in the Midwest to 1850, had little time or opportunity for specialized types of recreation. People were too scattered, transportation was too slow, and there was too much work to be done; even the children had chores. Not until the development of the automobile, the movies, and the radio were the farmers able to take much of a part in organized, commercial recreation.

In the case of the lower and lower-middle classes of the larger towns, they were usually too busy working long hours during this period to have much time or money for organized entertainment. However, since they lived in heavily populated regions, they had more commercial recreation available if they had the time and inclination. Eventually shorter work weeks meant that they had more time to indulge in leisure activities.

The upper-middle and upper classes of the cities usually engaged in the same activities as the other groups except they did it more lavishly. Many of them worked even longer hours than the poorer people in order to get still wealthier or for some other reason. On the other hand a large group of them did have more time and money to devote to recreation.

In the early rural Midwest, much of the recreation involved the everyday tasks of the pioneers. Women grew flowers. Hunting, fishing, and shooting the mark were especially popular among the men. The favorite targets at these shoots were nails driven part way into a tree or an inch square of white paper mounted on a black shingle. Targets were generally set up 75 to 100 yards away. A beef or barrel of whisky were the usual prizes. The marksman who hit the center of the target or drove his nail in furthest would win the hide and tallow; the second got his choice of hindquarters, the third received the remaining hindquarter, the fourth obtained the choice of front quarters, the fifth the other front quarter, and the sixth got the lead fired into the tree.

Men had cabin-and-barn raisings, militia-training days, log rollings, corn-husking bees, and wheat-reaping frolics; the women had picking, sewing, and quilting bees. The men usually accompanied their work parties with the consumption of ample amounts of corn whisky and large portions of food. Corn husking had an added attraction because the fellow who found a red ear of corn was allowed to kiss his favorite girl.

Men have always viewed feats of strength with admiration; in pioneer life these feats received added emphasis because physical strength and dexterity were necessary for pioneer tasks. Such sports as hurling the tomahawk, throwing the rail, tossing the long bullet or maul, lifting weights, tug of war, or gander pulling were widely engaged in. A person had to be agile and strong to pull the head off a live, squirming goose tied to the limb of a tree while riding horseback at full speed. Abraham Lincoln, an awkward country boy living in New Salem, Illinois, was among the most active in the sports of his community. His strength was illustrated by the fact that he could pick up a whisky barrel and drink from the bung hole.

Eating has always been a favorite pastime. The pioneers enjoyed eating huge meals of barbecued beef and hog, buffalo steaks, wild turkey, hominy, wheat cakes, corn bread, and a vast assortment of other delicacies. Francis Trollope noted in visiting Cincinnati that the only rural amusement in which she saw the people engaged was eating strawberries and cream in a lovely garden a few miles from town.

Courtship and marriage were also made a time of gaiety and frolic. Hugging and kissing and other pastimes engaged in by those in the throes of love were a form of amusement or exquisite torment. Some dating couples engaged in bundling, which consisted of hugging and kissing in the girl's bed. The custom originated from an attempt to save heat and light. The practice was usually chaperoned and the couple did not remove their undergarments so that temptation would be further removed. Despite these precautions, pregnancies occasionally occurred. Even this happening was largely forgiven, however, if the offending couple quickly approached the altar. Bundling in itself was not improper; it was equivalent to the later nineteenth-century buggy ride or the twentieth-century automobile drive.

Marriage too was a time of merriment for most and sadness for a few. It was a time of feasting and drinking accompanied by dancing and crude jokes. Sometimes weddings were staid and solemn affairs, and sometimes the only solemn part of the affair was the actual wedding ceremony. Sometimes the horseplay was unkind and even rough. Abraham Lincoln allegedly came close to breaking up a wedding party on one occasion. Although he was not invited to a double wedding ceremony in the Grigsby family, he went anyway. With the aid of a confederate, he switched the brides so that the grooms when escorted to their bridal chambers found themselves in the wrong bedrooms.

The charivari or "belling," a noisy concert for the newly weds, was often held a short time later. The usual way to quiet the noisemakers was with candy, cigars, or whisky depending on the nature and type of the callers.

Although churches in the early period were generally opposed to recreation, they did provide a form of entertainment. Camp meetings, which were supposed to bring about spiritual regeneration, often provided a break from loneliness and a chance to greet old friends and make new ones. People gathered from miles around to hear the circuit rider tell of the fire and brimstone of Hell and the glories of Heaven. As described by Peter Cartwright, the camp meetings had mourners and sinners, wailing for mercy, and convulsive jerkings of persons seized by the spirit. But despite these spiritual overtones, the sociability, sermons, and hymns still gave many people an emotional release and an exciting experience.

At first college commencements and school graduations were

turned into festive celebrations, but school officials soon converted them back into formal, academic channels. Every holiday became a period of recreation. In the case of Sunday the churches tried to save the Lord's day from desecration, but with little success. People of Yankee origin in the Midwest originally tended to emphasize Thanksgiving more than Christmas. As the years passed, however, Christmas won out. Both merchants wanting to sell gifts and churches desiring to stress the Christian significance of Christmas combined to put Thanksgiving in second place. People, however, still enjoyed Thanksgiving as a time of family association and good food. July 4 early became the time of patriotic speeches, parades, fireworks, and outings. On one fourth of July around 1850, 2,000 people gathered at Brownsville, Nebraska, for a barbecue and dance. There were enough buffalo, deer, oxen, sheep, hogs, and pigs slaughtered for the occasion to feed most of the people in the territory.

The Theater

For vicarious entertainment the stage in its myriad forms played a leading role in the Midwest. At first the taverns were the places where travelling performers, such as acrobats, magicians, tight-rope walkers, jugglers, and dog-and-pig trainers, appeared to entertain the townspeople. Concerts were occasionally given by musicians playing on such instruments as spinets, virginals, violins, and bass viols.

Cincinnati led the West in theatrical productions. In 1801 an amateur group there presented "The Poor Soldier" and "She Stoops to Conquer." Amateur productions were soon after given in St. Louis, Detroit, and other cities by newly formed "Thespian societies." About 1810 professional troupes of players appeared in the West and soon established circuits touching the larger towns. Professional actors directed by William Turner visited Cincinnati in 1811, 1815, and 1816. Cincinnati completed the building of a theater in 1820. The leading play cities of the Midwest were Cincinnati and St. Louis. Smaller midwestern towns also had an occasional visit from travelling players. Detroit, which was not in the circuit pattern, saw eastern companies in 1827, 1833, and 1834. By 1835 travelling companies were taking such plays as "Honeymoon," "Othello," and "Hunchback" all over the West. Playing leading roles in these productions were famous actors and actresses like Edwin Forrest, Junius B. Booth, Clara Fisher, Charles Kean, James H. Hackett, Dan Marble, and Helen Tree.

Although a number of productions were being presented in the Midwest by 1850, the actors and theater goers still faced certain problems. The people who attended were not always of the highest caliber. Toughs and prostitutes mingled in the crowds. Some men made themselves at home by standing on the benches in the upper tiers and spitting on the stage or into the boxes below. To try and combat this situation, Noah M. Ludlow barred both liquor and prostitutes from his St. Louis theater.

The theater was also hurt by the private lives of some of the leading actors. Kean was involved in so many scandals that he was finally hissed off the stage; Forrest's unsavory divorce case blighted his reputation; and Junius B. Booth alternated between drunken insensibility and insanity. His managers had to resort to all sorts of devices to get Booth on the stage in a relatively sober condition.

The theaters were generally most uncomfortable. They were dirty and rats occasionally ran to and fro. In winter the barnlike structures were cold and patrons and actors alike nearly froze. Lighting systems composed of candles and oil lamps smoked, dripped, and sputtered. Curtains and scenery often caught fire, and many theaters burned down. The seats were of rough planks and very uncomfortable. On western tours conditions were apt to be even worse. An old warehouse or barn might be used as a theater, and stage properties were improvised. Joseph Jefferson, in an early tour of Illinois, used old barns and even player-built structures for theaters.

Although Shakespeare remained the favorite fare of actors, the people seemed to prefer comedies, farces, melodramas, musical shows, and burlesques. The bill changed at theaters nearly every night. In 1839 a St. Louis theater set a kind of record by having 157 different plays in a single season. Even Shakespearean plays had dances, popular music, acrobats, and comedies inserted between the acts. Although "Our American Cousin," "The Green Mountain Boys of 1776," and "High Life Below Stairs" were popular, Shakespeare's greatest rival was probably John B. Buckingstone, author of "The Pet of the Petticoats," "A Kiss in the Dark," and at least 148 other plays.

To hold and tantalize the audiences, a variety of other productions were also developed. Equestrian dramas were introduced in which horses were actually used on the stage. Even "Richard III" was performed with the leading characters mounted on steeds. Ballet was introduced around 1850 to the consternation of some who were not used to seeing young ladies in such revealing circumstances.

PART III

THE DISRUPTIVE PERIOD IN THE MIDDLE WEST, 1841-1877

— 26 —

Indian Wars and Administration

By 1840 the "permanent" Indian barrier was established temporarily at the 95th meridian running from the Great Bend of the Missouri River up to the Red River of the North. West of the Missouri were transplanted Potawatomi, Seneca, Shawnee, Delaware, Kickapoo, Iowa, Chippewa, Sauk, Fox, Ottawa, Peoria, and Miami crowded into small reserves. To the west and north of these transplanted Indians were the Cheyennes, Arapahoes, Pawnees, and Sioux. To protect the white settlers and keep peace among the Indian tribes, an irregular line of garrisoned forts swept along the 95th meridian from Ft. Howard and Ft. Snelling in the North to Ft. Smith and Ft. Towson in the South. The federal government had every intention of giving permanency to this Indian country in the Great Plains. Companies of United States troops went into the Indian country to impress them with the power of the government, to hold councils to promote peace among warring tribes, and to protect caravans enroute to Oregon and Santa Fe. Some of the tribes made remarkable progress in adapting to their new environment and in improving their governmental, educational, and social conditions. Several new treaties were even made after 1840 with tribes living in Wisconsin and Iowa who ceded their lands in exchange for other tracts in Minnesota and Kansas.

But in the later 1840's the quest for gold, the Mexican War, and Oregon fever started the whites moving west. The government tried to clear the western lands of Indians as rapidly as possible, but the whites moved faster and the period 1849 to 1869 was a time of bitterness between the Indians who owned the western lands and the whites who wanted them. The government followed two procedures in dispossessing the Indians from the "Great American Desert" and the northern Middle West.

Between 1854 and 1866 the United States Government signed a series of treaties with various tribes, including the Omaha, Shawnee, Kickapoo, Choctaw, Chickasaw, Osage, Delaware, Cherokee, Comanche, Kiowa, Arapaho, Sioux, and Cheyenne which gave the government the right to build highways and railroads across Indian lands. In an attempt to prevent trouble in 1865, the government even went so far as to offer the Miniconjou Sioux of Dakota $10,000 annually for twenty years if they would withdraw from travel routes established across their lands.

In addition to buying right of ways, the government also began moving the Indians to smaller reservations. In the summer of 1851 Alexander Ramsey negotiated treaties by which the Sisseton and Wahpeton bands of Sioux gave up all their lands in Iowa and Minnesota except for a strip along the upper-Minnesota River which was set aside as a reservation for them. For this cession of 35,000,000 acres, the Sioux were to receive $1,665,000. Of the $420,000 actually paid out by Ramsey to the Indians in 1852, the traders immediately obtained $320,000 and soon after obtained most of the rest. Settlers rushing in before the treaties were ratified and the traders receiving most of the treaty money made the Siouan tribes angry; this animosity later found expression in murderous attack on the settlers.

In September 1851 Thomas Fitzpatrick assembled the chiefs of the plains tribes at Ft. Laramie. At this assembly the Indians promised to stop interfering with the emigrant route to Oregon and California and to allow the United States government to establish roads and posts within the Indian lands. The Indians also accepted more limited hunting grounds. The Sioux were tendered the Dakota Territory north of the Platte River, the Mandan and Grosventres were given a triangle just east of the Yellowstone River, the Assiniboin were assigned the region west of the Yellowstone, the Crows were given a large tract west of the Powder River, the Blackfeet were assigned the mountainous country around the headwaters of the Missouri, and the Cheyennes and Arapahoes were given an area between the North Platte and the Arkansas rivers. Once again the Indians were assured that they would not be further molested, but this promise was soon broken. In return for these cessions of land, the Indians were to receive $50,000 a year for fifty years in provisions, mechandise, domestic animals, and agricultural tools. The Senate unilaterally reduced the period of these annuity payments from fifty to ten or fifteen years. The Indians generally remained peaceful in spite of their resentment at this treatment.

Thomas Fitzpatrick made a similar treaty with the Comanche, Kiowa, and Apache tribes at Ft. Atkinson in 1853. These tribes promised to remain peaceful and allow United States posts and roads in their territories. For these concessions they were to receive $18,000 worth of goods annually for a period of ten years.

To pave the way for the organization of the Kansas and Nebraska territories and the opening of a central railroad route to the Pacific, Indian Commissioner George W. Manypenny in 1854 and 1855 was given the task of making treaties with these oft-moved Indians in order to move them again. This action was contrary to the promise made to the Indians that they would not be moved again. Ranging from north to south, the Omaha, Oto, Missouri, Sauk, Fox, Iowa, Kickapoo, Delaware, Shawnee, Ottawa, Kaskaskia, Peoria, Piankashaw, Wea, and Miami tribes ceded lands aggregating more than thirteen-million acres. Many of these tribes agreed to accept lands elsewhere and some of them secured small reservations within their former territories. All agreed to grant the right of ways across their lands for roads and railroads demanded by the government. Between 1854 and 1859 the eastern Indian tribes were either concentrated on small reservations or moved west out of Kansas and Nebraska. By 1860 most of Kansas and Nebraska and a corner of Dakota were freed of Indians.

As the Indians were consolidated in smaller areas, the whites rushed in to grab the vacated lands by law or force. By 1860 the slave and free-soil partisans in Kansas had temporarily stopped fighting one another and were concentrating on seizing Indian lands. With the whites encroaching on Indian lands and plundering the Indians throughout the western Middle West and with Indian dissatisfaction rising against the violations of treaty provisions and distribution of Indian annuities, battles and massacres were to be expected and they were not long in coming. In 1854 a small-scale war with the Sioux occurred in Nebraska because the Sioux killed and ate a footsore cow owned by a Mormon and a young West Point lieutenant did not know how to handle the affair. A year later General William S. Harney with 1,200 troops from Ft. Leavenworth caught up with Little Thunder's raiding band of Brule Sioux at Ash Hollow, massacred 136, and captured the rest. By his tactics Harney forced the Dakotas, Tetons, and Sioux to respect the Platte Valley Trail. But when the troops were pulled out for the Civil War, the Indians went on the warpath.

Of the semi-sedentary Indians of Nebraska, the Pawnee were the most belligerent. They occasionally raided the whites and in turn were attacked by the whites and the Sioux. They finally moved to Indian Territory (Oklahoma) in 1875 or 1876.

Although there were numerous small Indian raids in Minnesota during the period 1852 to 1861, it was not until after the Civil War began that the largest uprising occurred. This major uprising in 1862 came about largely because of broken treaties, the dishonesty of certain agents, and the greediness of the traders. The imediate causes stemmed from the withholding of Indian annuity payments due to government red tape and the raids of a few reckless braves in Meeker County, Minnesota, in August 1862. Little Crow and his band, disgruntled over their bad treatment and believing they too would be blamed for the August raids, went on a rampage. They began by attacking the Sioux agency near the junction of the Redwood and Minnesota rivers. New Ulm and Ft. Ridgely were also attacked, but these outposts managed to repulse the Indians. In all a region 200 miles long and 50 miles wide was devastated or depopulated. In a little over a week, the Sioux killed between 500 and 600 settlers and carried away several-hundred women and children into captivity.

The punishment of the Sioux was swift. General Henry H. Sibley was rushed to the troubled area; in September 1862 he defeated the Indians in a series of battles and freed a large number of the captive-white women and children. Through force and trickery he captured 2,000 Sioux and placed 400 of them on trial. Three hundred of these were sentenced to death for murder, arson, and rape. But President Abraham Lincoln pardoned all but 39 who were hanged on a single scaffold at Mankato late in December 1862. Of the remainder of the captured Sioux, they were kept in confinement for about a year. In February 1863

Congress abrogated all treaties with the Sioux, cancelled their annuities, and left them homeless. Three months later the captured Sioux were taken up the Missouri River into Dakota Territory. Many died enroute. Meanwhile Sibley went north to chastise the Sioux who had fled in that direction, and General Alfred Sully went into South Dakota to terrorize the Sioux who had fled west. There were some skirmishes and the whites perpetrated several massacres. In 1864 scouts were paid $25 for the scalp of any male Sioux Indian. The volunteer scouts collected $11,375. By 1866 all the Minnesota Sioux had been removed or driven out to the western Dakotas with the exception of 200 friendly Sioux who returned to their old Minnesota reservations. The Sioux paid heavily, innocent and guilty alike, for their uprising in 1862.

Trouble on a large scale next occurred in the area between the Platte and Arkansas rivers. There, the Cheyenne and Arapaho, upset by the gold seekers who violated their lands and drove out their game, began to raid the stage-relay stations and the wagon trains. In 1861 representatives of these two tribes were summoned to Ft. Wise where they were forced to relinquish all their former territory except for a small reserve along Sand Creek in southeast Colorado. The Cheyenne and Arapaho, however, continued their depredations and in the summer of 1864 even disrupted Ben Holladay's stage line. In the winter of 1864 when they drifted back to their reservations, Colorado wanted them punished for their misdeeds. Consequently in November 1864 Colonel J. M. Chivington, formerly presiding elder of the Nebraska Methodist Conference, went to the Sand Creek camp with two regiments of Colorado militia and with no pretense of apprehending the guilty raiders indiscriminately massacred over 100 Indian men, women, and children belonging to Black Kettle's band of Cheyenne. Chivington was later court martialed for his action; in 1865 Congress appropriated money to indemnify the relatives of these murdered Indians. As a result of this massacre, many of the Arapaho and Cheyenne went north to join the Sioux and relinquished their San Creek reserve. In 1869 those still alive were finally given a home in western Oklahoma.

After many battles and massacres, the United States government in 1867 finally decided to make the Indians wards of the government and move them to still smaller reservations. The peace commissioners at St. Louis decided to put the 53,000 northern-plains Indians in the Black Hills country of Dakota and the 86,000 southern-plains Indians in Oklahoma. At a council on Medicine Lodge Creek in October 1867, the commissioners forced the Kiowa, Comanche, Cheyenne, and Arapaho to accept reservations in Indian Territory. Lands in the Indian Territory, taken from the five civilized tribes (because of their alleged help to the confederacy in the Civil War), were also distributed to the Osage, Pawnee, Oto, Kansa, and to eastern Indians ousted from Kansas and Nebraska. At the Ft. Laramie Conference in 1868, the commissioners persuaded the Sioux to accept a permanent reservation in Dakota Territory, west of the Missouri River.

Although the Ft. Laramie and Medicine Lodge treaties virtually cleared the central plains of red men, there were still Indian uprisings. War began again in August 1868 when bands of Cheyenne, Arapaho, Kiowa, and Comanche under Chief Black Kettle obtained some rifles and started north to raid along the Smoky Hill and Saline River valleys in Kansas. Black Kettle's raids inspired a general uprising in the Southwest. General Philip Sheridan, commander of the army in the West, set out to round them up. He dispatched three expeditions; one from Ft. Lyon, Colorado; one from Ft. Bascom, New Mexico; and a main army from Ft. Hays, Kansas. His plan was to drive the Indians into the Washita River Valley and crush them there with the main army from Ft. Hays. The main force, commanded by Colonel George A. Custer, was joined by a regiment of Kansas frontiersmen near the north fork of the Canadian River. Finding a fresh Indian trail in the deep snow, Custer threw his orders to the winds and hastened directly to the Washita Valley where he found Chief Black Kettle and several-hundred Cheyenne and Arapaho braves encamped. He attacked and won and quickly withdrew before the other Indians in the valley could counterattack. His decisive victory broke the Indian resistance, and the erring bands were hustled back to their reservations. General Sheridan reported all quiet on the western front in 1869. But raids continued and General William T. Sherman, who replaced

Sheridan, was plagued with the Red River War which dragged on until November 1874 with some fourteen pitched battles.

In 1874 the rumored discovery of gold in the Black Hills, substantiated by a scientific expedition led by Colonel Custer into the area, set the stage for the final major Indian uprising in the Middle West. As the miners flocked into the Indian reservation, the Sioux became increasingly angry. The Sioux were also disturbed by the construction of the Northern Pacific Railroad and by the misappropriation and adulteration of their annuity goods. James A. Emmons, a newspaperman in Bismarck, reported this corruption in the Indian agency and was sued for libel by Secretary of War William K. Belknap. The New York *Tribune* investigated and found Emmons to be correct. Belknap resigned under threat of impeachment.

In 1875 the Sioux were out hunting buffalo. They were ordered to get back to their reservation by January 1, 1876, or be counted as enemies. Sitting Bull and Crazy Horse of the Teton Dakota said they had no intention of returning. General George Crook from Ft. Fetterman on the North Platte, General Alfred H. Terry from Ft. Abraham Lincoln, Dakota, and Colonel John Gibbon from Ft. Ellis, Montana, were sent out to bring them in. Early in 1876 General Crook suffered a minor defeat on the banks of the Redbud in an inconclusive battle with the Sioux. In June 1876 Terry sent Colonel Custer south along the Rosebud to swing around behind the Indians and keep them from fleeing into the Big Horn Mountains while the main force approached from the front. Instead of waiting for the main force to join him, Custer, smarting from a rebuke given him by General Ulysses S. Grant in connection with his testimony against Grant's brother in the Indian-agency scandal, decided to attack Sitting Bull at once and regain his glory. But he was foolhardy once too often. He and his entire command of 270 men were annihilated at the battle of the Little Big Horn. It was only a temporary victory for the Indians, however, for within a few months General Nelson A. Miles surrounded and defeated the Sioux in the Tongue River Valley. Sitting Bull escaped to Canada, but Crazy Horse was killed resisting arrest at Ft. Robinson in September 1877. After these defeats the Indian lands were reduced still more. The Brule and Oglala reservations in Nebraska were abandoned and the Indians were concentrated at the Pine Ridge and Rosebud reservations in South Dakota.

George A. Custer (1839-1876)
Army officer, killed at battle of
Little Big Horn
From *Dictionary of American Portraits* by Hayward and Blanche Cirker, Dover Publications, Inc., New York, 1967. *Reprinted through permission of the publisher.*

Sitting Bull (c. 1834-1890)
Sioux Indian chief
Courtesy Mercaldo Archives. From *Dictionary of American Portraits* by Hayward and Blanche Cirker, Dover Publications, Inc., New York, 1967. *Reprinted through permission of the publisher.*

John Brown (1800-1859)
Abolitionist and martyr
Painting by John S. Curry.

Levi Coffin (1789-1877)
Abolitionist, leader of the Underground
Railroad
From *Dictionary of American Portraits* by Hayward and Blanche Cirker, Dover Publications, Inc., New York, 1967. *Reprinted through permission of the publisher.*

—27—

Settlement of the Middle West

The migration trend most observable in the Midwest in the two decades after 1840 was the large influx of settlers from western Europe. Of these the great majority were Irish, German, and English.

In the five midwestern states east of the Mississippi, the increasing European immigration aided greatly in filling in the towns and hamlets after 1840. In Ohio in 1850, for example, 11.5 per cent of the population or 218,193 were foreign born. Of these 111,257 were German, 51,562 were Irish, and 25,660 were English. Overall this inflow of Europeans into the Lake Plains in the 1840's was demonstrated by the fact that these five states contained 640,000 foreign born in 1850, a figure equal to about one eighth of the total population of the area.

Other localized settlement trends and patterns were also observable. The settlement of northern Indiana, northern and central Illinois, and southern Michigan continued in the 1840's and 1850's. Indiana's population increased less rapidly after 1840. While its northern counties were settled by the overflow from the Chicago Road, its central portion was largely neglected until the 1850's. Because of the poor drainage of the sluggish streams north of the Wabash, many people believed that central Indiana was flooded. Settlement there was eventually stimulated by men like Henry L. Ellsworth, a Connecticut businessman, who made large purchases of land between the Wabash and Kankakee rivers in 1832 and circulated a book, *Valley of the Upper Wabash,* which outlined in glowing terms the advantages of the area.

The biggest settlement problem in Illinois was in populating the prairies. Settlers had a prejudice against treeless land, because forests furnished fences, firewood, game, protection from the elements, and a built-in drainage system. Even more important, settlers had to devise a method to break the tough sod. Before the steel plow was invented, this task was accomplished with a garantuan plow pulled by three-to-six yoke of oxen. Slowly, however, the prairies were settled and by 1850 all of Illinois was populated.

Across the Mississippi in Iowa, settlement increased steadily. By a series of treaties in the 1830's and 1840's, Iowa was cleared of Indians to make room for the whites. In 1846 Iowa came into the Union with its boundaries slightly reduced. The settlement of Iowa was greatly accelerated by the military-bounty warrants issued to veterans of the Indian and Mexican wars. Some fourteen-million acres of Iowa land were purchased with these military warrants, some of which had fallen into the hands of speculators. The peak of Iowa's migration occurred during the years 1854 to 1856 when 190,000 people arrived. By 1860 the population of the state stood at 674,913.

Settlement spread slowly from Iowa and Wisconsin into the forested-lake country of Minnesota adjacent to the Mississippi River. In 1837 treaties with the Sioux and Chippewa gave the United States a triangle of land between the Mississippi and St. Croix rivers. Into this triangle the first semi-permanent arrivals (the lumbermen) came within a few years. Towns such as Stillwater, Point Douglas, Osceola, and St. Croix Falls had their beginnings as saw mills. Farmers were lured into the cut-over areas by lumbermen who needed food for their logging camps. Many of the sawmill villages became the core of small agricultural communities.

Pierre Parrant, a Canadian voyageur, staked the first claim (1838) on the land that was to become St. Paul. A group of Swiss people moved into the St. Paul area in 1840 when they were evicted from their land around Ft. Snelling. St. Paul received its name from a log chapel dedicated to St. Paul, which was built by Lucian Galtier in 1841.

With the opening of the Mississippi River in 1847, a regular fleet of steamboats began operation between St. Paul and lower-river ports. St. Paul lands were put on the market in 1848 and immigration increased. People came up the Red River Trail in two-wheeled cars pulled by oxen. The Sauk River route later replaced the Red River Trail. By 1849 the major part of the white population in Minnesota was in the villages of St. Paul, Stillwater, and St. Anthony. By 1857 St. Paul alone had 8,000 people; and Minneapolis, laid out on lands of the Ft. Snelling Military Reservation in 1852, grew even faster than St. Paul. Minnesota, which became a state in 1858, had a population in 1860 of 172,023.

Missouri's population continued to grow despite its loss of population to the states further west. Although Iowa served in a lesser degree in the settlement of Oregon, Missouri became the "mother of states." Both the Oregon and California trails had their point of origin in Missouri; Missourians also claimed the distinction of opening up the Santa Fe Trail. In 1850 Missouri had the largest number of ex-residents in Oregon and California and the seventh largest number in Texas.

The beginning of settlement in Kansas and Nebraska can be attributed largely to transportation routes. The Santa Fe Trail crossed Kansas, the Mormon Trail crossed Nebraska, and the Oregon and California trails crossed them both. Although this was Indian country, a few stragglers began settling along the trails. In 1854 settlement rapidly expanded after the passage of the Kansas-Nebraska Act. The moving out of the Indians and the encouragement of white settlement in these territories were both part of a plan to obtain the transcontinental railroad for the region. This plan took on another, bloodier aspect with the influx of southern and northern partisans, each desiring to make the area an extension of their respective regions under the popular-sovereignty provision. By 1860 Kansas had a population of 107,206 and Nebraska 28,841.

Despite the slow settlement of the midwestern states west of the Missouri River and north of the 42nd parallel, the Midwest made a great gain in its total population during this period. From slightly more than one fifth of the U. S. population in 1840, it (with 9,096,716) was approaching one third of the nation's population in 1860.

— 28 —

Admission of Middle Western States

Admission of Iowa

With the influx of settlers, the midwestern states continued to enter the Union. Iowa, the sixth North Central state to be admitted to the Union, was given statehood in 1846. Prior to 1821 Iowa had undergone the same territorial perambulations as Missouri, described above. After 1821 Iowa, along with the rest of the area north and west of it, had no civil government until 1834, when it, Minnesota, and parts of the Dakotas were put under the jurisdiction of Michigan Territory. With the imminent statehood of Michigan in 1836, Wisconsin Territory was created and Iowa spent two years under its jurisdiction. In 1838 Wisconsin was delimited and Iowa Territory, composed of the area bounded by the Mississippi and the Missouri rivers, was created.

Iowa had two peculiar boundary episodes. In 1820 the "Honey War" occurred between Iowa and Missouri over thirteen miles of mutual boundary. Although both governors called out their militia, the boundary dispute was settled peacefully. It was referred to as the "Honey War" because the area in dispute had some bee trees and the taking of honey from one of these trees by a Missourian contributed to the dispute. Iowa acquired the dip in its southeast corner by a historical accident. In 1824 when the Sauk and Fox ceded their Missouri lands to the United States, the Indians kept a "half-breed tract" between the Des Moines and Mississippi rivers. Later when the Indians released it, it was acquired by Iowa.

The people of Iowa refused statehood in 1840 and 1842 because they did not wish to pay the additional taxes that came with a state government. Finally in 1844 Iowa voted for statehood, and the constitutional convention set the northern boundary at the Minnesota River. Congress agreed to admit Iowa, but with less area. Northern congressmen wanted to keep the new, northern states small in order to create as many states as possible and stay ahead of the South which was discussing the possibility of dividing Texas into five states. In 1846 Iowa reluctantly agreed to a compromise northern boundary of 43° 30′ and obtained statehood officially in December of that year. Florida had been admitted the previous year and thus the free-slave state ratio was still in balance.

Admission of Wisconsin

The seventh midwestern state to gain admission to the Union was Wisconsin. It was the last state in the original Northwest Territory to attain that status. In 1836 Wisconsin became a separate territory after having been a part of the Northwest, Indiana, Illinois, and Michigan territories. At the outset in 1836 Wisconsin Territory included the area north of Illinois and Missouri and east of the Missouri River. This ended after two years with the creation of Iowa Territory. At that time Wisconsin was pared down leaving only that portion of Minnesota east of the Mississippi River in excess of its present boundaries.

During the last twelve years that Wisconsin was a territory, the officials concentrated on extinguishing the Indian title. In 1848 only a triangular-shaped area in the east-central part of the state remained in the hands of the Indians. The whites of Wisconsin could hardly wait for Secretary of War Joel R. Poinsett to move out the Winnebago in 1840.

After dispossessing the Indians, the whites had the problem of not being dispossessed by other whites. Wisconsin settlers, like those of Iowa, established claim associations to prevent land speculators from grabbing the lands of bonified squatters. When the land sale occurred at Milwaukee in 1839, claim associations assured each farmer his land.

Despite the claim associations, the speculators were hard to control. There was a shortage of law which left the dishonest speculator considerable room in which to operate. Even harder to control were the corrupt and often absentee land-office agents and their cohorts. Jackson's Specie Circular, intended to help the small buyer and hinder conniving speculators and land agents, actually provided the latter a field day and nearly crushed the small landowner.

As in Illinois and elsewhere, land speculation also influenced the selection of the capital. James D. Doty, second territorial governor, bought land in the present-day Madison area and then used his influence to persuade the Wisconsin territorial assembly to locate the capital there.

Wisconsin had its great influx of population after the Panic of 1837. The high point of this deluge was in 1846, when 700,000 acres were sold in Wisconsin. Between 1842 and 1846 the population of Wisconsin increased from 46,000 to 155,000 and thus made the territory eligible for statehood.

At first a majority of the people in Wisconsin were reluctant to enter statehood and between 1841 and 1844 turned down the opportunity four times. There were two main reasons for their action. First, they did not want the higher taxes that came with statehood; second, they did not like the politics or proposals of the second territorial governor, James D. Doty (1841-1844). Not only was he a Whig while a majority of the people in Wisconsin were Democrats, but also Doty wanted a part of northern Illinois returned to Wisconsin, which would bring to Wisconsin a part of the huge Illinois debt. With the return of Henry Dodge to the governorship in 1845, these problems were resolved.

Finally in 1846 the people of Wisconsin voted six to one in favor of statehood. They had apparently decided that 500,000 acres of land for internal improvements and the right to choose their own public officials were sufficient advantages to offset the disadvantage of higher taxes. But the path to statehood was still rocky. The people turned down the first constitution because of boundary questions and a fundamental disagreement over what should be in the constitution. The Wisconsin voters were disgruntled over the fact that they received no extra land in either northern Illinois or the upper peninsula. Moreover, many persons were disturbed by "radical provisions" in the constitution which allowed married women to own property separate from their husbands, exempted forty acres or $1,000 worth of property in town from seizure for satisfaction of debt, forbade the creation of currency-issuing banks, and left the door ajar for Negro suffrage.

Even the second constitution of Wisconsin was liberal. It borrowed many of its provisions from the Michigan and New York constitutions. In Wisconsin the governor, legislators, and judges were all elected for short terms. A veto by the governor could be overridden by a two-thirds' vote of both houses. All native-born, white males were given the right to vote after one year's residence, and foreign-born, white males received a similar privilege after agreeing to a simple oath of allegiance. Small homesteads were exempted from seizure for debt, and married women were allowed to control their own property. A pay-as-you-go provision for the state government was also included. Negroes and most Indians could not vote. Even when a law was passed in 1849 allowing Negroes to vote, its validity was questioned until 1866 when it was upheld by the Wisconsin Supreme Court. Wisconsin had sufficient New England influence in the state to cause it to adopt the New England supervisor system of county government and the town, rather then the commissioner type of county government and the township prevalent in the Midwest.

Wisconsin began its statehood in 1848 with its capital at Madison and with Nelson Dewey, a Democrat, as governor. In its admittance Wisconsin was paired with Texas, although the latter had come into the Union three years before.

Admission of Minnesota

Minnesota, the next midwestern territory to attain statehood, did not enter the Union for a decade. Its earlier history had been intimately associated with fur traders, explorers, forts, and the Sioux and Chippewa Indians. The principal point of interest in

Minnesota from 1819 to 1849 was Ft. Snelling, which was begun by Lieutenant Colonel Henry Leavenworth and completed by Colonel Josiah Snelling who was commandant there from 1820 to 1827. The most influential civil official in Minnesota for the twenty-year period after 1819 was Laurence Taliaferro who was the Indian agent at St. Peter.

Minnesota in its earlier territorial stages had been divided between the Northwest Territory and the Louisiana Territory. As a result its governmental development had been disorganized. In part Minnesota had shared Iowa's territorial development and in part Michigan's. In 1846 and 1847 Morgan L. Martin of Wisconsin Territory introduced a bill to set up the territory of Minnesota, but Congress refused on the grounds that Minnesota had too few people. Stephen A. Douglas tried again in 1848 with similar results. When Wisconsin became a state in 1848, part of Minnesota was left with no government at all. Finally after considerable haggling, Minnesota became a territory in 1849. It had 4,000 inhabitants and included in addition to present-day Minnesota the portion of the Dakotas east of the Missouri River.

A great change in its population status occurred after 1851 when the Indian Department purchased a large part of western Minnesota from the Sioux. Within a year Minnesota's population had increased by 20,000; by 1860 Minnesota had over 172,000 inhabitants. But there was no rush for statehood because state taxes would be higher.

When Minnesota finally requested statehood in 1857, Congress passed the necessary enabling act despite southern opposition and some pleasantries about Minnesota being a violation of the Ordinance of 1787 which specified that only five states could be created out of the Northwest Territory. When the constitutional-convention delegates were elected, both the Democratic and Republican slates claimed to have won. Consequently each group drew up a constitution. Both sets of delegates drew from the constitutions of Wisconsin, Ohio, Michigan, Iowa, New York, and New Jersey. Since the constitutions were very similar, a compromise was worked out and the Democratic document was submitted as the official constitution. Minnesota entered the Union in 1858 with St. Paul as its capital.

Admission of Kansas

Like Missouri a generation earlier, Kansas, the ninth middle western state to enter the Union, became involved in the slavery controversy. Unlike the Missouri situation which was settled peacefully in a compromise, "Bleeding Kansas" became the battleground over the extension of slavery into the territories and as such became a major cause of the Civil War. In the 1820's Kansas had been dubbed a part of the "Great American Desert." Largely because of this it was set aside as Indian country in 1834 and left under the general supervision of Missouri for twenty years.

The Missouri Compromise of 1820 had provided that all the territory in the Louisiana Purchase north of 36° 30′ with the exception of Missouri was to be free. The South, however, wanted more northern area for slavery. Their chance came in 1854 with the Kansas-Nebraska bill. As early as 1844 the secretary of war had suggested the establishment of a territory to be called Nebraska west of Iowa to implement American emigration to the Oregon country. Stephen A. Douglas proposed its creation again in 1848. Four years later agitation began for the creation of a territory west of Missouri.

These movements would probably have come to naught except for the desire of Douglas and others to build a transcontinental railroad through the area. The idea of a Pacific railroad was probably begun by Asa Whitney, a New York merchant interested in the China trade. Douglas worked after 1844 to have the territory of Nebraska organized so that the railroad could go through that area. He wanted Chicago to be a great railroad terminal.

The South, on the other hand, wanted a southern route for the proposed railroad. With the organization of the New Mexico Territory in 1850, the South was in an excellent position to obtain the route because the territories were now organized all along the southern route.

If the central route was to have a chance, Nebraska had to be organized quickly and the Indians removed. The accomplishment of these goals encountered strong southern opposition. The South was opposed to the opening of this area not only because it would be a competitor for the projected transcontinental route, but also because under the Missouri Compromise it would be organized as a free territory. Only one major politician, Sam Houston, voiced opposition to the opening of the area because of the disruption and misery it would cause the Indians. In order to overcome southern opposition, Senator Douglas popularized the idea of popular sovereignty. This in effect would repeal the Missouri Compromise and allow the people of the territory to decide whether the state would be free or slave. Bills to organize Nebraska Territory under the Missouri Compromise were introduced twice during 1853 with no success. Then in January 1854 the bill was altered to allow popular sovereignty and to set up two territories (Kansas and Nebraska) rather than one. Because of these concessions the South approved and the territories were organized in May 1854.

The compromises that Douglas made on this issue were those that he felt he must make as the leader of a divided party to pass legislation he considered vitally important. He believed that popular sovereignty would solve the slavery controversy and obtain for him southern support necessary for his nomination and election to the presidency. Douglas also felt that by his concessions the central route would win out in its bid for the Pacific railroad, and this would be pleasing to his Illinois constituents as well as beneficial to his own, real-estate interests. Although his compromise did open up the area, it did not result in the panacea that he hoped for. Rather it let loose on the United States Pandora's Box. Not only did it not solve the slavery controversy, but it helped cause the Civil War and delayed the chartering of a transcontinental railroad until long after Douglas was in his grave.

The territory of Kansas included the area lying between the western boundary of Missouri and the eastern boundary of Utah. Between 1854 and 1860 this beleaguered territory had ten governors. Threats and sudden death accounted for the rapid turnover. Under the popular-sovereignty rule, both the North and the South decided that Kansas would be theirs. Even though the proslavery group in Missouri was closer, the North (especially New

England) was unwilling to give up without a fight. The headquarters of the contestants were Atchison, founded by the proslavery Missourians in 1854, and Lawrence, founded by the New England Emigrant Aid Society in the same year. The trouble came to a head in March 1855 when an election was held to determine the status of slavery in Kansas. The New England group sent out a large number of abolitionists, but they were far outnumbered by the 5,000 Missourians who crossed the border in waves to vote. The slavery forces carried the day by a vote of seven to one. Due to evidence of fraudulent voting, President Franklin Pierce called for a new election in May; again the slavery group won. The first capital of Kansas was the slavery stronghold at Atchison. The pro-slavery assembly immediately passed statutes to insure slavery; when the governor vetoed them, he was removed on charges of land speculation.

In the meantime the free soilers met at Topeka in October 1855 and established an abolitionist government. There were now two governments in Kansas. The pro-slavery sheriff of Douglas County, of which Lawrence was the hub, was shot trying to arrest abolitionists and enforcing the law as he saw it. To deliver the warrants to the many abolitionists in Lawrence considered responsible for the shooting, the federal marshall assembled an army of 800 bushwhackers who went into Lawrence and burned a part of the town. The free soilers armed with Sharp's rifles ("Beecher's Bibles"), named after the abolitionist pastor, Henry W. Beecher, retaliated in kind.

Also as a result of the Lawrence affair, the fanatical John Brown went to Pottawatomie Creek and hacked five pro-slavery men to death. The pro-slavery group had their revenge in clearing Pottawatomie Creek of every free soiler. A group of small wars took place in 1856. John Brown, alone, participated in raids on Franklin, Battle Mound, Sugar Creek, Osawatomie, and Black Jack. Both the free soilers and the slavery men began to organize armies, but the governor ordered them to disband and they did. John Brown kept the fire ablaze by liberating Negro slaves both in Kansas and Nebraska. The governor of Kansas and the president of the United States both offered rewards for Brown's capture. Brown did amazingly well in eluding his pursuers. His daring raids finally came to an end in his climactic and fatal attack on Harper's Ferry in 1859.

William C. Quantrill, the famous raider, also came to Kansas in 1857; and between Brown and Quantrill and their followers, life in Kansas was hazardous. During the three-year period 1856 to 1859, an estimated 56 to 200 persons were killed and around two-million dollars worth of property was destroyed. A part of this bloodshed, however, was over disputed land titles.

Meanwhile, political instability was the rule. Gerrymandering and non-registration of free-soil voters in 1857 assured victory for the pro-slavery group in the selection of the members for the constitutional convention. However, in the territorial election later in the year, the free soilers elected the delegates to Congress and to the legislature. But the slavery group continued to write the Lecompton Constitution. In the two elections held to ratify this constitution, the first was boycotted by the free soilers and the second by the slavery group. Despite the lack of support for the Lecompton Constitution in Kansas, President James Buchanan sent it to Congress with the recommendation to accept in order to keep peace in Kansas. Douglas opposed the acceptance of this constitution which he felt was an affront to the principle of popular sovereignty. It at first appeared, however, that Douglas' opposition would not prevent the admittance of Kansas as a slave state. William H. English of Indiana proposed a compromise which stated that if Kansas would accept the Lecompton Constitution, it would be admitted as a state and receive a large land grant. But Kansas still refused to accept the Lecompton document and the state's admission to the Union was delayed. In 1859 the Republican Party was established in Kansas and its ranks were swelled by the free soilers. Gerrymandering resulted in the constitutional convention of 1859 being dominated by Republicans, many of whom had come from Ohio and Indiana. Although the convention delegates obtained provisions from a number of constitutions, the Ohio constitution served as their main source. This Republican-inspired document, which forbade Negro voting, was approved by a two-to-one vote. After a controversy over the site of the capital, Topeka was selected. When Kansas asked Congress for admission under its free-soil constitution in December 1859, it was ignored.

Kansas had to wait until January 1861 when the Republican party was in control of Congress to be admitted to the Union.

Admission of Nebraska

Nebraska, whose development had been linked with Kansas' up to 1854, was the tenth midwestern state to enter the Union in 1867. Nebraska's territorial history was far less hectic than that of its sister state. By the time the Kansas-Nebraska Act became law, much of the land along the Platte River had been cleared of Indians. The Platte River Valley had long been important because of the Oregon and California trails which followed its winding course.

Although Nebraska had a number of territorial governors, their short tenures in office were due to less violent causes than their Kansas counterparts. President Franklin Pierce appointed Francis Burt, a South Carolina editor, as the first governor; he died of natural causes two days after taking the oath of office. Burt was succeeded by the territorial secretary, Thomas B. Cuming of Iowa, who became acting governor. Cuming, who was bribed by Omaha, was instrumental in having that town selected as the territorial capital. The following year Mark W. Izard was appointed governor, and Nebraska adopted the civil and criminal code of Iowa. The territorial governor's office of Nebraska was not a particularly sought after office. Nebraska was remote, and the office paid only $2,500. The most able and experienced of the territorial governors was William A. Richardson of Illinois, a friend of Douglas.

During its early territorial period, Nebraska was controlled by the Democratic Party. It was made a territory by a Democratic administration, its early governors were Democratic, and the first elected legislature had 27 Democrats and 12 Whigs. By 1859, however, the division of strength was nearly equal. In the election of that year, the Republican candidate, Samuel G. Daily, was chosen territorial delegate. In 1860 the Democratic J. Sterling Morton beat Daily by 14 votes; but because of the Republican control in Washington, Daily was seated. The persistent Morton ran again in 1862 and 1866, but both times was defeated by small margins. The Homestead Law strengthened the Republican position in Nebraska immeasurably. After the Civil War Nebraska filled up with Union veterans and became staunchly Republican.

In the period 1861 to 1863 Nebraska nearly assumed its present boundaries with the creation of Colorado, Dakota, and Idaho territories. Statehood in Nebraska was again opposed because it would increase the taxes. In 1866 the Republicans pushed through a constitution despite the opposition. This proposed constitution had a provision that Negroes could not vote. But the Republican Congress would not allow Nebraska in the Union with this anti-Negro clause. Nebraska reluctantly complied and became a state in March 1867. With statehood Nebraska received three-and-one-half-million acres of land for education, public buildings, and improvements.

Admission of the Dakotas

The Dakotas as territories had a very disorganized existence up to 1861. The Dakotas, with the exception of the small northern portion acquired by the United States in the Convention of 1818, were originally in the Louisiana and Missouri territories. After 1834 the sections east of the Missouri River were successively parts of the Michigan, Wisconsin, Iowa, and Minnesota territories. In contrast the western part of the Dakotas remained nominally in the Missouri Territory as Indian country until 1854, when it was incorporated as a part of the newly-established Nebraska Territory. When Minnesota became a state in 1858, the part of Dakota east of the Missouri River was left with no government. After several mass meetings, the residents of this unorganized part of Dakota finally persuaded Congress to create a new Dakota Territory, which not only united all of the Dakotas once more but also included Montana east of the Continental Divide and the northern half of Wyoming. In 1863 Idaho Territory was established, and Dakota Territory was reduced in size to include only the two, present-day Dakotas. Yankton was designated the territorial capital.

Many of Dakota's early settlements were connected with Indians, explorers, and forts. The Lewis and Clark expedition reached the Mandan village at Ft. Clark in 1804. Manuel Lisa, operating out of St. Louis, had trading posts in the Dakotas by 1808. John Fremont, Colonel Henry Atkinson, and Major S. H. Long also visited the Dakotas. In the 1850's the northern part of Dakota was considered as one of the four, possible routes for the transcontinental railroad and was surveyed for that purpose by General I. I. Stevens, governor of Washington Territory.

The forts in the Dakotas were legion. They included Forts Abercrombie, Lincoln, Buford, Clark, Pembina, Ransom, Rice, Totten, and Yates. Widely scattered they were built for reservation posts, defense against the Indians, protection for the building of the railroad, and protection of the mail routes.

The Western Land Company of Iowa, the Dakota Land Company of Minnesota, and the Homestead Act were especially important in the settlement of the Dakotas in the 1850's and 1860's. The removal of the Sioux in 1868 was followed by a five-year, settlement boom. By 1873 Dakota Territory had 20,000 people. In the 1870's the Black Hill's gold rush and the activities of James J. Hill of the Northern Pacific Railroad contributed greatly to the populating of the area.

North and South Dakota's approach to statehood was held up thirteen years after 1876 because the Democratic and Republican states were evenly balanced and each side thought the other would gain a political advantage if the Dakotas were admitted. Finally in 1889 the Dakotas, along with Montana and Washington, were granted statehood when the Republicans obtained a majority in Congress. The Republicans hoped in this way to insure a continuance of their party in power; a tactic which proved to be of little benefit.

Although the people of Dakota Territory had wanted to divide into two separate territories earlier, this division did not occur until they attained separate statehood in 1889. At that time they were divided on an east-west line designed to keep each of the two, large-populated areas together. They also divided up their public buildings and debt which had accrued during their joint territorial days. Upon their separation North Dakota retained Bismarck as its capital, and South Dakota selected Pierre as its center of government.

In the enabling acts for the admission of the Dakotas, Congress specified that these territories must follow certain guidelines in the writing of their constitutions. They had to renounce all claim to public or tribal lands, maintain a public, non-sectarian school system, and tax residents and nonresidents equally. Despite these provisions, the constitutions of these two states still reflected the Dakota residents' dislike of corporations, railroads, and banks.

— 29 —

Political Issues and Personalities

Slavery and Abolition

In the forty years after 1820, one of the leading political questions facing the United States was slavery. During most of the period, the people of the Midwest were divided on the subject. The controversy, given new emphasis by the Missouri Compromise of 1820, reached its crescendo in the Civil War. The West did not form a definite view on slavery until the 1850's when it was forced to take sides. Half the midwestern states came in under the pair arrangement made famous by the Missouri Compromise, in which the slave state of Missouri was paired with the free state of Maine. With the exception of Missouri, however, the midwestern states constituted the free state in these groupings. Indiana was matched by the admission of Mississippi; Illinois by Alabama; Michigan by Arkansas; Iowa by Florida; and Wisconsin by Texas. There was even a plan to pair Minnesota and Kansas with Kansas as the slave state, but Kansas refused to enter as a slave state and as a result Minnesota joined the Union without a partner. The Midwest was accustomed to this type of compromise and generally displayed little reaction to this pairing arrangement.

At the same time the Midwest was the scene of some abolitionist groups and underground-railroad activity. Benjamin Lundy, an ardent abolitionist, began the *Genius of Universal Emancipation* in 1821 at Mt. Pleasant, Ohio. Other abolitionists in the Ohio area included Charles B. Finney, Lyman Beecher, and Theodore D. Weld. Weld, who was busy in Ohio during the 1830's, converted James G. Birney to the abolitionist cause. A number of students and faculty left Lane Seminary in Cincinnati and went to Oberlin in a protest against slavery. In 1835 Oberlin began admitting Negro students. Ohio had an estimated 17,000 abolitionists in 1838.

Elsewhere in the Midwest, anti-slavery societies made slow progress. Elijah P. Lovejoy, trained as a Presbyterian minister, was a leader in the anti-slavery struggle in the 1830's as a newspaper editor in St. Louis, Missouri, and Alton, Illinois. In Wisconsin the first abolition society was formed in Racine County in 1840. The most prominent Wisconsin abolitionist was Sherman M. Booth, who was in turn editor of the *American Freeman* at Prairieville (Waukesha) and the *Free Democrat* at Milwaukee. Michigan had James G. Birney, who was a resident of that state when he was the Liberty Party candidate in 1840. In Minnesota Mrs. Jane G. Swisshelm of Kentucky joined the chorus late and began an abolitionist paper, the *Visitor,* at St. Cloud in January 1858.

Nearly every midwestern state had an underground railroad. An estimated 75,000 slaves escaped through these routes between 1812 and 1861. Levi Coffin, a longtime resident of Cincinnati, helped to dispatch 3,000 Negroes across Ohio and Indiana. Needless to say, these slave-escape routes were a great source of irritation to the South.

Even when a slave owner did find an escaped slave, he might not be successful in taking him south. In 1847 in Michigan, a Kentuckian tried to take his runaway slave, Adam Crosswhite, to Kentucky, but the citizens of Michigan would not allow it. Five years later Wisconsin was the scene of an equally famous, fugitive-slave case. Joshua Glover, who had escaped from his master in Missouri, came to work in a mill in Racine. His owner discovered his whereabouts. With the aid of some United States officials, the owner captured Glover and put him in a Milwaukee jail. Mobs from Racine and Milwaukee rushed to free him and the one led by Sherman M. Booth succeeded. Glover escaped to Canada. For the next six years, Booth was the center of a legal battle over the Fugitive Slave law. After several brief confinements in prison, President Buchanan finally pardoned Booth in 1861.

On the other hand, the people and constitutions of the mid-western states displayed tendencies that were decidedly unfriendly to Negroes and their partisans. In both Indiana and Illinois, slavery nearly succeeded in gaining a foothold. Illinois kept an indenture clause in its constitution of 1818 under which 700 to 800 slaves were being held on Illinois soil when that state joined the Union. Not until 1824 did Illinois conclusively vote for the exclusion of slavery. As late as 1837 Illinois generally opposed abolitionists. Elijah P. Lovejoy was driven out of St. Louis and later killed by a mob in Alton, Illinois, because of his abolitionist editorials. Missouri actually became a slave state by the Compromise of 1820. Later, most of the North Central states did not want free Negroes within their borders. Ohio favored colonization of Negroes outside the United States in the 1830's, partly because it did not want them coming into Ohio. Not until 1848 did Ohio repeal its black laws, which denied Negroes the right to testify against a white person and required them to post bond against becoming public charges. From the beginning Indiana refused Negroes the right to go to public schools and, in its second constitution of 1851, even denied Negroes the right to come into the state.

Yet another unfriendly gesture toward Negroes in the Midwest was the provision in all the state constitutions that a person must be white in order to vote. Wisconsin included a provision for Negro suffrage in the first draft of its constitution, but the clause was removed from the constitution that was adopted. Wisconsin did pass a law allowing Negroes to vote in 1849, but its validity was questioned until 1866 when it was finally upheld by the Wisconsin Supreme Court. As late as 1850 both Indiana and Ohio denied the suffrage to Negroes in their revised constitutions. Nebraska even tried to put a provision in its constitution denying the Negro the right to vote in 1867, but Nebraska had to delete this provision in order to obtain admittance to the Union.

Although the midwestern states still did not want Negroes within their borders, they did become more sympathetic to the slave after 1850. Seven events were primarily responsible. Attempts by slaveholders to recapture runaway slaves under the Fugitive Slave Act of 1850 left a bad taste in many a midwesterner's mouth. The repeal of the Missouri Compromise, "Bleeding Kansas," the Dred Scott decision, and the Lecompton Constitution angered

Dred Scott (c. 1795-1858)
Negro slave made famous by
Dred Scott v. Sanford

Courtesy New York Historical Society. From *Dictionary of American Portraits* by Hayward and Blanche Cirker, Dover Publications, Inc., New York, 1967. *Reprinted through permission of the publisher.*

Lewis Cass (1782-1866)
Secretary of War, Secretary of State,
Congressman, U. S. Senator

Engraving by John C. Buttre. From *Dictionary of American Portraits* by Hayward and Blanche Cirker, Dover Publications, Inc., New York, 1967. *Reprinted through permission of the publisher.*

"County Election"
Painting by George C. Bingham (1851)

others. Harriet Beecher Stowe's *Uncle Tom's Cabin* and John Brown's unsuccessful raid on Harper's Ferry furnished still more emotional fuel.

The Middle West was not strongly opposed to slavery in the South, but it did oppose extension of slavery into the territories. The midwesterner did not want slave labor present and competing on lands that he viewed as the exclusive domain of white men. The Kansas-Nebraska Act and then the Dred Scott decision convinced the people of the Midwest that the southerners were determined to invade every part of the United States with their slave-labor system. The South was so desperate in its attempts to push slavery into every corner of the Union that it deserted Stephen A. Douglas and split the Democratic Party when he stated that a territory could prevent slavery by not passing slave codes (the Freeport Doctrine) and when he would not support the Lecompton Constiution for Kansas. Douglas was willing to support popular sovereignty and give the South a chance to make the territories slave, but he wanted the contest to be fair. The South, feeling itself slipping, would settle for nothing less than the right to take their slaves into any territory with the guarantee that the federal government would protect them. This, the Midwest would not allow, and as a result the parties split, the Midwest went Republican, and the Union divided.

Public Land Policy

The Midwest continually used its political influence to obtain more liberal, land politics. The aspirations of the West on public-land policy were expressed by Thomas H. Benton. He wanted pre-emption, graduation in land prices, and eventually free land. He obtained his first goal in the Pre-emption Act of 1841, which permitted settlers, who had squatted without authority on Indian or unsurveyed land, first chance to purchase their land at the minimum price. Specifically, the act gave pre-emption rights to heads of families, bachelors over 21 years of age, widows, and aliens who had filed an intention of becoming citizens. People who already owned 320 acres were ineligible for a pre-emption claim. It also provided that ten per cent of the net proceeds from the sale of public lands was to be given to the state in which sold and the other ninety per cent was to be distributed among all the states and territories on the basis of their population. This latter provision became inoperative in 1843, because the South had inserted the phrase that this distribution would cease when the average tariff rate exceeded twenty per cent. Pre-emption as such continued until 1891, when it was repealed.

After an interlude in which the Free Soil Party (stood for free land and free men) reached its peak, Benton's second goal, the Graduation Act, was finally passed in 1854. The act provided that land held on the market for a long period of time was gradually reduced in price; from $1.25 down to $1.00 after ten years and with gradual reduction down to twelve-and-one-half cents an acre after thirty years.

The culmination of the liberalization of land laws occurred in 1862 with the passage of the Homestead Act. From 1852 to 1860 homestead bills were voted down by an alliance of South and East. But in the election of 1860, the Republicans, desiring to win, devised a platform formula pleasing to both the West and East. The winning compromise was free homesteads for the West and a high tariff and a national bank for the East. With the catalyst of the slavery issue, the Republicans were elected, the South seceded, and the West obtained free homesteads. The Homestead Act which became law in May 1862 provided that the head of a family or a person over 21 could receive 160 acres free. He had to live on the land five years and meet certain improvement requirements. This land-policy evolution demonstrated the growing political power of the West.

Middle Western Political Leaders

The number of leading, national politicians contributed by the Middle West prior to the Civil War was negligible compared to the number in the post-Civil War era. This is easily explained by the fact that the Midwest was a relatively new area and it took time for it to gain population and political influence. One of the first midwestern politicians of national significance was Senator Jesse B. Thomas of Illinois who devised the successful formula for the Missouri Compromise. One of the best-known politicians of the Midwest was William H. Harrison. He served as the territorial delegate from the Northwest Territory, governor of Indiana Territory, congressman, senator, a general in the War of 1812, and minister to Colombia prior to running for the presidency as a Whig in 1836. In 1840 he ran again and was successful. He was the first president elected from the Middle West (Ohio). His success proved to be short lived, however, because he died of bilious pleurisy a month after taking the presidential office.

One of the most colorful of the early midwestern politicians was James Shields. Born in Ireland he came to Illinois at the age of twenty one. In 1836 he was elected to the state legislature. Soon after he was appointed state auditor of Illinois. A Democrat, he once challenged his Whig critic, Abraham Lincoln, to a duel. Lincoln accepted with the understanding that they had to fight with broadswords at ten feet. They went to Missouri to duel; while there, they patched up their quarrel. Shields also served on the Illinois Supreme Court and as commissioner general of the Land Office in the Polk administration. He was a U. S. senator from Illinois for six years; Minnesota, one year; and Missouri, thirty-nine days. He also served as a brigadier general in the Mexican and Civil wars.

Another noted Democratic politician from the West was Thomas H. Benton of Missouri. Born in North Carolina, he moved to Tennessee and then to Missouri in 1815. He served as a United States senator from Missouri from 1821 to 1851. He lost his senate seat because he opposed the secessionists and favored the gradual abolition of slavery. His last official position was that of United States representative from 1853 to 1855. He ran for governor of Missouri at the age of seventy four in 1856, was defeated, and died of cancer two years later. One of the most outspoken and influential of midwestern politicians, he advocated sound money, opposed the national bank, championed a liberal land policy, opposed the annexation of Texas, and favored a

Thomas H. Benton (1782-1858)
U. S. Senator

Engraving by John Rogers. From *Dictionary of American Portraits* by Hayward and Blanche Cirker, Dover Publications, Inc., New York, 1967. *Reprinted through permission of the publisher.*

Salmon P. Chase (1808-1873)
Governor of Ohio, U. S. Senator, Secretary of the Treasury, Chief Justice of the United States

Courtesy National Archives, Brady Collection. From *Dictionary of American Portraits* by Hayward and Blanche Cirker, Dover Publications, Inc., New York, 1967. *Reprinted through permission of the publisher.*

Stephen A. Douglas (1813-1861)
U. S. Senator

Daguerreotype by Mathew Brady. Courtesy Library of Congress. From *Dictionary of American Portraits* by Hayward and Blanche Cirker, Dover Publications, Inc., New York, 1967. *Reprinted through permission of the publisher.*

Edwin M. Stanton (1814-1869)
Attorney General and Secretary of War

gradual abolition of slavery. He was an untiring representative of the active West. He represented them not only in the measures he advocated, but also in his manner of speech which was earnest, boastful, buoyant, and idealistic.

The Democrat Lewis Cass had a political career that paralleled William H. Harrison's. Born in New Hampshire, Cass began the practice of law in Zanesville, Ohio. A brigadier general in the War of 1812, he was with Harrison at the battle of the Thames. In 1813 he was appointed governor of Michigan Territory. He served as secretary of war and minister to France in the Jackson administration. Later he was elected to the United States Senate from Michigan and afterward was appointed secretary of state in Buchanan's cabinet. He often is given credit for developing the popular-sovereignty theory. Nominated as the Democratic presidential standard bearer in 1848, he was defeated by General Zachary Taylor.

John McLean, born in New Jersey, wandered west with his parents and was admitted to the bar in Ohio in 1807. He began his political life as a Democrat and served four years in the House of Representatives. In 1816 he was elected to a judgeship on the Ohio Supreme Court. He held the post of postmaster general in James Monroe's and John Q. Adams' administrations and was appointed an associate justice of the Supreme Court in 1829. He was partially responsible for the Supreme Court hearing the Dred Scott case which he wanted to use to strike a blow against slavery. Instead, Chief Justice Roger B. Taney obtained the upper hand and in effect made slavery legal in all the territories and in many states of the United States; a decision which hastened the outbreak of the Civil War.

Other cabinet members from the Midwest who served prior to the Civil War included Thomas Ewing of Ohio, who was secretary of the treasury under Harrison and secretary of the interior under Taylor; Edward Bates of Missouri, who was secretary of war under Taylor; Thomas Corwin of Ohio, who was secretary of the treasury under Millard Fillmore; Robert McClelland of Michigan, who was secretary of the interior under Franklin Pierce; and Edwin M. Stanton of Ohio, who was attorney general under James Buchanan.

The single Speaker of the House provided by the Midwest prior to the Civil War was John W. Davis of Indiana, who served in that capacity from 1845-1847. He was chosen permanent chairman of the Democratic National Convention in 1852.

Two other midwestern politicians, Salmon P. Chase and Benjamin Wade, well known for their bitter opposition to slavery, were elected to the Senate from Ohio in 1848 and 1851, respectively. Their unwillingness to compromise on the slavery issue helped to bring on the Civil War.

Two of the most prominent figures in the pre-Civil War era were Stephen A. Douglas and Abraham Lincoln of Illinois. Douglas was born in Vermont. Of small stature and great intellect, he was early dubbed, "the little giant." He moved to Illinois where he was admitted to the bar in 1834. A supporter of Andrew Jackson, he early became a Democratic leader in the West. He served as a member of the Illinois legislature and Illinois Supreme Court. A long time member of the U. S. Senate (1847-1861), one of his most noted accomplishments was the Kansas-Nebraska bill in 1854. This attempt to settle the "extension of slavery into the territories" peacefully with popular sovereignty resulted in bullets. Douglas' compromise position on the extension of slavery in the territories was made even more precarious in 1858. In their campaign for an Illinois senatorship in 1858, Lincoln and Douglas had a series of debates. In the one at Freeport, Lincoln asked Douglas if there was any way that a territory could keep slavery out prior to becoming a state. Douglas answered yes, that if a territory failed to pass slave codes, it would be possible to keep slaves out. Although this answer helped win him the senatorial election of 1858, it lost him the support of the southern wing of the Democratic Party, which felt that Douglas should have backed the Dred Scott decision. Douglas, who had run for the Democratic nomination for president in 1852 and 1856, finally obtained it in 1860 from the northern branch of the Democratic Party. Defeated by Lincoln, he died in 1861, having witnessed the beginning of the Civil War.

Lincoln, the Republican who defeated Douglas for the presidency in 1860, had a "rags to riches" story. Born in a log cabin in Kentucky, he moved with his migrant father, Thomas Lincoln, across Indiana and into Illinois. He served in the Black Hawk War and in his second attempt in 1834 obtained a seat in the Illinois legislature. Off to a slow start in both law and politics, he finally managed to win a seat in the U. S. House of Representatives in 1846. In Congress he worked with his Whig colleagues in opposing war with Mexico and introduced the "Spot Resolution," which questioned whether American troops were actually on American soil when attacked. Defeated for his efforts he remained only moderately active in politics until 1854, when he was again stirred to action by the Kansas-Nebraska affair. He made over fifty speeches on this issue. He helped in the formation of the Republican Party and supported John C. Fremont for president in 1856. Defeated for senator in 1858, he was nominated and elected president in 1860, a relatively untried national politician. The South took his election as a defeat for its cause and began state by state to secede from the Union. Lincoln was thus faced with a Civil War, which he battled through to a successful conclusion.

The Middle West and National Elections

Frontiersmen of the Midwest played the game of politics with great enthusiasm. Politics filled a social need and the first newspapers were established primarily to serve as political organs. Political opponents attacked each other with zest, and politicians found the friendship or control of one or more papers almost a necessity. Candidates could be nominated and launched easily, but in the early days it was in bad taste for a candidate to announce for office. He was supposed to be drafted. Much of the campaigning was done in person. Candidates tried to ingratiate themselves with voters by giving them a hand with their work for a few minutes. Political candidates were at all the meetings and they passed out free liquor.

In the national elections of this period, the Midwest reflected its views on political issues as much as can be shown in an election. In 1844 the Midwest went solidly for James K. Polk and manifest destiny, even though Polk was more southern and more pro-slave than the Midwest would have preferred.

Although extension of slavery into the territories was a dominant issue in all of the national elections between 1848 and 1860, the people and the candidates tried to disregard it. The election of 1848 was dominated by the Wilmot Proviso (provided that slavery would not be allowed in any area acquired from Mexico during the Mexican War), but both Lewis Cass and Zachary Taylor, a Mexican war hero, completely ignored it. The North Central states unanimously supported Cass, but they probably did it mainly because Cass was a Democrat and from Michigan rather than because of any particular issue. Again in 1852 the election was dominated by the slavery issue. This time it was the Compromise of 1850. Both the Democrats and the Whigs officially favored enforcement of the Compromise, but the Midwest and the nation somehow received a hint that General Winfield Scott, the Whig candidate, opposed it. Consequently this factor probably influenced the Midwest into going solidly for Franklin Pierce of New Hampshire as did most of the nation.

Unlike 1848 and 1852 the Midwest came solidly to grips with the extension of slavery into the territories in the elections of 1856 and 1860. In fact the Midwest played a leading role in the formation of the new anti-slavery party which replaced the disintegrating Whig Party. At Jackson, Michigan, in July 1854, one of the anti-slavery groups assumed the name Republican Party. Free Soilers, Anti-Nebraska Democrats, and Conscience Whigs flocked into this new party. The Republicans, running on a platform of repeal of the Kansas-Nebraska Act and the Fugitive Slave Act of 1850, were temporarily halted by the Know Nothings, a party dedicated to the policy of ignoring the major issues of the day. The widening split in the nation over the slavery issue was reflected in the votes of the Midwest in 1856. The four northernmost midwestern states of Iowa, Wisconsin, Michigan, and Ohio voted for the defeated Republican candidate, John C. Fremont. Missouri, Illinois, and Indiana voted for the victorious James Buchanan.

Again in 1860 the Midwest played a role in the Republican Party proceedings. The Republican convention met in Chicago at the newly-constructed Wigwam and, instead of nominating William H. Seward for president as they were supposed to, nominated Abraham Lincoln. Unlike 1856 the midwestern states in 1860 much more solidly supported the victorious Lincoln against Stephen A. Douglas. Only Missouri remained true to Douglas.

Several factors contributed to thte Midwest aligning itself with the Northeast against the extension of slavery. In the decade of the 1850's, an increasing number of East-West railroads were built. This meant that more of the western trade began to move east instead of south, and midwestern sympathies tended to shift with their trade. In addition, over a million settlers from New York, New England, and Germany arrived in the Middle West during the 1850's, and they were predominately anti-slavery. Moreover, the Republican Party had a provision for free land for the settlers (the Homestead Act) and many midwesterners liked this. Most important, however, the South talked of secession which the nationalistic Midwest could not stomach. The Middle West would compromise on slavery but not on Union.

Although the Midwest had only one state, Ohio, voting in the national elections in the period 1804 to 1812, it had eight by 1860. As the number of midwestern states and their respective populations grew, the political influence of the Midwest increased proportionately. Generally, the Midwest gave a majority of its votes to the Democratic Party at the national level. The only exceptions were 1840 when a majority of midwestern states voted for William H. Harrison and 1856 and 1860 when a majority voted for John C. Fremont and Abraham Lincoln. Moreover, the Midwest was usually on the winning side in the presidential elections. In the period 1804 to 1860 a majority of the midwestern states voted for the winning presidential candidate 13 out of 15 elections.

Abraham Lincoln (1809-1865)
President of the United States

Ulysses S. Grant (1822-1885)
President of the United States

Photograph by Alexander Gardner. Courtesy Peter A. Juley and Son. From *Dictionary of American Portraits* by Hayward and Blanche Cirker, Dover Publications, Inc., New York, 1967. *Reprinted through permission of the publisher.*

George B. McClellan (1826-1885)
Union general in Civil War

Courtesy New York Historical Society. From *Dictionary of American Portraits* by Hayward and Blanche Cirker, Dover Publications, Inc., New York, 1967. *Reprinted through permission of the publisher.*

— 30 —

Wars, Foreign Affairs, And the Middle West

Mexican War and After

Even though the Midwest had some qualms about the acquisition of Texas because of the slavery issue, it was generally agreeable to adding the increased area. Benton opposed the annexation of Texas because he feared that it would bring on a war with Mexico. However, when the Mexican War did occur a year later, largely because of the Texas issue and the United States claim that the Rio Grande was the southern boundary, Benton and the Midwest were generally favorable to putting Mexico in its place and acquiring from Mexico the territory that became the southwestern United States. A large number of volunteers for the Mexican War came from the upper-Mississippi Valley.

One of the most colorful marches of the war, which had its origin in the Midwest, was that led by General Stephen W. Kearney of Missouri. Kearney led 300 regulars and 1,350 Missouri volunteers 900 miles from Ft. Leavenworth to capture Santa Fe and then on to California to take control of the West Coast.

Although the Midwest generally supported the Mexican War, some midwestern Whigs denounced the Democrats for instigating the war. Senator Thomas Corwin of the Ohio Whig delegation put their position in bitter terms when he said: "If I were a Mexican, I would tell you: Have you not room in your own country to bury your dead men? If you come into mine, we will greet you with bloody hands and welcome you to hospital graves." When Abraham Lincoln, a little known Whig representative from Illinois, introduced his famous "Spot Resolution," questioning if American troops were actually on American soil (they were stationed between the Nueces and Rio Grande rivers) when hostilities began, he did not make himself particularly popular with his constituents. At least he was defeated at the next election.

On the whole the Middle West remained generally isolationistic in all other foreign affairs except expansion up to the Civil War and after. While the region was interested in expansion and defending the honor of the United States, other foreign relations were generally of little interest to this inland area. The Midwest did develop some opposition to the reciprocal tariff act signed with Canada in 1854, but this was because the Midwest felt it was losing markets for its agricultural products. Unless foreign affairs affected them directly, the people of the Midwest ordinarily displayed relatively little interest.

Civil War and its Aftermath

The Midwest played a vigorous role in the Civil War. This region not only made possible the election of Abraham Lincoln, the South's immediate reason for seceding, but it also contributed a large number of men to fight the war. Out of a total of approximately 2,775,000 troops in the Union forces, the North Central states furnished around 1,180,000 troops, plus a substantial number to the Confederate cause.

As is demonstrated by these figures, the Midwest was predominately in sympathy with the objective of saving the Union. The nationalism of this region would not allow the Union to be divided without a struggle. Yet there was strong sympathy for the South in certain sections, especially in Missouri and in southern Illinois, Indiana, and Ohio. Economically tied to the South, southern Ohio did not want war. Ohio refused to re-enact personal liberty laws in 1860 in an attempt to placate the South. Senator Corwin of Ohio was the chairman of the "Committee of 33," instituted in 1860 to prevent secession. This committee proposed an amendment to guarantee slavery in the South forever and Ohio ratified it. From the beginning of the Civil War, Clement L. Vallandigham, United States representative from Dayton, opposed it. He felt the fighting should end and there should be a compromise peace. Copperheadism also took the form of anti-war, secret societies in southern Ohio in 1864, but these societies accomplished little.

Southern Indiana had a similar organization, the Knights of the Golden Circle. Members of this organization wore hoods and resembled the later Ku Klux Klan. They changed their name to the Order of American Knights and still later to the Sons of Liberty. Their purpose throughout was to resist the northern prosecution of the war.

Like Ohio and other midwestern states, Indiana and Wisconsin were vigorous in resisting the draft. The people of Indiana felt that conscription entailed too much regimentation, and there was resistance in a number of counties. Although Wisconsin was generally for the Union, it strenuously resisted the draft and Republican suppression of civil liberties. The most serious rioting was in Port Washington in Ozaukee County, Wisconsin. Eighty people were arrested for resisting conscription. Many men went to Canada rather than serve in the army.

Although southern Illinois was frankly sympathetic to the South in early 1861, Douglas helped to keep it Union. The midwestern state that posed a real problem as to its allegiance was Missouri, a slave state. Missouri had a convention in February 1861 to decide on what course to follow. A resolution favoring war against the Union was defeated and a decision was postponed. Governor Claiborne F. Jackson, however, took steps to secede. On the other hand Frank P. Blair organized the Wideawakes, Republican marching groups, to protect the St. Louis arsenal. In April and May of 1861 the Wideawakes were mustered into federal service in lieu of the state militia that Jackson would not provide. Nathaniel P. Lyon, commanding the federalized Wideawakes, captured the state militia at Camp Jackson and a local civil war ensued. The state assembly met in night session, created a state army, and gave the governor virtual dictatorial powers. In August 1861 Lyon attacked the state forces under Sterling

Price. Assisted by Arkansas troops, Price defeated Lyon. Meanwhile, the moderates seized control and elected Hamilton R. Gamble as provisional governor. Price marched north in Missouri and won at Wilson's Creek and Lexington, but retreated before federal troops led by General John C. Fremont. Fremont irritated many Missourians by declaring martial law, heavily taxing southern sympathizers to care for unionist refugees, and freeing the slaves. President Lincoln countermanded this last action of Fremont. In October 1861 an assembly called by Jackson declared Missouri's secession from the Union. But the defeat of Price, commanding the state army, and the defeat of a Confederate force at Pea Ridge in northwest Arkansas, crushed Jackson's hopes of reestablishing his government in Missouri. Although raiding in Missouri continued, Missouri remained firmly in Union hands. In all, the state supplied around 110,000 troops to the Union armies and 50,000 to the Confederate cause.

The Midwest supplied a large part of the Union military leadership during the war. The most outstanding was Ulysses S. Grant, a West Pointer from Ohio who had fought in the Mexican War, had developed a drinking problem while in service in California, had failed at farming near St. Louis, Missouri, and was in his father's leather business in Galena, Illinois, when the war came. Given command of the Twenty-first Illinois Infantry, he demonstrated that he could discipline men and win battles. After trying a succession of other generals, Lincoln finally selected him to win the war for the North.

The second most noted midwestern general was General George B. McClellan. Also a former West Pointer, he was an official of the Ohio and Mississippi Railroad and lived at Cincinnati at the outbreak of the war. He began his career in the Civil War as a major general in command of all Ohio's troops. He was a thorough general and accomplished more as commander of the Union armies than any general save Grant. His main failing was that he was too slow and cautious in prosecuting the war. His most noted campaigns were in Virginia area. A good disciplinarian and defensive in military tactics, he displayed an indecision that prevented him from being a truly outstanding general.

General Irvin McDowell was also an Ohioan and a West Pointer. He was given command of the Army of the Potomac for a short time, but his disastrous defeat at Bull Run turned public opinion against him and he was replaced by McClellan. Later as commander of the Army of the Rappanhannock, he served with distinction at Cedar Mountain and the Second Battle of Bull Run.

Another of the succession of generals used by Lincoln in an attempt to win the war was General Ambrose E. Burnside of Indiana. Having fought at Bull Run, South Mountain, and Antietam, he was selected in the fall of 1862 to replace McClellan as commander of the Army of the Potomac. After being defeated by General Robert E. Lee at Fredericksburg, he was returned to a subordinate position and fought with Grant at the Wilderness and Cold Harbor.

Other interesting generals from the Midwest included George A. Custer of Michigan, Kit Carson of Missouri, and James Shields of Illinois. Custer, noted for his daring exploits, rose to the rank of major general in the Civil War. Kit Carson was brevetted a brigadier general by the federal government. His main task was keeping the Indians of the Southwest loyal to the Union. He died in his bed at the age of 59 in 1868. Shields supposedly defeated T. J. (Stonewall) Jackson at a small, bloody battle in the Civil War.

The Midwest also supplied a large number of political generals such as Carl Schurz, James A. Garfield, Rutherford B. Hayes, Benjamin Harrison, and David B. Henderson. They were called political generals because they received their commands largely because they were politicians and leaders of men. Several of them later reached the presidency and most of them entered politics after the Civil War. Out of eight congressmen elected in Indiana in 1866, for example, all had been in the Civil War. One had been a paymaster, one had been a captain, three had been brigadier generals, and one a major general.

Although the Midwest was the scene of few major battles during the Civil War, it was afflicted by numerous raids. Hardest hit were Missouri and Kansas. Missouri had a number of battles (described above) before it was certain that Missouri would remain in the Union. In 1863 Price took advantage of the removal of Union troops to move up to Jefferson City and Independence, but he was turned back at Westport by a federal force and driven out of Missouri. The worst problem in Missouri and Kansas were the raids carried out by guerrillas like Quantrill's raiders and the James H. Lane Brigade. William C. Quantrill had come to Kansas in 1857 and at first fought on both sides. Quantrill finally decided to join the Confederate cause. He ambushed federal troops in the area of Kansas City and killed 33. To stop these raiders the federal army locked up the wives and girl friends of the guerrillas to keep the latter from getting food, ammunition, and information. The building in which the Union soldiers imprisoned the women collapsed and four were killed and many others were injured. This made Quantrill and his men even more angry and in 1863 they sacked Lawrence, Kansas. Around 150 men were killed and 200 homes were burned. The loss was estimated at three quarters of a million dollars.

Senator James H. Lane of Lawrence used this episode to convince the War Department to issue Order Number 11, which required all rural families in Jackson, Cass, Bates, and (part of) Vernon counties to go into the garrisoned towns where they could be easily watched. Then all the grain, hay, and produce in those counties were destroyed so that they could not be used by the raiders. Many felt this federal order was worse than the raiders. At the same time the James H. Lane Brigade was engaged in burning and looting Confederates in the Kansas area. Around 1863 Lincoln setup the District of the Border between Kansas and Missouri in an effort to keep Lane's men from raiding into Missouri. In 1864 a new raiding force was introduced when Stand Watie's Indians were turned loose in Kansas. These raids were hard to stop even after the war was over.

Other raids in the Midwest were insignificant in comparison with those in Missouri and Kansas. In July 1861 Captain Adam Johnson, a Confederate officer from Kentucky, seized a ferryboat on the Ohio River and with the aid of thirty men crossed the river and captured a small Indiana town named Newburg. The invaders took what plunder they could find and left, having suffered no casualties. The next year General Kirby Smith invaded Kentucky and captured Lexington. General Lewis Wallace was dispatched to defend Cincinnati, but the expected attack did not occur. Later in 1863, however, General John H. Morgan crossed the Ohio River and attacked Corydon, Indiana. Three-hundred old men and boys, poorly armed, attempted to turn back Morgan; but when he began to shell the city, they retreated. Morgan then went north on a plundering expedition through Salem, Scottsburg, and Vernon, Indiana. At Vernon he began his retreat and most of his force was captured in Ohio. In 1864 a small Confederate force seized the American steamboat *Philo Parsons* at Windsor on Lake Erie. They were unsuccessful in their plan to free 3,000 southern prisoners held at Johnson's Island near Sandusky, Ohio.

Even though the Midwest was not the scene of many battles, it did serve as a vast reservoir of food, supplies, troops, and leadership for the Union during the Civil War. And although it divided slightly on such issues as conscription and how to handle the South, it was predominately in favor of keeping the South in the Union and the Negroes out of the territories.

After the Civil War the Midwest continued its peculiar combination of isolation and nationalism. Although the people of the region were generally little interested in foreign affairs, they were quick to take affront and threaten vigorous action if the affairs or honor of the United States were tampered with in any way. A combination of nationalism and economic shrewdness motivated the Midwest to support the United States in its attempt to collect damages from England for destruction of Union shipping during the Civil War. Known as the *Alabama* claims, they involved the destruction of Union shipping during the Civil War committed by vessels built in England and sold to the Confederacy.

— 31 —

Agriculture

Imported Plants and Animals

The original settlers coming over from Europe during the colonial period had brought with them plants and animals such as horses, cattle, pigs, peas, parsnips, turnips, carrots, wheat, rye, buckwheat, barley, oats, and apples. They had also gotten many plants from the Indians, including corn, pumpkins, squash, white potatoes, sweet potatoes, beans, tomatoes, rice, peanuts, peppers, watermelons, huckleberries, blackberries, strawberries, raspberries, cranberries, gooseberries, grapes, cherries, and plums.

Despite these earlier developments, however, the four decades between 1830 and 1870 were especially noted in agricultrue for the number of new strains of plants and breeds of domesticated animals brought into the United States. Shortly after 1800 the ministers in Spain and France, David Humphreys and Robert Livingston, purchased Merino sheep in those countries and shipped them to New York. During the 1820's much interest was displayed in these sheep by farmers in Indiana, Ohio, and Illinois. In the 1830's the midwesterners shifted their interest to the Cotswold, Southdown, New Leicester, and Saxony breeds which were larger and more productive of wool and meat.

Foreign cattle had been imported to the U. S. as early as 1795 to improve the midwestern cattle. Shorthorns came to the Ohio Valley from England in 1817. Although farmers at first thought Shorthorns were too fancy for them, they soon relented. Between 1820 and 1840 other western European breeds of cattle, including Herefords, Devons, Alderneys, Durhams, Guernseys, Ayrshires, Holsteins, and Jerseys, were imported into the Midwest. Indiana had large herds of Shorthorns, Devons, Durhams, Herefords, Ayrshires, Bakewells, Jerseys, and Holsteins by 1850. In Kansas in the 1870's an Englishman, George Grant, made a lasting contribution to cattle breeding. Desiring to raise either sheep or cattle, he purchased 69,000 acres from the Kansas Pacific Railroad near Victoria, Kansas. Having failed with sheep, he purchased a herd of long-horn cattle which he bred to black, English hornless bulls. This was one of the origins of Black Angus cattle in the United States.

There was a similar development in horses and mules. Most of the original pioneer horses in the eastern Midwest were small and scrawny. In 1832 Henry Clay imported a jackass from Spain which, crossed with horses, helped to begin the mule industry in Kentucky. German settlers brought Conestoga horses into Ohio, as well as Shakespeare, Messenger, and Diomede. French settlers introduced the Norman breed into Ohio in the late 1820's. Percheron stallions were brought in about 1851. With these new breeds coming in, the Midwest by 1840 became the largest producer of horses in the United States. Ohio, Indiana, and Michigan produced draft horses for the East and the Far West. Southern Illinois and Missouri were the suppliers for the South.

The hog industry had a similar origin and development. Breeds of hogs were brought in from England, China, and Spain. The United States also produced some breeds, such as the Chester (County) White of Pennsylvania and the Shaker hog (produced by Shaker farmers), one of the forerunners of the Poland China. Some of the breeds of hogs in Indiana were the Byfield, Woburn, Irish Grazier, Suffolk, Essex, Berkshire, and Poland China. With the influx of better breeds, the razorback began to disappear; by 1860 they were nearly gone. The average weight per hog on the Chicago market from 1856-60 was 228 pounds.

In the plant and seed line, red clover and timothy were introduced into Indiana in 1820, but they were grown very little until 1850. White clover and Kentucky Blue Grass also spread into the Midwest. Varieties of wheat in Indiana by 1850 included Red Chaff, Mediterranean, and Red Blue Stem. The average yield was 5 to 25 bushels per acre. Probably the most important seed for the drier sections of the Midwest was Turkey Red wheat brought to Kansas by Mennonite settlers from Russia in 1874. Sorghums, kaffir corn, soybeans, alfalfa, and sugar beets were also introduced into the area in the 1870's and 1880's. They had qualities which made them adaptable for dry land or irrigated farming.

Mechanization of Agriculture

An important development that accompanied the introduction of new plants and animals into the Midlands was mechanization. As late as 1800, large numbers of midwestern farmers were using wooden plows and oxen to break their land. In 1797 when Charles Newbold of New Jersey patented a plow made of cast iron, many farmers refused to use it because they believed that it would poison the soil. However, by 1825 Jethro Wood's cast-iron plows, costing about eight dollars each, were becoming plentiful. Despite its advantages, the cast-iron plow would not scour well. In 1833 John Lane of Chicago remedied this situation by inventing a steel plow, which would scour even in sticky soils. Four years later John Deere made his first steel moldboard from a saw blade. In 1838 plow manufacturing began to move from the blacksmith shop to the factory, and by 1845 there were seventy-three plow manufacturers making 61,334 plows annually. In 1858 John Deere alone was turning out 13,000 steel plows a year in his Moline, Illinois, plant. James Oliver of Indiana produced his first chilled-iron plow in 1869. Soon after F. S. Davenport and Robert Newton of Illinois perfected the first riding plow.

An even more elaborate set of inventions accompanied the perfecting of an implement for harvesting grain than for the breaking of the soil. By 1830 the scythe had been replaced by the cradle for cutting wheat. In 1833 Obed Hussey of Ohio produced a reaper (a horse-drawn conveyance). The following year Cyrus H. McCormick of Virginia perfected another. By 1846 these reapers were coming into vogue. McCormick built a reaper factory in Chicago in 1847 and within four years was turning out

John Deere (1804-1886)
Plow manufacturer

Courtesy Deere and Company. From *Dictionary of American Portraits* by Hayward and Blanche Cirker, Dover Publications, Inc., New York, 1967. *Reprinted through permission of the publisher.*

Cyrus H. McCormick (1809-1884)
Inventor and manufacturer of the reaper

From *Dictionary of American Portraits* by Hayward and Blanche Cirker, Dover Publications, Inc., New York, 1967. *Reprinted through permission of the publisher.*

William H. Russell (1812-1872)
Founder of the Pony Express

From *Dictionary of American Portraits* by Hayward and Blanche Cirker, Dover Publications, Inc., New York, 1967. *Reprinted through permission of the publisher.*

George C. Bingham (1811-1879)
Portrait painter

Self-portrait. Courtesy School District, Kansas City, Missouri. From *Dictionary of American Portraits* by Hayward and Blanche Cirker, Dover Publications, Inc., New York, 1967. *Reprinted through permission of the publisher.*

1,000 reapers a year. By 1852 an estimated 3,500 reapers were in operation in the Midwest.

Other modifications of the reaper were to follow. In 1843 George Esterly of Wisconsin invented a header. Fifteen years later C. W. and W. W. Marsh patented the "Marsh harvester," a reaper which by means of an endless apron delivered the grain to a table where two men could bind it. In 1878 John F. Appleby of Wisconsin patented the bird-bill knotter which made possible the grain binder. This knotter tied the wheat stalks in bundles rather than allowing them to fall loose and be tied by hand. William Deering and McCormick purchased the right to use Appleby's invention. As a result of the invention and perfection of the reaper, the number of men needed to cut and bind twelve acres of grain in a day had been reduced from twelve in 1840 to three in 1875.

Another aspect of harvesting grain was the actual removal of the kernels from the head. Although most of the wheat in the West in 1840 was beaten out by a flail or trampled out by animals, there were some stationary threshing machines in existence. The best machine on the market before 1840 was a machine invented by Hiram and John Pitt of Maine in 1836. It could thresh approximately twenty-five bushels per hour. Steam power did not replace horse power in operating these machines, however, until the 1860's. One of the largest manufacturers of threshing machines was Jerome I. Case of Wisconsin who turned to the manufacture of a variety of machinery after the Civil War. Later the thresher was further improved and remained the primary means of threshing grain well up into the twentieth century. Although the combine, which merged the binder and the thresher into one machine, was introduced into California in the 1880's, it did not become important even in the wheatlands of Kansas, Nebraska, and the Dakotas until after 1900. Its introduction into the eastern Midwest was even slower.

In the dairy industry, there was also a number of important inventions. W. F. Ketchum perfected the first successful mower in 1844. Hay rakes, both dump and side delivery, tedders, loaders, balers, and forks (for the unloading of hay) came along in the 1850's to greatly lessen the work in haying. In addition, there were also manure loaders and spreaders, shredding machines, corn shellers, and improved wagons. The dairy industry was also greatly aided by the invention of barb wire in 1874 by Joseph F. Glidden of DeKalb, Illinois. This made possible more systematic care of cattle. The cream separator was developed almost simultaneously in Denmark, Sweden, and Germany in 1878. A Frenchman developed the silo. In 1890 the milk tester was perfected by Dr. Stephen M. Babcock, head of the department of dairy husbandry at the University of Wisconsin.

Machines were introduced into other aspects of agriculture as well. Prior to 1850 seed was broadcast or planted by hand, but in that year seed drills began to make their appearance. Moses Pennock of Pennsylvania developed one of the most satisfactory ones. Corn planters and improved corn cultivators also appeared during the 1850's. The mechanical corn picker did not appear until 1890 and the corn binder two years later. The spring-tooth harrow was perfected by David L. Garver, a Michigan mechanic, in 1869. These inventions were very helpful to the Midwest during the Civil War and after to increase agricultural output and reduce manhours per unit of production.

—32—

Transportation

Land Conveyances

A number of different conveyances were used on the western traces and trails in the three decades after 1840. The most prevalent were wagons. The Conestoga, used in the settlement of the area east of the Mississippi, was replaced by the Murphy wagon manufactured in St. Louis. Sixteen miles in a day was a good distance for an oxen on the plains. Horses and mules, freighter wagons, and stage coaches were also plentiful. People migrating into Minnesota and the Dakotas on the Red River and Sauk River trails rode in two-wheel carts capable of hauling 800 to 1,000 pounds. The most unusual and inconvenient conveyances used were the handcarts pushed from Iowa City, Iowa, to Salt Lake City, Utah, by 3,000 Mormans around 1855.

Transportation companies were organized to operate on the western trails. Two stage lines came into being in 1850. One received a four-year contract to carry the mail from Independence to Salt Lake City; the other line made a monthly trip from Independence to Santa Fe. The most noted lines, however, were founded later. One of these established in 1858 was John Butterfield's Overland Mail line which followed a long, 2,800-mile semi-circular route connecting St. Louis, Ft. Smith, El Paso, Tucson, Los Angeles, and San Francisco. The trip took approximately three weeks, and two stages left St. Louis each week. The fare for passengers was $200. A second company, the Kansas City and Stockton Express begun in 1858, also connected Kansas and California.

Established in 1855, the largest freighting firm on the plains by 1860 was that of Russell, Majors, and Waddell. Not content with this accomplishment, however, William H. Russell, the plunger of the group, established a stage-coach line which merged into the Central Overland, California, and Pike's Peak Express. Russell also began the Pony Express from St. Joseph to San Francisco in 1860. It could deliver a letter between these two points in about 12 days. The Pony Express, which lasted about a year, as well as Russell's stagecoach venture, contributed to the financial collapse of Russell, Majors, and Waddell.

With the secession of the southern states, the Butterfield Overland Mail Line was transferred to the Platte Valley route. In 1862 Ben Holladay acquired both the Butterfield line and the Central Overland, California, and Pike's Peak Express. When he sold out to Wells Fargo in 1866, Holladay had succeeded in consolidating the northern stage lines to California into one company.

The standard freighting outfit of 25 freight wagons, a mess wagon, oxen, and miscellaneous equipment cost around $19,000. One of these heavy, canvas-covered wagons, drawn by six teams of mules or six yokes of oxen, could haul approximately 5,000 pounds of freight. The cost of freighting added greatly to the price of goods in the West. For example, the cost of flour and potatoes in the western Midwest was 20 to 30 cents a pound; onions, 35 to 50 cents a pound; and a box of matches, 50 to 75 cents.

For the passengers there were Concord coaches, manufactured by Abbott-Downing Company of Concord, New Hampshire. These swaying coaches, seating nine passengers, rolled through the Platte Valley, pulled by six horses or mules. They averaged about six miles per hour including stops. By the end of the Civil War the fare was around 27 cents a mile. The coming of the railroads hurt the wagon-and-stagecoach trade, even though they continued to distribute freight and passengers from the railroad stations until the advent of taxis and trucks.

During this period the horse was nearly indispensable in the Midwest. Droppings in the streets, and livery stables were a sign of the times. The livery stable and the blacksmith shop were the centers of interest and gossip. The narrow-rimmed wheels of wagons and buggies cut deep ruts during the rainy periods. Hitching posts connected with iron chains surrounded the court house. Business was conducted with a horse and wagon. A good, gray trotter and a glistening black buggy appealed greatly to the young ladies up to the turn of the century.

Steamboats

The rapid increase of steamboats on the western waters was indicated by their growing numbers. In 1820 there were 60 steamboats on western streams; in 1834, 230; in 1842, 450; and in 1860, 1,000.

There was a high incidence of accidents on these vessels. They hit sandbars and snags and their boilers blew up. Explosions could occur at any time, but racing made it more likely. Steamboat Bill and the *Whipporwill* are immortalized in a ballad which tells how the *Whipporwill's* boiler blew while racing the *Robert E. Lee.* The *New Orleans,* the first steamboat on the Ohio River, served as a packet to Natchez until it struck a snag and sank. The *Vesuvius,* built in 1814, grounded on a sandbar the same year and burned to the water's edge in 1816. The *Walk-In-The-Water* was wrecked in a gale near Buffalo in 1826. The *Tennessee* hit a log above Natchez in 1823 and 30 passengers were drowned. The *Constitution* burst a boiler and 11 persons were scalded to death. In 1832 the *Brandywine* burned near Memphis with the loss of 110 persons. These accidents caused the state and national governments to take action. In the 1830's the states passed laws ordering the safe handling of steamboats. Congress also appropriated money to remove river snags and sand bars. Between 1822 and 1860 the federal government spent three-million dollars on snag-removal projects. This helped, but there were still accidents. *Lloyd's Steamboat Directory of 1856* contained descriptions of 87 major steamboat disasters due to explosions, fires, snags, and collisions. One of the worst accidents occurred near Memphis, Tennessee, in 1865, when the steamboat *Sultana's* boiler blew. The vessel was swept by fire and 1,500 passengers were killed. All told over 400 vessels were sunk or damaged with losses amounting to about nine-million dollars. Despite its tremendous popularity, steamboating's profits were held down by accidents, cutthroat competition, and poor management. Few companies were able to make six percent on their investment. After 1860 steamboating rapidly declined because of the competition of the railroads.

Life and travel on the steamboats were colorful and exciting. The boat crews were generally rough and ready fellows. The dress of a boatman generally consisted of a red-flannel shirt, a blue jacket, brown trousers, and a fur cap. Cards and gambling were prevalent on board the passenger steamers. Natchez was the rendezvous for gamblers, prostitutes, and boatmen.

Passenger fare downstream from Louisville to New Orleans was $75.00 in 1818. By 1835 it had dropped to $25.00. Upstream fares were 60 per cent higher. As the streams became more navigable and the steamboats improved, their speed increased. In 1814 it took the *Enterprise* 25 days to go from New Orleans to Louisville. In the 1850's a steamboat could make the same trip in five days.

The steamboat served a major function in the trade and commerce of the Midwest from 1830 to 1870. Steamboats virtually took over the fur trade in the late 1830's. They also hauled much of the midwestern agricultural produce south and had a large passenger trade. As early as 1834 there were 126,278 tons of shipping on the Ohio and Mississippi rivers. The commerce of the Mississippi Valley in 1852 was an estimated $653,976,000, of which a large percentage was transported on steamboats. This North-South trade helped to hold the South and Midwest together in the 1840's and 1850's. The building of East-West railroads helped to cause a shift in this alignment and in part explained why in 1860 the Midwest stayed with the East in the Civil War. Except for local packets, the Mississippi River was closed to navigation below Cairo in 1861 for the first time in 160 years. Although steamboats had a revival after the Civil War, it was limited by the coming of the railroads.

Railroads

Canal building had hardly begun in the 1820's and 30's when railroads began to replace them. With the success of steam-driven boats, engineers decided that the steam engine might also be used to propel wheeled vehicles. George Stephenson's *Rocket* proved the practicability of steam railroads when it pulled a train weighing thirteen tons on the English Liverpool and Manchester Railroad at an average speed of 15 miles per hour in 1829. In time the advantages of railroads over canals were realized. Railroads provided more rapid transportation, they were cheaper to construct, they could be built nearly anywhere, and they were not affected by floods, ice, or droughts.

One of the first railroads chartered in the United States was the Baltimore and Ohio in 1827. It was begun by some Baltimore merchants who wished to obtain some of New York City's commerce with the West. The ground-breaking ceremony for the road occurred in Baltimore on July 4, 1828. At first there was some doubt as to whether horse power or steam power would be used on the road. But Peter Cooper's *Tom Thumb* won the day for steam in 1830 when it travelled the 13 miles from Baltimore to Ellicott's Mills in 75 minutes. Although the B and O's first 13 miles were completed by 1830, it did not reach the Ohio River until the 1850's.

The West followed the B and O project with great interest and began to plan on building railroads of its own. In Ohio the first railroad charter was granted to the Ohio and Steubenville in 1830, but it never got past the charter stage. The Mad River and Lake Erie Road (Springfield to Sandusky) received its charter in 1832. Construction, however, did not begin until 1835 and the first 30 miles were not completed until five years later. The first locomotive on this road was the *Sandusky,* which had been built at Patterson, New Jersey, and transported to Ohio via the Erie Canal. It was the first practical locomotive west of the Appalachian Mountains. Construction on the Mad River and

Lake Erie road bogged down for lack of money and was not completed until 1848.

Of the 24 railroads chartered in Ohio during the decade from 1830 to 1840, only one was actually built at that time. By 1850 Ohio had 300 miles of railroad. The Little Miami Railroad in conjunction with the Columbus and Xenia roads and the Cleveland, Columbus, and Cincinnati Railroad opened lines between Cincinnati and Sandusky, and Cincinnati and Cleveland in 1851. Two years later the New York and Erie built the New York Central to Toledo. During the same year the Pennsylvania Railroad was extended to Crestline, Ohio, where it joined the Cleveland, Columbus, and Cincinnati line. Railroads consolidated after 1865, and by 1880 Ohio had 5,655 miles of track.

Governor James B. Ray of Indiana advocated the construction of railroads as early as 1827. Six railroad charters were granted by the Indiana legislature in 1832. The Lawrenceburg and Indianapolis Railroad was the first to be vigorously promoted. Although stock subscriptions abounded, money was hard to raise for the 88-mile project. A one-and-one-quarter-mile section with a horse-drawn car was opened near Shelbyville in 1834. Indiana's first real railroad, the Madison and Indianapolis, was begun in 1836. The first nine miles were completed by 1838. In that year probably the first steam locomotive in Indiana was used on this line. The first 28 miles of the Madison and Indianapolis cost Indiana $1,624,603. It was finally completed to Indianapolis in 1847. The Monon line from New Albany to Chicago was opened in 1854. In the same year access to Indianapolis from Crestline, Ohio, was attained by the Bellefontaine and Indiana Railroad. Goods could now be sent from Philadelphia to the western border of Indiana through Springfield, Dayton, Crestline, and Richmond (or Crestline and Indianapolis) to Terre Haute. The mileage of Indiana railroads jumped from 228 in 1850 to 2,163 in 1860.

Michigan began chartering railroads in 1832 and quickly established 19 railroad corporations. The Erie and Kalamazoo line opened one of the first railroads in the West between Toledo and Adrian in 1836. It was 33 miles long and its locomotive was the *Adrian*. In 1837 Michigan borrowed $5,000,000 in an attempt to complete three railroads and two canals. But the eastern banks collapsed before the routes were completed in 1840, and Michigan was left with a number of half-finished projects. One of these railroads was the Detroit and St. Joseph chartered in 1832. Known as the Michigan Central, it had been constructed from Ann Arbor to Detroit by 1840, a distance of 44 miles. In 1846 the John M. Forbe's group purchased the unfinished Michigan Central and Michigan Southern from the state for $2,500,000. Within three years this group had built the Michigan Central Railroad to New Buffalo on Lake Michigan and had established a water connection to Chicago. Both the Central and the Southern were continued westward in 1851 and were completed to Chicago in 1852. By 1870 Michigan had 1,638 miles of railroads.

Illinois had early railroad dreams. In 1825 a company was incorporated with a capital stock of three-million dollars to build a railroad connecting Vincennes, Danville, Paris, and Chicago. Early in 1833 a bill to charter the Chicago and Illinois Railroad failed in the Illinois senate by one vote. No actual building was done, however, until after 1837. In that year the Illinois legislature committed Illinois to the creation of more than 1,300 miles of railroad in addition to canals and turnpikes. The total cost was to be ten-million dollars. When Illinois took stock in 1839, it had spent more than $10,000,000 and had only the Northern Cross Railroad and one canal which held any promise of future returns. The Northern Cross which connected Quincy and Springfield was completed in 1842. The locomotive on the line had mechanical difficulty and the line was soon abandoned. Eastern capitalists opened it in 1849 as the Sangamon and Morgan Railroad.

Cincinnati and St. Louis, concerned with the growing commercial importance of Cleveland, Toledo, Detroit, and Chicago, resolved to build a railroad of their own. Although the idea was suggested in 1832, a charter for the railroad was not granted by Ohio and Indiana until 1848 and by Illinois until 1851. This was the origin of the Ohio and Mississippi Railroad. It was begun in 1852 and the first 26 miles were completed two years later. Lack of funds delayed its completion until 1857. This road made possible a railroad trip from Baltimore to St. Louis, if one changed trains five times, crossed two rivers by ferry, and made two short trips by steamboat. Other railroads reaching the Mississippi River in the 1850's and 1860's included the Rock Island in 1854, the Northwestern (at Clinton, Iowa) in 1855, and the Illinois Central (at Dubuque) in 1869.

Chicago's first railroad was the Galena and Chicago begun in 1848. Successful from the outset, the railroad reached Elgin in 1850. Its first locomotive was a second-hand engine named *Alert* (later renamed *Pioneer*) purchased from the Michigan Railroad. Meanwhile, the Michigan Central and the Michigan Southern built westward toward Chicago and reached it is 1852. A few years later the Chicago, Burlington, and Quincy and the Rock Island connected Chicago with the Mississippi River; and the Chicago, Alton, and St. Louis connected Chicago to St. Louis. Chicago also had a rail connection with Indianapolis. By 1860 Chicago was well on its way to becoming the hub of the railway system and after the Civil War it outdistanced all competitors. By 1875 the New York Central, Pennsylvania, Erie, Baltimore and Ohio, and Grand Trunk had all reached Chicago. In 1879 Illinois had 7,578 miles of railroads.

In 1836 the Wisconsin territorial assembly asked Congress for a railroad from Lake Michigan to the Mississippi. Although some surveys were made, no railroads were built in Wisconsin until 1847 when the Milkaukee and Waukesha was begun. It started service in 1851. Alexander Mitchell organized the Milwaukee and St. Paul in 1863. Four years later this line joined with a railroad in Minnesota to give St. Paul its first out-of-state railroad connection. In 1874 this consolidated line became known as the Chicago, Milwaukee, and St. Paul. By 1860 Wisconsin had 891 miles of railroads; seven years later, 1,030 miles. As of 1860 the Old Northwest had about one third of the 30,000 miles of railroads in the United States.

Across the Mississippi, the lines were fewer and longer. Although Missouri had a flood of projects, only five became important railroads. The Missouri Pacific began building west from St. Louis in 1851 and reached Kansas City in 1865. The other four were the Hannibal and St. Joseph completed in 1859, the North Missouri, the Platte City line connecting St. Joseph and Kansas City, and the Cairo and Fulton line. Although Missouri had invested $23,000,000 in railroads by 1860, the Civil War almost destroyed them.

In Iowa most of the early railroads were extensions of roads built west from Chicago. Several of them ran to Council Bluffs. The Chicago and Northwestern reached there in 1856; the Rock Island and Chicago, Burlington, and Quincy four years later. By 1873 the Chicago, Milwaukee, and St. Paul Railroad also had a branch in northern Iowa.

Minnesota's early ventures in railroading turned out badly. In 1858 Minnesota voted $5,000,000 in special bonds for railroads. Of this only $2,250,000 was actually issued for which Minnesota received 240 miles of discontinuous, ill-graded road beds. Several Minnesota banks collapsed partly because of these bonds. Within six years after entering Minnesota in 1867, the Chicago and Northwestern Railroad had crossed the state. Probably the most important railroad in Minnesota was begun in 1873 by James J. Hill. He took over the St. Paul and Pacific Railroad with an indebtedness of $33,000,000. He extended those two "streaks of rust" to the Red River Valley. With the help of settlers whom he encouraged to settle in Minnesota and North Dakota, he built a railroad empire known as the Great Northern. By 1883 he had completed it to Helena, Montana, and a decade later to Puget Sound. Another important line originating in Minnesota was the Northern Pacific chartered in 1864 to extend from Lake Superior to the Pacific. The Northern Pacific moved westward very slowly until 1869 when Jay Cooke took over its management. He sold bonds and built the road from Duluth to Bismarck. The panic of 1873 ruined Cooke and construction stopped. The western terminus of the road remained at Bismarck until 1878 when building was resumed under Henry Villard. By 1883 he had extended it to Tacoma, Washington.

Kansas and Nebraska were also noted in railroading for the part they played in the building of transcontinental railroads. Railroad fever struck Kansas in the early 1860's. Out of the 1,100 Kansas railroad companies that were chartered, an estimated 200 companies built track. Kansas greatly overbuilt and the result was disaster. Two of the most important roads in Kansas were the Kansas Pacific and the Atchison, Topeka, and Santa Fe. The Kansas Pacific linked Kansas City and Denver by 1870. Organized in 1859 under the leadership of Cyrus K. Holliday, the Atchison, Topeka, and Santa Fe connected Kansas City and Santa Fe by 1865. The Chicago, Rock Island, and Pacific also built out of Kansas City. Eventually both of these roads were built to the Southern Pacific to form transcontinental lines. A smaller railroad, the Missouri, Kansas, and Texas, was built south from Topeka and reached the Kansas border in 1870.

Although the Kansas-Nebraska Act organized both the Kansas and Nebraska territories, the first transcontinental railroad built crossed only Nebraska. In 1853 Congress appropriated money for the survey of five possible railroad routes to the Pacific. Secretary of War Jefferson Davis had them surveyed. The northernmost route ran from St. Paul to the mouth of the Columbia River, the second followed the Platte River route to California, the third ran west from Kansas City along the Kansas River, the fourth followed the 35th parallel west from Ft. Smith, and the most southern route ran along the 32nd parallel. After the surveys the North and South still could not agree on a route. Stephen A. Douglas introduced a bill for three transcontinental routes in 1855, but it died in the House of Representatives. It took seven years and the secession of the South before a route could be selected.

In July 1862 Abraham Lincoln signed into law an act providing for the building of a railroad from the Missouri River to the Pacific Ocean. Council Bluffs was selected as the eastern terminus. The Union Pacific was to build west from Council Bluffs, and the Central Pacific was to build east from San Francisco. For building the railroad, the companies were to receive a 400-feet right of way, building materials from the public domain, ten sections (and later 20 sections) of land for each mile of railroad completed, and a subsidy in government bonds at the rate of $16,000 a mile in level country, $32,000 in the plateau regions, and $48,000 in the mountains. The Central Pacific began building almost immediately, but the Union Pacific did not begin until 1865. Because of slowness of construction by the Union Pacific, the meeting place had to be moved east twice; the place finally selected was Promontory Point, Utah. The lines met there in May 1869 and the first transcontinental railroad was opened. Nebraska's next most important railroad was the Chicago, Burlington, and Quincy which reached Council Bluffs in 1869, Kearney in 1873, and Denver in 1882.

The Dakotas' important railroads were again principally continuations of eastern roads. The Illinois Central was continued to Sioux Falls and Yankton after 1818. The Chicago and Northwestern was built into Watertown, South Dakota, in 1873. The Chicago, Milwaukee, and St. Paul was built through South Dakota in sections. It entered South Dakota in the 1870's, was extended in the 1880's, and finally reached the West Coast by 1910. It was South Dakota's only transcontinental route.

North Dakota was more liberally blessed with railroads. The St. Paul and Pacific Railroad reached Wahpeton in 1873. In the same year the Northern Pacific was extended to Bismarck on its way to the Pacific, and James J. Hill began building the railroad that became the Great Northern, the second transcontinental railroad passing through North Dakota's borders. By the 1890's the Great Northern, Northern Pacific, Minneapolis and St. Paul, and the Sault Ste. Marie railroads were all operating in North Dakota.

Railroads up to 1890 posed a great many problems in construction and operation. The major difficulty in construction was raising the money. In the early period legitimate as well as irresponsible promoters were allowed to print bond and stock certificates with little restraint. Many of these companies went broke. If, as in the Midwest in the 1830's, the states pledged their credit to railroad building, they often went broke too. In 1840 Ohio, Indiana, Illinois, and Michigan all had debts of around $15,000,000, which were largely the result of canal and railroad building. Eastern and European money financed much of this building. In Wisconsin most of the money for railroads came from local citizens since eastern investors thought these railroads were too speculative. Some 6,000 Wisconsin farmers mortgaged their lands for five-million dollars for railroad building in the years 1850 to 1857. When the railroads crashed in 1857, so did the farmers. Similarly in Kansas in the 1880's, railroads were overbuilt, and both local and eastern money was lost.

The railroad financing problem was ameliorated by the national government policy of ceding public lands to railroad companies. In 1850 Stephen A. Douglas obtained a liberal land grant for the Illinois Central Railroad which served as a precedent for later subsidies to railroads. This grant gave the Illinois Central a generous right of way plus six sections of land adjacent to the right of way for each mile of railway constructed. In 1852 a general law was passed providing that if a railroad met certain conditions it could receive 100 feet of right of way, additional land for stations, and the right to cut lumber on the public domain. In the case of the Union and Central Pacific Railroad companies, which built the first transcontinental railroad, they not only received 20 sections of land but also subsidies ranging from $16,000 to $48,000 for each mile of track completed. The Atchison, Topeka, and Santa Fe, the Kansas Pacific, and the Northern Pacific also received extremely large grants of public land. The Santa Fe received 17,000,000 acres, the Union Pacific, 20,000,000 acres, and the Northern Pacific, 44,000,000 acres. Grants of land given to railroads in the Midwest included one fourth of the acreage in Minnesota; one fifth in Wisconsin, Iowa, Kansas, and North Dakota; and one seventh in Nebraska.

Another related problem involved in railroad building was financial collusion. The Credit Mobilier scandal in the building of the Union Pacific was a case in point. Composed of leading stock holders in the Union Pacific, it was established as a construction company to build the railroad. It made exorbitant profits and gave bribes and offices to public officials in order to keep from being examined too closely. Another case occurred in Wisconsin where the La Crosse and Milwaukee Railroad obtained land grants from the state by bribing the governor and legislature with bonds worth $900,000. It did not take many of these actions to convince the public that railroad companies were not honest.

In construction railroads had the problem of shack towns. Similar in function to trail-end cattle towns and mining towns, shack towns followed the railroad gangs as they built track. These towns had the usual quota of bartenders, prostitutes, and gamblers associated with quick wealth and single, hard-living laborers. Only the completion of construction put an end to this type of demoralizing influence.

Another construction problem was the determination of the best material for road beds and the material to be used for the rails. Railroads were laid on wood timbers rather than stones, because wood settled more evenly when frost went out of the ground. Rails at first were made of hard wood topped with a thin strip of iron. But since these iron strips loosened and caused accidents, builders soon replaced them with solid iron rails.

The gauge of the railroads up to 1863 was also a major construction and operational problem. Ohio's first railroad, the Mad River and Lake Erie line, had a gauge of four feet, ten inches. The Ohio and Mississippi Railroad completed in 1857 had a six-feet gauge. Other gauges used included five feet, and five and one-half feet. Not until 1863 with the building of the Union Pacific did Congress establish a uniform gauge for railroads at four feet, eight and one half inches.

Another operational problem in the earlier locomotives was that their boilers, like the steamboat boilers, blew up. There were also collisions with other trains and animals. Occasionally, a locomotive would "strike a cow and cut it into calves," as one humorist put it. Harriet Martineau reported that during her travels in the 1830's a shower of sparks often greeted the passengers. Her own shawl had 13 holes burned in it. Eventually many of these mechanical problems were eliminated.

The influence and contributions of railroads in the Midwest were great. They played a large part in populating the western portion of the Midlands. Within a few years after 1869, the Northern Pacific, Kansas Pacific, Missouri Pacific, Santa Fe, Burlington, Rock Island, and Great Northern all became household words. It was largely through them that western Iowa, western Minnesota, the Dakotas, Kansas, and Nebraska became habitable and inhabited. The railroads wanted to populate these lands in order to have products and passengers to haul. The Union Pacific spent $885,412 in advertising land for sale and the Burlington, $969,500. Passenger fares and freight charges were often refunded to families who moved into an area within two years after the building of a railroad. Railroads also sold much of their land cheap and on easy terms in order to get settlers. James J. Hill did everything from growing wheat to bringing in pure-bred bulls to stimulate settlement in the Great Northern area. Towns grew up in the wake of the railroads moving west. The Illinois Central even used a standardized plan in laying out towns. Streets running east and west were named for trees and those running north and south were numbered. Railroads brought in the settlers and hauled out the produce. They made land valuable because they furnished the facilities to transport products to market.

—33—

Religion

Two of the leading problems facing the midwestern churches in the period 1840 to 1865 were their positions on the abolition of slavery and the Civil War. Although there were some church members who were staunch abolitionists in the period before 1840, the vast majority of people had little feeling on the subject. Much of the western abolition movement stemmed from a religious revival began in western New York in the 1820's by Charles G. Finney. Theodore D. Weld became a disciple of Finney's abolition movement during this time. Weld went west in 1831 and won recruits for his cause in the Western Reserve. Since Weld believed the Mississippi Valley would decide the issue, he selected Lane Seminary in Cincinnati for his headquarters. Having failed to obtain the support at Lane they desired, Weld and his followers moved to Oberlin College in 1835. A year later Weld's colleague, James G. Birney, began publishing the *Philanthropist.* By 1837 Weld and his abolition evangelists claimed 200 societies with around 15,000 members in Ohio. Although their numerical strength in Indiana, Illinois, and Michigan remained small, they made a noise in the Midwest far out of proportion to their numbers.

Another vocal minister pushing the abolitionist cause was Elijah P. Lovejoy in the St. Louis area. He began as a newspaper man in St. Louis and then went to study for the ministry at Princeton Theological Seminary. On his return to St. Louis, he began denouncing slavery in his religious paper the *Observer.* Forced out of St. Louis because of his views, he went to Alton, Illinois, where he continued his attacks against slavery. After having several presses destroyed by mobs, he was finally killed by a mob in 1837. His martyrdom helped the cause of abolition more than his life and writings.

While there were a few avid abolitionists in the churches, most of the churchmen were only lukewarm on the subject. The Ohio Methodists disliked the agitation of the evangelical abolitionists and denounced them in their General Conference of 1835. Again in 1836 the Ohio and Michigan conferences, among others, expressed regret at the actions of the abolitionists. Abolitionist ministers were disciplined for their agitation. One abolitionist group even withdrew from the Methodist Episcopal church in 1840, partly because of the latter's stand on the slavery issue.

During the 1840's, however, feeling became stronger on both sides, and the moderates lost control. In 1845 the Baptists split over the slavery issue, and the Methodists followed a few months later. These split churches almost immediately began to squabble over who would get the border states including Missouri. There were also lawsuits over the division of common property such as book-publishing plants. The Old School Presbyterians managed to straddle the fence and stay together, but the New School Presbyterians separated. With these fissions the churches grew faster partly as a result of the competition engendered. As the breach between the North and South continued to widen, the ecclesiastical bonds, along with the political and social, snapped, and war proved the final result.

When the Civil War came, the midwestern churches were strong in their support of the northern cause. The northern Presbyterians and Methodists made strong statements on their support of the Union. The Ohio Baptist convention in 1862 issued a typical patriotic resolution. They declared it their Christian duty to give their prayers, sympathy, support, and cooperation to the government and the armies "in their endeavors to crush the wicked rebellion."

Although the northern and southern Episcopalians set up separate organizations during the war, their relations remained so cordial that they united immediately after the war. Relations among most of the North-South Protestant churches, however, were not this congenial during the war. The northern Baptist and Methodist churches, for example, with the cooperation of the military, took over their counterpart's churches in the South and installed new church officials. An interesting case in this regard occurred in St. Louis in 1862 when Dr. Samuel B. McPheeters of the Presbyterian church was deposed by the military because McPheeters refused to declare his loyalty to the United States. McPheeters protested to the attorney general and it eventually came to President Lincoln's attention. Lincoln said he did not want the government or the military interfering with the operation of the southern churches, but his declaration was occasionally ignored. The next year Lincoln was informed that an order of the War Department gave possession of all Missouri Methodist Episcopal churches, South, to the northern Methodist bishops. Lincoln ordered the secretary of war to rescind this order for all loyal areas and to keep its action to a minimum in rebel areas.

— 34 —

Education in its Seedbed Years

Public Schools

The seedbed years, in which public education in the Midwest received its real start, were 1837 to 1860. Because of the educational activity, this twenty-three years has also been designated the educational awakening. During this period state legislatures took an active part in passing laws and establishing sound administrative policies for their public school systems. Ohio in 1837 created the office of superintendent of the common schools. Samuel Lewis, a self-educated lawyer, was chosen to fill the position. He was supposed to gather information, stimulate interest in, and report on the common schools. In his first sweeping report, Lewis advocated the creation of high schools and libraries, revealed the mismanagement of the school lands, and stated that far more money was needed to adequately support the schools. He recommended laws that would allow school districts to borrow money for buildings, establish local school supervision, and require educational and financial reports. He also proposed the creation of a state-school journal. The Ohio law passed in 1838 embodied many of his recommendations. It provided for a school census, a common-school fund, a two-mill, county education tax, and county and township supervision of the schools. A backward step was taken in 1840 when the office of state superintendent was abolished and his duties turned over to the secretary of state. Not until 1853 was this ground recovered, when a new law re-established the office of state superintendent, levied a state educational tax, and made the schools free.

In Indiana Caleb Mills of Wabash College took the lead in

advocating a public-school system for the state. In 1846 he published the first in a series of six annual "Addresses to the Legislature." With the exception of the fifth address which preceded the convening of the constitutional convention in 1850, all were issued on the opening day of legislative sessions. In these he called attention to the deplorable educational conditions, outlined needed reforms, and urged the legislature to pass desirable educational legislation.

The educational provisions in the Indiana constitution of 1851 and the school law of 1852 reflected his influence. Unfortunately, one phrase in the Indiana constitution, providing for the creation of a "general and uniform system of common schools," was interpreted so narrowly by the state supreme court that all local school taxes were declared unconstitutional, because they would vary from county to county and thus destroy the uniformity of the system. As a result free public schools could operate only for two months a year, because the state common school fund could not provide more. Some districts with paying students used the rate bill to increase the length of the school term, but free, public education for more than two months a year was not provided until after 1867.

In Illinois free public schools had such advocates as Ninian Edwards and Abraham Lincoln. In 1837 and 1841 the Illinois legislature revised the school laws to make them more uniform and equitable. Taxation for the schools, however, did not really begin until 1845 and it took another decade before a general, free, public educational system was a reality.

Although Michigan had benefited from its sister states' mistakes in administering school lands, its public education still progressed slowly. In 1835 the state constitution made education a branch of the government. Two years later the legislature created the office of superintendent of public instruction and appointed John D. Pierce to the office. Pierce had been instrumental in framing the 1837 law which provided that the superintendent would manage the school lands and supervise the schools. The 1837 law also provided for state and local taxes and local boards which were to implement the educational program. In addition to Pierce, Michigan also had the educational leadership of Isaac E. Crary. Despite their efforts, however, Michigan was slow in adopting free public schools. Schools supported largely by parents of the students remained dominant until 1869. In 1856 three-month terms were the rule in the free schools.

The laws on education passed by the Michigan territorial legislature applied to Wisconsin at the time of its separation from Michigan. After 1840 Wisconsin passed laws on public education which generally followed the lead of Michigan. The number of public elementary and secondary schools in Wisconsin rapidly increased in the two decades prior to the Civil War. Private schools, however, made very little headway. Of the 105,000 children between the ages of five and 20 in 1850, 58,000 were in Wisconsin's 1,425 public schools and less than 3,000 were in private schools.

Although Iowa passed an ambitious law in 1839 providing for a common school in each school district of the territory and free education for all white citizens between four and twenty-four years of age, the state was able to only partially implement the act. Improvement, however, was rapid during the next two decades.

High schools began to develop in the period 1840 to 1860. Both Cleveland and Columbus, Ohio, began high schools in about 1846. One of Illinois' first high schools was established in Chicago by William H. Wells in 1856. In addition to preparing students for college, these high schools also prepared teachers to instruct in the common schools.

Despite increased funds and better state laws, the educational system in the Midwest still had serious drawbacks. In 1847 the average monthly salary of a male teacher in Ohio was $15.42; Michigan, $12.71; and Indiana, $12. Salaries for women teachers averaged about half that of men in these three states. Although schools grew in number during the 1850's, their development was spotty. Indiana illustrated this. Indianapolis had no public schools during the years 1857 to 1860; Terre Haute, 1854 to 1860; and Muncie, 1853 to 1857. With the expanding population, adult illiteracy even increased from 38,100 in 1840 to 72,710 in 1850. Fortunately, this trend was finally reversed during the 1850's and adult illiteracy dropped to 62,716 by 1860.

Colleges

Although denominational colleges for the training of ministers were the dominant form of higher education up to 1860, state supported colleges were also appearing on the scene. The University of Missouri was established in 1839, the State University of Iowa in 1847, the University of Wisconsin in 1848, and the University of Minnesota in 1851. Of the 73 colleges founded in this period that have survived, 61 were privately supported and 12 publicly supported. Colleges generally had small attendance. In 1849 Governor Paris C. Dunning of Indiana reported that Asbury (DePauw) had 295 students; Franklin, 145; Hanover, 183; Indiana, 197; and Wabash, 148. The newest innovation in colleges, developed during the 1840's, was the Normal school. It was an outgrowth of the Institute and was the forerunner of the Teacher's college.

In general mortality among the colleges founded prior to 1860 was high. Out of 43 colleges established in Ohio during the period, only 17 survived. Missouri only retained eight out of 85. Many of these colleges were dependent on eastern money and when it was not forthcoming they closed. Fifteen different religious denominations founded colleges west of the Alleghanies prior to the Civil War and many of the churches did not have enough money to support them. The midwestern colleges also had the problem of obtaining qualified teachers, because the best ones preferred to stay in the eastern colleges. Even the state institutions were short on funds, facilities, and qualified instructors, as well as qualified students. Legislatures viewed colleges as a good place to cut expenditures in case of ememgency.

As a result college training in the West was in name only and the faculties were overworked and underpaid. During his 30 years at Hanover, John F. Crowe served as vice-president, member of the board of trustees, financial agent, and an instructor in logic, history, literature, and political science. For these many tasks, an educator might receive $500 to $600 per annum. An instructor at Oberlin in 1843 said that he was unable to pay for the clothes he wore.

As if this were not enough problems, splits over slavery and denominational issues muddied the waters of college administration still more. Slavery proved especially divisive at Western Reserve and Illinois College. The Plan of Union established by the Presbyterians and Congregationalists to jointly found colleges in the West began to disintegrate in 1837. Some denominations established colleges mainly for the purpose of eliminating a nearby rival, denominational institution. All of these factors helped to explain the high mortality rate among early midwestern colleges.

Adjuncts to Education

A number of innovations in education came to the Midwest in the two decades before 1860. Johann H. Pestalozzi's pedagogical ideas were introduced but made little impression. Most teachers preferred rote learning and a birch switch to kindness and investigation. Friedrich Froebel's kindergarten was made known to the Midwest by Mrs. Carl Schurz. She began one of the first at Watertown, Wisconsin, in 1856. The basic principle of kindergarten was to instill the beginnings of creative activity and group participation in the pre-school child. More state laws providing for public-library associations were passed. Indiana, for example, passed a law in 1843, providing for the establishment of public libraries, and by 1850 Indiana had 151 of them. Michigan boasted that during this period it acquired its first agricultural college, its first state-supported Normal, and its first state superintendent of public instruction.

The idea of public education gained a great following in the Midwest prior to the Civil War. Many had come to believe with James W. Grimes, newly elected governor of Iowa in 1854, that education was the great equalizer and the best preventer of pauperism and crime.

—35—

Art and Sculpture

Alexis de Tocqueville's statement that there was a dearth of artists in America because most of the energy was directed at conquering the new land was certainly true in the early Midwest. Fine arts on the Middle Border were viewed by many as a waste of time and impractical. Despite this attitude some art and sculpture were produced in the early Midwest.

At the beginning much of the art that was present was centered around Cincinnati. Seven years after the Frankenstein family arrived in Cincinnati, Godfrey Frankenstein became president of the Academy of Fine Arts in that city. In 1839 he held an exhibit of 150 items, the first art exhibition of importance in the Midwest. Nicholas Longworth was also a generous patron of the arts in the Queen City.

The sculptor, Hiram Powers, for a time brightened the artistic scene at Cincinnati with his presence. Clerking at first in a Cincinnati store, his sculpture gained the notice of Nicholas Longworth who financed his trips to Washington and Europe. Powers' most famous work was the feminine nude figure, "Greek Slave." The New York or New Orleans banker who wanted one of the six versions of the "Greek Slave" had to pay $4,000 for it. This statute even took the general public by storm. For a generation parlors across the country contained miniature copies of the "Greek Slave." Henry James wrote an excellent description of the statuette and the people who possessed it: "So undressed, yet so refined, even so pensive, in sugar-white alabaster, exposed under little glass covers in such American homes as could bring themselves to think such things right."

James H. Beard, noted as a portrait painter, settled at Cincinnati in 1834. He enjoyed painting animals almost as much as people. One of his best paintings was "The Long Bill," depicting a store scene. When Harriet Martineau visited Cincinnati, she was impressed with Beard's portraits of children, but she also noted his conceit and his contempt for Boston which bespoke his provincialism.

Henry K. Brown, a sculptor from Massachusetts, also joined the Cincinnati group about 1836. His most noted work was the equestrian statute of "George Washington" which was placed in Union Square, New York City.

Thomas B. Read had been a cigar maker, a grocery clerk, and a female impersonator before Nicholas Longworth took him under his wing and financed his art education in New York. Although Longworth reproached Read for his playboyish attitude while in New York, Read's spirits were not dampened. He wrote the poem "Sheridan's Ride," on Henry W. Longfellow's urging and painted the poet's children. He also painted a seven-by-eight-feet canvas of the "Children of Marcus L. Ward" which was noted most for its size. His repetitious painted versions of a man bouncing on a horse (a painted rendition of his poem) were comic in their badness.

Another painter of Cincinnati, William H. Powell, received a commission in 1846 to paint a historical picture for the Capitol Rotunda in Washington, D. C. His contribution was "Discovery of the Mississippi." A little later the Ohio legislature commissioned him to paint "Perry's Victory on Lake Erie" for the state capitol at Columbus. Although he was to receive $5,000 for the picture, he spent so much time on it that he asked $15,000. He received $10,000. In 1865 the United States Congress asked him for an enlarged replica of the picture which was placed in the Senate wing.

After coming from England, Thomas Cole stayed briefly at Steubenville, Ohio. He was important in midwestern painting primarily because of the scenes he painted. He was intrigued by the wilderness around him. "The Expulsion from the Garden," the "Landscape with Woodsman," and the "Oxbow" reflected his love of nature. He painted clouds with trailing blue mists and crags that glittered. When Cole returned to Europe in 1829, William C. Bryant wrote that Cole had fixed the living image of America on his canvass – the placid lakes, the running streams, the deserts, and the rocks. Cole was an early member of the Hudson River School of painters.

In Indiana Christopher Garrison, the first lieutenant governor of the state, was among the first artists in the state. Most of the early artists, however, such as Charles A. Lesueur, Lucy Sistaire, and David D. Owen centered around New Harmony. An exception was Jacob Cox of Indianapolis who combined portraits and a few landscapes with his tinsmithy. Cox's favorite subject for landscapes was Fall Creek located near Indianapolis.

James O. Lewis, who arrived in Detroit in 1824, was one of Michigan's first portrait painters. He painted, among others, a picture of Lewis Cass. Earlier at St. Louis, he had copied a picture of Daniel Boone and painted a number of Indian portraits. He also painted the Michigan aboriginese for the United States government.

Another portrait painter, Portugese-born Manuel J. de Franca, studied under Thomas Sully at Philadelphia and then wandered West. He passed through Pennsylvania and Kentucky and finally reached St. Louis, where he perfected his style. His drawing and placing of figures were similar to Sully's, but the colors were darker.

Missouri had one of the best pre-Civil War painters in the Midwest. George C. Bingham, brought to Missouri by his family in 1819 at the age of eight, portrayed midwestern and river themes. He briefly attended the art school at the Pennsylvania Academy and then returned to Missouri to paint. Among his best river paintings were "Fur Traders Descending the Missouri," "The Jolly Flatboatmen," and "Raftsman Playing Cards." Among his other most outstanding pictures were "The County Election" and "The Verdict of the People," which displayed democracy in action, and "Order No. 11," which was a protest against the federal order stripping western Missouri of all produce in order to stop Confederate guerillas operating in the region.

A whole group of painters, referred to as "Painters of the Amerind," wandered over the upper-Mississippi Valley in the period up to 1865. Chief among these was George Catlin of Pennsylvania who painted over 600 pictures of the western

Indians. He painted many Indian portraits as well as landscapes where Indians and buffaloes played subordinate roles.

Seth Eastman, whose technique was inferior to Catlin's, learned his draftsmanship at West Point. At Fort Snelling, Minnesota, in 1830, he made numerous drawings of the Sioux and the Chippewa. He later used his drawings to make illustrations for Schoolcraft's six-volume work on the Indians and to make a series of nine pictures for the Indian Affairs Committee of the House of Representatives.

A third painter in this group was John M. Stanley. Although he was more conscious of Indian racial characteristics than Eastman, his style was more tedious. A rover he was in the Willamette Valley, in the Southwest with General Phil Kearney, with Governor Isaac Stevens when the latter left St. Paul to find the best route for a northern transcontinental railway, and in Hawaii. Always with paintbox in hand, he even painted portraits of King Kamehameha and his Queen in the island kingdom.

Another Amerind painter, George Winter, did for the Miami and Pottawatomi what Catlin and his cohorts did for the more western Indians. Winter painted Kick-Ke-Se-Quah and O-Shaw-Se-Quah on the Wabash before these Indians and their kinsmen were ejected from the area.

— 36 —

Architecture

Architecture in the Midwest was as conventional and as diversified as architecture elsewhere in the United States. Probably the most distinctive type of architecture in the early Midwest was the rectangular log cabin, but even it had been used by frontiersmen long before they arrived in the Midwest. The eastern Midwest had timber, limestone, sandstone, and the proper clay for bricks to use as building materials. And although the houses were primarily log and later clapboard, there were also brick and stone houses. As early as 1802 Zanesville, Ohio, had two brickyards. By 1815 Cincinnati had 250 brick houses out of a total of 1,100 dwellings. By 1850 Indiana and Ohio, as well as other portions of the Midwest, were dotted with brick and stone houses. The main architectural styles were the simple rectangular for the humble and a Greek Revival for the more pretentious.

Further west on the plains where the people were short on timber, brick, and stone, many of them fell back on sod as building materials. Sod (soil with grass on it), however, would not keep out the elements or the insects, and so the people imported lumber as rapidly as possible to construct more repellant, clapboard houses.

The most distinctive types of architecture in the Midwest were displayed in the churches, courthouses, and capitol buildings. Again at first they were simple, rectangular buildings, but later brick and stone were used and they became local monuments. Although most of the later court houses and capitols reflected the American Greek Revival in architecture, there were other architectural types and combinations. Many churches and academic buildings were also of the Greek style, but some were also influenced by the Gothic and Romanesque types of architecture. Not until after 1900 did many state, church, and educational buildings begin to take on the appearance of more functional office buildings (like the state capitols at Pierre or Bismarck) or Swiss mountain homes.

Among the Midwest's architects, one of the earliest was Colonel Joseph Barker, who designed the famous southern-style Harman Blennerhasset mansion in 1799. Located on an island in the Ohio River, 16 miles below Marietta, it cost around $40,000 to construct. It consisted of a two-story, hip-roofed, central building, 30 by 52 feet, with smaller buildings on either end, connected to the main house by circular colonnades.

Another early Ohio building associated with a noted Ohio architect was Manasseh Cutler Hall at Ohio University (Athens), built in 1817 under the direction of Benjamin Corp, a carpenter-architect of Marietta. Federal in style, it was a three-story brick with plain windows and a square shaped cupola with a dome-crowned clock tower.

An architect of early Ohio noted for his taverns was Jonathan Goldsmith. He designed the Rider Inn, a frame building of New England vintage at Painesville, Ohio, in 1822. Two other taverns built by Goldsmith in the same neighborhood were Mountain House and Old Stage House.

Among the architects involved in building the Illinois state capitol at Springfield in 1837, the most noted was John F. Rague of Springfield. The capitol building, constructed of native stone, was of a Greek style and had Doric porticoes and a copper-clad dome. Although Rague won the competition for the drawing of the plans, he received little attention for his work. Two years later he prepared the plans for the Iowa state capitol at Iowa City in his Greek Revival style. After leaving Springfield, Rague settled at Milwaukee where he designed the Phoenix building, several school houses, and North and South halls on the University of Wisconsin campus. In 1854 he moved to Dubuque, where among other buildings, he designed the city hall, the county jail, and some schools and private homes.

The Ohio state capitol at Columbus begun in 1838 had a number of architects associated with its construction. In the architectural competition, first place went to Henry Walter of

Cincinnati, second place to Martin Thompson of New York, and third place to Thomas Cole. Alexander J. Davis of New York was also made a consultant to devise a workable building plan. Architects W. Russell West, N. B. Kelley, and Isaiah Rogers later actually supervised the construction. The building resulting from all this planning and supervision was of the Greek Revival style, 304 feet long by 184 feet wide. Constructed of limestone, it had four Doric plastered facades and a central rotunda, 65 feet in diameter, which was crowned by a dome reaching to a height of 120 feet. Its construction took 23 years.

One of Indiana's most prolific courthouse architects was John Elder, who came to Indianapolis from Pennsylvania in 1833. Before moving on to California seventeen years later, he designed a number of courthouses including those at Frankfort, Columbus, Rushville, and Connersville. A representative example of his architecture was his Connersville courthouse. It was a Doric temple set on top of a Roman-like, lower story. It was flanked on either side by two-story wings and had an octagonal cupola on the roof. The total cost of construction was $20,000.

In Ohio one of the best examples of a courthouse of the Greek Revival style was in Montgomery County in Dayton. Designed by Howard Daniels, an architect from Cincinnati, and constructed of white Dayton stone in the years 1848 to 1850, it was a form of Ionic temple with six columns across the front. The roof, stairway, and floors were composed of solid masonry, and it had a central winding stairway built in a cantilevered style.

Joseph Willis of Logansport, Indiana, was noted especially for his work on buildings for the Institute of the Deaf and Blind and the Masonic Hall in Indianapolis. The latter, constructed in 1849, was a two-story, Doric temple set upon a basement. Built of brick covered with stucco, it was 63 by 110 feet and its front columns were 33 feet high. It cost $20,000 to build.

The old St. Joseph County Courthouse at South Bend, Indiana, built in 1854 and 1855, was also of classic derivation. Designed by Van Osdel and Olmstead of Chicago, it was a two-story temple of Corinthian design, set upon a high podium with irregularly spaced columns. As a finishing touch, it had an elaborate octagonal cupola, housing a clock on the roof.

Of a completely different construction was the Fort Street Presbyterian Church in Detroit designed by A. and O. Jordan, architects. Built in 1855 in a crisp English Gothic style, it had a corner tower, a slender spire 230 feet in height, and flying buttresses at the corners. The cost of the church and lot was about $77,000.

Another English Gothic style church, Christ Church in Monument Circle in Indianapolis, was designed by William Tinsley, an architect originally from Ireland. Christ Church had an open timber roof and a lacy wooden screen. Tinsley also designed buildings for Indiana University, Wabash College, and the University of Wisconsin. At the latter he drew the plans for Bascom Hall.

Architects Henry J. Cobb and Charles S. Frost of Chicago were especially noted for their designing of the Potter Palmer mansion at 1350 Lake Shore Drive. Built in 1882 this house was of the wooden Gothic style.

PART IV

THE MIDDLE WEST COMES OF AGE, 1864-1900

— 37 —

The Indians' Last Frontier

The Little Big Horn was the last major Indian war in the Middle West. There were other skirmishes and massacres after this but no major Indian campaigns. The increasing number of whites and the decreasing number of buffalo made further effective Indian resistance impossible. Whereas in 1870 there were an estimated seven-million buffalo on the Great Plains, by 1885 the buffalo herds were almost extinct. The great slaughter of buffalo was in the period 1872-74 when three railroads hauled well over one-million buffalo hides out of the southern plains. The Indians fought to save the buffalo, but to no avail. When the buffalo were gone, the Indians were more controllable. Since they no longer had their travelling commissary they had to stay on the reservation and eat agency rations. Attempts at raiding, however, continued until 1890. In 1878, for example, a small band of Cheyenne under Dull Knife fled the Ft. Reno reservation and killed about forty settlers in western Kansas.

In Minnesota the major Indian problem consisted of persuading the Indians to settle on their new reservations. The Chippewa were to be concentrated in the Cass, Leech, and Winnibigoshish lakes area. As an added attraction to the Chippewa, the government provided the reservation with oxen, farm implements, a sawmill, carpenter, blacksmiths, farm laborers, and a physician. But the Indians still did not move in very fast. After ten years, 800 of the 2,100 Chippewa were on the reservation in 1875; it took ten more years to get the bulk of the rest of them there. In 1889 the Nelson Act provided for the settlement of all the Chippewa on the Red Lake and Blue Earth reservations. These two reservations were just a small part of the original reservation given to the Chippewa in 1863.

After 1876 Indian agency activities generally consisted of herding the Indians on to reservations and providing them with enough food to subsist. In 1889 a variation on this theme occurred among the Teton-Sioux when they learned a mystic dance which was to bring them a Messiah that would deliver them out of bondage. Sitting Bull was again involved. Although he fled to Canada after his defeat in 1877, he had returned to the United States in 1881 and surrendered. After spending two years in prison, he was allowed to return to his former home near the Standing Rock Agency in South Dakota. Sitting Bull was among those who took up the Messiah craze. The settlers, alarmed by this unusual activity, called for soldiers. In the melee accompanying his attempted arrest, Sitting Bull and several of his followers were killed.

A few weeks later in a bungling attempt to disarm another band of Sioux, 200 Dakota warriors, women, and children were massacred by a large force of soldiers at Wounded Knee Creek. This engagement brought a belated end to the Indian wars in the Middle West.

After 1871 the United States government dispensed with the fiction that Indian tribes were independent nations and ceased making formal treaties with them. This was done partly because Indian strength had decreased and partly because the House of Representatives, who had to appropriate the money for the Indians, felt that they should be consulted in Indian affairs. With the government beginning to treat the Indians like individuals, tribal organization began to disintegrate. The Dawes Severalty Act (1887) and the Burke Act (1906) were passed which permitted an Indian to own and sell individual holdings. Each Indian head of a family was allotted 160 acres with lesser amounts for bachelors and unmarried women. In practice this simply continued the decrease in lands owned by the Indians. Many Indians were incapable of caring for their own land, and unscrupulous whites were present to exploit the inexperienced red men. By 1900 approximately two thirds of the Indian lands of 1887 were no longer in Indian hands. Minnesota was a classic example. Of the 2,800 Chippewa there in 1909, 80 per cent had lost their lands to whites within the previous twenty years. About all these

Indians had received in return for their lands from the whites was disease. Sixty per cent of the Chippewa had tuberculosis, 30 per cent had trachoma, and 20 per cent had syphilis. In 1909 the Indian office finally became alarmed enough about the land swindlers to take steps to get back the Indian land that had been improperly acquired. This court action resulted in a little land and money being returned to the Indians. In 1934 the Indian-land situation was finally improved by the Indian Reorganization Act (Wheeler-Howard Act), which forbade land allotments and the sale of Indian lands except to other Indians. The act also provided credit facilities for Indians who wished to own land, gave Indians the right to form corporations, and granted a large measure of self government to the Indians. In an attempt to right another injustice, the Indians were also finally admitted to full citizenship in 1924.

Indian education was improved and increased after 1873 with the establishment of reservation boarding schools and agency boarding schools. Non-resident boarding schools, such as Haskell Institute (1884) at Lawrence, Kansas, and the Carlisle, Pennsylvania, School (1879) were among the best educational facilities. Teachers in the Indian schools were largely incompetent until they were removed from the spoils system and put under civil service. Educators generally experienced difficulty in obtaining the cooperation of older Indians who resented innovations in their way of life. Often Indian parents would not allow their children to attend school. In 1891 a compulsory education act was passed which empowered the commissioner of Indian affairs to enforce attendance of children at Indian schools. Usually the government schools tended to emphasize industrial and agricultural education, which they felt to be most useful to the Indians.

— 38 —

Population and Settlement

Urbanization and Immigration

There were three main population trends in the Midwest during the period 1860 to 1900: urbanization, increased immigration from Europe, and settlement of the trans-Missouri River states.

Urbanization was especially evident in the Midwest east of the Mississippi River. This is the period that Arthur M. Schlesinger entitled *The Rise of Cities* in the *History of American Life* series. Although this effect may have been more noticeable in the Northeast than in the North Central states, it was still significant in the latter. By 1900 the midwest had a rural population of 16,166,485 and an urban population of 10,166,519 compared to 13,170,111 rural and 4,194,000 urban in 1880.

Although industrialization was the chief cause of this urbanization, the loneliness of country life, the drudgery of farm work, and the end of cheap fertile land also caused people to move to town. In addition, a majority of the 900,000 immigrants who arrived in the Midwest in the 1880's settled in the cities.

The European emigration to the United States after 1860 was similar to that prior to 1860 except that the number increased and the people now came from all parts of Europe rather than just from northwestern Europe. By 1900 Chicago had 587,112 foreign born; Cincinnati, 57,961; Cleveland, 124,631; Detroit, 96,503; Milwaukee, 88,991; Minneapolis, 61,021; and St. Louis, 111,356. The total foreign born in the United States was 10,356,644, and the Midwest had 4,158,474 of these. Of the five leading nationalities composing the foreign born in America (German, Irish,

English, Canadian, and Swedish), the Middle West had a larger percentage of German people than any other region in the United States and large percentages of the other four.

Settlement of the Trans-Missouri River Area

After 1860 the area of greatest settlement activity in the Midwest was the tier of four states across the Missouri River. A number of factors contributed to this development. First, the states adjacent to this area were filling with people and they furnished the reservoir to flood the Great Plains. From 1880 to 1890 Iowa, Missouri, and the states of the Old Northwest contributed more than one-million pioneers to the advancement of the frontier. Second, the Homestead Act of 1862 attracted many people to the West. Third, railroads such as the Union Pacific, Santa Fe, Illinois Central, and Great Northern brought in settlers by advertising, special rates to immigrants, and special land sales. Fourth, gold rushes such as those to Pike's Peak and the Black Hills also caused a westward movement of people. Finally, high prices for agricultural products during the Civil War encouraged people to go West where they could obtain more land to raise crops. After the war returning soldiers told of the land available in the West and this began a new land rush.

Settlement in the pre-war era touched only eastern Kansas and Nebraska. Settlers, moving further into Kansas after the Civil War, ran into new problems of settlement for which they had to find solutions. A shortage of wood for building and heating was one of the most difficult. To meet this house-building problem until they could afford to purchase imported lumber for a wood-frame house, they constructed either a dugout, a rectangular hole covered with poles and sod; a half dugout, which was half underground and half above-ground; or a sod house, built completely above ground and made of turf cut into bricks from two to three feet in length. Although these shelters were very unsatisfactory, they had to suffice until other building materials could be acquired.

To partially solve the fuel problem, these pioneers burned buffalo chips, hay, or sunflower stalks. The reason for Kansas becoming the "Sunflower State" was apparently due to this heating problem. The original settlers had planted sunflowers to use for fuel and these sunflowers spread volunteer all over the semi-arid West.

Because of the shortage of wood, fences at first were also nearly nonexistent. Some made use of the Osage Orange named after the Indian tribe in whose territory it grew. These trees would grow rapidly, even in dry Kansas, and would produce a cheap and effective fence. Later barbed wire came into vogue, but in many cases the settlers could not afford to buy it.

But a worse problem than the scarcity of timber or even than unfriendly Indians was the lack of moisture. A person might find a stream or dig a well to provide water for the family and the animals, but there was still insufficient water for the crops. To meet this problem, the western settler either left the land in pasture and raised livestock, or else he tried to summer fallow and produce low-moisture, consuming plants such as sorghum, kaffir corn, and Turkey wheat. But even dry farming was a gamble, especially west of the one-hundredth meridian, and the battle with the elements was always in doubt.

Settlements in Kansas after the Civil War tended to follow the transportation routes. Towns like Wichita, Wellington, and Dodge City, for example, sprang up along the Santa Fe Railroad. By 1880 Kansas was sparsely settled to the ninety-eighth meridian, and by 1900 it was thinly populated to its western edge. Although the states to the east had furnished most of the people for this settlement, European emigrants also moved to Kansas after the Civil War. Kansas by 1900 had 126,685 foreign born of which German, Swedish, Irish, and Russian were the most numerous.

Representative of these groups were settlements in Saline, McPherson, and Ellis counties. In 1868 one of the principal Swedish settlements in the Kansas wheat country was established in Saline and McPherson counties in the Smokey Hill River Valley. They purchased twenty-two sections of land from the Kansas Pacific Railroad. At first Saline was their market center; after a railroad was built to Lindsborg, this became their center.

At intervals through the years they held Swedish pioneer festivals to revive their European customs. Some of their favorite dishes were dried herring, potato sausage, jelly meats, Swedish hard tack, pork meat balls, Swedish peppermint candy, and ligonberry preserves.

A group of German-Russians also settled in the Smokey Hill River Valley in Ellis County in 1876. They had treked from Prussia to Russia in the latter eighteenth century when Catherine had thrown open large tracts of land to them. All went well until 1871 when the czar decreed that these Germans must perform military service and become members of the Russian Orthodox church. Again they moved to escape limitations on their freedom, and this time they came to the United States. They built a village at Herzog, Kansas, in the European style and went out from their homes each day to farm their forty-acre strips. They built small, square houses with sharply peaked roofs and connected their barns to their houses. Their favorite foods were cabbage soup, sauerkraut, clabbered milk, oat cakes, plain boiled potatoes, watermelons, and sunflower seeds.

The settlement of Nebraska followed the same pattern as neighboring Kansas. Again the transportation routes played an important role in the settlement. In Nebraska the important transportation routes were originally the Oregon Trail, the Mormon Trail, and later the Union Pacific Railroad. Like Kansas the Homestead Act and the railroads were instrumental in populating it. Nebraska had the nation's first entry made under the Homestead Law. It was filed by Daniel Freeman, a Union soldier, on a claim to a quarter-section lying along Cub Creek near Beatrice, Nebraska, on January 1, 1863. Between 1863 and 1895, 68,862 persons in Nebraska received title to 9,609,922 acres of land under the Homestead Act. Like Kansas, Nebraska drew population largely from adjacent states, but it also obtained people from Europe. By 1900 Nebraska had 177,347 foreign-born residents of whom a large plurality were German.

Overall, both Kansas and Nebraska made phenomenal growths in population. From a low of 136,047 persons in 1860, their joint population grew to 2,536,795 by 1900.

The Dakota country began to fill slowly after 1860 when

people from Iowa, Minnesota, Wisconsin, and Illinois began to move in. They were attracted by the Dakota Land Company of Minnesota and the Western Land Company of Iowa. The problems of settlement in the Dakota Territory were very similar to those in its two sister states to the south.

Although the whole Dakota area was established as a single territory in 1861, the southern area was populated faster than the northern section because of the latter's greater remoteness. The first settlements were made in the Sioux River Valley in 1857 at Flandreau and Sioux Falls. Some 500 people were in Dakota by 1860. The Civil War, Indian wars, droughts, grasshoppers, and the absence of a railroad discouraged settlement in the early 1860's. With the removal of the Sioux to reservations and the building of the Illinois Central Railroad, which connected southeastern Dakota to Chicago, the settlers began to move in rapidly after 1868. Dakota had 20,000 people by 1873. A year later the Black Hills' gold rush caused another population boom. By 1875, 15,000 miners were in the Black Hills, even though it was Indian country and federal troops had tried to keep them out. In 1876 Deadwood was founded as a gold-mining town. The "Wild West" made its last glorious stand in the Black Hills' mining region with an abundance of dance halls, street brawls, murders, thieves, prostitutes, and gamblers.

Except for the mining interlude, the area that became North Dakota had a parallel development to that of South Dakota. To attract settlers, the Northern Pacific Railroad conducted an experiment in wheat growing under Oliver Dalyrymple. The Great Northern, under the management of James J. Hill, also strove to encourage settlement in the northern part of Dakota Territory. That they were somewhat successful is demonstrated by the population growth. From a low of 4,837 in 1860, Dakota's population had spiralled to over 720,000 by 1900.

A normal pattern of migration into the Dakotas can be demonstrated by the Garland family. Hamlin Garland's family first lived near Onalaska, Wisconsin; from there they moved to a farm two miles west of Hesper, Iowa; then to Mitchell County (near Osage), Iowa; and finally in the 1880's to the Dakota Territory. Many of the families who settled in the western part of the Middle West were similar restless pioneers.

Dakota Territory also received a large number of immigrants from Europe. Out of a total population of 720,716 in the Dakotas, 201,599 were of foreign ancestry. Norway, Canada, Germany, and Sweden were the largest contributors. O. E. Rolvaag portrays the arrival and the life of one of these groups, the Swedes, in the Dakotas in his *Giants in the Earth.*

To the east in Minnesota, settlement dropped off in the early 1860's. The Sioux uprising was enough to frighten all but the most stout-hearted. But the Indians were soon defeated and removed to reservations and the influx of people began again. In the three-year period 1863 to 1866, 9,529 homestead entries for 1,237,733 acres were made in Minnesota. After 1879 James Hill of the Northern Pacific was also active in Minnesota trying to attract new settlers. Throughout the period up to 1900, the Indians were pushed into smaller areas and the "excess" lands opened to white settlement.

The largest foreign influx into Minnesota in the 1880's and 90's was Scandinavian. Resembling the country of their birth, Minnesota had attracted 115,476 Swedes and 104,895 Norwegians by 1900. Some 400 Minnesota towns had Swedish names. While visiting in Sweden, Henry Adams noted somewhat expansively that all the Swedes he saw had either been in America or were on their way over. One day he saw a party of five young men and women get on the train he was aboard, bedecked with wreaths and flowers. He supposed they were a wedding party, but as he later discovered they were just emigrants bound for Minnesota.

After 1860 Iowa was a transition area in the settlement pattern. People continued to flow in but many also left. The Garlands, for example, went through on their way to Dakota. Immigrants driving ox teams with a crate of chickens tied in back and livestock walking behind were often observed passing through Iowa towns.

Iowa prior to 1900 had developed into the type of settlement pattern that Lewis Atherton described in his *Main Street on the Middle Border,* when he said that villages a few miles apart speckled the midwestern countryside. Farmers with only horses or oxen for transportation had to have a market center within twelve miles in order to get there and back in time to do the evening chores. Among the most important stores and shops in these agricultural towns were the post office, gristmill, general store, and blacksmith shop. Urbanization in Iowa, generally, was built on agriculture rather than on industry.

Iowa, too, grew in population, but less rapidly than some of its neighbors in the forty years after 1860. Its total population almost quadrupled during the period, and in 1900 it ranked sixth in the Middle West in the number of foreign-born residents. Of these people of European birth, Germans were by far the most numerous.

Missouri was even more in the middle than Iowa in the population shuffle after 1860. Missouri not only lost population to the western states but also to the southern states because of the secessionist sympathies of many of its citizens. Missouri also served as a battle ground between North and South during the Civil War and many persons moved out to escape this.

After the Civil War, Missouri became a peculiar mixture of ordinary Americans, Anglo-Saxon stock in the Ozark Mountains, and a large number of persons of German extraction in the St. Louis area. Out of Missouri's 216,379 foreign born in 1900, over half were German. Ireland and England contributed the next largest groups of foreign-born residents to Missouri.

Urbanization and Summary

In contrast to the seven midwestern states west of the Mississippi River, the five states east of the Mississippi had been much more influenced by urbanization. In comparing the two sections, the states west of the Mississippi were 29 per cent urbanized while those east of the Mississippi were 45 per cent urbanized. Of the 14 cities in the Midwest in 1900 with over 100,000 population, eight were east of the Mississippi and three of the remainder were just across the river on the western bank of the Mississippi.

Among the eastern midwestern states in 1900, Illinois enjoyed two distinctions. It was the only state that had a larger urban than rural population and the only one that had a city of over one million population.

Chicago, which gave Illinois both of these distinctive characteristics, had early became the transportation center of the Middle West. The city was built around the loop which was the city's financial and shopping center. The middle class filled the east-side residential district, the foreign born filled the west side, and Chicago's very rich inhabited the North Shore's Gold Coast. Around the fringes and within the sections themselves were the thousands of factories that produced Chicago's industrial products.

Illinois' neighbor, Indiana, had within its borders the center of population of the United States. This distinction had come to Ohio in 1860 and had moved on into Indiana in 1890. In 1900 this "spot" was located near Columbus, Indiana. This ever westward-moving "spot" was indicative of the westward migration that was taking place in the Midwest.

Although many of the people who were rapidly increasing the population and filling the cities of the eastern Midwest in 1900 came from other states or from the region's own rural areas, a significant number, approximately 16 per cent, came from Europe. Germany contributed the most people to each of these five states with the exception of Michigan; it had more Canadians. Overall, the leading foreign-born populations in these five states were German, Canadian, Irish, English, Swedish, and Norwegian in that order. For the Midwest as a whole, it had over four-million foreign born, of which about 30 per cent were German, 9 per cent Swedish, 8 per cent Irish, 8 per cent Canadian, 7 per cent Norwegian, and 7 per cent English.

— 39 —

Political Issues and Personalities

Civil War and Reconstruction

National elections were probably an even poorer index of midwestern feeling on issues in the period after 1860 than before. On the basis of the national elections, however, a majority of the Midwest apparently favored radical reconstruction for the South, Negro suffrage, high tariff, sound money, the Homestead Act, veteran's pensions, imperialism, and aid to business.

Although a majority of the leaders and people in the Midwest tended to favor the Republican Party and its principles, there were also large blocks of dissent. Therefore, a survey of the leading political figures and issues in the Midwest in the period 1860 to 1900 reflected both Republican and anti-Republican sentiment.

Although a majority of people in the Midwest greatly favored the northern position in the Civil War, there were those who were opposed to the war, the draft, and the suppression of civil liberties. Indiana had a group known consecutively as the Knights of the Golden Circle, the Order of American Knights, and the Sons of Liberty. They opposed the war and on one occasion even helped Confederate prisoners to escape. Indiana, Ohio, and Wisconsin, among others, had riots against the newly introduced draft. Many also objected to Lincoln's suspension of habeas corpus, arbitrary arrest, and suppression of newspapers.

A southern sympathizer who was one of Lincoln's most bitter political foes was Clement B. Vallandigham, Democratic congressman from Ohio. After leaving Congress in 1863, he critized the Abraham Lincoln administration so violently that he was tried by court martial and sentenced to imprisonment. Lincoln changed the sentence to exile in the Confederacy. Escaping, he went to Canada and from there ran unsuccessfully for governor of Ohio in absentia in 1864.

On the other hand the Midwest had a large number of Republicans who were considerably more radical in their approach to the Civil War, the status of the black, and the treatment of the South than Lincoln. Probably the most noted of these was the Ohioan, Benjamin F. Wade, who led the fight for a stringent reconstruction policy for the South. As president pro tem of the Senate, he was also instrumental in having Andrew Johnson impeached. Since he was next in line for the presidency, he may have had an ulterior motive.

Edwin M. Stanton of Ohio was another noted Radical Republican. Appointed attorney general in Buchanan's cabinet, he was retained by Abraham Lincoln and made secretary of war. He remained as secretary of war in Johnson's administration until the latter decided Stanton was a spy for the Radical Republicans and attempted to remove him. To support Stanton, Congress passed the Tenure of Office Act, which provided that the president must have the concurrence of the Senate to remove an appointed official from office. When Johnson disregarded this act and removed Stanton, Congress used this action along with other vague charges as an excuse to impeach Johnson.

As is evident from the vote on conviction in the Senate, not all the Republicans in the Midwest were as radical as Wade and Stanton. Seven Republicans committed political suicide by voting against the conviction of Johnson; four of whom were from the Midwest. These men were Senators James W. Grimes of Iowa, John B. Henderson of Missouri, Edmund G. Ross of Kansas, and Lyman Trumbell of Illinois. All were denounced and castigated by their home states for their action and each was defeated in the next election. These men refused to bend to the intolerant passions of the period and for their honesty and foresight they were subjected to scorn, ostracism, and abuse.

Actually Stanton came out little better for his shabby part in this travesty. Appointed a justice of the Supreme Court by President Ulysses S. Grant, he died a few days after receiving the office.

Another important middle western Republican involved in

Johnson's impeachment trial was Salmon P. Chase of Ohio. From 1849 to 1855 he served as United States senator and vigorously opposed the Kansas-Nebraska Act and the extension of slavery into the territories. He then served two terms as governor of Ohio and was an unsuccessful candidate for the Republican presidential nomination in 1860. Appointed secretary of the treasury in Lincoln's cabinet, he was extremely successful in obtaining the funds to carry on the Civil War. In 1864 he resigned as secretary of the treasury and shortly after was appointed chief justice of the Supreme Court. In that capacity he presided over the impeachment trial of President Johnson, a task which he performed with dignity and fairness.

Corruption in Government

In the late 1860's and early 1870's, the Midwest furnished political leaders who were both involved in corruption and fought against it. Although personally honest, General Ulysses S. Grant of Illinois, who was elected president in 1868, allowed corruption to occur all around him. Even Schuyler Colfax of Indiana, Grant's vice-president, added a taint to his administration. Colfax, originally a Whig editor in Indianapolis, obtained a seat in Congress in 1855 and served a total of fourteen years in that position, the last six of which he was Speaker of the House. After being elected to the vice-presidency in 1868, he was accused of complicity in the postal frauds and the corruption involved in the building of the Union Pacific Railroad (Credit Mobilier scandal). Although nothing officially was proved against him, Colfax left office under a cloud.

The Midwest also contributed the "whisky ring." Centered in St. Louis it was exposed in 1875 by Benjamin H. Bristow, newly appointed secretary of the treasury. It was composed of wealthy distillers, aided by the chief clerk in the treasury department and Grant's private secretary, Orville E. Babcock, who defrauded the government of over $1,650,000 in taxes. Babcock, implicated in the conspiracy, escaped largely through Grant's unwise intervention in his behalf.

Benjamin Harrison, who was an ex-Senator from Indiana, a corporation lawyer, a grandson of William H. Harrison, and an ex-Civil War brigadier general was also involved in corruption during his campaign for the presidency in 1888. In the Midwest this election chicanery was best illustrated in Indiana where the Republicans increased their chances of winning by buying votes. There the notorious Dudley letter, written by a party chairman telling the party machine to put a lieutenant over each bloc of five votes and pay them to vote, came to light. Despite such Republican shenanigans, Grover Cleveland still polled 100,000 more popular votes than Harrison. Due to the distribution of the votes and the nature of the electoral-college system, however, Harrison won a majority of the electoral votes (233-168) and the election.

The Midwest also provided men who fought against political corruption on the basis of principle or for less laudatory reasons. For example, the reaction in the Republican Party against Grant's nepotism, corruption, and inefficiency had its roots in the Midwest. The Liberal Republican movement began in Missouri in 1868. Carl Schurz and Benjamin G. Brown were the main originators. Carl Schurz had come to the United States from Germany in 1852. After practicing law and serving as a brigadier general in the Union army, he made a tour of the South and reported the conditions he found there. Shortly after he became editor of the St. Louis *Westliche Post* and in 1869 was elected United States senator from Missouri. Schurz's co-worker in the Liberal Republican movement was Benjamin G. Brown of Missouri. Also a Union brigadier general, he was elected to the United States Senate in 1863 and to the governorship of Missouri in 1871.

The Liberal Republicans, holding their national convention in Cincinnati, favored a more lenient policy toward the South, civil service reform, and a lower tariff. For their presidential candidate they made the mistake of choosing Horace Greeley, lifelong foe of the Democrats and low tariff. Brown was chosen for the vice-presidency. The Democrats ate crow and endorsed both Liberal Republican candidates at their convention in Baltimore. Despite the combined efforts of the Liberal Republicans

Rutherford B. Hayes (1822-1893)
President of the United States

Carl Schurz (1829-1906)
Journalist, U. S. Senator, Secretary of the Interior

From *Dictionary of American Portraits* by Hayward and Blanche Cirker, Dover Publications, Inc., New York, 1967. *Reprinted through permission of the publisher.*

George H. Pendleton (1825-1889)
U. S. Senator

Engraving by W. G. Jackman. From *Dictionary of American Portraits* by Hayward and Blanche Cirker, Dover Publications, Inc., New York, 1967. *Reprinted through permission of the publisher.*

William McKinley (1843-1901)
President of the United States

James A. Garfield (1831-1881)
President of the United States

Courtesy National Archives, Brady Collection. From *Dictionary of American Portraits* by Hayward and Blanche Cirker, Dover Publications, Inc., New York, 1967. *Reprinted through permission of the publisher.*

Benjamin Harrison (1833-1901)
President of the United States

Courtesy Benjamin H. Walker. From *Dictionary of American Portraits* by Hayward and Blanche Cirker, Dover Publications, Inc., New York, 1967. *Reprinted through permission of the publisher.*

Morrison R. Waite (1816-1888)
Chief Justice of the United States

Marcus A. Hanna (1837-1904)
Industrialist and U. S. Senator

and the Democrats, Grant continued his tainted administration for another term.

An issue closely related to corruption and often contributing to it was patronage. There were many politicians in the Midwest as elsewhere who favored this political-spoils system. However, at least three midwestern political leaders on the national level received acclaim for their struggle against the evils of the spoils system. Roscoe Conkling, Republican senator from New York, for one, did not like President Rutherford B. Hayes' ideas on patronage. For example, when an investigating committee revealed mismanagement in the New York customs, Hayes ordered Chester A. Arthur and Alonzo B. Cornell to make reforms. When they did not comply, he suspended them.

Similarly, President James A. Garfield, an ex-Union major general and an eight term U. S. congressman from Ohio, stood firm against improper patronage. At the beginning of his administration, Thomas L. James, the new postmaster general, uncovered graft involving star-route contracts in the West. Assistant Postmaster General Thomas W. Brady and Stephen W. Dorsey, secretary of the Republican National Committee, were both involved. Garfield allowed the investigations to take their course and for this he was badly maligned by members of his party.

Actually Garfield turned out to be an inadvertent martyr against the spoils system and for civil-service reform. In July of 1881 he was shot by a disappointed office seeker, Charles Guiteau. Garfield died from the wounds three months later. The circumstances of Garfield's death gave great impetus to the civil-service reform movement.

Another Ohioan, George H. Pendleton (Democrat) was also very instrumental in the civil-service campaign. In 1864 Pendleton had been the unsuccessful vice-presidential candidate on the Democratic ticket. Four years later his name was attached to an idea to pay off the Civil War debt in paper money. Defeated on this proposal in the Democratic party, he for a time joined the Greenback movement. In 1879 he was elected to the Senate and became chairman of the committee on civil-service reform. He fought vigorously to improve the public service and in 1883 he helped bring forth the Pendleton Bill, the basic act establishing the merit system in public service. This act established a bipartisan commission of three to set up rules and policies for the administration of the federal civil service. In the classified service, as civil service was called, there were to be no political assessments or removals for political reasons. The classified list could be expanded by action of the president.

Disputed Election of 1876 and the Rise of Big Business

Two midwestern political leaders also played roles, one active and one passive, in the disputed election of 1876. Hayes was the Republican candidate for president and David Davis of Illinois was almost placed on the electoral commission that selected the president.

In this noted election Samuel J. Tilden, the Democratic candidate, received a majority of over 250,000 votes, but he obtained only 184 electoral votes, one short of election, to 165 for Hayes. Twenty electoral votes in the states of South Carolina, Louisiana, Florida, and Oregon were in dispute. To settle this matter Congress established an electoral commission composed of five representatives, five senators, and five justices of the Supreme Court. The senators and representatives were to be half Republican and half Democratic. The Supreme Court members were to be broken down into two Democrats, two Republicans, and one independent. The partisan members were easy to select but the independent proved impossible to find.

Supreme Court Justice Davis of Illinois came nearest to being an independent. He had helped Lincoln obtain the Republican nomination in 1860; for his efforts he was appointed to the Supreme Court in 1862. A millionaire landowner and lawyer, he was selected as the National Labor Reform Party presidential candidate in 1872. He accepted and ran from the security of the Supreme Court bench. His political independence was further demonstrated in 1877 when he accepted a Democratic senatorship from Illinois. Since accepting the senatorial seat made Davis unavailable for the electoral commission, the fifteenth man chosen turned out to be a Republican. As a result Hayes obtained all twenty disputed electoral votes and the presidency by a vote of 8 to 7. In this instance a man from the Midwest possibly altered the course of United States history by accepting a seat in the Senate.

The Civil War, in addition to restoring the Union and ending slavery, speeded the overthrow of the landed aristocracy and placed the economic and political power of the nation in the hands of the rising industrialists and financiers. This was done largely through the Republican Party, which turned the South temporarily into a Republican "rotten borough" and kept the agrarians of the South and West from uniting by waving the "bloody shirt." President Grant was the front man for the businessmen as they took over control of the country. Later Republican presidents like Benjamin Harrison and William McKinley, especially, continued this trend.

Whereas President Grover Cleveland had wanted to lower the tariff in order to reduce the treasury surplus, President Harrison, who was very business oriented, thought a better way to meet the problem was to raise expenditures. The 1889-1890 Congress thus became the first "billion-dollar" Congress. The Republicans spent some of this surplus on veterans. Harrison said that this was "no time to weigh the claims of old soldiers on apothecary scales." Corporal James Tanner, commissioner of pensions, took this admonition literally and was so liberal that he had to be dismissed.

Besides spending, Harrison's administration was also noted for the McKinley tariff, the Sherman Silver Purchase Act, and the Sherman Anti-Trust Act. This tariff, bearing the name of Senator William McKinley of Ohio, raised tariff duties and warmed the hearts of the protectionists. Both of the other acts bore the name of Senator John Sherman of Ohio. The silver purchase act provided for the coinage of 4,500,000 ounces of silver per month. The Sherman Anti-Trust Act was theoretically a second major dent in governmental laissez faire (the Interstate Commerce Act was the first). But despite the fact that these last two acts appeared to be anti-business, neither had much effect in reducing the power of big business in the country; the overall tone of Harrison's administration was very pro-business.

McKinley, whose most trusted lieutenant was the dedicated

businessman, Senator Mark Hanna of Ohio, not only went along with a solid-gold plank and high tariff in his administration but also many other policies that were favorable to the interests of big business.

Labor, Agriculture, and the Populist Movement

On the other hand the Midwest also provided a large number of the political leaders who championed the cause of labor and agriculture. President Hayes, for example, found himself attacked by the midwestern congressional leadership over the amount of money in the economy and the coinage of silver. Actually, Hayes was partly a victim in this affair, because both the Coinage Act of 1873 and the Resumption Act of 1875 had been passed prior to his taking office.

The Coinage Act of 1873, referred to as the "Crime of 1873," had suspended the coinage of silver. The Resumption Act of 1875 (effective in January 1879) further reduced the amount of money in circulation by returning the country to the gold standard. This trend toward deflation was resented by the inflationist group. In 1878 this group in the House reacted by passing the Bland-Allison Act over Hayes' veto. As originally pushed through the House under the leadership of Richard P. Bland of Missouri, it provided for the free and unlimited coinage of silver. Unwilling to go this far, the Senate at the insistance of William B. Allison of Iowa altered the bill so that the treasury could buy only two to four-million dollars of silver bullion a month for coinage.

The Greenbackers, who favored more paper money in circulation, also had a noted leader from the Midwest. He was James B. Weaver of Iowa who had served as a brigadier general in the Civil War.

Probably the strongest anti-business movement coming partly out of the agarian Midwest, however, was the Populist movement. It had its beginnings soon after the Civil War and its causes were legion. Farm prices declined steadily from 1865 to 1897 except for a temporary boom in the 1880's. Wheat, for example, dropped from $1.06 in the period 1870-1873 to 63 cents in the period 1894-1897. There was also a shortage of money, especially in the rural areas. The railroads also contributed to the farmer's plight. Farmers of Kansas, Nebraska, Iowa, Minnesota, and Dakota maintained that it took one half of their crop of wheat or corn to get it to market. Still the railroads did not become wealthy, because they had overbuilt and did not have adequate business. In addition, trusts beset the farmer on every side. Items he had to buy were kept high by the plow, fertilizer, or machinery trusts. The prices of the items he had to sell were kept low by lack of demand and marketing trusts. Since the rural areas were short on capital, interest on farm mortgages was high and it finished grinding the farmer down. After 1887 interest rates ranged from eight to twenty-four per cent.

The high point in midwestern discontent came in the decade after 1887 because of a peculiar combination of circumstances. People pushed into western Kansas and Nebraska in the 1870's and 1880's. There was a lot of rain during these years and the people thought this area was a garden spot. Western land companies using eastern money loaned up to the full value on western farms in 1886 and 1887. This tempted the midwesterners into over-expansion, over-investment, speculation, and extravagance. Speculation reached its peak in 1887 in midwestern towns like Omaha, Lincoln, Kansas City, Atchison, Topeka, and Wichita. Kansas towns installed street-car systems and railroads on borrowed money. The end of the boom came in 1887 when a drought began that lasted a decade. Chinch bugs, grasshoppers, hail, and early frosts accompanied the dry spell. The cattle industry collapsed and the lending easterners lost their investments. People began to move east from the arid West. In 1891, 18,000 prairie schooners crossed from Nebraska into Iowa. One third to one half of the counties in Kansas, Nebraska, and South Dakota had smaller populations in 1900 than 1890. Those people remaining in the central and eastern part of these states almost starved and they formed a discontented group ideally prepared for political and economic panaceas.

The first of the farmer organizations to express this discontent after the Civil War was the Patrons of Husbandry (the

Grange) founded in 1867 by Oliver H. Kelley, an ex-Minnesota farmer and clerk in the United States bureau of agriculture. The Grange's purpose was to improve the political, economic, and social status of the farmer. The Grangers began to take over the state legislatures and to fix the maximum rates for railroads. They were elated by the case of *Munn v. Illinois* in 1876, which stated that the state legislature could set railroad rates in intrastate commerce. By 1874 the Grange had 1,500,000 members. Illinois, Wisconsin, Iowa, Minnesota, Kansas, and Nebraska had the most. But as economic conditions improved after 1877, the Patrons of Husbandry declined.

In the Midwest the Grange was succeeded by the Northern Alliance which had its beginning sometime during the 1870's. New York claimed the organization began there in 1877, and Kansas claimed credit for founding it in 1874. In either case the first really effective Alliance organization was begun in Chicago, Illinois, by a farmer-turned-editor, Milton George, in 1880. He publicized the Alliance idea in his *Western Rural* and the Alliance began to spread. At first the Alliance proved most popular in Kansas, Nebraska, Iowa, and Minnesota. It claimed 100,000 members by the time of its third national meeting at St. Louis in October 1882. Slipping after 1882, hard times put it back on its feet by the time of the Minneapolis meeting in October 1887. At this time it began to work with the Southern Alliance that had been founded in Texas. The Alliances tried to merge but they could not agree on name, Negroes, or objectives. Since the Southern Alliance had about two or three times the membership of the northern branch, the former tended to take over and speak for the movement. The midwestern group did have a national paper published by Jay Burrows, president of the Northern Alliance, at Lincoln, Nebraska, and numerous local papers. The main emphases of the Alliances at first were social and economic. They had dinners and discussion groups as well as cooperatives for buying, selling, and insuring.

At first they tried to work through the major parties, but found themselves frustrated at every turn by clever politicians. In 1890 they decided to establish an independent political party. The Alliances were aided in this endeavor by the Union Labor Party,

James B. Weaver (1833-1912)
Populist political leader and Congressman
From *Dictionary of American Portraits* by Hayward and Blanche Cirker, Dover Publications, Inc., New York, 1967. *Reprinted through permission of the publisher.*

William J. Bryan (1860-1925)
Political leader and Secretary of State
From *Dictionary of American Portraits* by Hayward and Blanche Cirker, Dover Publications, Inc., New York, 1967. *Reprinted through permission of the publisher.*

Philip D. Armour (1832-1901)
Meat packer
From *Dictionary of American Portraits* by Hayward and Blanche Cirker, Dover Publications, Inc., New York, 1967. *Reprinted through permission of the publisher.*

Eugene V. Debs (1855-1926)
Socialist leader
Courtesy Tamiment Institute Library. From *Dictionary of American Portraits* by Hayward and Blanche Cirker, Dover Publications, Inc., New York, 1967. *Reprinted through permission of the publisher.*

which had been founded in Cincinnati in 1887 and had polled a large number of midwestern votes. In June 1890 a convention met at Topeka to establish an agricultural party. The convention was composed of 41 Alliance men, 28 Knights of Labor, 10 members of the Farmers Mutual Benefit Association, 7 Patrons of Husbandry, and 4 Single Taxers. They decided to call it the People's Party and select nominees for Kansas state offices. Nebraska, South Dakota, North Dakota, Minnesota, Michigan, and Indiana also picked Populist candidates. The Populist movement became a crusade under the leadership of James B. Weaver, Ignatius Donnelly, Jerry Simpson, and Mary E. Lease. Weaver of Iowa was elected to Congress in 1879 and 1885 and in 1880 was the Greenback candidate for president. Ignatius Donnelly of Minnesota served three successive terms in the House of Representatives after 1863. Originally a Liberal Republican, he became in turn a Greenbacker and a Populist. Considered a leading genius in the Populist Party, he was twice nominated as vice-president on the Populist ticket. Jerry Simpson, who had formerly been a ship captain on the Great Lakes for twenty-three years, gained his political notoriety after moving to Kansas in 1878. Gaining fame as a man of the soil who wore no socks, he was elected to Congress for two terms in the 1890's on the Populist ticket. Hamlin Garland described him as a personable man with a pleasing voice. The fourth in this group was Mary Lease, also of Kansas, who went down in political history for her many speeches in the Populist cause and the phrase, "What you farmers need to do is to raise less corn and more hell."

In the election of 1890 the Populists made amazing inroads in Missouri, Kansas, Nebraska, North and South Dakota, Minnesota, and even Indiana. After several meetings in 1891 and 1892 at Cincinnati, Indianapolis, and St. Louis, the Alliance and its allies decided to run the Populist ticket as a third party in the presidential election. The seasoned campaigner, General James B. Weaver, was chosen as the nominee for the presidency. The Populist Party was billed as the last attempt to save agricultural America from the jaws of industrial America. Its platform favored labor unions, government ownership of railroads, free silver, postal-savings banks, graduated income tax, exclusion of immigrants, eight-hour day, direct election of senators, and one term for president. Overall the Populist Weaver made a tremendous showing for a third-party presidential candidate in 1892; he received 22 electoral votes and over one-million popular votes. In 1894 the Populists remained strong. They received 48 per cent of Nebraska's popular vote, 30 to 47 percent of Kansas' and South Dakota's, 15 to 29 percent of North Dakota's and Minnesota's, and about 14 percent of the votes in the rest of the Midwest. In all the Populists elected seven representatives and six senators at the national level.*

Grover Cleveland, who had been elected to his second term in 1892, disturbed the midwestern labor-and-agricultural interests still more. Cleveland spent most of his second administration combatting the Panic of 1893 and his remedies were not popular with the above groups. He had the Sherman Silver Purchase Act repealed to stop the drain on gold. Then he saved the gold standard by repeated sales of gold bonds using the services of J. P. Morgan and other New York bankers who made a profit on the transactions. He broke the Pullman Strike in Illinois against the wishes of the Illinois governor, John P. Altgeld. He also ignored the demands of Jacob S. Coxey (Coxey's Army) who led 336 men from Ohio to Washington, D. C., in 1894 to request a $500,000,000 public-works appropriation.

With this background the midwestern labor-and-agricultural leaders approached the election of 1896 with great vigor. Of the issues involved the silver issue received the greatest play and it brought forth a number of midwestern political luminaries on both sides of the issue. On the negative side were Senator Mark Hanna and his Ohio colleague, William McKinley. On the positive side were William J. Bryan, the silver-tongued orator from Nebraska, and Richard P. (Silver Dick) Bland of Missouri. Ignatius Donnelly, in commenting on Bryan's endorsement and theft of the silver plank from the Populists, remarked that Bryan went to *Coin's Financial School* and stole the textbooks.** Bland, who was a veteran congressman from Missouri, was an enthusiastic

*Wooed back into the Democratic Party in 1896, they withered after that election.

**Coin's Financial School (1893) was a tract written by William Harvey which extolled the virtues of unlimited coinage of silver.

advocate of free coinage of silver and as noted earlier was co-author of the Bland-Allison Act of 1878.

Whereas the Republicans chose William McKinley of Ohio as their candidate in 1896, the southern and western agrarians in the Democratic Party got in the saddle, repudiated Cleveland and the gold boys, wrote an inflationist platform, and nominated Bryan after he mesmerized them with his "Cross of Gold" speech.

The election proved to be a struggle between the agrarian South and West on one side and the new capitalist group on the other. The Republicans waged an expensive campaign. McKinley delivered speeches from his front porch in Canton, Ohio. Hanna extracted four-million dollars from the money interests to provide the voters with pamphlets, campaign speakers, bands, and parades. Mortgage holders threatened foreclosure and manufacturers threatened loss of jobs if Bryan were elected. Bryan was ridiculed as a baby Demosthenes and for his over-emphasis on silver. In contrast Bryan took his $300,000 campaign fund and toured 29 states talking directly to five-million people; Bryan lost by one-half million votes.

Summary

As has been noted in the discussion above, the Midwest came into its own in the period 1860 to 1900 as far as persons supplied to top, national-government posts were concerned. A numerical listing further substantiates this conclusion. The Midwest supplied six presidents, three vice-presidents, six secretaries of state, ten secretaries of the treasury, twelve secretaries of war, one secretary of the navy, five attorney generals, eight postmaster generals, thirteen secretaries of the interior, four secretaries of agriculture, four Speakers of the House of Representatives, and nine justices of the United States Supreme Court, including three chief justices. In addition, the Midwest also supplied four unsuccessful presidential candidates and seven unsuccessful vice-presidential candidates for the major parties and numerous presidential and vice-presidential candidates for the minority parties.

That the Middle West was also both influential and a bellwether in national politics was indicated by the fact that a majority of the midwestern states was on the winning side nine out of ten times in presidential elections. Another interesting fact about midwestern participation in national politics was that a majority of midwestern states voted Republican nine out of ten times in the period 1860 to 1900. This is in marked contrast to the period 1800 to 1860, when a majority of the Midwest went Democratic in all but three elections, and of those three the midwestern states split equally between the major parties in two elections. Two contributory factors to this complete political about face were probably the industrialization in the Midwest after 1860 and the Civil War.

— 40 —

Middle Western Views On Foreign Affairs

The New Orleans Mafia Affair

In this period the Midwest generally displayed a combination of economic nationalism and isolationism. The Chicago *Tribune* displayed some of this attitude in the Mafia affair in 1891. The Mafia controversy involved Italian subjects from Sicily who settled in New Orleans. Some were allegedly members of the Mafia Black hand society, who engaged in vendettas, primarily with other Sicilians. In the process of ferreting out the criminals, an American chief of police was murdered. Although suspects were brought to trial for his murder, none was convicted. A number of people in New Orleans then decided to take the matter into their own hands. They marched on the jail and lynched eleven Italians who had either been acquitted or were being held as suspects. The Italian government demanded indemnity for the persons lynched and punishment of the lynchers. When Secretary of State James G. Blaine tried to explain the gap in federalism that kept the national government from taking action in the case, the Italian minister in Washington would not be reconciled and continued to complain. Blaine finally told the Italian diplomat that he did not care what the latter thought of United States institutions; that the United States had never taken orders from a foreign nation and it was not starting now. In commenting on Blaine's statement, the *Tribune* complimented Blaine on his "vigorous assertion of American rights" which took away "the breath from the monkey and hand-organ man and he at once changed his tune." After more furor the United States government finally paid the Italian government a $25,000 indemnity to smooth relations.

Imperialism and the Spanish-American War

As late as 1895 at the peak of the crisis over the Venezuela-British Guiana boundary dispute, the Midwest still retained an anti-British feeling. Vice-president Thomas Marshall of Indiana recalled how small boys chanted on the Fourth of July:

> Fee, fi, fo, fum, I smell the blood of an Englishman
> Dead or alive, I'll have some. Fee, fi, fo, fum.

This feeling in the United States helped to account for President Grover Cleveland's and Secretary of State Richard Olney's vigorous statements on what would be done in settling the dispute between England and Venezuela. England remained calm and finally allowed the United States to survey the line. The boundary which was drawn by the United States and accepted by the disputants in 1899 turned out to be much more agreeable to the British than to the Venezuelans.

It is difficult to assess the reasons for the Midwest's willingness to enter the Spanish-American War. President William McKinley and Senator Mark Hanna, both of Ohio, displayed some reluctance toward going to war. The warlike clamor of the newspapers and the cruelties of General Valeriano Weyler in Cuba undoubtedly had a great effect on the favorable attitude of the Midwest toward the war. Then when the *Maine* was sunk in Havanna harbor, the Midwest, along with the rest of the United States, was ready for war. Although the Kansas City *Star* insisted that "a great nation can afford to take time to be perfectly just," in deciding how the *Maine* was sunk, a majority of the midwestern newspapers and people were inclined toward war. The Spanish flag was burned by a group of students in Omaha and by a mob of people in Chicago. McKinley bowed to public sentiment and sent a war message to

Congress on April 11, 1898. A little over a week later, war was declared.

The midwestern states immediately raised regiments of troops for the engagement but the war was so short that only a small number of the troops saw action. Kansas raised four regiments and none of them reached the battle zone. North Dakota furnished more than a regiment, of which some served in General Arthur MacArthur's brigade in the Philippines. One Minnesota regiment also saw active duty in the Philippines. Out of Iowa's four mobilized regiments, one man was killed and 134 died of disease. Ohio supplied 15,354 men for the war, of whom 240 died of disease. Nebraska had special representation in Colonel William J. Bryan of the state national guard. But he and his troops were unable to get to Cuba fast enough and Theodore Roosevelt, second in command of the Rough Riders, beat him there and obtained more glory out of the affair. General Frederick Funston of Ohio and Kansas gained great notoriety in 1901 when he was successful in capturing Emilio Aguinaldo, the Philippine rebel leader, who had continued to fight the United States after the Spanish-American War was over. General William R. Shafter of Michigan also received praise for his conduct of the land war in Cuba. On the other hand his superior, General Russel A. Alger of Michigan, who was secretary of war, was severely criticized for the unpreparedness of the United States Army at the outset of the war.

Largely as a result of the war and the stage of development of the United States, the U. S. launched out into imperialism around the turn of the century. In the Peace of Paris of 1898 ending the Spanish-American War, the United States acquired the Philippines, Puerto Rico, and Guam. Some midwesterners, apparently viewing imperialism as a natural outgrowth of the expansion in North America, were favorable to the acquisition of these foreign territories. President McKinley, after prayer, decided that he had no alternative. He was supported especially by such midwesterners as Albert J. Beveridge of Indiana and John C. Spooner of Wisconsin.

On the other hand there were midwesterners like Champ Clark of Missouri and Senator Richard F. Pettigrew of South Dakota who favored expansion but opposed the Philippine policy.

Clark said Spain had tried for 300 years to subjugate the Filipinos and had failed, and the United States was foolish for trying. He thought the United States should restrict itself to the acquisition of the British West Indies, the Bahamas, the British North American possessions, and Cuba. Pettigrew said that he had received a marriage certificate from the Philippine Islands, which contained the signatures of over 1,000 people. Only two of them had had to make a mark for their signature. "These," he said, "are the people we are trying to conquer and deprive of their liberty in spite of the fact that they were our allies and helped us fight Spain. We ought to say to the Filipinos, establish your own government. The country belongs to you, and we will protect you."

The Midwest also had vigorous opponents to any type of imperialism. Among these were William J. Bryan and Carl Schurz. Although Bryan lent his influence to pass the Treaty of Paris in 1898, he did it largely so that he could make imperialism an issue in the 1900 presidential campaign. Bryan maintained that there was no warrant for imperialism in the Bible. He argued that the command, "Go ye into all the world and preach the gospel to every creature," had no Gatling-gun attachment. Carl Schurz said he voted for Bryan in 1900 as a protest against McKinley's imperialism, even though he opposed Bryan's free-silver stand and felt that Bryan was the evil genius of the anti-imperialist cause. Although the people of the Midwest, like the rest of the United States, were divided on imperialism, they were apparently satisfied with the continuing growth and power of the United States.

Ship Subsidies and the Tariff

On topics like the Panama Canal and subsidies to merchant shipping, the Midwest was somewhat disinterested. Although the people of the North Central states were proud of the accomplishment of building the canal, they were not too interested in its use.

Because of his commercial interests, Mark Hanna of Ohio was very interested in the Panama Canal and also very favorable to passing a ship-subsidy bill. He was unsuccessful in this and he said it was because he couldn't get the midwestern Republicans interested in the project. Examples of attitudes that killed the ship subsidy were displayed in the Vincennes *Western Sun* and the Goshen *Democrat.* The *Western Sun* in 1901 pointed out that the shipyards were running a year behind schedule in their orders and that 112 new ships of 16,120 gross tons had been turned out in August. These facts satisfied the *Sun* that no subsidy was necessary to increase the merchant marine. Especially vitriolic, the Goshen *Democrat* in 1901 commented that the ship-subsidy rogues or treasury tappers could not decide whether they would steal nine-million dollars per year or six million. The *Democrat* concluded that they would probably compromise on twelve-million dollars, since none of them would feel badly about robbing the public of a few million.

On the topic of tariff the Midwest had long tended to favor high duties. This region had supported the high-tariff provision in Henry Clay's American System and had also supported protectionist tariffs like the Morrill Act of 1861, the McKinley Act of 1890, and the still higher Dingley Tariff of 1897. However, the Dingley Tariff may have been too high even for some midwestern Republicans who began talking of reciprocity. According to some midwestern newspapers, however, this reciprocity idea was just window dressing. The Indianapolis *Journal* in 1901, for example, remarked that no one need worry about the Republican reciprocity craze. In the case of McKinley, the paper contended that his view of reciprocity was simply expanded protection. The *Journal's* view on McKinley's reciprocity proved to be largely true. He did little on the matter. In the election of 1908 the Republicans again talked about revising the tariff and everyone supposed they meant downward. When they finally did get around to revising the tariff in 1909, however, they passed the Payne-Aldrich Tariff which increased the duties still more. A group of insurgent Republicans including Albert J. Beveridge of Indiana, Joseph L. Bristow of Kansas, Moses E. Clapp of Minnesota, Albert B. Cummins and Jonathon P. Dolliver of Iowa, and Robert M. La-Follette of Wisconsin led the fight against this higher tariff in the Senate but they lost. Congress also tried to pass reductions on single items (popgun tariff bills), but President William H. Taft vetoed them. Taft did favor a reciprocal tariff with Canada, but the insurgent midwestern Republicans and many others from the region opposed this. As in 1854 the Midwest feared the lower duties of Canadian reciprocity would apply only to agricultural goods which would again aid the manufacturers and hurt the farmers.

— 41 —

Agriculture and Lumbering

Cattle Range Industry

By 1900 there were several distinctive patterns of agriculture in the Midwest, varying with the soil, climate, terrain, and background of the people. In addition there had been changes in each of these agricultural areas due to changes in laws, mechanization, scientific agriculture, urbanization, and transportation.

Percentage-wise, the greatest development in agriculture in the latter part of the nineteenth century took place in the area west of the Missouri River. As a whole, the wide-open spaces of this drier area led to greater independence and lawlessness and a cattle-range industry. The cattle industry of the western Midlands was related to the development of the Great Plains and went through several stages of development. First the buffalo had to be killed if the cattle industry was really to flourish. This was accomplished after 1870 by men like "Buffalo Bill" Cody who shot buffalo by the hundred. His killing of them was somewhat defensible, because many of the buffalo were used to feed railroad crews building the Kansas-Pacific Railroad. Others killed them for sport or for the hides. In the three years 1872-74, three railroads carried more than 1,350,000 hides from the southern plains. The buffalo on the northern plains were next to go and they were nearly exterminated by 1885.

At first the states on the western fringe of the Middle West, such as Missouri, Kansas, and Nebraska, simply served as railheads for the cattle brought up from Texas. As the railroads were built west, the terminal cow towns moved with them. The long drive from Texas began in 1865 or 1866 when the Missouri Pacific Railroad reached Sedalia, Missouri. In 1867 operations were shifted to Abilene, Kansas, on the Kansas-Pacific Railroad. Cattle came to this town via the 600-mile Chisholm trail. Ellsworth, Newton, and Wichita also served as terminal cattle towns. When the Santa Fe Railroad reached Dodge City in 1872, it had a cattle boom. It also became a center for buffalo hunters. By 1875 Dodge was the cattle market for the Southwest and it held that position for ten years. Between 1875 and 1879 one-million beeves were delivered to Dodge. William B. (Bat) Masterson and Wyatt Erp were brought in to insure peace. In Dodge City the graveyard was designated "Boot Hill" because so many died with their boots on. In Nebraska Schuyler became the terminal point for Texas cattle on the Union Pacific in 1870. As the railroad was built west, the terminal point moved to Kearny and then to Ogallala and Sydney. Most long-lived of the Nebraska cow towns, Ogallala had about 100,000 Texas cattle driven there each year between 1886 and 1896. All together some 4,000,000 cattle went over the long drives. In the middle eighties, these long drives virtually ended. By that time, the Middle West had passed quarantine laws to keep out Texas fever and the railroads had finally reached Texas.

Since the cattle business was profitable and the Great Plains had the grass for cattle, Kansas, Nebraska, and then the Dakotas began to develop cattle industries in the 1860's which became firmly established by 1880. A large part of the cattle to stock these northern ranges came from Texas. Numerous cattlemen's associations were established to set up rules for summer and winter grazing; keep newcomers out of filled ranges; keep a record of various brands so that the owner could claim his cattle; and protect the cattle and cattlemen from Indians, cattle thieves, sheep men, and homesteaders.

usually had access to a river or creek for water. Ranchers ordinarily tried to stay at least fifteen miles away from their nearest neighbor. This was a man's country. Women disliked the loneliness and isolation. The most colorful events in ranch life were the roundups and the drive. Roundups occurred in the spring and fall. They were for the purpose of branding the calves and of cutting out the prime beef to be driven to the railroad for shipment to market. The length of the drive depended upon the distance of the ranch from the railroad.

The optimum number of cattle for a drive were 2,500 to 3,000 managed by 16 to 18 cowboys. On the trail the cattle were strung out in a long line, with the strongest cattle in the front. They were kept moving by pointers (cowboys ahead), pairs along the sides, and dragmen in the rear to push the cattle. It was a hard, dirty, sometimes dangerous job. But even at this after the round up and drive, the other tasks of ranching, riding fence, and putting up hay were drab by comparison.

The heyday of this first ranching period was 1880 to 1885; then it collapsed. Too many people moved west, went into the cattle business, and flooded the market. This was the period when Theodore Roosevelt moved to North Dakota to enter the cattle business. Other causes of the collapse were the severe winters and blizzards in the years 1885 to 1887, President Cleveland's order forbidding the leasing of Indian lands to cattlemen, and the coming of the homesteaders and the sheep men.

At first the cattlemen fought the homesteaders because their farms and fences marred the landscape. Later in the 1880's the cattlemen fought the homesteaders, because the latter cut the cattlemen's barbwire fences which often enclosed land not belonging to the cattlemen. In his report of 1884, for example, the commissioner of the United States General Land Office reported 32 cases of illegal fencing, averaging more than 138,000 acres per enclosure. After 1885 the government and homesteaders began to win and the ranches were reduced in size. The only solution was for each rancher to fence his range, restrict his herds to reasonable size, and insure plenty of hay for winter. This was the end of the romantic era in ranching. The six gun was replaced by barbed wire and the windmill. But the change did mean better cattle, because breeding and feeding were now more closely controlled.

In addition to modifying the cattle ranch, the windmill and barbwire also aided the farmer in the settlement of the West. The Great Plains were better adapted to cattle raising than to grain farming, but this did not stop the farmers from coming under the auspices of the federal government and the Homestead Act. Although the Homestead Act was beneficial to the small farmer, it did contain some loopholes and disadvantages. In addition to speculators and railroads obtaining the lion's share of the best lands (about 6 to 1), there were also large land swindles. Moreover, a bonafide settler could only acquire 160 acres under the Homestead Act and this was not enough land to make a living in the dry West.

Supplementary acts were passed in an atempt to improve the situation. The Timber Culture Act of 1873 allowed homesteaders to expand their holdings to a more workable size. The Desert Land Act of 1877 provided that a person could get a preliminary title to 640 acres if he made an initial payment of 25 cents an acre. If after three years he could prove that he had irrigated a portion of the land and was willing to pay an additional dollar an acre, he received final title. Designed to help the homesteader, it was actually of more benefit to wealthy ranchers who were not above using a little fraud to obtain land. In 1904 Congressman Moses P. Kinkaid of Nebraska pushed through a law which allowed homesteaders to obtain 640 acres in 37 counties of northwest Nebraska. Although the Kinkaiders had a hard time of it in their tar paper shacks and soddies, many of them proved up their land. Two other general homestead laws were passed later. One in 1909 provided for homesteads of 320 acres in dry-farming areas. A second in 1916 allowed 640 acres to be homesteaded for stock raising.

Dry-Land Farming

The problems faced by the dry-land farmers moving into Kansas, Nebraska, and the Dakotas were staggering. They often became the victims of large ranchers who did not want them cluttering up the range. In many areas there was little or no water. The windmill proved a partial solution in these areas where the winds constantly blew. Not until 1890, however, could most farmers afford the $1,000 for a well and a windmill. But even the windmill did not provide sufficient water for farming. Although irrigation was a possible solution, only a small part of the area had water available for irrigation and irrigation was expensive. Moreover as of 1900 only about one-two hundredths of the potential irrigable land was irrigated. Although Congressman Francis G. Newlands of Nevada tried to improve this situation with an irrigation act in 1902, irrigation still proceeded very slowly.

A more important way in which the farmers tried to combat the lack of moisture was with dry farming. Hardy W. Campbell of Nebraska was the great evangelist for dry farming. He advocated the growing of low moisture crops like Turkey Red, Kharkov, and Crimean wheat; special varieties of oats, barley, and rye; milo maize; Sudan grass; and kaffir and Jerusalem corn. He favored dry-farming techniques such as summer fallowing (allowing a part of the land to lay idle for a season with periodic cultivation in order to store moisture), deep disk harrowing (rather than plowing) to keep the stubble on top of the ground and check wind erosion, and the planting of wind breaks to restrict the sweep of the wind and to retain moisture.

Consequently, because of the geographical conditions present, the most colorful and abundant of the grains grown in Kansas, Nebraska, and the Dakotas was wheat, king of the grain country. Although wheat was grown first in the western Midwest in 1839, it did not become a major crop until the 1870's. Although horses drawing binders and stationary threshers, capable of threshing thousands of bushels of wheat per day, did most of the harvesting as late as 1900, the fourteen-foot combine (a header and thresher in one machine, pulled by eight horses or a steam tractor) had already been introduced into the region from California.

Farming in the Eastern Middle West

In the more moist areas of the eastern Middle West, farming was less of a gamble and the standard of living was at least slightly better. In 1900 the composite American as compiled by the Twelfth Census was representative of this more easterly midwesterner engaged in diversified farming. According to the census, this person was of western European stock. His civil, political, and social makeup was Anglo-Saxon, sharpened and intensified by his fresh contact with nature. Physically, the average American male was five-feet, eight-inches tall and weighed 150 pounds. His family consisted of a wife and two children, a third child having died in infancy. His age was thirty-seven and he expected to live thirty years more. His wife was thirty-five, five-feet, four-inches tall, and weighed 126 pounds. They had been married ten years. The two children were pursuing their studies in public schools. Both parents had received a common-school education but had not attended high school.

Their home was a farm near Columbus, Indiana, in the southern part of the state. The farm contained 137 acres, eighty of which were under cultivation. Although estimated in value at $3,500, the farm had a mortgage of five-hundred dollars. Fairly well supplied with livestock, the average farmer owned three horses and mules, three cows, six beef cattle, eight sheep, and eight hogs. During the preceding year, the farm had produced 500 bushels of corn, 200 bushels of oats, 45 bushels of potatoes, and 12 tons of hay. His annual income from the farm was $540. This average family ate well, consuming 1,250 pounds of wheat flour, 600 pounds of oat and corn meal, 750 pounds of meat, 750 pounds of potatoes, 100 pounds of butter, and 300 pounds of sugar. The greatest coffee drinkers on earth, the family consumed one pound a week. In one year the head of the family smoked 20 pounds of tobacco and drank seven gallons of liquors and 75 gallons of beer. His stoves consumed three tons of coal and 14 cords of wood. Since gas and electric lights had not reached his rural district, he used five gallons of kerosene per year for lighting. Members of the family used the mails lavishly, sending 220 letters, 40 postal cards, and 60 packages annually. For clothing the family expended annually one-hundred dollars. Although the farmer seldom attended church, he and his family were numbered among the adherents of a Protestant church. His wife and children were regular Sunday school attendants.

In contrast to this composite midwestern farmer of 1900, there were also more prosperous specialized farmers like the fictional Farmer Russell. Russell owned eighty acres of land and specialized in dairying and fruit raising. He had a hired man that he provided with a neat tenant house and $300 a year in cash. The day began at five o'clock in the morning when the hired man hurried to the barn, fed and groomed the cows, and cleaned the stalls. Russell helped with the milking. The milk was carried to an adjoining milk-room, where it was poured into an electric cream separator. Placed directly into shipping cans, the cream was hauled to the creamery by a trolley with a freight car attached. The cows, instead of picking a poor living from uncertain pastures, were fed a scientific ration of grain and ensilage in comfortable stalls. The water for the barn, house, lawn, and milk room was supplied by a windmill and a tubular well. The grain crops were planted, cultivated, and cut by horse-drawn equipment. The orchards were carefully cultivated, sprayed, and tended.

Farmer Russell's business arrangements were cared for in a similar careful manner. He had a telephone. To keep informed on market prices and world affairs, he took two daily papers. He kept a simple set of books, and he knew where he stood financially at the end of each year.

In addition to farmers of these two types, there were many other farmers more prosperous and less prosperous. But in nearly every case, there was a great deal of hard physical labor and plain living on these farms.

Agricultural Production

Since the Midwest contained large areas that had a favorable climate and rich soils, it was only natural that it was the largest producer of agricultural products in the United States in this period. The region had early acquired this distinction in several crops. Ohio ranked first in wheat production among the states in 1840 and in corn and wool in 1850. In 1840 the Midwest as a whole led in the production of swine, horses, mules, and wheat. Twenty years later it had 32 per cent of the improved land and produced 55 per cent of the wheat, 48 per cent of the corn, 31 per cent of the barley, 68 per cent of the flaxseed, 37 per cent of the hay, 36 per cent of the sheep, 30 per cent of the dairy cows, 36 per cent of the swine, and 37 per cent of the horses and mules. In addition the Midwest was also second in oats, flax fiber, potatoes, and cattle. Among the individual midwestern states in 1860, Ohio was first in the nation in the production of flaxseed, wine, and sheep; Indiana in hogs; and Illinois in wheat and corn. By 1880 Kansas was first in the production of wheat.

In 1900 the Middle West was still leading in improved land and agricultural products. This section with 25 per cent of the land area had 54 per cent of the improved farm land. From these farms came 73 per cent of the nation's corn, 67 per cent of the wheat, 81 per cent of the oats, 58 per cent of the hay, 63 per cent of the barley, 52 per cent of the potatoes, and 63 per cent of the rye. In animals the Midwest contained 64 per cent of the nation's swine, 26 per cent of the sheep, 52 per cent of the horses, and 23 per cent of the mules. In number these twelve states had 47 per cent of the nation's cattle and in value 53 per cent. In the 40 years after 1860, the Midwest improved percentage-wise in nearly every one of its major agricultural production areas.

Farm Problems

Even in areas where rich soils and moderate climate were present, the Middle West, like the rest of the rural United States, had farm problems. And as one would expect, the farm problems were the greatest in the submarginal areas of the Midwest. Farmers are by nature gamblers and those living in the semi-arid and less fertile areas of the Midwest gambled most. Some problems were perennial, some were temporary, some came from within the agricultural community, and some came from without.

Probably the most perennial problem of the farmer was nature. A few examples will suffice. Around 1850 Ohio wheat production declined because of winter killing, rust, blight, and chinch bugs. Seven years later Nebraska was plagued by droughts and grasshoppers. In the years between 1873 and 1877, the Dakotas, Iowa, Kansas, Minnesota, and Nebraska were infested with Rocky Mountain locusts. A modest boom which began in 1877 when it started to rain again came to an abrupt end after 1877 when late and early frosts, hail, drought, chinch bugs, and Hessian flies returned. Droughts and dust storms were the inevitable result of cultivation and low moisture. Dust storms of the late 1880's in Kansas were so bad that a man, standing in the middle of a village street, could hardly see the street lights burning on either side. People who had gone confidently to Kansas a few years before returned east with the slogan, "In God we trusted, in Kansas we busted." In August 1901 the temperature soared from 90 to 110° in Missouri, Iowa, Kansas, Nebraska, and there was no rain. At Topeka the Kansas River was so dry that grass grew in the center of the river bed. Pastures were burned so severely that growers of stock rushed their cattle, sheep, and hogs to market to keep the animals from starving. About one third of the total midwestern corn crop was destroyed.

Another of the farmer's perennial problems were farm prices which were too low to meet his expenses and afford him a fair profit. Between the early 1870's and middle 1890's, the price of wheat dropped from $1.07 to 63 cents a bushel and corn from 43 to 30 cents a bushel. These low prices were caused largely by overproduction and lack of control over markets. Overproduction in turn was caused by several factors. First, the farmers produced crops indiscriminately for an unknown market. Second, increasing amounts of land were rapidly put in production. In the period 1860-1900, for example, over 500,000,000 acres of land were put under the plow. Third, mechanization greatly increased production. As an indication of this, the man hours required to produce a bushel of corn declined from four and one-half hours in 1855 to 41 minutes in 1894; and a bushel of wheat from four hours in 1830 to ten minutes in 1894. Fourth, scientific agriculture, including fertilization, improved crop rotation, and better plants and animals, made possible greater production per acre.

As the prices went down, the farmers were also met by rising costs and greater overhead. As early as the 1850's, a contemporary estimated that a farmer in Iowa would need around $1,800 in order to get started. By 1890 the price of land, livestock, and machinery had all increased so that more money was needed to start farming. The value of farm land in Iowa, for example, increased from $10 an acre in 1870 to $50 in 1890 and to $100 in 1910. In 1900 a walking plow cost $14, a cultivator $23, a drill $50, a twine binder $140, and a good team of horses $220. Overall, the value of machinery used on midwestern farms more than doubled between 1860 and 1900.

Transportation rates also seemed exorbitant to the farmer. Those living in Kansas, Nebraska, Iowa, Minnesota, and Dakota in the 1880's and 1890's had to pay one bushel of wheat or corn to get two bushels to the Chicago market. Short hauls were expensive too. There was often little competition among routes and the railroads charged as much as they could. Actually the railroads made small profits because they had overbuilt and the farmers were charged for their mistakes.

Farm credit was scarce and expensive. In the earlier history of the Midwest, there was a shortage of banks in the rural areas, and there was the natural tendency of credit to concentrate in the urban areas. Up to 1900, at least, even when a farmer could obtain a loan, it was at an exorbitant rate; six to twenty per cent per annum.

As a result of these problems the farmers of the Midwest, particularly in the western Midwest, felt very mistreated in the period of the 1880's and 1890's especially. This unrest revealed itself in the Farmers' Alliances and the Populist movement described earlier which blossomed out in this period.

Lumbering

One of the richest pine regions in America originally lay in the upper-Mississippi Valley in the states of Michigan, Minnesota, and Wisconsin. As early as 1830 the conquest of the forests began and lumbering became one of the primary frontier industries. Lumbermen were among the first arrivals in northern Michigan,

Wisconsin, and Minnesota. By 1858 the upper-Wisconsin River alone had 107 sawmills. The chief markets for these lake-state pines were in the treeless plains of Illinois, Iowa, and states westward.

Since the first lumberjacks were largely from New England, they brought with them the legend of Paul Bunyan and Babe, the great blue ox, and the "state-of-Maine" lumber camp. This camp had one building about 30 by 40 feet with side walls about two feet high. The walls were built of logs and the roof was made of stakes covered with evergreen boughs or clay. The building was so low inside that a man could not stand erect in more than two thirds of its width. It had a fireplace in the center and on one side a field bed extending the full length of the building. The men slept with their heads toward the wall. Rough tables across one end of the building served as the dining area. In the 1880's and 1890's this type camp was replaced by a more elaborate one. At first double-bitted axes and later saws were used to cut the trees. Many men got hurt or killed by falling or rolling logs. Although there was no work on Sunday, thirteen-hour days were the rule on the other six days.

The boom period in the midwestern lumber industry was 1860 to 1910. For a time the lumbering and railway interests practically controlled Wisconsin. The lumber barons exploited the Wisconsin timber and left the state poorer. When they had cut the best timber, they simply abandoned the cutover areas. Lumbermen in Minnesota also cut timber on government land and were seldom caught. Forest fires also took their toll. In 1871 at the same time as the Chicago fire, Michigan had a forest fire that left 3,000 families homeless. The rapid decline of the lumber industry in the Midwest is shown by the fact that the Midwest produced 49 per cent of the nation's lumber in 1900 and seven per cent in 1930. In 1900 Wisconsin was first in lumber production in the United States and in 1930, in fourteenth place. Michigan showed a similar pattern. In 1890 Michigan was first in all fields of lumbering activity and by 1935 had dropped to nineteenth place.

—42—

Mining and Manufacturing

Mining

In addition to agricultural crops, the people of the Midwest also obtained many other products from the earth and water bodies of the area. Coal in the Midwest was noted as early as 1679 by Father Hennepin. Christopher Gist took some samples back with him to his employers in the Ohio Company in 1751. In 1787 Manasseh Cutler noted coal areas on his Ohio map. By 1840 large quantities were being mined in Ohio, Illinois, and Indiana. Although the grade of coal in the Midwest was generally lower, this region produced about 32 per cent of the nation's bituminous coal in 1900.

Copper mining was once very important in the Midwest especially in the Keweenaw Copper Range of Upper Michigan. Mining having begun about 1842, the big copper rush to the area occurred in 1846 when several thousand people arrived. Calumet and Hecla Company owned the richest copper mines in Upper Michigan and paid $160,000,000 dividends on $10,000,000 invested. In 1889 Michigan was the greatest copper-producing area in the world. In 1900 it was still producing 21 percent of the nation's copper ore. Its decline occurred after 1910 when shallow mines in the West replaced Michigan's deep ones.

One of the most colorful periods in the Midwest was born with the discovery of gold in the Black Hills in about 1875. It not only attracted men like "Wild Bill" Hickock and women like "Calamity" Jane to Deadwood, but it was also partly responsible for the Battle of the Little Big Horn and Custer's Last Stand. Although a substantial amount of gold was mined in the Black

Hills, South Dakota's production in 1900 was only about four per cent of the nation's total.

The most abundant mineral in the Midwest was iron. Iron ore was mined soon after 1800 in Ohio. By 1835 the Hanging Rock area (Jackson, Lawrence, Scioto, and Uinton counties) became most important. In the 1840's iron ore was discovered at the present-day site of Negaunee, Michigan. The first range to be developed there was the Marquette Range. The "Soo Canal" and Civil War put it in business. It was followed by the Menominee and Gogebic ranges which were developed in the 1870's and 1880's.

A geologist reported iron ore in northern Minnesota in 1865, but little was done about it until the 1880's. The Vermillion Range was opened in 1884. The Minnesota Iron Company was instrumental in this. Mining operations began in the great Mesabi Range in 1892. In 1901, 9,004,890 tons were taken out of 30 mines in the Mesabi. The Cuyuna Iron Range was not opened until 1911. United States Steel and J. J. Hill were early developers of the mines and railroads in this area. Port Arthur, Two Harbors, Duluth, Superior, Ashland, Escanoba, Marquette, and Michpicoten handled the ore. In 1900 this Great Lakes region produced 80 per cent of the nation's iron ore, and 30 years later 88 per cent. Mesabi was the largest single producer followed by the Cuyuna Range.

The Midwest also produced varying amounts of phosphate, clay, sand gravel, rock, petroleum, natural gas, gypsum, zinc, and chalk. The 40 per cent of United States limestone produced in the southern Midwest was very important for building stone as well as for iron smelting. Despite its huge deposits of high-grade iron ore and large quantities of some other selected minerals, the Midwest was low enough in other minerals that the total value of minerals produced in 1900 in the Midlands was only about 30 per cent of the nation's total.

Manufacturing

Manufacturing was the last economy to come to the Midwest. At first midwestern industries used the streams and rivers for power. Later coal was a main fuel and still later electricity became the dominant form of energy. At the population poured into the Midwest, it quickly developed a labor pool. The Midwest had a great abundance of agricultural and extractive raw materials. Transportation was soon present in the form of boats, wagons, trains, and trucks. With its own large population and access to the rest of the nation and the world, it had little problem in finding a market.

The Midwest developed a wide range of industries. Certain ones were especially outstanding. With its large numbers of hogs and cattle, the Midwest early developed a meat-packing industry. At first most of the butchering was done on the farms for home use. After 1818, however, meat packing as an industry came into existence west of the Alleghenies. During the period 1810 to 1830, herds of cattle and hogs were driven to the southern plantations and eastern industrial areas. The difficulties experienced on these drives encouraged the development of local slaughtering houses. Cincinnati, favorably located at a place where drover's trails and water transportation met, became the first important meat-packing center in the Midwest. By 1840 this "Porkopolis of the West" had 62 slaughter houses. Ten years later it packed 27 per cent of the meat products of the West.

Within fifteen years, however, Chicago, as a result of the coming of the railroads, was the leading western packing center. In 1900 the chief packing plants of Chicago were Armour and Company, Swift and Company, Nelson Morris and Company, Anglo-American Provision Company, Libby, McNeill and Libby Company, Fairbank Canning Company, Schwarzschild and Sulzberger Company, Continental Packing Company, and Thomas J. Lipton Company. These plants employed a quarter of a million of Chicago's population. The capacity of the Chicago yards at that time was 75,000 cattle, 80,000 sheep, 300,000 hogs, and 6,000 horses. In addition to the regular meats, the packing houses also produced as by-products such items as phosphorus, fertilizers, glue, pepsins, glycerine, wool, bristles, hair, felt, skins, eggs, butter, lard, oleo, tallow, and soap. Although Illinois with Chicago as its center had 40 per cent of the meat packing, nearly every midwestern state had a packing industry in 1900. Other leading meatpacking cities in 1900 were Kansas City, Kansas, and Omaha, Nebraska, tied for second, with St. Louis, Missouri, and Sioux City, Iowa, next in importance.

A second major food processing industry in the Middle West was the flour and meal industry. Flour mills were set up first in Chicago and St. Louis and in other major cities of the Ohio Valley. As early as 1836 Cleveland's wheat and flour exports were valued at more than $1,700,000. The flour and meal industry was the largest industry in Indiana in 1860. In 1870 it was also largest in Illinois and second largest in Minnesota. Ten years later it was first in Wisconsin. After the turn of the century, the center of the flour-milling industry moved to the twin cities of Minneapolis and St. Paul and Kansas City.

A third food industry that early developed in the Midwest was distilled liquors. The pioneer farmers of the West turned corn into whisky because it was easy to transport. They could get two gallons of whisky out of a bushel of corn. By 1850 Cincinnati was the greatest distilling center in the world. After 1860, however, much of the industry shifted to German communities in Missouri, Wisconsin, and Illinois. In 1900 Illinois was the first in the distilling of spirits in the nation, and the Midwest had 59 per cent of the nation's distilling industry.

Other important food industries in the Midwest included dairy products, canned fruits and vegetables, bakery products, and miscellaneous food preparations. A few examples of leading, food-processing cities were Green Bay, Wisconsin, noted for cheese; Battlecreek, Michigan, for Post and Kellogg breakfast cereals; Cedar Rapids, Iowa, for Quaker Oats; and Minneapolis, Minnesota, for flour milling.

Other agricultural and lumber-processing industries in the Midwest included printing and publishing, rubber products, lumber products, furniture, paper products, and leather products.

Most of these industries were widely spread. Saw mills, tanneries, and paper mills developed early. In 1850 Cincinnati was the leading furniture-manufacturing city in the West. Less than fifty years later, Grand Rapids, Michigan, became the furniture capital of the United States. Des Moines was noted for its hosiery and woolen mills and its fur and leather factories. Green Bay, Wisconsin, was noted for its napkin and tissue plants. Rubber manufacturing was somewhat more centralized at Akron, Ohio. B. F. Goodrich built a rubber factory there in 1869. In the 1930's Akron, with thirty rubber plants, used forty per cent of all the rubber produced in the world, manufactured 125,000 tires daily, and produced 32,000 different rubber articles from rubber bands to balloons and dirigibles.

The Midwest also had industries based on products mined and extracted from the soil. The Midlands made an early start in the iron industry. In Ohio an iron furnace was in operation at the mouth of Yellow Creek in 1808; another was operating at the mouth of the Licking River in 1810. Three Ohio furnaces, reported in the census of 1820, had an annual output of 1,187 tons with a value of $109,000. The Hanging Rock district in Ohio became an important iron-producing area after 1830. The first important manufacture of crucible steel in the United States began at Cincinnati in 1832. Southern Ohio soon lost its early lead. By 1900 the Youngstown area of northern Ohio was developing as a steel area with the ore pouring in by lake vessels from the Lake Superior iron ranges.

Among the early industries based on iron in the middle west were safe and vault manufacturing. As early as 1900 Ohio had 61 per cent of this industry.

With its booming agriculture, the Midwest also naturally developed a farm-machinery industry. At first farm machinery was produced in blacksmith shops, but by 1840 it was moving to the factory. Cyrus H. McCormick built his factory in Chicago in 1847 and by 1860 he was turning out 4,000 reapers a year. In 1858 John Deere at Moline, Illinois, was producing over 13,000 steel plows annually. One of the largest manufacturers of threshing machines was Jerome I. Case of Wisconsin who diversified in farm-machinery production after the Civil War. Illinois, however, remained the leader in this area with 41.5 per cent of the nation's agricultural-implement production in 1900.

Overall development of manufacturing in the Midwest was rapid and continuous. The shift of manufacturing to the Midwest was demonstrated by the fact that the statistically-derived center of industry in 1850 was near Mifflintown, Pennsylvania, and by 1900 it was near Loudonville, Ohio. As of 1900 the Midwest accounted for 34 per cent of the manufacturing done in the United States.

— 43 —

Labor

Agricultural Labor

Up until 1850 labor was extremely scarce in the Midwest. The people of the Old Northwest, who entered the territorial stage under the Ordinance of 1787, were not allowed to have slaves. A few persons in Ohio, Indiana, and Illinois, however, evaded this provision up to 1820 by keeping indentured servants. In 1810 Indiana had 250 indentured servants and in 1818 Illinois had 800. Missouri, entering the territorial stage under the Spanish land law, had slavery, a condition continued by the Compromise of 1820. The number of slaves in Missouri, however, was low.

Despite the shortage of agricultural labor in the pioneer years, wages were low. The usual wage of a farm laborer in the first half of the nineteenth century was $7 to $15 a month plus room and board. Without board the pay of an agricultural laborer was about fifty cents a day in 1800. By 1860 this had increased to $1.50 or even $2.00. Even after 1860 when the population had increased in the Midlands, farm labor was still scarce. Labor was needed for the new industrial development, and the manufacturer could usually pay better wages than the farmer. As of 1900 the farm laborer was still only receiving on the average about $10 a month plus room and board. Without board the average wage was still $1.50 to $2.00 a day. Agricultural laborers in the Midwest were not organized and their total number was low. As of 1920, their wages had increased some, but they were still below industrial wages. A farm laborer might receive $15 to $25 a month plus room and board, or $1 to $3 a day without board and room.

Industrial Labor

Because of their numbers, industrial laborers received much more attention than agricultural. Industrial laborers were not particularly numerous in the Midwest prior to 1860. The average wage in 1800 for unskilled labor was 90 cents a day. It had increased to $1.00 a day by 1825 and remained at that figure until about 1860. By 1900 the average wage had climbed to $1.50 a day. Skilled labor made about twice as much. Although these were not high wages they were higher than those received in Europe. Thomas Mooney, an Irish traveller in the United States in 1850, wrote of the wonderful opportunities for laborers. He said that no worker received less than 70 cents a day or $4.20 a week. The laborer could get food, room, and laundry for $2.50 and save up $1.70 per week. With land only $1.25 per acre, he could save up enough in a year to buy 80 acres of good land in the West. Actually these wages were not very high for a single man and if the man were married and had a family, these wages were hardly sufficient to exist on.

Poverty did exist in midwestern cities in the 1840's and 1850's. But it was not as horrible as in Europe, because there was the frontier in America to serve as an escape valve. However, the early mills in the Midwest were often unsanitary and unhealthy places in which to work. The 12 to 15 hour day was common in 1832. Child labor was prevalent. Immigrants poured in during the forties and fifties, crowding the cities and providing competition which resulted in even lower wages.

The factors chiefly responsible for the development of labor organizations in America were the coming of the Industrial Revolution, the concentration of labor in the urban areas, and the changing economic position of the worker. The artisan in a small shop or on a small plot of ground was far more independent than the person who worked in a factory and lived in a tenement. Moreover, labor organized because of unsanitary slums, long hours, low pay, exploitation of women and children, and failure to obtain justice in the courts.

Although eastern unionization began around 1830, the Midwest did not experience much union activity until after 1860. The Brotherhood of Locomotive Engineers, first of the great railroad brotherhoods, was organized as the Brotherhood of the Footboard in Detroit in 1863. The Knights of St. Crispin, basically a shoemakers organization, was founded in Milwaukee in 1867. Its greatest strength, however, was in the East. The Midwest also had many members in the National Labor Union (1866) and the Noble Order of the Knights of Labor (1869). In 1881 the Knights of Industry, strong in the Middle West, and its daughter organization, the Amalgamated Labor Union, issued a call for a convention to set up a closer relationship among the craft unions. The American Federation of Labor which grew out of this did not actually federate until 1886.

Two of the most sensational events that occurred on the midwestern labor scene prior to 1900 were the Haymarket Riot and the Pullman Strike. In February 1886 the workers struck at the McCormick works in Chicago in an attempt to get a closed shop. McCormick locked out the workingmen. On May 3 a riot occurred at the McCormick plant. The following day a mass meeting was held at Haymarket Square in Chicago, where some anarchists spoke in protest against the shooting of strikers by police. During the course of the meeting, police surrounded the group and an unknown hand hurled a bomb that killed one policeman and wounded several others. In the fight that ensued, ten more people were killed including six policemen. As a result eight anarchists were arrested and brought to trial for murder. Although no trace of the bomb thrower was found nor the fact established that any of the accused were involved with him, all eight were found guilty. Four were hanged, one committed suicide, and three received life imprisonment. The labor movement, blamed for this mob action, received a violent setback. In 1893 Governor John P. Altgeld braved public opinion and pardoned the three who had been imprisoned.

The Panic of 1893 with its accompanying unemployment and distress plunged the labor world into a series of strikes. The number of wage earners involved in strikes in 1894 reached almost 700,000, surpassing the mark set in 1886. The most serious disturbance again took place in Chicago as the result of drastic wage cuts by the Pullman Palace Car Company. The employee's cause was championed by the American Railway Union, an industrial-type union, newly formed by Eugene V. Debs, a union organizer from Terre Haute, Indiana. When the company refused to submit the dispute to negotiation, the American Railway Union ordered its 150,000 members to cease handling Pullman cars on all roads. Although the strike affected 23 lines in 27 states and territories, the heart of it was Chicago. There, gangs of hobos and criminals took advantage of the occasion to loot, burn, and kill. The damages, direct and indirect, were later estimated at $80,000,000. Despite Governor John P. Altgeld's refusal to ask for federal troops, President Grover Cleveland sent them anyway. On July 3 the federal government secured from a federal circuit court an injunction which forbade Debs, his union, or any person from interfering in any manner with the operation of the railways. On the next day two-thousand troops were dispatched to Chicago under General Nelson A. Miles. On July 10 Debs was arrested on a charge of conspiracy in restraint of trade under the Sherman Antitrust Act; a week later he was further charged with violation of the injunction of July 2. Debs received six months in Woodstock prison. The national government's vigorous action broke the back of the strike and it collapsed a few weeks later.

The reasons for strikes at the turn of the century in the Midwest were innumerable. A few examples will illustrate their diversity. At Hammond, Indiana, in September 1901, a strike of the printers against W. B. Conkey company occurred. Conkey refused to recognize the printer's union or to pay higher wages. Many of the 250 strikers left to find work in other cities. There was also a strike against the Chicago meatpackers for higher wages and better working conditions, which Upton Sinclair wrote up vividly in his book, *The Brass Check*. The strike accomplished little. A steel strike was also in effect in September 1901 which had some affect in the Midwest. All together some 36,757 strikes involving 6,728,084 strikers occurred in 181,407 establishments between 1881 and 1905 in the United States. Of these, the Midwest had 30 per cent of the strikes and strikers and 33 per cent of the establishments involved.

—44—

Money and Banking

During the generation following the Civil War, the Midwest and South were especially depressed economically. They felt the deflationary policies of the government were ruining them. In 1873 the coinage of silver was suspended. Although none was being coined at the time, within three years discoveries and international actions caused the price of silver to drop so that it would have come back into circulation. As a result the so-called "Crime of 1873" became the issue on which the agrarian West and South blamed their troubles. The Resumption Act of 1875, which returned the country to the gold standard in January 1879, further reduced the amount of money in circulation. As a slight concession to the soft-money group, a small per cent of the greenbacks ($347,000,000) issued by the government during the Civil War was left in circulation. In 1878 the inflationist group, led by men like Richard P. Bland of Missouri, passed the Bland-Allison Act over President Rutherford B. Hayes' veto. This bill ordered the treasury to buy two to four-million dollars of silver bullion monthly for coinage. Silver certificates were also to be issued by banks upon the silver dollars deposited. A second silver-coinage bill, the Sherman Silver Purchase Act, passed in 1890, provided for the coinage of 4,500,000 ounces of silver per month, which was double the amount provided in the Bland-Allison Act. Despite these silver-purchase acts, money in circulation declined while business increased. The situation was made worse by the fact that the government was paying off its bonds, thus reducing the amount of bonds on which national bank notes could be issued. Bank notes in circulation declined $126,000,000 between 1886 and 1890.

Money became even more scarce after the Panic of 1893. Not

only had the Republicans spent money rapidly, they had also passed the high McKinley Tariff which reduced the tariff receipts. This caused such a reduction of gold in the treasury that President Grover Cleveland felt that he must have the Sherman Silver Purchase Act repealed and sell government bonds to save the gold standard. The inflationist wings of both parties were disturbed by Cleveland's actions. In 1896 the Democrats repudiated Cleveland and chose William J. Bryan on a free-silver platform. But the inflationist group was unsuccessful. Bryan was defeated and the Republicans in 1900 passed the Gold Standard Act which kept the United States on a deflated currency basis.

—45—

Railroads

Railroading after 1870 underwent expansion, consolidation, increasing government control, and modernization. Midwestern railroads increased from 11,055 miles (36 per cent of the U. S. total) in 1860 to 85,575 miles (44 per cent of the nation's total) in 1900.

Even more noticeable was the consolidation that took place in railroads after 1870. This consolidation paralleled the combination of capital in industry. Its purpose was to secure greater efficiency, eliminate competition, and obtain greater profits. Cornelius Vanderbilt took the lead in this from 1853 to 1858 in combining 18 small roads into the New York Central. To reduce the disasters of unlimited competition, the railroads set up pooling agreements in the 1870's and 1880's. But when the Supreme Court in the Trans-Missouri Freight Association case in 1898 stated that pooling was a violation of the Sherman Anti-Trust Act, railroad companies began to consolidate again. During the period from 1898 to 1904, the number of consolidations in railroads increased rapidly by means of purchase, lease, and control of stock. It was slowed temporarily in 1904 by the Supreme Court decision in the Northern Securities case.

The Northern Securities Company had been created in 1901 as a result of a struggle between the Edward H. Harriman interests, that controlled the Union Pacific and Southern Pacific, and the J. P. Morgan-J. J. Hill combination, which dominated the Great Northern. The contest was to determine which of the giants would control the Northern Pacific, which in turn controlled the Chicago, Burlington, and Quincy. Each wanted the Burlington because it ran into Chicago and because it tapped a rich agricultural and industrial area. The price of Northern Pacific stock jumped from $100 to $1000 within a few days.

Dwight L. Moody (1837-1899)
Evangelist

From *Dictionary of American Portraits* by Hayward and Blanche Cirker, Dover Publications, Inc., New York, 1967. *Reprinted through permission of the publisher.*

James J. Hill (1838-1916)
Railroad promoter

William T. Harris (1835-1909)
Hegelian philosopher, educator

From *Dictionary of American Portraits* by Hayward and Blanche Cirker, Dover Publications, Inc., New York, 1967. *Reprinted through permission of the publisher.*

James B. Angell (1829-1916)
Educator, diplomat

From *Dictionary of American Portraits* by Hayward and Blanche Cirker, Dover Publications, Inc., New York, 1967. *Reprinted through permission of the publisher.*

Having fought each other to a standstill, they compromised by organizing the Northern Securities Company, a holding company representing both sides which would control the stock of the Great Northern and Northern Pacific. Attacked as a monopoly and a violation of the Sherman Anti-Trust Act, the Norther Securities Company was dissolved by order of the Supreme Court in 1904.

However, despite this setback, the railroads were still highly consolidated by 1906. Of the 228,000 miles of railroads in the United States on that date, about two thirds were in the hands of seven groups. Nearly all these groups had track in the Midwest. The Vanderbilt roads with over 22,500 miles controlled the main routes from New York to Chicago; the Pennsylvania interests with 20,000 miles dominated the East-West roads beginning in Pennsylvania and Maryland; the Morgan system with 18,000 miles predominated in the Southeast; the Gould roads with 17,000 miles and the Rock Island lines with 15,000 miles held sway in the Mississippi Valley; the Hill roads with over 21,000 miles monopolized the Northwest; and the Harriman roads controlled the central and southern transcontinental routes. Moreover, these seven groups received approximately 85 per cent of the railroad earnings.

— 46 —

Religion and Reform

Religious Groups and Directions

The midwestern churches benefiting most from the post-Civil War immigration were the Catholic and the Lutheran. Many of the Catholics went to the cities although some like the German-Russian group that went to Ellis County, Kansas, settled in the rural areas. Between 1870 and 1910 around three-quarter million Swedes, Norwegians, and Danes came to America and a majority of them settled in Minnesota. By 1900 Minnesota had over a million people of Scandinavian origin. Wisconsin, the Dakotas, Illinois, Michigan, Iowa, and Kansas drew large numbers also. Although the Northmen were primarily Lutheran, the growth of that church was not as great as one would have expected. Only about one fifth of these immigrants joined Lutheran churches in America. They simply remained unchurched. This poor record of membership was partly due to the struggle between the conservative and liberal elements in the church and partly to the fact that church membership was less compulsory in America.

With the influx of Jews from Germany, a new, aggressive Jewish leadership developed. In 1875 this Reform Judaism centered in the Midwest at the newly established Hebrew Union College in Cincinnati. The first president of the college was Isaac M. Wise, who was a prime mover in the Union and Reform movements. Although Wise's Reform Judaism accepted the moral laws of the Mosaic code, it rejected the ceremonial and rabbinical regulations which it considered out of date. It also emphasized the universal nature of Judaism rather than the restoration of a Jewish state in Palestine.

Another German group coming in after the Civil War were the Mennonites. Catherine the Great had attracted them originally to the Dnieper Valley of Russia. But in 1870 the Czar put restrictions on their religion and said they must put in 20 years of forestry service in lieu of military service. As a result many of them came to the Midwest. One group settled in Reno, McPherson, Marion, and Harvey counties in Kansas around 1874. Excellent farmers, they were thrifty, God-fearing people. They followed the New Testament and their ministers were often elected laymen. They were historically conscientious objectors, opposed to the taking of oaths, and against settling their disputes in secular courts.

A new, revivalist period came after the Civil War and the leading evangelist of the movement was Dwight L. Moody of Chicago. He served as the president of the Chicago Y.M.C.A. from 1865 to 1869. In 1871 he was joined by Ira D. Sankey, whose singing added greatly to Moody's success. His sermons were simple, but full of conviction, spirit, and emotion.

Missions to the Indians were continued after the Civil War. In 1876, for example, Reverend C. L. Hall and his wife became Congregational missionaries to the Berthold Indians of Dakota. In 1904, 4,000 of South Dakota's 20,000 Indians were members of the Protestant Episcopal church. Some writers like Hamlin Garland believed that the Indians' former culture and religion were more colorful than that foisted on them by the white man. The missionaries, however, felt the white man's Christianity was far more uplifting and beneficial to the Indians than the latter's own religion and culture.

Avenues of reform carried on by the churches prior to 1900 included the Young Men's Christian Association, the Chautauqua, and the Christian Endeavor. Even though all three of these originated outside the Midwest, all were soon in operation there. The Y.M.C.A. had as its purpose the furnishing of wholesome recreation for young people and to introduce them to the church. The Chautauqua was originally initiated to train Sunday School teachers, although it later broadened out into all phases of education. The third group, the Christian Endeavor Society, was founded to bring together thousands of young people of many denominations to discuss problems of Christian service.

The church also underwent some criticism during the 1880's. Many people were disturbed by the principle of evolution which had been announced by Charles Darwin. Many believed evolution was in conflict with the Genesis account of creation. Some men like John Fiske and Lyman Abbott quickly arose to popularize the idea that evolution was not necessarily contradictory to the Bibical story. To the sneer, "So you think your ancestor was a monkey, do you!" Abbott replied that he "would as soon have a monkey as a mud man for an ancestor."

The liberals and conservatives also divided over "higher criticism." This referred to the attempt of Biblical scholars to put the King James version into modern English and to utilize in translation the increased knowledge that 300 years of Biblical scholarship had produced. The question of the inspiration and the accuracy of the scriptures was also hotly debated. A number of heresy trials grew out of this, including one involving Henry P. Smith of Lane Theological Seminary in Ohio. A distinguished Presbyterian scholar, he was convicted of doubting the complete accuracy of the original manuscripts of the Bible.

The church people were even more disturbed by such men as Robert G. Ingersoll of Illinois and Ed Howe of Kansas. Ingersoll, a lawyer, author, and politician, was most noted for his opposition to the Christian religion. He attacked particularly the doctrine of Hell, which he said made man an eternal victim and God an eternal fiend. "Such a doctrine," he said, "gives to the Holy Ghost (the dove) the beak of a vulture and fills the mouth of the Lamb of God with the fangs of a viper." The church, he said, has given nothing to the world except cruelty and superstition. Ingersoll also argued that the writer of Genesis must have been a savage, because Genesis stated that Jehovah worked almost six days to make the things of the world; to make the sun, moon, and stars had required only a part of the afternoon of the fourth day.

Howe, who was the editor of the *Globe* in Atchison, Kansas, had migrated there from Indiana. Referring to himself as a materialist, he blasted away at formal religion year in and year out.

Howe was apparently embittered by the actions of his father, a religious circuit rider in northern Missouri. His father had ruled the family with an iron hand and had caused his family great embarrassment by having affairs with female converts who found him attractive.

By 1890 the churches of the Midwest were being influenced by big business, science, and urbanization. Successful businessmen were often put on church boards, and churches began to use the methods of business. Religion in the new expensive churches was more formal and less spiritual. In the cities there was a liberalizing attitude toward theater going, card playing, and dancing. Ministers found it convenient and popular to deliver short sermons. The Bedford *Daily Mail* in September 1901 commented that this desire for short sermons did not necessarily signify that church people were less devoted to the cause of religion than they used to be. It simply meant that the churches were keeping abreast of the increasing tempo of the times. The Bedford editor was a firm believer in the maxim, "brevity is the soul of wit." The September 5, 1901, issue of the Cleveland *News and Herald* was even less charitable in its summation of the status of religion. It contained this little story about two people contemplating matrimony. "He – I am afraid my religious views are not the same as yours dear." "She – That need not necessarily make any difference. We both belong to the same golf club."

To meet the challenges of urbanization, secularization, and big business control, church groups used different approaches. One approach, used by some fundamentalist groups, was stated to be a return to the ideas of the early church. This movement was especially strong in the Methodist church. As a result large numbers of these people, especially in the rural areas, separated from the parent churches and formed new denominations. Between 1880 and 1925 some 25 of these pentecostal bodies came into being and many of them occurred in the Midwest. These sects were formed largely of the poorer and less-educated groups in the city and country.

These fundamentalist movements were just another aspect of the fundamentalist-modernist struggle. The fundamentalists tended to emphasize the virgin birth of Christ and the divine inspiration and literal interpretation of the Bible. From the beginning of the controversy, the Moody Bible Institute of Chicago was a main center of fundamentalism.

Another approach were the communal, religious experiments such as the Christian Catholic Apostolic church of Zion, established just north of Chicago in 1895 by John A. Dowie. In his community Dowie built a publishing house, a tabernacle, a bank, a college, and candy and lace factories. In 1901 he announced himself Elijah the Restorer and made plans to extend the influence of Zion's church throughout the world. A virtual dictator in Zion, he was deposed in 1906 by a revolt of his followers.

Yet another widespread reaction to urbanization and big business was social Christianity. This approach had been expressed in the Y.M.C.A. and Y.W.C.A. movements and in books like Charles M. Sheldon's *In His Steps*. Sheldon, a Kansas preacher, explained the personal conduct that would lead to Utopia. The hero in his book always considered the question, "What Would Jesus Do?" in making every decision. The result was an exemplary life.

In a yet more active role, Washington Gladden, a Congregational minister in Columbus, Ohio, was a representative spokesman for socialized Christianity. The bitter contests between capital and labor and the accusation that the churches were the agents and tools of capitalism made the churches squirm. Ministers like Gladden tried to answer this challenge. In a series of volumes, *Workingmen and Their Employers* (1876), *Applied Christianity* (1887), and *Tools and Men* (1893), Gladden, although not a socialist, attacked the maltreatment of labor by capitalists. In more general terms he said that the trouble with the church was that it had concentrated its energies upon believing things about Christ and had ceased believing Him. Gladden believed that as soon as the church was revitalized, it would become the inspiring agency of the social movement. He prophesied that the time was drawing near when the Christian organization would be able to discern and declare the simple truth that religion was simply love for God and men.

A few years later the University of Chicago became a center in the Midwest for the teaching and application of social Christianity. The movement there was led by men like Shailer Mathews, A. W. Small, and Charles R. Henderson. Another pastor in Chicago, Harry F. Ward, working in the stockyards' district, was also a champion of social Christianity. He actually applied the doctrine in the field as it affected the lives of families.

Reform Movements Outside the Church

Another outgrowth of this social Christianity in Chicago, although not directly related to the church, was the work of Jane Addams at Hull House. Addams was of a fairly wealthy family. Her father owned a sawmill and flourmill at Cedarville, Illinois, and had once been elected state senator. In the early part of the 1880's, she spent two years in Europe for her health. While in East London Market on a Saturday evening, she was deeply impressed by poverty. Returning to the United States she decided to do something about the slum areas of Chicago. Patterning her experiment after Toynbee Hall in London, she and Ellen G. Starr rented in 1889 the second floor and the large, first-floor drawing room of a large house built in 1852 by one of Chicago's pioneer citizens, Charles J. Hull. It was located at the junction of Blue Island Avenue, Halstead Street, and Harrison Street. In 1890 the owner of the house, Miss Helen Culver, generously gave them a free lease-hold to the entire house. Although a prosperous section of the city in the 1850's, the middle-class Irish and Germans had moved out, allowing the area to be repeopled with poor, immigrant Russian-Jews, Italians, and Greeks. To these groups Miss Addams and her colleagues began their ministering. Facilities at Hull House included nurseries, sewing rooms, reading rooms, a coffee room, a dancing room, and three public baths. Hull House social workers washed newborn babies, prepared the dead for burial, nursed the sick, and cared for the children of working mothers. As the years passed the enterprise expanded and the buildings of Hull House by 1930 occupied the greater part of a city block. It included cooperative buildings for working girls, a building for men and boys, a gymnasium, a cafeteria, and a music hall.

Although not a new approach, the struggle for temperance was in a sense a part of social Christianity. Excessive drinking undoubtedly led to crime, disease, and poverty. Two of the greatest forces for temperance, the Woman's Christian Temperance Union organized at Cleveland, Ohio, in 1874 and the Anti-Saloon League of America (1895), had been founded largely by persons living in midwestern country towns. They used laws, lectures, sermons, and education to aid their cause. Around the turn of the century, the most notorious liquor fighter was Carrie Nation of Medicine Lodge, Kansas. She used the hatchet to chop up saloons and other places selling alcoholic beverages and tobacco. In whatever manner accomplished, the states did begin to go dry and after World War I the eighteenth amendment was ratified by the states and prohibition was put into force. But prohibition was not very successful. It was opposed by those who made money from liquor sales and by those who enjoyed drinking fermented beverages. As a result of the opposition from these groups, the eighteenth amendment was repealed in 1933 by the twenty-first and the legal sale of liquor began once more.

— 47 —

Crime in Society

That the midwestern reformers and ministers of this period had their work cut out for them was illustrated not only by the abundance of run-of-the-mill sinners and selfish individuals, but even more strikingly by the criminals and hoodlums that were present. Some of this lawlessness may have stemmed from the feeling of individuality developed on the frontier. Many of the crimes in the Midwest after the Civil War had distinctive frontier flavor. Among the most infamous gangs were the James boys, the Daltons, and the Youngers. At one time the James brothers were blamed for every unsolved crime in the state of Missouri. Among the gangs who robbed and murdered in Kansas, none was more notorious than the Daltons, sons of a farmer-preacher, who chose the wrong road. Their climactic escapade was a double-bank holdup in broad daylight in the town of Coffeyville, Kansas, in October 1892. Five of the brothers rode into town and were doing fine until the citizens opened fire. Four Daltons along with four Coffeyville citizens were killed. The fifth Dalton was wounded, captured, and sentenced to 14 years in prison. The sixth Dalton's horse went lame and he missed the Coffeyville fracas. He later formed another gang that was of an inferior quality.

One of the leading gangs in Minnesota was one led by Thomas C. Younger. Younger and his gang tried to rob the First National Bank of Northfield, Minnesota, in 1876. Part of the gang was killed in this hold-up attempt; Thomas and two of his brothers were captured. They were given life terms and only one lived to be pardoned in 1903.*

*Needless to say the Midwest continued to have crime and criminals after 1900. The most noted change in the lawless was that with increasing technology, they tended to urbanize and mechanize.

Among the most colorful lawmen who were employed to stop these killers and despoilers were Wyatt Erp, Bat Masterson, and Bill Hickock. The number of men that Hickock killed is a matter of conjecture. Originally from Illinois, this sinewy six-footer wore his blond hair in a long bob which reached his shoulders. He also wore a large drooping mustache that covered much of the lower part of his face. A fancy dresser, Hickock sometimes wore a Prince Albert coat, checkered trousers, a silk vest embroidered with colored flowers, and a cape with a flowered silk lining. He took great pride in his boots which cost as much as $60 a pair. The tops were of black shiny leather, embossed with various curves and spirals, and the heels were two inches high. He carried his two ivory-handled, silver-mounted revolvers in a wide sash of scarlet silk.

He lived as long as he did because he was an excellent shot. Witnesses said he could stand in the center of a road, 65 feet wide, spot first to one side and then the other, fire in both directions simultaneousy, and put a bullet through a fence post on both sides of the road. He could put three bullets through a tin can thrown thirty feet in the air before it touched the ground.

Because of Hickock's expertness with weapons, he served as marshal in the wide-open Kansas cattle towns of Ft. Riley, Hays City, and Abilene during the period 1866 to 1872. In 1876 at the age of 39, Hickock was killed in a saloon in Deadwood, Dakota Territory, by a shot in the back by Jack McCall.

— 48 —

Era of the New Education

Elementary and Secondary Schools

The thirty years after 1860 have been dubbed the "Era of the New Education." Actually this period was not noted for its novelty in education as much as for its increase in public education. Between 1860 and 1900 the average attendance at public schools jumped from 61 days to 152 days. Statistics in the Midwest revealed similar increases in public education. The number of high schools in Ohio increased from 161 in 1860 to 567 in 1880. Indiana increased the amount of money spent for elementary education from $824,643 in 1860 to $6,534,298 in 1900. During the same period in Indiana, the number of elementary teachers grew from 7,357 to 15,617.

This increased emphasis on schools was due to prosperity, more stable communities, and increasing population. As the frontier was settled, people had more time and inclination for schooling. The newer states of the Midwest were slower in starting schools just as they were slower in acquiring people. The first public school in Dakota Territory was not established until 1860 at Bon Homme. Two years later the Dakota territorial legislature passed a law which provided for free, elementary schooling for all white children between the ages of five and twenty one. Minnesota passed a law in 1865 providing for the establishment of school boards. In Kansas a township high-school law was passed in 1881.

The growth of public schools was also aided by constitutional provisions and court interpretations. The Illinois constitution of 1870 specified that the legislature should "provide for a thorough and efficient system of free schools whereby all the children of this state may receive a good common-school education." Shortly after this law was passed, the Illinois state supreme court ruled that this was a minimal requirement which did not prevent the establishment of high schools. The most eloquent statement on this latter principle was made by Chief Justice Thomas M. Cooley of the Michigan state supreme court in the Kalamazoo case in 1874. This case was a friendly suit brought to determine whether Kalamazoo had the right to establish a high school, hire a school superintendent, and to levy taxes to pay for them. In his decision Cooley argued that the state in creating the common schools and the university had intended to provide a complete system of schools, and the high school was the necessary transition from the common school to the university.

As the high schools developed, their course offerings were enriched. More foreign languages, sciences, mathematics, and history were added. When the high schools in Iowa, Ohio, and elsewhere became larger, they offered two or more parallel curricula with some electives.

To help the high schools in fulfilling their function of preparing students for college, the University of Michigan in 1871 began sending out committees of professors to visit high schools to approve graduates for entrance into college. To aid the University of Michigan and other colleges in this task, state accreditation agencies were established to check on the quality of high schools. Later, to make the accrediting system still more uniform, regional agencies were created. The North Central Association, established in 1894, was the third one of these created, having been preceded by the New England Association in 1885 and the Middle States and Maryland Association in 1892. Although the North Central group was especially concerned with the accreditation of schools in the Midwest, it expanded its operations beyond these twelve states.

The quality of public schools was also improved by men like William T. Harris, superintendent of the St. Louis public schools. When Harris became superintendent in 1868, less than two decades had elapsed since Missouri had established the state-school fund and St. Louis had levied its first school tax and created its first high school. Harris' first goals were to retain and expand the system of flexible and frequent promotions in the grades. He also instituted ability sectioning. To improve administration he established a scheme for district supervision. Each principal of an upper-grade school served as a supervisor of the primary schools from which his pupils came. The principal was required to visit every school in his district once a week, to talk to the teachers and principals, to observe instruction, and to report to the superintendent. In addition to visiting the elementary schools, the principal also had to administer his own school and do some teaching. Harris felt a principal should never lose direct contact with students in the classroom. Harris introduced the kindergarten into St. Louis in 1873; by 1880 St. Louis had 50 public kindergartens. He also introduced evening schools with vocational classes and a city Normal school which was separated from the high school. Large building programs were completed under his supervision to keep pace with the growing population. Music, drawing, and gymnastics were added to the curriculum. Harris believed that a city superintendent should not only administer the school property and records, but also supervise the course of study and methods of instruction, inspire teachers for self improvement, and educate the members of the school board on the nature of quality education. One of the methods used by Harris to further his own education was to visit other city-school systems such as those in Cincinnati, Chicago, and Cleveland.

A middle-of-the-roader in educational philosophy, Harris wanted to conserve and transmit the achievements of the race. He wanted a balance between science and social science. He later became editor-in-chief of Webster's *New International Dictionary* and general editor of Appleton's International Education Series. From 1889 to 1906 he admirably filled the position of United States commissioner of education.

Despite the improvements in and enlargement of the public elementary and secondary schools, educational progress in the Midwest was spotty and inadequate. Education was always far behind the needs of the people and the school-age population was constantly increasing. The average pupil attended a one-room school where he was instructed by a young woman who had little training beyond the elementary school and had more interest in matrimony than instruction. During a term of 140 days, the average student spent 70 per cent of his time on formal subjects, mechanically taught, in which the idea of discipline was predominant. His mathematics and spelling had little connection with the society in which he lived; and his grammar, penmanship, and reading were badly directed. The school he attended was supported largely from local taxation and the teacher's income was around $300 a year.

The favored child might "enjoy" a school year of around 200 days, while his contemporary in the poorest community might receive only three months or less. The best prepared teachers had a little professional training beyond high school, while those at the other extreme had not even completed elementary school. The richest course of study included such subjects as drawing, geography, history, literature, music, physical training, natural science, and a foreign language. On the other hand the poorest community offered only the fundamentals of reading, writing, spelling, and arithmetic. For them McGuffey's reader, Ray's arithmetic, Webster's "blue back" speller, Harvey's grammar, and the *Eclectic History and Geography* were standard textbooks. Under the best conditions reading was an introduction to classics suited for children. Under the worst it was a formal study of fragments and unrelated material.

In some cities, school buildings and equipment were built and selected with attention to convenience, health, and utility. The best schools had large playgrounds with play equipment and shade trees. The buildings were of masonry and practically fireproof. These buildings had central-heating systems, indoor playrooms, gymnasiums, showers, rest rooms, and ventilated lockers. Children drank from continuous-stream drinking fountains. There were electric lights, chemical fire extinguishers in the corridors, and adjustable desks in the classrooms.

At the other extreme in the poorest rural districts, the schools might be little better than cattle sheds with practically no equipment. There was either no ventilation or too much. A heating stove or fireplace supplied the heat. Those near the source of heat would perspire, and those at a distance would be cold. One drinking cup at an open well was used by all with the resulting possibility of typhoid and other diseases. Toilet facilities consisted of small, unheated, unsanitary buildings some distance from the main school building. School cleaning, when done, was usually accomplished with a broom or feather duster which stirred up the dirt and germs. Educational equipment consisted of a few books and slates. A blackboard was considered a luxury. The superintendent of schools at Green County, Wisconsin, for example, reported in 1869 that only 89 of the 120 rural schoolhouses were in fair condition and only 54 had adequate outhouses.

At best security of tenure was small and at its worst the teacher was at the mercy of local politicians. Some privileged teachers received $100 a month for 9 or 10 months, while others received that amount or even less for the whole year. In Kossuth County, Iowa, in 1864, male teachers received an average of $5.62 a week and female teachers received an average of $3.58 a week. Twnty years later the average weekly salary was $24 for males and $20 for females.

Growth of Colleges

The generation after 1860 witnessed the greatest increase in the number of midwestern colleges in its history. Ohio State University along with the Universities of Kansas, Illinois, Nebraska, South Dakota, and North Dakota made their appearance. The two largest, state-supported types of colleges established during this thirty years, however, were the Normals, created to train public school teachers, and the agricultural colleges. But even in this period the number of private colleges established far outnumbered the public ones. Of the 99 colleges begun during this period that survived, 62 were private and 37 were public.

The founding of colleges at public expense was greatly facilitated by the passage of the Morrill Act in 1862. This was Senator J. S. Morrill's second attempt to pass such legislation. In 1859 he had secured the passage of a college-aid bill but it had been vetoed by President James Buchanan. It had provided for an appropriation of 20,000 acres of public land to a state for each of its United States congressmen. The grant was to be used to aid colleges that emphasized agriculture and mechanic arts within their course of study. Buchanan vetoed it because he said that the federal government was short on money and could not afford the grant to the states, that the states would hurt public land values by dumping this land on the market and the federal government would lose millions, that the federal government could not enforce state expenditures for colleges, and that the colleges were teaching enough agriculture anyway.

With the South out of the Union, Morrill reintroduced his bill in 1862 and it was passed by Congress and signed into law by President Abraham Lincoln. The new bill contained two major changes. The amount of land per member of congress to be donated to the state had been increased from 20,000 to 30,000 acres and the colleges receiving the money had to teach military tactics. The latter provision was undoubtedly added because the nation was at war.

In most cases in the Midwest, the Morrill land grants were either given to established state universities or to state colleges founded especially to receive the grants. There was an argument over the type school that was to be founded with the money. The strict constructionists felt the phrase "to teach such branches of learning as are related to agriculture and the mechanic arts" should be interpreted strictly. The broad constructionists felt the study of mathematics, science, and language should also be added in order to enable the student to understand the principles of business, agriculture, and living. The broad constructionalists generally won out and the land-grant colleges retained or obtained a firm liberal-arts base.

At the outset, the agricultural colleges and departments established by the Morrill Act had great difficulty in attracting students. The farmers did not feel that any college instructor could teach them or their children how to farm. What was even worse was that the "cow colleges" actually had little to teach because scientific agriculture was in its infancy. In addition, many of the rural students did not have the educational background to do college work and many agricultural departments had to set up classes to meet these deficiencies. Women were admitted in the 1860's and 1870's at Kansas State, Iowa State, Michigan State, and the Universities of Illinois and Nebraska partly to increase enrollments. Home economics departments were also added partly for the same reason. Despite their efforts, however, colleges specializing in agriculture and the mechanic arts had a small enrollment up to 1900.

Although the Morrill Act was a help, land-grant colleges were still short on funds and within a decade after 1862 they were again asking for funds from Congress. Morrill, who remained true to his educational crusade, began a campaign for annual money grants to colleges endowed by the land-grant act. After he had introduced such a bill many times, the second Morrill Act finally became law in 1890. It provided that the federal government would give an annual grant of $15,000 to each land-grant college, which would increase $1,000 a year until the figure reached $25,000. This maximum was then to be a permanent amount to be given to the colleges each year.

To provide better trained instructors for the rapidly expanding public-school systems, the states decided to establish county and state Normals. Many high schools also initiated pedagogical courses for the same purpose. The curriculum of the Normal school was limited. Since there were few specialized books in education or school administration, the Normals concentrated on a review of the basic subjects and practice teaching. Although many of the early Normals lacked the facilities and faculties that they should have had, some like the ones at Normal, Illinois, and Ypsilanti, Michigan, had exceptional teachers and courses of study.

Although many Normal schools came into existence between 1860 and 1890, they were unable to prepare enough teachers. There was a shortage of trained teachers at the outset, and with the rapidly increasing student population, the Normals had difficulty in even maintaining the status quo. This shortage of trained teachers was especially noticeable in the rural areas. As of 1900 most of the rural teachers still obtained their licenses by examination after attending a Normal school for a short time or with no teacher training at all.

One of the best of the Midwest's colleges and universities

by 1890 was the University of Michigan. James B. Angell had become president there in 1871. Under his leadership, Michigan became a leader of the nation's public colleges in three areas. It had the largest attendance, enjoyed the highest income, and offered the greatest number of undergraduate and professional courses.

While the University of Michigan meant academics and administration to President Angell, it had a far different connotation to many of the students. Although some associated study with a university, others were more concerned with their social life and clothes. Michigan male students were noted for their outrageous wearing apparel. Enormous four-in-hand cravats with knots more than two Inches long, stiff stand-up collars, horseshoe stickpins, suede gloves, bamboo canes, and white spats were in vogue. To appear more ridiculous, they "sported" three-inch checks and plaids in their full jackets and skin-tight trousers.

The "coeds," whose parents had decided that college was the place for their "darlings" to pursue a male, as well as possibly a course of study, were more conventional in attire. Skirts were floor length, except for the "rainy daisy," introduced in this period. This skirt, as its name suggests, was designed for rainy days. Extending only to the ankles, it allowed the girl much more freedom of movement. Some contemporary papers reported that girls with trim ankles wore this skirt when "there was not a cloud in the sky." For their daring they were denounced by ministers and were considered "fast" by the general populace. As to other incumbrances, the girls wore corsets that reduced their normal waist measurements significantly. Since "dainty feet" were prized, shoes were high on the ankle and usually a size too small. Tight kid gloves and enormous hats balanced precariously on a swirl of hair completed the ensemble.

To the collegiate youth dates were nearly as important as clothes. The boys usually took the initiative in this (or at least the girls allowed them to think so) and romances at the University of Michigan generally followed a prescribed pattern. As freshmen they met the Ann Arbor girls at church and Sunday school; as sophomores and juniors, they found the girls at Ypsilanti (Normal) responsive; and as seniors they finally received some attention from the freshmen coeds. Then after graduation, they returned home and married the girls who lived across the street. This schedule was not invariable. If it had been many Michigan coeds would not have been in college.

— 49 —

The Blossoming of Literature

The greatest blossoming of literature in the Midwest probably occurred in the 50 years after the Civil War. Even during much of this period, however, many of the midwestern literary lights moved to the East in order to find a more congenial atmosphere for writing. Those who remained in the Midwest generally gravitated to St. Louis or Chicago. Cincinnati had ceased to be the literary capital of the West.

One of Ohio's greatest literary lights during the period was William D. Howells, born at Martin's Ferry in 1837. Although he had little formal education, he did receive a systematic literary education from his duties as printer and reporter on his father's paper. In 1860 he made a pilgrimage to New England, which he chronicled in *Literary Friends and Acquaintances.* In this work he related how he liked Nathaniel Hawthorne, got on badly with Ralph W. Emerson, and could not understand Henry D. Thoreau. At the beginning of the Civil War, he was appointed United States consul to Venice, where he remained four years. On his return from Europe, he stayed in the East. Although he served on the staff of the *New York Times, Tribune,* and *Nation,* his most noted work was done as editor of the *Atlantic Monthly* and *Harper's Monthly.* He wrote more than twenty novels and several volumes of poetry. Although several of Howell's books were romances and descriptions of his life and travels, his greatest fame came from his realistic novels such as *A Modern Instance* (1882), *The Rise of Silas Lapham* (1884), *A Hazard of New Fortunes* (1890), and *The Landlord at Lion's Head.* Prudish about sex, his novels had realism about catastrophes. Train wrecks and fires were his most prevalent disasters. His characters, including the heroes, died of brain fever, sudden sickness, suicide by poison, shootings, railroad accidents, and tuberculosis. Al-

William D. Howells (1837-1920)
Novelist, editor of *The Atlantic Monthly*
From *Dictionary of American Portraits* by Hayward and Blanche Cirker, Dover Publications, Inc., New York, 1967. *Reprinted through permission of the publisher.*

Samuel L. Clemens (1835-1910)
Novelist, lecturer

Hamlin Garland (1860-1940)
Novelist
From *Dictionary of American Portraits* by Hayward and Blanche Cirker, Dover Publications, Inc., New York, 1967. *Reprinted through permission of the publisher.*

William A. White (1868-1944)
Kansas newspaper editor, owner of *Emporia Gazette,* writer
From *Dictionary of American Portraits* by Hayward and Blanche Cirker, Dover Publications, Inc., New York, 1967. *Reprinted through permission of the publisher.*

though Howells' realism was narrow, it was exactly drawn. In his older age Howells became philosophically a socialist, but he continued to wear a fur-lined overcoat and live in all the luxury money could provide. In 1909 he was chosen president of the American Academy, and six years later he was awarded the National Institute's gold medal for distinguished work in fiction.

Other noted Ohio lights included Paul L. Dunbar and Zane Grey. Dunbar, known as the Negro poet of Dayton, was born in 1872 and died at the age of 34. The son of a former slave, he worked as newsboy and elevator boy while attending high school. Dunbar won the praise of William D. Howells in 1895 with *Majors and Minors.* The following year Howells wrote an introduction to Dunbar's *Lyrics of Lowly Life,* which established Dunbar as a popular poet. Dunbar was most successful with his dialect poems.

Zane Grey, born in Zanesville, Ohio, in 1875 was originally a dentist. He soon left that profession, however, to become a writer. Unsuccessful at first, he became very popular with the publication of his *Riders of the Purple Sage* in 1912. Extremely prolific on the wildwest theme, he produced over 50 novels before his death in 1939.

Indiana had an even greater outpouring of literature during the half century after the Civil War than Ohio. By 1914 Hoosier pens had produced 15,000 volumes of which a great majority had been written since the Civil War.

One of the earliest of Indiana's post-Civil war writers was General Lewis Wallace. Born in Indiana in 1827, he spent most of his life at Crawfordsville where he practiced law. He fought in the Mexican War and the Civil War. His first major work, *The Fair God,* an elaborate romance about the conquest of Mexico, appeared in 1873. A chance conversation with the skeptic Robert G. Ingersoll led Wallace to do research on the character and life of Christ, the basis of *Ben Hur: A Tale of the Christ* (1880). Although he wrote several other books, none compared in popularity to *Ben Hur.*

The next noted Indiana author in point of time was Edward Eggleston, an itinerant Methodist minister, born in Indiana in 1837. Unlike Wallace he based his novels on the surroundings he knew. By far his best was the *Hoosier Schoolmaster* (1871). It was distinguished for its local color and realism in depicting rural conditions in Indiana at the end of the Civil War. This book was based on the experiences of his brother George C. Eggleston, who taught in a rural Indiana school and was also an author in his own right.

Another Indiana writer known primarily for one work was James M. Thompson. Born in Indiana in 1844, he was raised in Georgia and served in the Confederate Army. He then moved back to Crawfordsville, Indiana, where he spent most of his adult life. A civil engineer and lawyer, he was also an enthusiastic naturalist. He spent considerable time exploring the swamps of the southeastern United States with a canoe, bow, and arrow. He was the state geologist of Indiana from 1885 to 1889. His books reflected his experiences with nature, the South, and Indiana. One of his earliest works was *The Witchery of Archery, Byways, and Bird Notes.* His southern experience was reflected in books like *Stories of The Cherokee Hills* (1899). *Alice of Old Vincennes* (1900), by far his most noted work, had its setting in Indiana. A romance about George R. Clark and the Northwest Territory, it was full of patriotism, sentimentality, and social status.

One of the leading Indiana poets was James W. Riley. Born at Greenfield, Indiana, in 1853, he was the son of a lawyer. In his early years he travelled with a circus and a medicine show and painted houses and signs. Eventually he gravitated into journalism and obtained a job with *The Indianapolis Sentinel.* A bachelor, he made his home with the widow of a Civil War veteran. He began writing poetry at about 20 years of age. He often used the Indiana dialect and became known as "The Hoosier Poet." His public reading of his poems such as "When the Frost is on the Punkin," "Out to Old Aunt Mary's," "Good Bye, Jim," and "The Old Swimmin' Hole" was very popular. Also known as "The American Burns," some of his chief volumes of verses were *Afterwhiles* (1887), *Pipes O'Pan at Zekesbury* (1888), and *Rhymes of Childhood* (1891). Riley wrote of every-day life in rural Indiana, of home and old times, of childhood, and simple pleasures and pains. His poetry had an optimism and nostalgia far removed from the realistic searchings of other late nineteenth-century authors.

Another Indiana poet, William V. Moody, born at Spencer, Indiana, in 1869 had little in common with Riley except a home state. Moody, the son of a steamboat captain, attended Harvard and returned to the University of Chicago to teach English. After seven years he left teaching to write full time. He nearly starved in the process. His favorite medium of expression was blank verse. Concerned with man's relationship to God, his great poetic trilogy consisted of *The Fire Bringer* (1904), which dealt with the Prometheus legend; *The Masque of Judgment* (1900) which explored the eventual meaning to God of man's destruction; and the *Death of Eve* (1901), which pictured Eve as the agent of reconciliation between God and man.

At Shelbyville, Indiana, Charles Major wrote *When Knighthood was in Flower* (1898) while waiting for prospective legal clients. Ostensibly told by Sir Edward Caskoden, master of the dance, the plot of the book was based on the romance of Mary Tudor and Charles Brandon. Although this overly sentimental work had fleeting popularity, the works that have made his name live were his juvenile books such as the *Bears of Blue River* (1901). Little noted at the time of publication, they became classics in children's literature.

Another Indiana author of children's stories, Annie F. Johnston, was born at Evansville in 1863. Her father, a Methodist minister, died when she was two and her husband, a widower with three children when she married him, died three years after their marriage. She wrote to support herself and three children. On a visit near Louisville, Kentucky, she was impressed with the aristicratic bearing and character of a little girl who had the temper of her grandfather, an old Confederate colonel. This occurrence was the basis for *The Little Colonel* (1895), the first in a series of 12 popular volumes centering about this little heroine. In search of a healthier home for her stepson, she also lived in Arizona, California, and Texas; these climes also formed a back drop for some of her other children's books. Mrs. Johnston entertained thousands of children with her characters who had integrity and love and lived in a world of goodness and virtue.

Indiana's greatest contribution to the muckraker group at the turn of the century was David G. Phillips, born at Madison, Indiana, in 1867. As a reporter he worked for the Cincinnati *Commercial Gazette* and the *New York World.* Although Joseph Pulitzer liked Phillips as a newspaperman, he disliked the latter's depiction of him in the newspaper novel, *The Great God Success* (1901). During the period 1901 to 1911, Phillips devoted himself largely to writing realistic novels. Always a reformer, his novels invariably debunked something. Although his attack on the Senate in *Treason in the Senate* (1906) earned him Theodore Roosevelt's dislike and the muckraker brand, his book did help to bring about the popular election of senators. One of his favorite subjects for debunking was the upperclass woman whom he felt was spiritually and mentally weak. This latter crusade helped to bring on his death at the hands of a paranoiac, Fitzhugh C. Goldsborough, in 1911. Goldborough hated Phillips for his portrayal of American women generally and especially for Phillips' description of Margaret Severance in *The Fashionable Adventures of Joshua Craig.* Goldsborough believed that the character Margaret Severance was based on the life of his sister.

One of the leading historians in Indiana prior to World War I was Albert J. Beveridge. Born in Ohio in 1862, he attended Asbury College (later DePauw University). A Republican United States senator from Indiana for two terms, he was defeated for that office in 1912 when he ran under the banner of Theodore Roosevelt's Progressive Party. After his defeat he concentrated more of his efforts on writing and in the period 1916-1919 published his four-volume *Life of John Marshall.* He won the 1920 Pulitzer Prize for this biography. In 1928 two volumes of his incomplete life of Abraham Lincoln were published posthumously.

One of Illinois' leading lights was Finley P. Dunne, born in Chicago in 1867. He spent most of his life as a newspaperman on the *Times, Evening Post, Times-Herald,* and *Evening Journal.* Writing under the pseudonym of Mr. Dooley, a saloon keeper of Archy Road in Chicago, his essays were enlivened with homely similes and Irish-American humor. Although some of the earlier articles contained considerable Irish sentiment and prejudice, many were based on intelligence and humane principles. In discussing the poet's fate in one of his columns, Dunne had Dooley explain that as soon as a poet wrote a good piece of poetry, he should either commit suicide or else not publish any more poetry. Using Rudyard Kipling as an example, Dooley said: "That's what happens to a poet when he's found out, an' no poet can escape. The Amalgamated Assocyation iv Baraboo has become th' society f'r th' previntion iv Kipling, th' Stock Exchange is readin' th' polis gazette, and ye' won't any more hear Kipling mintioned in th' pulpit than ye will th' Bible."

Supposedly the original of Dunne's Mr. Dooley was an old-time saloon keeper of Chicago named James McGarry, who worked as night bartender at a place on Dearborn Street near Madison. McGarry was a born philosopher and his sayings were flavored with dry humor.

Dunne gained notice as an author when his columns were collected in book form. The second of his volumes, entitled *Mr. Dooley in the Hearts of His Countrymen,* appeared in 1899. He dedicated this second volume to the English publishers that had pirated his first volume, *Mr. Dooley in Peace and War.* One of the last of these collections of his columns was *Mr. Dooley on Making a Will* in 1919.

Wisconsin's leading author during the first part of the twentieth century was Hamlin Garland. Born in West Salem, Wisconsin, in 1860, he moved with his family at an early age to Iowa. In 1884 he went to Boston to study and to further his literary career. Although he travelled widely in the United States to obtain inspiration for his books, his most noted novels came out of his own childhood experiences. His best were *A Son of the Middle Border* (1917) and *A Daughter of the Middle Border* (1921). For the latter he received the Pulitzer Prize in biography. Other noted works among his voluminous writings included *Main-Travelled Roads,* a book of short stories (1891), and *Companions on the Trail* (1931). Although much of his writing was conventional chronicling, some of his books like *A Son of the Middle Border* displayed a mastery of realistic detail and sketches such as "Under the Lion's Paw" revealed a strongly rebellious attitude against the status quo.

Among Wisconsin's other authors was Zona Gale. Born at

Portage, Wisconsin, in 1874, Miss Gale was best known for *Miss Lulu Bett*. Educated at the University of Wisconsin, she worked a few years as a reporter on the *New York World* and then returned to Wisconsin to spend most of her life in Portage. She was an untiring writer and wrote more than 25 major works before here death in 1930. The caliber of her work declined in her later years. She was a local colorist with a touch of sentimentality and realism.

Missouri had an outstanding triumvirate of writers before World War I, the most noted of whom was Samuel L. Clemens (Mark Twain). Born in Florida, Missouri, in 1835, he was raised in the river town of Hannibal, Missouri. His experiences in this river town gave him a background for his two most popular books, *The Adventures of Tom Sawyer* (1876) and *The Adventures of Huckleberry Finn* (1884). At an early age he worked as a printer. He next became a steamboat pilot and worked in that capacity until the Civil War halted traffic on the Mississippi. Some of his experiences as a pilot were related in *Life on the Mississippi* (1883). He spent two weeks with a troop of Confederate volunteers and then deserted and went to Nevada with his brother Orin. *Roughing It* (1872) was based partly on this trip west and partly on a later trip to Hawaii. Tired of prospecting, he obtained a job as a reporter on the Virginia City *Enterprise*. Here he began to use the pseudonym Mark Twain (a call of river men meaning two fathoms), a name which had been used previously by a retired river pilot working for a New Orleans paper. To escape a duel, Clemens migrated to California around 1864. Clemens' first book, *The Celebrated Jumping Frog of Calaveras County and Other Sketches* (1867), was very popular. The San Francisco *Alta California* sent Clemens to Europe, and his irreverent letters about European customs and traditions sent back to the paper were published as *Innocents Abroad* in 1869. Although he reaped a fortune from his writing, his lavish style of living and bad publishing and investment ventures put him in bankruptcy. He made a worldwide lecture tour, paid his debts, amassed another fortune, and built a mansion at Redding, Connecticut. A born worrier his last years were tormented by tragedy and speculation about the hereafter. He was involved in political campaigns and was a vigorous anti-imperialist. Like Garland, his writings displayed a mastery of detail and a certain rebellious spirit. He died on his return from Bermuda in 1910. Among his other important works were *The Prince and the Pauper* (1882), *A Connecticut Yankee in King Arthur's Court* (1889), and the *Mysterious Stranger* (1916). This last work displays the profound pessimism of his later years.

The second of the triumverate was Eugene Field, who qualified as a midwesterner by his birth in St. Louis in 1850. Three years in three different colleges and a trip to Europe were his preparation for journalism. He worked on several Missouri papers but his best years were spent in Chicago as a contributing editor for the *Chicago Record*. His first humorous skit, *The Tribune Primer* (1882), was reprinted from the *Denver Tribune*. His daily column of "Sharps and Flats" in the *Record* was the source from whence came *A Little Book of Western Verse* (1889). This *Book of Western Verse* is a queer mixture of ballads of Red Hoss Mountain, lullabies, Old English ballads, tales of infant mortality, and much gossip cleverly versified.

The third of the group whose name has probably faded most is Winston Churchill, born in St. Louis in 1871. A graduate of the United States Naval Academy, he edited the *Army and Navy Journal* and later *Cosmopolitan Magazine*. In 1898 his first novel, *The Celebrity*, appeared. It was followed in 1899 by *Richard Carvel* and in 1901 by *The Crisis*. Both war novels, *Richard Carvel* had its setting in Maryland during the Revolutionary War and *The Crisis* in St. Louis during the Civil War. These two were his most popular works.

One of the most noted Kansas writers was Edward W. Howe. Born in Indiana in 1853, Howe moved with his family to Missouri at the age of three. He never attended high school but did receive two honorary bachelor of literature degrees. He published the Atchison, Kansas, *Globe* and later *E. W. Howe's Monthly*. In literature he is most noted for *The Story of a Country Town* (1883), a book in which he points out the smugness, meanness, cruelty, and boastfulness of a small town in an even more striking fashion than Sinclair Lewis did in *Main Street* or Sherwood Anderson did in *Winesburg, Ohio*, a generation later.

— 50 —

Newspapers

In the period 1830 to 1860, midwestern newspapers were affected by the movement toward a penny press and by the invention of the telegraph. A change in the postal laws in 1845 favored cheaper, local circulation of newspapers. With the telegraph, telegraphic columns became a leading feature and news associations grew as wires lengenthed. With their own wire services, the newspapers of inland cities like Chicago, Cincinnati, and St. Louis became independent of the New York Papers.

After the Civil War the main trends affecting midwestern newspapers were syndication, consolidation, mechanization, and soft-pedaling of editorial opinion. The man referred to as the father of the newspaper syndicate was Ansel N. Kellogg, founder of the Barbadoo, Wisconsin, *Republic*. He built his syndicated, shoe-string venture into a $200,000 business, supplying 1,400 papers by 1875.

One of the first of the newspaper chains was begun by Edward W. Scripps of Illinois. After going to Cleveland in 1878, he established the Cleveland *Penny Press* and soon began the formulation of the first newspaper chain in the United States. By 1901 his chain included the Cleveland *Press,* St. Louis *Chronicle,* Cincinnati *Post,* Covington *Kentucky Post,* San Diego *Sun,* Los Angeles *Record,* Seattle *Star,* Spokane *Press,* Tacoma *Times,* and San Francisco *News.* At its peak the Scripps chain included 34 newspapers. Scripps collaborated with Milton A. McRae and others in establishing the Newspaper Enterprise Association in 1902 which supplied syndicated features, cartoons, and pictures to papers of the chain. To compete with Associated Press in telegraph news, Scripps helped form the United Press. Under the management of his son, Robert P. Scripps, the Scripps papers became the Scripps-Howard chain.

Mechanization came to newspapers in many forms. The extension and perfection of the electric telegraph, better railway and postal service, an increase in the number of ocean cables, invention of the telephone and wireless all increased the speed and efficiency by which news could be collected and disseminated to the readers. The actual production of newspapers was aided by such inventions as the typewriter, the typesetting machine, the automatic press, and the linotype machine. These happenings made possible large newspaper circulations and larger newspapers.

The soft-pedaling of editorial opinion that developed after the Civil War was probably due largely to the business manager winning out over the editor. Advertisement was the most lucrative part of the newspaper business; if a paper antagonized certain portions of the population, it received neither advertisements nor subscriptions. Syndication and especially news services like Associated Press and United Press also contributed to less editorializing and to more uniformity and objectivity in reporting.

Of the Middle Border editors and publishers after the Civil War, however, some remained partisan and some independent. Murat Halstead, born in Butler County, Ohio, in 1829, was editor of the Cincinnati *Commercial,* later the *Commercial Gazette.* Halstead exercised a powerful position in the Republican Party in Ohio and his newspaper reflected it.

On the left bank of the river at Louisville, Kentucky, was an editor on the other side of the political fence. Although technically not in the Midwest, his newspaper and influence still crossed the Ohio River. Henry Watterson, who had been a colonel in the Confederate Army, became editor and part owner of the Louisville *Journal* in 1866. Two years later the *Democrat* and *Journal* merged to form the Courier Journal. A liberal Democrat he trained his editorial guns on the corrupt Republican party in 1872. He was so angry at Samuel J. Tilden's defeat by Rutherford B. Hayes in 1876 that he threatened to lead 100,000 armed Kentuckians on Washington to obtain justice. In his later years he quarreled with Grover Cleveland and had great difficulty in swallowing William J. Bryan's free silver.

A more politically independent publisher was William R. Nelson of the Kansas City, Missouri, *Star.* Having served his apprenticeship on the Ft. Wayne *Sentinel,* he arrived in Kansas City in 1880. Although the usual price per copy for newspapers there was five cents, he sold his newly-established *Star* for two cents. In 1901 he merged the *Times* and the *Star.* Nelson launched many crusades. Although he detested comic strips, he finally allowed them in his paper. The Kansas City *Star* had the largest circulation of any paper west of Chicago.

On the eastern side of Missouri at St. Louis, Joseph Pulitzer began his American success story. Born in Budapest, Hungary, in 1847, Pulitzer came to the United States at the age of 17. He served in the Union Army and after the war went to St. Louis where he secured a position as reporter on the *Westliche Post,* a German-Republican newspaper. He became managing editor and part owner. After he joined the Democratic Party, he decided to sell his interest in *Westliche Post.* In 1879 he purchased the St. Louis *Dispatch* and the *Evening Post* and united them in the *Post-Dispatch.* This venture made his fortune. In 1883 he purchased the New York *World* and built it into a leading newspaper. Pulitzer's use of sensationalism to sell newspapers became his hallmark. The epithet "yellow journal" was first applied to the *World* by its competitors on Sunday, November 19, 1893, when it issued the first colored supplement in America. One of the features in this supplement was the "Yellow Kid," a cartoon drawn by Richard F. Outcault of Lancaster, Ohio. It depicted a buck-toothed youngster in a single sacklike garment. In addition to colored comics, Putlizer also indulged in garbled headlines such at "A Bride but not a Wife," "Baptised in Blood," and "Love and Cold Poison." These methods enabled Pulitzer to run his circulation into the hundreds of thousands. In 1895 William R. Hearst also entered the sensational game and between the two of them helped bring on the Spanish-American War. Pulitzer's most lasting contribution was the establishment of the Pulitzer Prize awarded for the best in all types of literary endeavor.

The Emporia *Gazette,* a small paper, became one of the most influential papers in Kansas because of its editor, William A. White. Born in Emporia, Kansas, in 1868, White became owner and editor of the *Gazette* 27 years later. White's editorial against Populism, "What's the Matter with Kansas?" brought him notice throughout the United States. A liberal Republican, he remained in the Republican fold constantly except in 1912 when he supported Theodore Roosevelt on the Progressive ticket. White once referred to Thomas C. Platt, the New York boss, as a slimy reptile of poltics. White early advocated preparedness and entry of the United States into World War II.

An editor and publisher of a newspaper noted particularly for his isolation and conservative Republicanism was Robert R. McCormick of the Chicago *Tribune*. Born in Chicago in 1880, he was a lawyer and soldier as well as an editor. Under his leadership the *Tribune* played an influential role in making the Midwest more isolationistic and Republican.

The Midwest had avid newspaper readers. Its favorite type was the weekly. In 1927 Illinois and Iowa ranked first in the number of weeklies in the United States with 500 each. Thirteen years later, the Middle Border had 43 per cent of all the weekly newspapers published in the United States.

—51—

Music

Music on the early Middle Border tended to be tuneful and popular, rather than proper and classical. Group singing, without accompaniment, was conducted in churches. Singing masters conducted groups in Cincinnati, Marietta, and other villages as early as 1802. Instrumental music also developed. Although pianos were scarce, flutes and fiddles were more prevalent. Self-taught men often played at dances and social gatherings. As the century wore on, instruments became more numerous and more children received music lessons.

Midwest composers did produce a number of popular tunes. Daniel D. Emmett of Ohio launched one of the original black-face minstrel shows in New York in 1843. Of the dozens of minstrel songs he wrote, "Dixie," "Turkey in de Straw," "Whar Ye Been So Long," "Old Dan Tucker," "De Boatman's Dance," and "My Old Aunt Sally," were among the most famous. The South adopted "Dixie" as its sectional song during the Civil War, even though it had been written by a northerner. Influenced by the abolitionist movement, Benjamin R. Hanby wrote "Darling Nelly Gray" while attending Oberlin College in 1856. Other Ohioans like Oley Speaks wrote on the "Road to Mandalay," Earnest R. Ball wrote "Mother Machre," and Tell Taylor wrote "Down by the Old Mill Stream."

Wisconsin produced an unusually large number of the Midwest's popular song writers. Dr. William S. Pitts wrote "The Little Brown Church in the Vale" after a visit to Chickasaw County, Iowa. Eben E. Rexford wrote the words for "Silver Threads Among the Gold." Sanford F. Bennett and Joseph P. Webster contributed "In the Sweet By and By." Carrie J. Born composed the music for over 300 songs including "A Perfect Day."

Another prolific song writer, Charles K. Harris, wrote 125 songs of which "After the Ball is Over," "Break the News to Mother," "Hello, Central, Give Me Heaven," were among his most famous. His most productive period was at the beginning of the twentieth century.

"Home on the Range" was written by two Kansans, Brewster Higley and Dan Kelley. Thurlow Lieurance of Wichita was an authority on Indian music and composed "By the Waters of Minnetonka." Emporia, Kansas, in 1912 was also the site for the Kansas Music Competition Festival, the first of its type held in the United States.

In addition, the Midwest played a part in other musical crazes and phases that passed through the United States. The first songs in the Midwest were the ballads and European tunes brought in by the pioneers and the evangelical religious songs made famous by the circuit-riding preachers and evangelists. In the 1840's the black-face minstrelsy came into vogue. In addition to the minstrel songs of Daniel D. Emmett, the Midwest also enjoyed the songs of Stephen C. Foster of Pennsylvania. By 1860 Foster had written such favorites as "Susanna," "Old Uncle Ned," "Old Folks at Home," "My Old Kentucky Home," "Massa's in de Cold Ground," "Old Black Joe," and "Camptown Races." The Civil War supplied "Tramp, Tramp, Tramp," and "Tenting on the Old Camp Ground." After the Civil War came ragtime, blues singing, and jazz. Like the black face minstrelsy, all three of these were partial outgrowths of the Negro culture in the United States.

— 52 —

Recreation

Religious, Political, and Educational Events

Throughout the nineteenth century, the church condemned many forms of recreation ranging from the theater to card playing and dancing. Dancing was denounced as an incitement to fornication, card playing and dicing as the paths to swindling and stealing, and the theater as a haven for loose actors who degraded the morals of those who watched them. By the turn of the twentieth century, many churches came to realize that a new course of action must be followed if they were to hold the people. If they disapproved certain commercial amusements, they learned that they must provide substitutes. The churches established libraries, gymnasiums, and assemblies and provided games, concerts, sociables, suppers, bazaars, festivals, raffles, and even bingo. The church-affiliated Y.M.C.A. and Y.W.C.A. also developed to provide recreation for the young people. Many churches objected to this compromise with the devil and would have no part of it. Revival meetings continued to be prevalent, but many of them had a more subdued tone. Churches tried to have a rounded program so as to have something for everyone, but the churches had an increasingly difficult time holding their own against the many competitive activities and entertainments.

Political speeches and oratory, whether on the fourth of July or any other time, originally had a wider appeal than the theater. Orators, at the drop of a hat, would start pouring forth flowing sentences and classical allusions, and people came to listen. Salmon P. Chase, Stephen A. Douglas, Abraham Lincoln, and William J. Bryan, to mention only a few, were popular speakers.

At the turn of the century, James B. Clark noted that 10,000 paying attendants turned out in Missouri to hear Bryan speak. Although political rallies and orators continued to draw crowds in the Midwest, attendance was increasingly viewed more as a duty than as a festive pastime.

Lectures and Chautauquas also supplemented the educational and recreational fare of the people. Personalities as diverse as P. T. Barnum, Samuel L. Clemens, Ralph W. Emerson, Josh Billings, Bret Harte, Elizabeth C. Stanton, and Frederick Douglas appeared on the western lecture circuit. The Vincennes, Indiana, *Western Sun* in 1901 noted that Bob Fitzsimmons had taken up lecturing as a side line. On the basis of this, the paper went on to observe, people may now expect a series of joint debates to be held between the Honorable James J. Corbett and the Honorable Robert Fitzsimmons.

Chautauqua, originated as a course or Sunday school teachers in 1874, soon swept the country. Described as "a cross between a camp meeting and a country fair," it was a curious combination of inspirational talks, jugglers, magicians, boy whistlers, and jubilee singers. It even encouraged sports such as baseball for the men and croquet for the women. Since it was under the supervision of the churches, the Chautauqua had a highly moral tone. Drinking and smoking were forbidden, and a Methodist dining tent or Christian Endeavor ice cream tent provided the refreshments.

Dancing

Dancing was a perennial type of entertainment. In the rural Midwest, any occasion was suitable for a dance. A log rolling, a barn raising, a corn-husking bee, a fourth-of-July celebration, or a wedding were all excuse enough for a dance. Virginia reels, country jigs, shakedowns, or square dances were the order of the day and night. The fiddler often furnished the music for such tunes as "Money Musk," "Fisher's Hornpipe," "The Irish Washerwoman," and "Turkey in the Straw." In some rural areas where instrumental music was not available or was not allowed, the young people sang the dance tunes such as "Buffalo Gals," "Billy Boy," "Captain Jinks," and "Round and Round the Mulberry Bush." Dances were just as popular on the sod-house frontier as in the Ohio Valley. Women were more scarce there and the men had to search the plains to find a partner. A young girl or a grandmother sometimes had to suffice.

By the 1850's the developing urban Midwest not only had the jigs and reels but also exciting new dances like the waltz and polka. Wealthier people might have a small orchestra to supply the music in luxurious surroundings. The middle class often attended public balls, staged by popular clubs, that charged 25 cents to one dollar for admission. For the poorer people of the larger cities, there were the less respectable dance halls where one might dance and drink and view a cheap variety show for less than a quarter. Some of these places of entertainment were filled with respectable mechanics and dress makers; others were crowded with prostitutes and underworld characters. Rural communities were shocked by these amusement places which they associated with the wicked city. But even though these dance halls were not the best type of entertainment, they still provided recreation for great numbers of people. Some of the leading dances by the turn of the century included the waltz, polka, military march, quadrille, and a series of reels. Another dance step coming into vogue was the two step which was made popular by the lively music of John P. Sousa and his famous band. His "Washington Post," which gave its name to the two step in foreign countries, was often played at the more fashionable dances.

The Theater in Myriad Forms

Among the most shocking recreation was the burlesque staged by enterprising showmen who advertised their wares as living tableaux in which men and women appeared in almost the same state as Adam and Eve in the famous garden. Later feminine jiggling and wiggling were added to further captivate the audiences. The Madison Street Opera House in Chicago advertised burlesque girls in their "close-fitting, flesh-colored silk tights" as being far more attractive than if they had no costume on at all.

Beginning in the 1840's, serious plays were satirized. Even Shakespeare and grand opera came in for their share in such productions as *Much Ado About a Merchant of Venice* and *Lucy Did Lamm Her Moor*. Variety shows which foreshadowed vaudeville also appeared. Magicians, ballad singers, strong men, burlesque dancers, bloomer girls, and female ministrels might all appear on the same bill.

Burnt-cork players in minstrel shows, such as the one staged by Dan Emmett, also became increasingly popular after 1840. They specialized in shuffling dances, jokes, and Negro dialect and simulated Negro songs. These productions were especially appropriate for the showboats that plied the Mississippi and tied up at village landings to present farce and melodrama, minstrel shows, and musical extravaganzas to eager audiences.

Undoubtedly, one of the leading stage innovations developed in the latter part of the nineteenth century was vaudeville. Growing out of the mid-century variety show, this mixture of comedy, melodrama, and burlesque became the principal commercial amusement of the urban democracy. By the 1880's Chicago had two vaudeville houses and St. Louis had three. Traveling companies took vaudeville to every hamlet. One of the leading vaudeville starlets was Lillian Russell, born Helen L. Leonard in Clinton, Iowa. Her forte was gowns and songs like "Kiss Me Mother, Ere I Die." She entered the employ in 1900 of Joe Weber and Lou Fields, owners of the New York Weber and Fields Music Hall.

Vaudeville consisted of nearly every kind of act. Acrobats, trained animals, tricks, stunts, sentimental ballads, bicycle riders, Magicians, dancers, and short comedies were all included. Will Rogers even got his start in vaudeville twirling a rope and commenting on everyday happenings in his whimsical manner.

Despite its competitors, the legitimate stage did live on as a source of entertainment, especially for the more socially elite. Every large city had its fashionable play houses, such as McVicker's and Hooley's in Chicago, which welcomed the stars of the legitimate stage. Even the popular theaters, usually called opera houses in the Midwest, interrupted their usual programs to present *Macbeth, King Lear,* and *Othello.* To direct and play the leading roles in the legitimate theater were people like John Drew, Charles Frohman, Julia Marlowe, Otis Skinner, Ethel Barrymore, Neil Burgess, and E. H. Southern. In addition to Shakespeare, other legitimate stage fare that appeared at he local midwestern opera houses during the 1890's included *His Excellency the Governor, Captain Jinks of the Horse Marines, Richard Lovelace, Vanity Fair, In a Woman's Power, Rip Van Winkle, Ben Hur, Lady Huntsworth's Experiment,* and *The Case of Rebellious Susan.* Representative theatrical fare was illustrated by the performances scheduled for the small towns of Indiana during a week in December 1898. They included a group of Shakespearean plays, several Broadway comedies, a minstrel show, a musical comedy, some melodramas, and a variety show. Many of the midwestern theater goers enjoyed these presentations. A more discriminating William A. White, however, commented in 1897 that there might be worse theatrical companies than those visiting Kansas, but no one had ever described them.

Also for the social and cultural elite were the symphony orchestra concerts, operas, and operettas. At mid-century Jenny Lind had paved the way for the tours of European artists such as Fritz Kreisler, Madame Schumann-Heink, Trivador Nachez, Josef Hofman, Harold Bauer, Fannie Bloomfield-Zeisler, Whitney Tew, and Estelle Liebling. Walter Damrosch and Theodore Thomas tried to introduce the Midwest along with the rest of the United States to classical music. Slowly the larger cities of the Midwest began to organize symphony orchestras of their own.

Grand opera received its first permanent home in America with the completion of the Metropolitan Opera House in 1883. It was supported and attended by people of the Gould and Vanderbilt class. After entertaining the wealthy set of New York, the opera company would make an annual post-season tour of leading U. S. cities including Chicago, Cincinnati, and St. Louis. There the society people were given the opportunity to emulate their social counterparts in New York City. During the opera season of 1901, the larger cities of the Middle West were favored by such offerings as Suzanna Adams in *La Boheme;* Madame Breval in *Tosca;* Madame Eames in *Il Trovatore;* Madame Sibyl Sanderson in *Manon* and *Romeo et Juliette;* Madam Semblrich in *Ernani, L'Elisire d' Amore,* and *Lohengrin;* Miss Fritze Scheff in *Carmen;* Madame Ternine in *La Gioconda;* Alvarez in *Le Cid* and *Othello;* and Edouard de Reszke in *Die Walkure* and *Ernani.* Despite a few humble music lovers in the upper galleries, grand opera became one of the most exclusive and fashionable forms of entertainment.

The Circus and Wild-West Shows

Undoubtedly, the greatest innovator of them all in the last half of the nineteenth century was Phineas T. Barnum. He kept a finger on the public-recreation pulse and gave the people what they wanted. He produced in rapid succession such individuals, animals, and acts as the Feejee mermaid, General Tom Thumb, a bearded lady, trained fleas, Madame Rockwell, Joice Heth, alleged nurse of George Washington, a woolly horse, and white elephants from Siam. Probably his most sensational triumph was his presentation of Jenny Lind, the Swedish Nightingale.

The circus, which had its beginnings in the little menageries and bands of itinerant acrobats, was extremely popular in the rural Midwest. The West saw its first circus of sorts around 1819. By the 1830's around 30 rolling shows were making their tours of the country. Buckley and Wick boasted eight wagons, forty horses, and thirty-five performers. Not until about 1850 did the combination of wild animals, a ring beneath the big top, acrobats, clowns, and horsemanship merge to form the true circus. The Mammoth Circus of Howe and Mabie reached Chicago in the 1850's. There it unexpectedly met a competitor, the Grand Olympic Arena and United States Circus. In the 1850's Barnum also entered the circus field with the Grand Colossal Museum and Menagerie, which later became the Greatest Show on Earth. Although William C. Coup was the prime mover in establishing the Greatest Show on Earth and James A. Bailey became the true circus king, it was still Barnum's reputation that packed the main tent. Joining forces with Coup in 1871 and Bailey after the great circus fire in 1880, Barnum brought together with immense fanfare the largest collection of wild animals, curiosities, acrobats, equestrian performers, and clowns ever assembled. There were giraffes from Africa and cannibals from the Fiji Islands, Admiral Dot (successor to Tom Thumb) and Esau the Bearded Boy, more elephants than ever before, and even a hippopotamus. By the turn of the century, Barnum and Bailey had many rivals including Ringling Brothers and 39 other major circuses plus many smaller ones.

Hamlin Garland gave a description of the reception of the circus on the Middle Border. He recalled that when the circus came to town, the roads were crowded with every type of conveyance (wagons, buckboards, and buggies) bringing the farm families into town for a holiday. After eating their basket lunches, the crowd flocked to see the show. The bands blared forth the signal for the opening march. There it all was — the ring master with his whip, the cry of the popcorn and candy vendors, the white-faced clowns, the terrifying swings on the flying trapeze, and the ever-present sawdust. When the last performance was over and exhibition viewed, the tired holiday makers journeyed homeward in the gathering dusk, the children asleep on the hard wagon floor. It was not surprising that the family felt they had received entertainment enough to last them for many months.

A variation on the circus theme was the wild-west show engineered by such men as Buffalo Bill (William) Cody. After success in plays like *The Scouts of the Plains* and *The First Scalp for Custer,* he established his Wild West Rocky Mountain and Prairie Exhibition. With his traveling crew, he presented all types of fare for the small boys who thronged to watch his performances. At first Cody featured Indians, cowboys, wild Texas steers, Sitting Bull, and Annie Oakley. Later he turned to military campaigns with such battles as Tien Tsin and the capture of Peking as subjects for portrayal. In one particular extravaganza, he presented the capture of the Boxers, the scaling of the walls, the turning of the Gatling guns on the fleeing foe, and the relief of the legation. When Buffalo Bill's Wild West Show and Congress of Rough Riders of the World visited Bedford, Indiana, in 1901, the local *Daily Mail* described the pageant as a veritable kindergarten of history, teaching equestrianism, primitive savagery, and military tactics with horsemen and heroes of nearly every nation on earth. There were over 1,200 men and horses in all; admission was just 50 cents for adults and 25 cents for children.

Another wild west show especially enjoyed by the people of the westernmost tier of states in the Midwest was the rodeo. It consisted of roping and riding events. People used to working with horses and cattle enjoyed watching and participating in the roping of calves and the riding of bucking horses and charging steers. Oftentimes a noted western figure was present to add luster to the occasion.

Fairs and Expositions

An event also growing out of the daily life of the rural midweserner was the county and state fair. Its reason for being lay in the exhibits of cows, pigs, chickens, pumpkins, corn, tomatoes, jellies, pies, and fancywork. Farmers and their families competed eagerly for the blue ribbons which testified that the recipients were the best homemakers, cattlemen, and tillers of the soil in their communities. The first agricultural society in the Midwest was organized at Vincennes in 1809. A decade later a cattle show, sponsored by the Scioto Agricultural Society, was held near Chillicothe, Ohio. The first state fair in the Midwest occurred near Detroit, Michigan, in 1849. It was followed in quick succession by state fairs in Ohio, Indiana, Iowa, Illinois, and other midwestern states. Although exhibits were most important at first, the side-shows gradally overshadowed them. Trotting matches began to draw such large crowds that they virtually supported the whole fair. At first commercial amusements were not allowed, but by 1850 they were an important feature of the fair. The forty-eighth exhibition of the Indiana

State Fair held at Indianapolis in September 1901 illustrated the trend in fairs. An advertised $30,000 in premiums and $7,500 in purses were awarded to the winners of the exhibits and the trotting and pacing races. Other outstanding attractions were concerts given by John P. Sousa's band and prize drills presented by the Odd Fellow's Lodges. A person could attend all these grand attractions for only 50 cents.

Expositions or world's fairs were simply larger examples of exhibition fever. Generally, however, they tended to show the cultural, industrial, and historical development of the nation and the world, rather than displaying only agricultural products. Two of these held in the Midwest around the turn of the century were the World's Columbian Exposition (celebrating Columbus' discovery of America) held at Chicago in 1893 and the Louisiana Purchase Exposition held at St. Louis in 1904. In commenting on these world's fairs, Finley P. Dunne, through the medium of Mr. Dooley, said:

> F' one man that goes to a worruld's fair to see how boats is made, they'se twitty goes to see the hootchy-kootchy, an' that's where the wan lands finally. They may not do th' city anny good, but they're good f'r the people in it. An' they do th' city good in wan way. If a city has wan fair, it never has to have another.

Sports Events

The Midwest as a frontier area early took great delight in watching, betting on, and even participating in the more brutal sports of cockfighting, bearbaiting, wrestling, and boxing. Abraham Lincoln was known to have supervised a cockfight as had George Washington and Andrew Jackson before him. By the latter part of the nineteenth century, however, this type sport was generally left to the rougher element of society. This latter group attended the sporting halls where cockfights, dogfights, and "rat worries" were held.

Wrestling and boxing followed a different sequence. At first they were extremely popular on the frontier, then they had an eclipse, and then after 1900 they became respectable again. Wrestling among the keel-boat men, lumber men, and other rougher elements was a brutal affair. Biting, kicking, and gouging were allowed. The perennial fighters allowed their thumbnails to grow long and even filed them to a sharp point so they could more easily burst the eyeball of an opponent. One traveler in the Midwest judged the respectability of the inns by the number of ears the innkeepers had missing. Although Abraham Lincoln of New Salem, Illinois, was noted as a wrestler, his bouts followed more humane rules.

The original bare-knuckle fight was nearly as brutal as the gouging match of the frontier. The match often continued until one or the other of the contestants was unable to get up. By 1900 gloves, bells, and the Marquis of Queensbury rules had been adopted to make the sport less brutal. Although the Midwest had many minor prize fights, it did not furnish the locale or participants for major fights until more recent times.

All types of races were also favorite spectator sports in the Midwest. Foot races were a common occurrence at frontier gatherings. Owners of horses meeting on the road often staged impromtu races to see whose steed was the fastest. Although Cincinnati early developed a saddle-horse track and Louisville later became the home of the Kentucky Derby, the Midwest largely stayed with harness racing in which horses were harnessed to a cart and later a sulky for trotting or pacing horses. In addition to racing on established tracks, harness races also became an important feature of county and state fairs.

At the turn of the century, bicycle races became very popular. They in turn were succeeded by automobile and airplane races. Indianapolis became the home of the famous "500," an auto race that occurred on Memorial Day each year. Over 100,000 people attended this race annually to see accidents at high speed and to see racers attain increasingly higher average speeds for the 500 miles. Types of races included matches between almost anything that would move including ponies, greyhounds, rabbits, soapboxes on wheels, swimmers, skaters, and boats.

Midwesterners also enjoyed watching or participating in sports that involved a ball or reasonable facsimilie. These included baseball, softball, basketball, football, tennis, badminton, golf, polo, hockey, bowling, and croquet. Although cricket was early imported from England, it was too slow for Americans. Baseball and softball slowly evolved from it and replaced it. Chicago had four baseball clubs in 1858. The nation's first professional team, the Cincinnati Red Stockings, took the field in 1869. Before long the larger cities had set up professional clubs of their own. These clubs formed the National League in 1876, and they soon had a friendly rival in the American Association. In 1897 the American Association collapsed; two years later it was succeeded by the American League. After a brief struggle for supremacy, the National and American associations decided to divide up the larger cities and teams. Popular interest in baseball was further enhanced by the World Series, created in 1903, in which the best team from each association had a post-season series of games. Some of the midwestern professional teams in these associations included the St. Louis Browns and Cardinals, the Chicago Cubs and White Sox, the Cincinnati Red Sox, the Cleveland Indians, the Detroit Tigers, and the Milwaukee Braves.

Although baseball was also played at the public-school and college level, it was more popular as a professional sport. On the other hand football and basketball, which also had professional teams, were more popular at the public-school and collegiate level. Football was of English origin. It slowly evolved into its present form among the eastern colleges. Although it was too rough a sport for older men, they enjoyed watching the physical contact of the younger men. It appealed to the same atavistic instinct as boxing. By 1900 it had spread to the colleges of the Midwest. By far the most dazzling team in the Midwest in 1901 was the Universiy of Michigan eleven, coached by Fielding H. Yost. The record of his team during the season was sensational: Michigan, 550 points; opponents, 0. Michigan beat Chicago 22-0; Iowa, 50-0; Northwestern, 29-0; Ohio State, 21-0; Indiana, 33-0; and the University of Buffalo, 128-0. So much clamor arose over the Michigan team that the excitement had to be satisfied with a post-season game. The Football Coach's Association matched mighty Michigan with Stanford of California. The contest was scheduled for New Year's Day, 1902, in Pasadena, California. Although the railroad day coaches and the California water and heat upset the Michigan squad, they still beat Stanford 49-0. After considerable debate, this was finally dubbed the first Rose Bowl contest.

Rules had to be revised in the 1890's and in 1905 to make the game a little less rough because of the large number of fatalities. Educators also objected to the emphasis on commercial college athletics to the detriment of academics. But the bulk of the alumni of the colleges felt that intercollegiate football was germaine to college life and must be preserved. Football brought out large crowds in the Midwest at the public school, collegiate, and even professional level.

Basketball probably obtained most public attention at the public-schol level in the Midwest. It was one of the few popular American games whose origin could not be traced to England. As an instructor at the Y.M.C.A. training school in Springfield, Massachusetts, in 1891, James A. Naismith became aware of the need for an indoor sport that would take the place of baseball and football during the winter months. Basketball, the result of his thinking, was an almost immediate success. Although professional teams did appear, basketball, spread by the Y.M.C.A., remained largely an amateur sport. Largely because of the midwestern craze for high-school basketball, it became one of the leading sports in the Midwest.

For the fullest enjoyment of such new sports as tennis, croquet, polo, and golf, a new institution, the country club, came into being in the 1880's. Although one of the first of these was the Brookline Country Club near Boston, they soon spread to the Middle West. A country club at Chicago was one of the first in the region. Such country clubs, composed of the socially elite, allowed the wealthy to engage in sports without impairing their snobbishness. Both croquet and lawn tennis. which were introduced from England after the Civil War, were popular at country clubs, partly because they were sports that both men and women could participate in. Polo, also introduced from England during the 1870's, was a good country-club game, because only the wealthy set, found in such surroundings, could afford it. The country club's greatest contribution to recreation was golf which was finally introduced into America from Scotland in 1888. At first the democracy laughed at the enthusiastic gentlemen in red coats making holes in the turf with a stick and chasing little white balls. But erelong it moved westward taking Chicago, Milwaukee, and St. Louis by storm. Courses were rapidly built, and the game that had been the special property of the elite soon became the most popular game of the middle class. In addition to popular participation, golf and tennis over the years developed numerous prize tournaments for the professionals. Croquet remained largely a family diversion, and polo remained the recreation of the wealthy. Miniature golf, which combined features of croquet and golf, was of more recent origin, and its popularity varied from year to year. Two other diversions of the country-club set were badminton and archery. In their reintroduction to America, both of these sports had a genteel flavor. The *Harper's Weekly* described an archery tournament at White Stocking Park in Chicago in 1879 at which the contestants were of such social refinement that courteous dignity prevailed throughout. Although the democracy later picked up these sports; they, like croquet, remained family diversions.

Two other ball sports that were extremely poplar in the Midwest were softball and bowling. Bowling, originally known as nine pins, became an important indoor sport for middle-class midwesterners during the winter. Softball became a popular sport for company teams and public schools.

Transportation Activities

In addition to races, transportation served other recreational purposes. Walking, bicycling, horseback riding, boat riding, sleigh riding, or buggy riding were enjoyable ways to exercise, court one's best girl, or see the sights of the city and countryside. Trolleys, trains, automobiles, and airplanes increased the amount of scenery that one could see in a given time. Automobiles also increased the distance one could go for a date and for recreation. A Sunday afternoon drive became a family institution in the Midwest.

Such transportation sports as bicycling, swimming, skating, and skiing were very important in modifying women's clothing. Bicycling was particularly popular during the 1890's. The drop frame made it even more tempting for women. Despite Victorian objections, long skirts began to retreat before the need for leg freedom.

Although women did swim and bathe in public in the 1840's, they were fully clothed and only in the presence of other women. By the 1890's mixed bathing was considered respectable, but women were still fully clothed. Not until the 1920's and 1930's did brief bathing suits for women appear. Again, the needs of the sport had overcome the prudery of society. Although ice skating and skiing did not call for a reduction in women's clothing, they did require a modification that would allow greater freedom. The result was slacks and tight-fitting leggings. In roller skating, as in tennis, the temperature was warmer and the skirts became shorter to allow maximum movement and coolness. By a few years after its introduction in 1863, roller skating quickly spread into the Midwest. By 1880 Chicago had a skating casino that accommodated 1,000 skaters and 3,000 spectators. People danced, raced, and courted on skates.

Bicycles, trolleys, trains, and automobiles made excursions, amusement parks, and resorts popular. Amusement parks with swings, bears, band music, and Punch-and-Judy shows had been present at mid-century. But with faster means of transportation, more people went and amusements became more elaborate. Many trolleys ended at an amusement park where people could dance, ride roller coasters, merry-go-rounds, and ferris wheels and see the animals. For example, Chicago had Cheltenham Beach, noted for barbecues and clam bakes, and St. Louis had Forest Park Highlands. At these parks people also watched balloon ascensions, barnstorming airmen, parachute jumpers, baseball games, and bicycle races. As a result of faster transportation, zoos, beaches, resorts, and amusement parks became only a few minutes away.

Drinking, Gambling, and Parlor Games

People also engaged in recreation which was less commendable. Drinking of alcoholic beverages and gambling with cards and dice had long been a pastime for many people. In pioneer days a jug of corn whisky or hard cider was usually available for every festive occasion for those who wished to indulge. In the mining camps, railroad shack towns, and end-of-trail cow towns, whisky, gambling, and women were mixed with reckless abandon. This combination often led to a loss of large sums of money and killings. Many cowboys coming in from cattle drives had not seen a woman or tasted a drink for six months; with their wages burning a hole in their pockets, they were eager to remedy this situation. In mining and shack towns, the men had no family life and so they spent their idle hours gambling, drinking, and wenching.

Although many of the small towns of the Midwest under the Puritan influence of the church had a minimum of drinking or gambling, a little was always present. In the Midwest's larger cities and in some of the frontier towns, these activities were more free and open. The saloon, with its free lunch of pickled pig's feet, stacks of rye and white bread, and cheeses, was the poor man's club. Although violence and loss of money through drinking or gambling often accompanied his visit, he still enjoyed the companionship of people in a festive atmosphere, a far cry from the cramped and unhappy drabness of his own home and family. The church tried to stop this drink-and-card obsession by moral persuasion and by offering substitute entertainment. The business groups tried to stop it with longer working hours. Other groups tried to legislate and educate to stop drinking and gambling, but with limited success. Gambling with cards and dice, on the other hand, was greatly reduced by legislation. But private gambling and betting were extremely difficult to curb, because people liked to take a chance for a thrill or in hopes of wininng a fortune.

Card playing, when done for diversion only rather than for

gambling, was one of that large group of recreational pastimes known as parlor games. Parlor games included card games like whist, euchre, poker, Sancho Pedro, bridge, pinochle, hearts, rook, and canasta, and other indoor activities such as billiards, ping pong, chess, checkers, anagrams, Chinese checkers, bingo, dominoes, and dozens of others. Whist was the fashionable card game in the early Middle West. Later it was replaced by bridge and pinochle. Generally these games were accompanied by conversation and comradeship in home gatherings.

Clubs and Lodges

Still another avenue of entertainment and enlightenment developing after the Civil War was the infinite number of clubs, lodges, and organizations. The Midwest had many "joiners." For the farmers there was the Grange or Patrons of Husbandry, the largest rural, social organization. Meetings were usually held in a local schoolhouse. Although the bleak little building with its crude desks might be bare and cheerless, the hanging oil lamps, the heat of a large wood stove, and the presence of laughing people transformed it into an attractive meeting place. Farm families would come from miles around to spend a long evening over a potluck supper and simple amusements. Programs consisted of speeches, recitations, songs, rituals, country dancing, folk games, and refreshments.

For the urban midwesterner and later for his rural counterpart as well, the number of lodges from which he might choose was endless. Although freemasonry crossed the Atlantic in colonial days, it received a cool reception until after the Civil War. After 1880 the people, feeling a need for something different, began to join various fraternal orders in large numbers. Some 500 fraternal organizations were in operation by the turn of the century. At that time the Odd Fellows, Masons, and Knights of Pythias were among the most popular, a position which they continued to hold in the Midwest. These and hundreds of other organizations, such as the Ancient Arabic Order of Nobles of the

Mystic Shrine, the United Order of Druids, the Tribes of Ben Hur, and the Independent Order of Gophers, furnished a social environment in which men could play cards, participate in rituals, make business contacts, eat meals, and escape from home for an evening.

Women followed the lead of the men in joining organizations. There were temperance and suffrage organizations, auxiliaries formed on the lines of the men's organizations such as Eastern Star, Daughters of Rebekah, and daughters of Isus, associations like the Women's Relief Corps and Lady's Aid, and a wide array of social clubs. There were Shakespeare and Beethoven circles, sewing circles, noon-day rest clubs, bridge clubs, gardening clubs, and hundreds of others.

PART V

PROGRESSIVISM, CONSERVATISM, AND PRAGMATISM IN THE MIDDLE WEST, 1900-1940

— 53 —

Population and Settlement

Distribution of Population

Population trends after 1900 in the Midwest were largely a continuation of those just prior to 1900, but there were modifications. Urbanization continued unabated. From the 40 per-cent urban population that the North Central states had in 1900, it had increased to about 58 per cent by 1940. Only five midwestern states, Iowa, Kansas, Nebraska, and the Dakotas remained predominately rural. During the forty-year period, the Middle West had jumped from one to two cities of over one-million population (Detroit having joined Chicago in this) and from 14 to 28 cities of over 100,000. As in 1900 the vast majority of these larger cities was found east of the Mississippi River.

As for the distribution of population in the Midwest, the area by 1940 had an average population of 70 to 80 persons per square mile. Density was greatest in the southeastern portion (Ohio, Indiana, Illinois, southern Michigan and Wisconsin) where large sections had 100 to 150 per square mile. In much of northern Michigan, Wisconsin, and Minnesota and western North Dakota, South Dakota, Nebraska, and Kansas, there were only five to 10 persons per square mile. The number of rural settlement units, based upon an average family of five persons, indicated that the Midwest had an average of three to five farmsteads per square mile; in actuality, however, the marginal areas varied from fewer than one per square mile in the west and north to more than 10 in the more densely populated sections of the east and south. The dispersed farmstead usually constituted the basic rural settlement unit. Composed of a house, barn, outbuildings, yard, orchard, and garden, a rectangular farmstead usually covered two acres.

Although the Middle West still had a shifting population in 1940, it had no particular direction. People were simply looking for greener pastures in the city, the country, north, south, east, or west. The frontier movement in search of new land had apparently left its imprint on the American mind even after the free land was gone.

The total population of the North Central states like that of the rest of the United States was continuing to increase. Although the population of the Midwest had grown from around 26,000,000 in 1900 to approximately 40,000,000 in 1940, its percentage of the total United States' population had dropped from about 34 per cent to approximately 31 per cent. In part this was due to the increased settlement of the western United States, a fact which was demonstrated by the westward movement of the center of population from Columbus, Indiana, in 1900 to a spot near Carlisle, Indiana, in 1940.

Immigration

Probably the greatest changes in the population pattern after 1900 took place in the type and number of European immigrants coming to the United States and to the Middle West. The starting point of the heavy emigration to the United States was shifting from northwestern Europe to southeastern Europe. This changing immigration picture was due largely to the stability and increasing industrialization of western Europe and the increasing population pressures, instability, and persecution in eastern Europe.

Beginning even before 1900, popular sentiment was growing to stem this tide of immigrants. Many reasons were given. The frontier and free land were exhausted. Anarchists and agitators spewed out of Europe were coming to plague the United States. The new immigration from eastern Europe was difficult to assimilate; they bred crime and became pawns of corrupt political bosses. There was objection to the competition of these Europeans and Asians who were satisfied to work for less money. Then there was the nationalistic reason that America should be for Americans, that is, those immigrants already in residence. In 1901 the Cincinnati *Commercial* sounded this note by saying that America had too long been the dumping ground of Europe and that the United States' immigration laws should be stiffened to keep out Europe's undesirables.

Throughout this debate, labor and the lower middle classes tended to favor drastic limitation on immigration; the railroads, industrial capitalists, and upper classes tended to favor unrestricted immigration. Armour's company of Chicago encouraged their foreign-born laborers to invite their friends over to work in the meat plant. The western railroads and the states of Michigan and Wisconsin among others advertised for immigrants until 1914. The advertisements sent to Europe usually stressed the economic advantages that could be enjoyed by eneregtic Europeans who crossed the Atlantic.

Those favoring immigration restriction gradually won out. Prior to 1900 the Chinese were excluded as well as certain social, mental, and physical undesirables. In 1917 illiteracy became a bar to entry and four years later the door was closed to a crack with the Emergency Quota Act. This was made permanent by the National Origins Act of 1924, which when implemented five years later allowed 150,000 in per year. Western Europe was favored by the quotas, and immigration became a trickle.

By 1940 this immigration restriction had had a definite influence on the number and type of foreign born coming to and in the North Central states. The United States immigration figures in the second two decades as compared to those of the first two decades of the twentieth century revealed the change. Austria's and Hungary's output to the United States dropped from over three million to 75,000; Italy's from over three million to a little over 500,000; Russia's from over two and one-half million to 63,000; and Greece's from 350,000 to 60,000. The Midwest, drawing about 30 per cent of the newcomers who came to the United States, was affected accordingly. The total foreign born in the Midwest dropped from 4,762,796 in 1900 to 3,348,937 in 1940. Of this group, the leading nationalities were considerably different from those of 1900.* Of the first five in 1900, Germany was still first and Canada third. But the other large foreign elements showed the effects of the new immigration. Poland was second, Italy was fourth, and Russia was fifth.

*The leading foreign nationalities in 1900 were German, Irish, English, Canadians, and Swedish.

— 54 —

Indians and Negroes

Indians

The Midwest contained another group of citizens, that although there were born in America, were accepted even less readily than the immigrants. These were the Indians of which the Middle West in 1940 still had a relatively large percentage, usually located on out-of-the-way reservations. Of the 334,000 Indians in the United States in 1940, 71,350 or about twenty-one per cent were located in the twelve North Central states. South Dakota ranked first in the number of Indians in the Midwest with over 23,000. Minnesota and Wisconsin were in second place with over 12,000 each. The largest reservations in the Middle West were located in Wisconsin, South Dakota, North Dakota, Nebraska, Minnesota, Michigan, and Kansas.

In the Dakotas, the Sioux predominated. Of the many Dakota reservations, the Rosebud, the Pine Ridge, and the Standing Rock were the best known. As an example, the Rosebud Reservation, with its three-million acres of rolling, sparsely timbered land in southern South Dakota, was the home of some 7,000 Sioux Indians. The Sioux, descendants of nomadic buffalo hunters, preferred ranches to farms. This was fortunate, because the majority of their land was semi-arid with brakes and ravines useful only for raising stock. To aid the Indians in the pursuit, the government had established a cattle-placement agency which loaned calves and heifers to Indians desiring a start. In addition, the Indian boarding school stressed courses in cattle raising and allowed the boys to work part time and use their earnings to purchase cattle. The Dakotas also had other Indian tribes. For example, the Turtle Mountain Agency had about 5,000 Chippewa, and the Cheyenne River Reservation contained about 3,000 Cheyenne.

Minnesota's largest Indian tribe was the Chippewa. The consolidated Chippewa agency with its 6,000 Indians was the leading reservation. Minnesota's Indians existed on hunting, subsistence agriculture, and government aid. Although their literacy had improved, many were still diseased.

Wisconsin and Nebraska had Winnebago interspersed among other Indian tribes. The most noted reservation in Wisconsin was the Great Lakes Agency which had some 4,000 Indians.

In general, the Middle West in 1940 had a diversified Indian population. This diversity was demonstrated by Kansas which had slightly more than 1,000 Indians composed of Kickapoos, Sauks, Foxes, Potawatomi, Munsee, and Chippewa. To make this heterogeneity even more pronounced, a large number of these Indians had white ancestors on their family trees.

Although the Indians remaining in the Middle West were improving in educational and economic status, it was a slow process. Most of them lived in submarginal, isolated areas. Those who had managed to overcome their cultural tradition and adopt white man's ways still found themselves unacceptable as integral members of the white community. Because their number was so small and their homes so remote in the Midwest they did not constitute a serious minority problem, but on the other hand neither were they really a part of American life.

Negroes

Another minority group also poorly received in the Midwest were the Negroes. One of their most noted characteristics was their growing number. In 1860 the Midwest had 184,239 blacks, about two percent of its total population. By 1900 this figure had grown to 495,751, still about two percent of the total population, and in 1940 to 1,420,318, 3.7 percent of the total population.

Whereas the Indians were primarily rural, the Negroes by

1940 were predominately urban in the Midwest. Approximately eighty percent of these blacks lived in urban areas and 67 percent of the total lived in 24 cities of 100,000 or over in population. In these northern urban areas, segregation of the blacks was present, and it was increasing through increased emphasis on segregated housing.

The black ghettos which were generally in a run-down part of the city had a much larger population per square mile than their white counterparts. The crime and delinquency rates among Negroes were also much higher than that of the whites, and the black educational level was considerably lower. Although the midwestern blacks had more privacy, freedom of action, and independence than their southern brethren, they were still discriminated against. Approximately 83 percent of the blacks were manual laborers or in domestic or personal service while less than three percent were in the professions. Although lynchings of Negroes were much less frequent in the Midwest than in the South (5 out of a total of 104 in 1900, for example), riots, another indicator of bad racial relations, were present. East St. Louis, Illinois, had a race riot in 1917 (39 Negroes killed), Chicago in 1919 (38 persons killed), and Detroit in 1943 (25 Negroes and nine whites killed). Although the Midwest was some improvement over the South in the amount of freedom, wages, and economic and political opportunities, it was still not the land of equality that the southern blacks had envisaged when they migrated to the Midwest.

— 55 —

Cultural Characteristics

The most significant characteristics of midwestern culture in the period 1890 to 1940 were its moderate prosperity, its equalitarian tradition, its optimism, its agressiveness, its conservatism, and its diversity in homogeneity. These qualities stemmed in part from its abundant resources, favorable climate, continental position, and rural-urban distribution and in part from the people who settled in the region. Until 1830 the Middle West was settled largely from the South (especially Kentucky, Tennessee, Virginia, and North Carolina); this gave the area a touch of southern flavor and culture. With the completion of the Erie Canal in 1825, the immigration route shifted from the Ohio River to the Great Lakes, and people from New England and the Middle Atlantic states began to flow in, followed by sturdy immigrants from western Europe. In the late nineteenth century, the type of immigration into the Midwest began to change again. The number of incoming Swedes, Germans, English, Irish, and Canadians declined sharply, and by 1901 southeastern Europe was contributing the most people to the Midwest. However, in 1940 the people of the Middle West were still predominately of western European ancestry.

Through their words and deeds the people of the Middle West by 1940 displayed the traits of character and philosophy such as conservatism, individualism, competitive spirit, independence of thought, and a firm belief in democracy which are generally accepted as being characteristically American. Because of its heterogeneous population, the speech of the midwesterner was a representative compromise of the various geographic regions. He had a drawl more pronounced than the easterner, but less than the southerner or westerner.

The average midwesterner's set of values, which included morality, conservatism, and democracy, were summed up by William F. Butler in 1873 after visiting the Midwest. He said that he had heard an earnest midwesterner declare that he believed all religious, political, social, and historical teaching could be reduced to three sources: "the Sermon on the Mount, the Declaration of Independence, and the Chicago Republican Platform of 1860."

One American trait of character, demonstrated very clearly in the midwesterner, was the tendency to eat too fast and work too hard. European travelers could not understand why an American would wait thirty minutes for a meal and then gulp it down in five. They said the American boys' ambition was to work hard, to get old, and to get in the grave as soon as possible. This gospel of hard work and thriftiness was exemplified by Robert Howlett, a farmer from Lyndon, Michigan. In September 1901 he went to Detroit to spend a week's vacation at his son's home. It was his first vacation in fifty years, and he declared it would be his last. After spending one day in idleness, the habit of hard work took such a hold on the eighty-four-year-old Howlett that he insisted on helping build a fence around his son's lot. He said that if he knew he was to die on an afternoon, he would work that day at least until noon.

Thus the Midwest, with its population fairly evenly distributed between urban and rural, presented a moderately prosperous society. Many of the immigrants and native populace in this section lived on farms, but many also lived in the cities. Although the cities contained many middle-class neighborhoods, they also had slum areas like Halstead Street in Chicago, where Negroes, unassimilated immigrants, and downtrodden native whites abounded. In addition, the North Central cities had business tycoons, most of whom in the final analysis made their money from the soil. In Cincinnati was the Longworth family, whose ancestor had made a fortune in real estate. Detroit boasted the Newberrys, Algers, Trowbridges, and Russels; all descendents of lumber and real estate magnates. Chicago was the site of the Swifts, Armours, and Cudahys (meat packers), and McCormicks (farm machinery). Dry goods also produced fortunes in the Windy City; Marshall Fields, Potter Palmers, and Leiters.

On the western edge of the Middle West, there was a small, rural-urban population with a more frontier society, interspersed with immigrant and Indian minorities. Ranch life there was lonesome (especially for the women) and guests were welcome. There was a saying that ranch families could tell in the morning whether they were going to have visitors during the day by the absence or presence of dust rising in the distance. Most of the prairie towns were little more than grain elevators or fort outposts. For a resident of this region, a pistol and a horse were standard equipment.

Although the Midwest was still 42 percent rural in 1940, urbanization was having increasingly significant effects on the midwesterner. More midwesterners were becoming appreciative of cultural achievements. Specialization of talent was becoming more valuable and respectable. The old "jack of all trades" concept of the rural frontier was on the wane. Voluntary association of people had increased and the interdependence and proximity of industrialization and urbanization had cut down on individualism and the laissez-faire idea of democracy. The new limited frontiers made people realize that the old wasteful use of resources must be replaced by careful utilization or there would not be enough to go around. City life had made people aware that they might not have a job and so were interested in the security that such devices as labor unions, social security, and insurance could give them.

Forgetting the admonition of the poet that all are equal in the grave, even the democratic Midwest had a touch of social inequality that seemed to become more pronounced as the twentieth century progressed. Although the midwesterner had a feeling of equality, he still spoke of living across the tracks. There was a fluidity of classes and yet class lines were firmly drawn. Every town had its social elite and each group tended to ape the ways and words of the class that they inwardly decided were their social betters. Again the Midwest demonstrated a notion of social status that was uniquely American.

The abundance of resources in the Middle West hed helped

produce at least two other attitudes in the American. One was wastefulness and the other was optimism. Both had been modified by 1940. Harriet Martineau had remarked on the way the American farmer had farmed his land carelessly and gotten wealthy at the expense of soil and timber. With the end of limitless land in 1890, Americans began to use conservation practices and be less wasteful of the soil, but the habit of extravagant usage was hard to break.

The optimism in America was early expressed in the hundreds of utopian groups who felt they could create a perfect society in America. This boundless faith in the destiny of America was still expressed after the turn of the twentieth century. Henry D. Lloyd of Chicago wrote that the smoke nuisance in the cities would be abolished and so would the cities themselves. The new rapid transit would make possible complete suburbanization. Every house would be a center of sunshine and scenery, and every school would become a garden school. The famous Nebraska orator and politician, William J. Bryan, writing in 1925, conceived of a national destiny for the United States, surpassing the glories of the present and the past. He said, "Behold a republic increasing in population, in wealth, in strength, and in influence, solving the problems of civilization and hastening the coming of a universal brotherhood – a republic whose history is as the shining light that shineth more and more unto the perfect day." Even one of the leading historical scholars of the day, Frederick J. Turner, concluded from his study of the frontier that America would never succumb to the Old World's despotic rule of class or dictator. He perceived in America a trend toward "social justice under freedom," accompanied by the welfare and progress of the common man which would lead to ultimate peace. He was not certain America could save the world but he believed that it could preserve and expand democracy.

Probably because of its physical and cultural factors, the Midwest had come the nearest of any section of the United States in 1940 to producing the American that Hector St. John de Crevecoeur described in 1782 in his *Letters From An American Farmer:*

> What then is the American, this new man? . . . Leaving behind him all his ancient prejudices and manners, he receives new ones from the new mode of life he has embraced, the new government he obeys, and the new rank he holds. He becomes an American by being received in the broad lap of our great *Alma Mater.* Here individuals of all nations are melted into the new race of men, whose labors and posterity will one day cause great changes in the world . . . .

Or as Governor Frank O. Lowden of Illinois so succinctly stated it, the Mississippi Valley had been the birthplace of the American culture.

— 56 —

Politicial Issues and Leaders

Progressive Period

The Midwest and its political leaders played an important part in the issues of the period 1901 to 1941. Generally the Midwest continued to support the Republican Party and its conservative, business-oriented philosophy. In the 1930's a majority of the midwesterners were disenchanted enough with President Herbert Hoover and the depression to vote Democratic at the presidential level in an election or two. The Republican nature of the Midwest, however, was more illusion than reality. The Midwest was badly splintered on nearly every domestic issue and their political leaders revealed a similar tendency.

The Midwest influenced and in turn was influenced by Progessivism, which had part of its roots in the midwestern Populist movement and was popularized by the muckrakers. As Progressivism developed, it early went urban in cities under such men as Samuel M. Jones in Toledo and Tom L. Johnson in Cleveland and then washed over into state politics with the election of reformers like Governor Joseph W. Folk of Missouri, Robert M. LaFollette of Wisconsin, and Albert B. Cummins of Iowa. All of these men took up the cudgel against the champions of enrenched privilege and party bosses. That the Midwest had its share of urban corruption to fight was pointed out in Lincoln Steffens' *Shame of Cities* (1904). Although the Midwest had a tradition of opposition to entrenched privilege, this region like the rest of the United States often found it difficult to keep corruption and special privilege weeded out. One of the ways the midwestern reformers used to fight entrenched inequities was

Jane Addams (1860-1935)
Social reformer, founder of Hull House

William H. Taft (1857-1930)
President of the United States, Chief Justice of the United States

Melville W. Fuller (1833-1910)
Chief Justice of the United States

Robert M. LaFollette (1855-1925)
Governor of Wisconsin, U. S. Senator

with the passage of initiative, referendum, and recall laws which were partially successful.

As a part of this movement to regulate business and support the weak, Senator Shelby M. Cullom of Illinois was especially noted for his support of more stringent interstate commerce laws. His goal was to make the Interstate Commerce Commission, established in 1887, into a powerful, regulating agency beneficial to the public.

As a side issue, Senator Joseph B. Foraker (Republican) of Ohio became involved in a controversy with President Theodore Roosevelt over the latter's dismissal of a group of Negro troops in Brownsville, Texas. One of the Negro troops had been involved in a criminal act and when the group refused to reveal the name of the guilty man, Roosevelt dismissed the whole group. Although Foraker continued this debate up to 1907, Roosevelt emerged the victor.

Both an insurgent Republican and a conservative Republican from the Midlands were involved on opposite sides in the R. A. Ballinger-Gifford Pinchot controversy. While in office Theodore Roosevelt had pushed conservation rapidly. One of his chief lieutenants in this enterprise was Gifford Pinchot, head of the new forestry service. When President William H. Taft took office, he favored conservation also but he questioned Roosevelt's withdrawals by executive order. At the same time he did encourage Congress to withdraw lands necessary for public welfare. Taft's problem came in the allegedly fraudulent patenting of the Cunningham coal claims in Alaska. L. B. Glavis investigated and said Secretary of the Interior Ballinger, formerly legal council for the Cunningham interests, was trying to push through his former company's patents without investigation. Glavis appealed to Pinchot and Pinchot appealed to Senator Jonathan P. Dolliver of Iowa for aid. Because of their disloyalty in appealing to a senator and not to him, Taft dismissed both Glavis and Pinchot. Pinchot rushed to Theodore Roosevelt and Roosevelt took Pinchot's side. This split the Republicans still more and the insurgent Republicans backed Roosevelt. The whole affair obscured Taft's contribution to conservation.

Taft also ended up on the side of the conservatives in the

fight over limiting the powers of the Speaker of the House. In the Benjamin Harrison administration, the Speaker had obtained nearly dictatorial powers in order to expedite business through the House. Some felt that this system restricted legislative power to too small a group. Speaker Joseph G. Cannon of Illinois became the target, because as leader of the standpatters he pushed through the Payne-Aldrich tariff, downgraded conservation, and stopped temperance and labor legislation. In 1910 a coalition of Democrats led by Champ Clark of Missouri and insurgent Republicans led by George W. Norris of Nebraska set out to clip Cannon's wings. When they got through, the Speaker's chairmen-and-committee appointing powers had been reduced, and the Speaker was eliminated as chairman of the Rules Committee.

Despite these conservative stands of President Taft, he actually accomplished many reforms during his administration including the Postal Savings and Parcel Post acts, natural resource laws, Mann Elkins Act (strengthened Interstate Commerce Commission), an act separating the departments of Commerce and Labor, an act requiring publicity of sources and expenditure of funds in federal campaigns, and innumerable anti-trust prosecutions under the Sherman Act. But despite these progressive measures, Taft was still labeled a conservative, a dangerous title in this Progressive era.

As had happened in 1872 the Republican insurgents, again with the Midwest as their focal point, set out to capture the Republican Party in 1912 and ended up by creating a new party. In January 1911 they formed the National Progressive Republican League with Senator Robert M. LaFollette as its leader. The League criticized Taft and favored progressive legislation on tariffs, trusts, banking, and conservation.

Meanwhile, Theodore Roosevelt had become politically active again. After his hunting trip, he felt too young to retire. He had sided against Taft in the Pinchot affair, supported the Progressives against the Taft candidate in New York, and in August 1910 made his famous speech on new nationalism at Osawatomie, Kansas. In this speech he came out in favor of federal regulation of trusts, tariff revision, conservation, graduated income tax, direct primaries, labor legislation, and recall. After LaFollette had the

Progressive Party well under way, Theodore Roosevelt decided to be its leader and its candidate for president. In February 1912 he accepted the candidacy that he had asked seven governors to offer him. The Progressives flocked to him en masse. The frustrated LaFollette remained with the Republican Party. Roosevelt entered the Republican primaries in states holding them and won most of them. Roosevelt undoubtedly was the favorite of the people, but Taft's steam roller ran over Roosevelt as the latter's had crushed LaFollette in 1908. Taft's hand-picked delegates from the South and his hand-picked committee on credentials made Taft's selection certain. Roosevelt stalked from the hall claiming foul play. The insurgents then reassembled at Chicago where they established an independent progressive party and chose Theodore Roosevelt as its standard bearer. They set out to save the nation under the symbol of the bullmoose and the theme song, "Onward Christian Soldiers."

The most exciting event in this out-of-the-ordinary campaign and election occurred in October 1912, when Roosevelt was harmlessly but spectacularly shot in the glass case by an unhinged man at Milwaukee, Wisconsin. In the election the split in the Republican ranks gave the election to the Democrats. Although Woodrow Wilson obtained 435 electoral votes to 96 for Roosevelt and Taft, the latter two combined received over 1,000,000 more votes than Wilson. The most unusual event of the election was that Roosevelt, the third-party candidate received over 700,000 more votes than Taft, the regular Republican candidate.

In 1924 LaFollette set out again to establish another progressive party, composed of Socialists, Farm-Laborers, and insurgent Republicans, as a challenge to the Republican Party. This time LaFollette was able to retain leadership of the movement and he received the nod to be the standard bearer for the National Conference of Progressive Political Action. A life-long reformer it was only natural that LaFollette should finally head a reform ticket. Over the years he had favored parcel post, postal savings, a separate Department of Labor, an eight-hour day, child-labor laws, and woman suffrage. Extremely reformist this party stood for public ownership of railroads, abolition of judicial review, election of federal judges for ten-year terms, direct nomination and election of the president, initiative and referendum in the federal government, and a referendum for a declaration of war (except in case of invasion).

For the first and last time the American Federation of Labor gave its support to a third party. With labor support LaFollette's progressive party made a fair showing. It received nearly five-million popular votes and 13 electoral votes. Despite the defection of this vote, however, the Republicans still won a landslide victory — over seven-million vote plurality.

Although the original progressive party of 1912 had been defeated, the Progressive movement was kept alive in President Woodrow Wilson's New Freedom. Wilson wanted to protect the man on the rise and keep big business fair and efficient. He obtained downward tariff revision in Underwood-Simmons, increased control of banking in the Federal Reserve Act, and more control of business in the Clayton Anti-Trust and the Federal Trade Commission acts. Although the South and East probably had a larger part in Wilson's administration than the Midwest, the latter had some influence. Vice-President Thomas R. Marshall of Indiana presided over the Senate and Champ Clark of Missouri was Speaker of the House. William J. Bryan was secretary of state. The insurgent Republicans from the Midlands joined the Democrats in approving the income-tax and direct-election-of-senators amendments. Senator LaFollette took a leading role in passing the Seaman's Act which required improved working and living conditions on board inland-waterway and ocean vessels.

An interesting midwestern political movement began in North Dakota in 1915. The Non-Partisan League, under the leadership of Arthur C. Townley, had its beginning when a member of the legislature allegedly told some farmers that they had "better go home and slop the hogs." The Non-Partisan League decided that rather than slop the hogs or start a new political party, it would take over one of the major parties and pass laws to help agriculture. In North Dakota it seized the Republican Party; in Minnesota, the Farmer Labor Party; and in Wisconsin, it joined LaFollette's Progressive group. In North Dakota where the league was most successful, it reduced freight rates, passed a grain-grading law and a law guaranteeing bank deposits, and established a state-owned bank, elevator, and flour mill. By 1920 the League had nearly collapsed. Corruption and lethargy contributed to its demise.

Prohibition which came in part out of World War I was was strongly supported by the Midwest. The rural element of the Middle West had long been a supporter of temperance. Westerville, Ohio, was headquarters for the Anti-Saloon League and Wayne B. Wheeler of Columbus was an Anti-Saloon League leader. In 1917 Representative Andrew J. Volstead of Minnesota even got his name attached to the act that defined what an alcoholic beverage was.

Conservatism in the 1920's

In 1920 the Midwest supplied a large part of the national executive leadership that was noted for its corruption. The man in charge of this shady administration was President Warren G. Harding, originally a small-town, newspaper man and senator from Ohio, who had mediocre talents and was a poor judge of character. His cabinet varied greatly in competence. Those cabinet members from the Midwest seemed to be among the least competent. Henry C. Wallace of Iowa, secretary of agriculture, was good; but Henry M. Daugherty of Ohio, attorney general; Will H. Hays of Indiana, postmaster general; and Edwin Denby of Michigan, secretary of the navy; were poor. Denby was in on the Teapot Dome scandal by which government oil lands were leased to private interests under suspicious circumstances. Daugherty seemed always to be closer to corruption than he should have been.

During Harding's term in office Congress passed the higher Fordney-McCumber tariff, reduced taxation slightly for the higher income groups, cared for the disabled war veterans, and passed a stringent immigration law. Worn out by two and one-half years in office and harrassed by scandals, Harding died in San Francisco in August 1923 on his return trip from Alaska.

Warren G. Harding (1865-1923)
President of the United States

Courtesy Library of Congress. From *Dictionary of American Portraits* by Hayward and Blanche Cirker, Dover Publications, Inc., New York, 1967. *Reprinted through permission of the publisher.*

John M. Hay (1838-1905)
Diplomat, Secretary of State, author

Courtesy Library of Congress, Brady-Handy Collection. From *Dictionary of American Portraits* by Hayward and Blanche Cirker, Dover Publications, Inc., New York, 1967. *Reprinted through permission of the publisher.*

Frank B. Kellogg (1856-1937)
U. S. Senator, Secretary of State

Courtesy Library of Congress. From *Dictionary of American Portraits* by Hayward and Blanche Cirker, Dover Publications, Inc., New York, 1967. *Reprinted through permission of the publisher.*

John J. Pershing (1860-1948)
General, Army Chief of Staff

Courtesy Library of Congress. From *Dictionary of American Portraits* by Hayward and Blanche Cirker, Dover Publications, Inc., New York, 1967. *Reprinted through permission of the publisher.*

During the Calvin Coolidge administration, the Midwest was probably most upset with Coolidge over his vetoes of the McNary-Haugen bills, which were to absorb some of the agricultural surpluses. The midwestern farmers along with their counterparts in other sections tried but could not gather the votes to pass these bills over his vetoes.

Also in the 1920's the Midlands produced an even more infamous politician than Harding. After the war an anti-foreign reaction in the United States produced a red scare and a revival of the Ku Klux Klan. In Indiana the leader of the Klan was an illiterate Texan by the name of D. C. Stephenson. Preaching hatred for Catholics, foreigners, Jews, and Negroes, he first ran on the Democratic ticket. Swamped there he turned to the Republicans. Supported by 400,000 voters he moved into Indianapolis as governor of the state. His rule, marked by vice and betrayal, finally collapsed in 1926 when he was convicted of murdering a girl who had been his mistress. He retired to the state prison at Michigan City.

The More Liberal 1930's

In the Midwest, as elsewhere, the depression of the 1930's also produced strange political phenomena. In Kansas in 1930 emerged Dr. John R. Brinkley, a red-goateed, aggressive young medic, who had made a fortune by allegedly restoring masculine virility in older men by making goat-gland "transplantations." Attacked by the Kansas City *Star* and the medical profession as a fraud, he was eventually deprived of his license to practice medicine in Kansas. He decided to turn to politics and ran for governor. His broadcasting station and a whirlwind tour made him many friends, and he might have won the election if the officials had not thrown out many of his write-in ballots.

Of a far more commendable type but also extremely individualistic was George W. Norris, a liberal Republican from Nebraska. Born in Ohio he had been a teacher, lawyer, and judge before serving in the House and Senate. He had been a leader in the unhorsing of Speaker Joseph Cannon in 1910, opposed to World War I, and an advocate of the League. His name was in the Norris-LaGuardia Act of 1932, which outlawed the "yellow dog" contract. He introduced the Lame Duck Amendment (Twentieth) six times before it finally passed Congress and was presented to the states for ratification. His perseverance also helped to bring about the establishment of the Tennessee Valley Authority which had been a source of contention from World War I to the time of its creation in the early 1930's. A Republican he was popular enough in Nebraska to run as an Independent for the Senate in 1936 and win.

The Midwest also produced two other noted political figures who were even more noted than Norris for their perseverance in the face of defeat. They were the Socialists Eugene V. Debs of Indiana and Norman Thomas of Ohio. Debs, who was originally a union organizer, was the perennial Socialist candidate from the turn of the century through 1924. Debs even ran his last race from the Atlanta federal penitentiary, where he was incarcerated for his militant, anti-World War I activities. Norman Thomas, a former Presbyterian minister, began his unsuccessful races as the Socialist candidate for the presidency in 1928. His track record for seeking the presidential office was nearly as impressive as Debs'.

A Summary

Although the Midwest did not have as many national office holders during these four decades as during the previous generation, it still had an impressive box score. The Midwest supplied two presidents (three with Hoover), four vice-presidents, two secretaries of state, three secretaries of the treasury, five secretaries of war, four secretaries of the navy, three attorney generals, four postmaster generals, nine secretaries of the interior, seven secretaries of agriculture, five secretaries of commerce, five Speakers of the House, and eight justices of the U. S. Supreme Court, including two chief justices. In addition the Midwest supplied four unsuccessful presidential candidates and six unsuccessful vice-presidential candidates for the major parties as well as many unsuccessful vice-presidential candidates for the minor parties.

The Midwest had almost the same political-bellwether and Republican record in this period as in the 40 years preceding. A majority of the midwestern states were on the winning side nine out of ten elections and voted Republican in all but three of these ten elections.

Despite its mavericks, special problems, and Republican learnings, however, the Midwest by 1940 was becoming an increasingly integral political part of the main stream of United States history. Improved transportation and communication were making the United States a unified nation in fact.

— 57 —

Foreign Affairs

Imperialism and Tariffs

In foreign affairs around the turn of the century, imperialism became the dominant question of the day. In this President William McKinley took a positive position favoring acquisition of colonies and markets. In this policy he was strongly backed by fellow midwesterners such as Senator Albert J. Beveridge of Indiana, Senator John C. Spooner of Wisconsin, and Secretary of State John Hay of Ohio. John Hay, who was noted for his Open Door (trade) policy in China and his acquisition of colonies, was the key man in American imperialism at the turn of the century.

Tariffs during this period were generally higher. The stage for this was set by the Payne-Aldrich Tariff of 1909. Although this tariff was supposed to revise the duties downward, it instead increased the duties slightly over the protective Dingley Tariff of 1897. Albert J. Beveridge of Indiana, Joseph L. Bristow of Kansas, Moses E. Clapp of Minnesota, Albert B. Cummins and Jonathan P. Dolliver of Iowa, and Robert M. LaFollette of Wisconsin led the fight in the Senate against this higher tariff but they lost the battle. Congress later tried to pass reductions on single items (popgun tariff bills) but President Taft vetoed them. Taft later favored a reciprocal tariff with Canada, but the same insurgent Republicans in Congress fought this lower tariff because they said it would help the manufacturer and hurt the farmer.

Although the Democratic Underwood-Simmons tariff of 1913 reduced duties somewhat, this trend ended with the Democratic administration of Wilson. The Republicans used the agricultural distress and the nationalism kindled during World War I to rush through an "emergency" tariff in 1921, which pushed rates up particularly on agricultural products like wheat, corn, meat, wool, and sugar. This high tendency was reinforced by the Fordney-McCumber tariff of 1922 and the Hawley-Smoot Act of 1930. Having decided that they could not pass a lower tariff, Congress turned the lowering of tariffs over to the executive branch in the Trade Agreements Act of 1934.

The business group of the Midwest generally favored high tariffs and a large number of farmers also believed that their prosperity depended upon high duties. As in the case of imperialism there was considerable division on the tariff question, but a majority apparently believed strongly enough in economic nationalism to want to protect the home market for home production whatever the cost.

World War I

When World War I came along in 1914, the Midwest following its isolationistic bent wanted to stay neutral. Some of the minority groups, however, expressed their sympathies. In July 1914 a group of Americans of Czechoslavakian and Yugoslavian origin displayed their sympathy for Serbia in a demonstration in the Czechoslovakian district of Chicago. The Chicago Poles met the next month in a protest movement against Russian despotism. On the other hand, the Midwest also had a large number of German birth who were sympathetic to Germany, but generally were intimidated into silence. The Midwest, however, primarily Anglo-Saxon in origin generally ignored these demonstrations and minorities of both persuasions, mildly sympathized with England, and strove with President Woodrow Wilson to be neutral in thought. But then midwestern businessmen made loans to England, Germany marched across unoffending Belgium, Germany began to use the submarine, and the Midwest was propagandized with the idea that American honor on the seas was being trampled on. A majority of midwesterners, despite the large German minority, decided it was time to fight Germany. Although men like William J. Bryan, George W. Norris of Nebraska, and Robert M. LaFollette of Wisconsin fought hard against breaking relations with Germany, arming merchantmen, and finally American entrance into the war, they were defeated. Bryan resigned as secretary of state in 1915 because he did not feel America was being neutral in its relations with England and Germany. When the vote for war was taken, both Norris and LaFollette joined a number of their midwestern colleagues in voting against the declaration, but to no avail. America, including the Midwest, was ready for war.

In all the Midwest furnished about 1,431,000 troops for World War I, which was about 30 per cent of the U. S. Armed Forces employed in the war. The North Central states also made some special contributions to the war effort. General John J. Pershing, commander of the American Expeditionary Forces in Europe, was from Missouri. Columbus, Ohio, furnished Edward V. Rickenbacker, known as "America's Ace of Aces" in World War I. As for the aircraft used in World War I, many of them were built by the Lincoln and Packard Motor companies in Michigan. The first American soldier killed on the battlefield in France was from Indiana.

During the course of the war, some middle western officials were over zealous in their prosecution of the war. People with pro-German sentiments were occasionally mistreated, and the teaching of German was banned in some schools. Some students undoubtedly joined this crusade in order not to have to study German. The American Protective League, a volunteer secret-service organization made up of frustrated snoopers, originated in Chicago. Established for the purpose of ferreting out anyone that was suspected of being anti-American, it occasionally invaded the constitutional freedoms of American citizens. It at one time had 13,000 members in Chicago alone. Minnesota set up a "Commission of Public Safety" to enlist the home guard to protect the state. German sympathy was quiet in the face of this show of force. Kansas attempted to Americanize foreigners and used the American Protective League to ferret out disloyalty.

Nebraska also had an intolerant administrative group that restricted the liberties of Nebraskans in the name of winning the war. The national government went a little overboard in prosecuting those who looked or sounded slightly disloyal, and the national government was well supported in this by intolerant people in each of the North Central states.

Other developments of the war period included the wheatless and meatless days originated in Wisconsin to save food. Wisconsin also passed an educational bonus bill in September 1919 which paid Wisconsin servicemen thirty dollars a month up to thirty-six months for attending school. This idea was picked up by the federal government for use in the post-World War II period. Although the first steps for the American Legion were taken in Paris, the name of the organization and tentative draft of its constitution were originated at St. Louis in May 1919.

Between the Wars

After the war Wilson tried to keep America in international affairs by advocating that America join the League of Nations. Although opinion was divided in the Midwest on entrance into the League, a majority seemed to favor isolation and "Return to Normalcy." Ohio furnished both presidential candidates in 1920; Governor James M. Cox who said he was for the League and Senator Warren G. Harding who hazily maintained that he favored international organization. Harding won and he and his party took it as a mandate not to approve American entrance into the League, whether that was the desire of the American people or not.

The Midwest did have a well-known figure at the national level in foreign affairs during the latter half of the 1920's This was Frank B. Kellogg of Minnesota, who had been a United States senator and ambassador to England. He was appointed secretary of state by President Coolidge in 1925. In 1927 and 1928, Kellog reluctantly became involved in the Kellogg-Briand pact. Signed by many nations of the world, this pact was to outlaw war as an instrument of national policy. Although high sounding on paper, the invasion of Manchuria by Japan in 1931 displayed its weakness.

By the 1930's the Midwest was more isolationistic than ever. A series of stringent neutrality acts were passed partly at the urging of Senator Gerald P. Nye of North Dakota. Nye, as head of a Senate committee, investigated the huge profits of the American munitions industry in World War I and tried to prove that these companies were responsible for American entrance into the war. Many people were convinced and agreed to legislation designed to prevent the U. S. from entering another foreign war.

— 58 —

Developments in Agriculture

Western Middle West

Mechanization was probably the most significant development in agriculture in the period 1900 to 1930. Although mechanization was important throughout the Midwest, it was probably most important in the wide-open fields of the western half of the North Central states. Among other farming tools, the disk harrow and steam tractor of 1900 and later the internal combustion tractor and combine were probably most important in the expansion of grain production.

Ranching probably changed less between 1900 and 1940 than did grain farming in the drier reaches of the Midwest. Although better strains of cattle were developed and the pickup truck began to replace horses in ranching, many of the procedures remained the same. Brands were still used because fences were not always trustworthy. Most of the drives, however, were mechanized and cattle rode to market. The refrigerator car and the packing plants helped make Americans a beef-eating people and the cattle industry a permanent part of the economy. But ranch life remained somewhat isolated and lonely, and the color of former days was reserved mostly for the rodeo and the movies.

Generally in describing either a ranch, dry land farm, or a combination thereof in the 1930's, the description would be similar to one made in 1900. At the later date, there were still ranchers who owned 10,000 to 400,000 acres of grazing land and thousands of head of cattle. For example, one of the largest ranches in South Dakota in the 1930's was the Diamond A, located at Eagle Butte. It contained 400,000 acres and 10,000 head of

Nebraska Sand Hills cattle

Indiana Amish farm

cattle. There were also large dry-land farmers who had a corresponding number of acres for grain farming with many hired men and the latest mechanized equipment.

There were also many places like the 1,040 acre ranch near Gordon, Nebraska, on the edge of the sandhills. The owner combined cattle ranching and grain farming. The ranch contained about 100 cattle on 400 acres of pasture land. The other 640 acres were devoted to grain farming. Half of this 640 acres was allowed to lie fallow each season while the other half was planted to wheat and rye. The buildings consisted of a house, a garage, a small barn, and a number of other outbuildings. The operator of this ranch was not unduly prosperous. He worked long hours from May through October and was always at the mercy of the elements.

Eastern Middle West

Similarly in the more moist areas of the eastern Midwest, the basic outlines of farming were very similar in the 1930's to what they had been a generation earlier. The farm was generally larger and more mechanized but the routine was essentially the same.

A look at a farming community in Hancock County, Iowa, would illustrate this. These farmers were corn and hog men. Out of the fertile black loam that covered their 200 to 300-acre farms came great abundance. Hancock County's crops were valued at over $4,500,000 and its livestock at over $3,000,000. Three fourths of the farm dwellings had electricity. Freshly painted outbuildings usually included a barn, hog houses, chicken houses, corn cribs, a machine shed, a granary, and a silo. A high school education was considered a necessity for the sons and daughters, and each fall an increasingly large number of the children entered Iowa State University at Ames.

There was still hard physical labor even on the later-day farm. Up at dawn the farm family had twice a day to do chores: feeding the beef cattle and hogs; bringing in the milk cows from pasture; watering, feeding, and milking them; and cleaning out the barn. Caring for the poultry, the garden, and the house usually fell to the womenfolk.

In the spring the race began to get the ground plowed and oats planted. During March a Hancock farmer might spend all day with his tractor and plow in the field and half the night in the sow pens, helping the sows to bear their young. In April he plowed for corn and May he planted it. The corn had to be cultivated thrice before the oats ripened in August. Fall pigs came in September, and October was devoted to picking corn and hauling it to the cribs or to market. And throughout, farm produce rolled to market in the form of oats, hogs, poultry, eggs, and milk.

Other owners of diversified farms in the Midwest lived similar lives under similar conditions. Some like those in Hancock County, Iowa, had more fertile soil and thus were more prosperous. Others specialized more in one crop or another. Around Holland, Michigan, it might be fruit growing and sugar beets; around Mankato, Minnesota, or Green Bay, Wisconsin, it might be dairying; or around Syracuse, Indiana, corn and other grain crops; but in all these places, the life of the farm family was very similar.

Prosperity and Recession

Despite his perennial problems of increasing costs and decreasing prices, the farmer of the Middle Border enjoyed relative prosperity in the period from 1897 to 1919. Increased gold discoveries increased money in circulation. The rapid expansion of the agricultural area was slowing down. In comparison to the period 1870 to 1890 when fifteen-million acres were put under cultivation annually, the period 1900 to 1910 had only four-million acres added each year. The Federal Farm Loan Act of 1916 set up federal land banks where farmers could borrow money at a low rate of interest. World War I brought farmers to the peak of prosperity. Wheat rose in price to two dollars a bushel. Another source of prosperity was the unearned increment that farmers who owned their land gained from the rising price of land. For example in Iowa, the value of an acre of land in 1870 was $10; 1890, $50; 1910, $100, and 1920, $220.

Beginning in 1919, however, the bottom fell out for the midwestern farmer. The national government attempted to ameliorate this agricultural recession by passing remedial legislation. Among agricultural acts passed for this purpose were the following: the Stockyard Act (1921), insured that stockyards could not combine to hold down the prices on stock which they purchased; the Capper-Volstead Cooperative Act (1922), exempted farm co-ops from anti-trust laws; the Agricultural Marketing Act (1923), set up an intermediate credit bank in each federal land-bank district to extend intermediate loans; the Agricultural Marketing Act (1929), authorized the Federal Farm Board to loan $500,000,000 to cooperative associations and stabilization corporations which were to buy farm surpluses and store them until the prices went up to insure more orderly marketing; the Farm Relief and Inflation Act (1933), paid farmers to take acreage out of production and to cut down on livestock production and also authorized federal land banks to issue two-billion dollars in four per cent bonds to refinance farm mortgages at a low interest rate; the Farm Mortgage Foreclosure Act (1934), made possible an extension of loans to farmers to enable them to recover property already foreclosed; the Rural Electrification Administration (1935), created to provide low cost electricity to farmers; the Soil Conservation and Allotment Act (1936), paid farmers to take land out of production and to build up the fertility of their soil; and the second Agricultural Adjustment Act (1938), paid farmers for restoring soil fertility, for taking land out of production, and for storing surpluses to be sold in lean years.

Despite this legislation, however, agriculture continued its downward spiral. The same old factors of over-expansion, overproduction, farming marginal land, rising costs, and declining prices again contributed to the farmer's plight. Two-dollar wheat had caused farmers to pay too much for land, and go too far in debt, and to plow up blow land on the drier margins. When the prices of corn, wheat, cattle, and hogs dropped one half between 1919 and 1921, the farmers were forced to pay back with one-dollar wheat, loans which they had contracted when the price of wheat was two dollars. Overhead spiralled with mechanization. Between 1890 and 1940 the value of farm machinery increased seven fold. Overproduction, which in essence meant increased production or a dropping off of demand stemmed from many causes. There was a cessation of war demands, greater competition in the world market as foreign countries got back in production, and the impoverishment of Europe. Dietary and style changes along with a decreasing rate of population growth cut down the market for agricultural goods. The increased use of hybrid seeds and fertilization of the soil generally increased production. Even the replacing of horses by automobiles, trucks, and tractors increased costs to the farmer and increased production, because the horses were no longer eating a part of the agricultural produce. Another basic cause of the agricutural recession was the fact that the farmer no longer had the unearned increment of rising land values to fall back on. Land values in Iowa, for example, dropped from $220 an acre in 1920 to $120 in 1930 and to $70 in 1935.

During this recession, interest, taxes, and prices of manufactured goods stayed up, and farmers were forced to the wall. The bankruptcy rate per thousand farms jumped from .21 to 1.20 in the period 1920 to 1926. Farm mortgages rapidly increased and land values dropped one half. Tenantry rose from 38 per cent in 1920 to 42 per cent in 1930. Economic conditions got even worse during the early 1930's and were accentuated by a terrible drought in the western Midwest in the years 1934 to 1936 that completed the farm crash. Although New Deal policies aided the farmer a little, agriculture did not really recover until World War II brought greater demand and higher prices for agricultural products.

Production

Despite their many problems, however, the farmers of the nation continued to produce. And although many additional acres of farmland were put under cultivation in the forty years after 1900, the Midwest held its own percentage-wise in production. In 1940 the Midwest produced 71 per cent of the nation's corn, 59 per cent of the wheat, 82 per cent of the oats, 67 per cent of the barley, 49 per cent of the hay, 31 per cent of the potatoes, and 83 per cent of the rye. In the animal line the Midwest contained 60 per cent of the nation's hogs, 55 per cent of the horses, 14 per cent of the mules, 27 per cent of the sheep, and 46 per cent of the cattle. In the total value of all agricultural products sold, the Midwest was first among the regions with 45 per cent.

As for the individual state production in the United States in 1940, Iowa was first in the nation in oats, hogs, horses, total livestock, and corn. Wisconsin was first in hay and dairy cows; Kansas in wheat; and North Dakota in rye. Although the Midwest had slipped percentage-wise in the 40-year interval in wheat, hay, potatoes, sheep, and mules, these slippages were small, and the overall midwestern agricultural production was nearly twice that of any one of the other three regions.

— 59 —

Mining and Manufacturing

Mining

Percentage-wise the Midwest dropped slightly in mineral production in the generation after 1900. One of the earliest minerals of commercial importance in the Midwest was salt. Ohio, alone, in 1840 had produced 297,000 bushels. In 1940 the Midwest had 54 per cent of the nation's output, and of this Michigan alone accounted for 28 per cent of U. S. salt production.

Lead, also, early became an important product in the Midwest. The Frenchman Julian Dubuque moved into the Fever River district in northwest Illinois around 1789 to mine the lead in the area. Forty years later, thirteen-million pounds of lead were being mined there annually. Moses Austin moved to the St. Louis area in 1798 and sank the first lead shaft and built a shot tower on a cliff at Herculaneum. Missouri proved in the long run to be a better source of lead than Illinois. In 1940 Missouri, with 38 per cent of U. S. production, was the leading lead-producing state in the Union.

In coal and copper, the Midwest between 1900 and 1940 declined in its percentage of production. In bituminous coal, for example, the Midwest had dropped to 23 per cent, a nine per cent reduction in its percentage of production. Similarly copper production in Michigan in 1940 had dropped from 21 per cent to five per cent of the nation's output.

In contrast iron-ore production in the Midwest increased. It grew by eight percentage points up to 88 per cent of the U. S. total in 1930 and then dropped off to 83 per cent by 1940.

Overall, however, the Midwest declined in total mineral production in the 40-year period after 1900. It dropped nine percentage points to 21 per cent of the nation's total mineral production by 1940.

Manufacturing

The Midwest had some interesting developments in manufacturing in the first four decades of the twentieth century. One of these developments involved steel production. Soon after 1900 U. S. Steel decided to build a steel-production complex on the southern shore of Lake Michigan. To serve as a foundation, the company covered the swamps and dunes of the area with a 15-feet layer of silt pumped from Lake Michigan and then built the largest steel plants in the nation there. The company hauled in train loads of black soil so that grass, trees, and shrubs would grow. In 1906 when this newly created city received its charter, it was named after Judge Elbert H. Gary, chairman of the board of directors of United States Steel. By 1940 the Gary-Whiting-East Chicago-Hammond region placed second only to the Pittsburgh-Youngstown area in steel production. The Youngstown and Gary areas made it possible for the Midwest to have approximately 43 per cent of the iron and steel production of the United States in 1940.

Automobile manufacturing also settled in the Middle West. Although Cincinnati had originally led in the carriage and wagon trade, Detroit gradually developed a strong carriage industry. Then in 1900 the revolution began. The "horseless carriage" industry was invented, and the industry centered in eastern Michigan. Ransom E. Olds, who was first at Detroit, moved to Lansing in 1901 when his Detroit factory burned. Olds originated the Reo. Its name was taken from his initials. Henry Ford, off to a slow start in Detroit, began his success with a low-priced Model T in 1909. He developed the assembly-line principle in 1914, and by 1927 he had manufactured fifteen-million Model T's. The Buick Company, named after inventor David Buick, was begun at Flint in 1903 by Benjamin Briscoe. The Oakland, which

Henry Ford (1863-1947)
Automobile manufacturer

Orville and Wilbur Wright
(1871-1948) (1867-1912)
Aviation pioneers

was the forerunner of the Pontiac, was started at Pontiac, Michigan, by a carriage maker named Edward Murphy in 1908. The Chrysler Corporation had its inception in the Maxwell-Briscoe Motor Company started in 1904. Walter Chrysler bought it out in 1919. The growth of the automobile industry was indicated by the increase in production from 187,000 cars and trucks in 1910 to 4,472,286 cars and trucks in 1940. Its magnitude was also indicated by the fact that Detroit's automobile and other industries in the late 1930's utilized 75 per cent of the rubber, 70 per cent of the plate glass, 57 per cent of the malleable iron, 40 per cent of the mohair and lead, 33 per cent of the nickel, 25 per cent of the steel, 15 per cent of the aluminum and an almost equal amount of the tin, zinc, hardwood lumber, and cotton used in the United States.

Generally, by 1940 the bulk of midwestern manufacturing was centered in the five states east of the Mississippi River. Of the 191 major industrial and diversified centers in the Midlands, all but 21 were north of the Ohio River and east of the Mississippi. These 170 manufacturing cities in Illinois, Indiana, Ohio, Michigan, and Wisconsin formed the western half of the great manufacturing belt of America. The five states east of the Mississippi reported 31 per cent of the national factory production in 1940 compared to 6 per cent for the seven states lying west of the Mississippi. Among export items, motor vehicles in 1940 came largely from Michigan, meat products from Iowa and Illinois, rubber products from Ohio, printing and electrical goods from Illinois, and paper and leather products from Wisconsin. For the Midwest as a whole the metals and machinery industries accounted for more than half the entire manufacturing output. Cities like Flint, Youngstown, Detroit, Canton, South Bend, Grand Rapids, Dayton, Cleveland, Erie, and Toledo were primarily devoted to the manufacture of basic steel, machinery, automobiles, and metal products.

Other specific examples of midwestern cities with industries built on extractive raw materials in 1940 included Detroit with the largest stove-manufacturing, adding-machine, pharmaceutical, and electrical-refrigeration plants in the United States; Elkhart, Indiana, with Miles laboratories; Indianapolis with Ely Lily pharmaceutical company; Dayton, Ohio, with the National Cash Register Company; Hannibal, Missouri, with the largest Portland Cement plant; Cleveland, with a huge petroleum refinery; Zanesville, Ohio, with Weller Pottery and Cincinnati with Rockwood Pottery; South Bend, Indiana, with Studebaker, Bendix, and Singer Sewing Machine; Kenosha, Wisconsin, with Nash automobiles and Simmons beds; Racine, Wisconsin, with Johnson's Wax; Ft. Madison, Iowa, with the Shaeffer Fountain Pen Company; Elgin, Illinois, with watches; Newton, Iowa, with the largest washing-machine company (Maytag); Muscatine, Iowa, with the largest button industry; and the St. Clair River towns in Michigan with Morton and Diamond salt and Garwood and Chris Craft boats.

Thus, the Midwest over the years became not only the bread basket of the United States but also the metal basket. In 1940 the Midwest not only produced 45 per cent of the agricultural products of the nation but also 37 per cent of the manufactured goods.

— 60 —

Labor on the Defensive

Despite the national character of labor unions such as the American Federation of Labor and the railroad brotherhoods, the Midwest did have a few distinctive labor movements and happenings after 1900. One of the most interesting was the Buck Stove and Range Company case of St. Louis in the early 1900's. The Buck Stove Company obtained an injunction from the supreme court of the District of Columbia forbidding officers and members of the American Federation of Labor not only from including the plaintiff's products in the "We Don't Patronize" list of their official publication, but also from referring to the dispute in print or by word of mouth. This incredible injunction was obeyed as far as the unfair list was concerned, but otherwise ignored. Although Samuel Gompers, John Mitchell, and Frank Morrison were all sentenced to prison for violating the injunction they evaded prison terms because of legal technicalities.

One small segment of the labor movement in the Midwest took a slightly different turn because of the presence of Socialist leaders like Victor L. Berger of Milwaukee, Wisconsin, and Eugene V. Debs of Terre Haute, Indiana. In 1897 these two cooperated in founding the Social Democratic Party in America. Debs was the perennial candidate for president on the Socialist Party through 1924. He was also involved along with Daniel DeLeon and William D. Haywood in the founding of the radical Industrial Workers of the World organization in Chicago in 1905. Berger was the Socialist mayor of Milwaukee and later a United States representative. Because of the red scare in the United States, however, he was not allowed to take his congressional seat from 1918 to 1922. Debs and Berger and their associates did much to make Socialism more acceptable to the American workmen.

Probably the most indigenous union in the Midwest in more recent times was the United Auto Workers originally affiliated with the Congress of Industrial Organization. It appeared in 1935 with the purpose of organizing all laborers in auto factories into industrial unions. Largely a Michigan union, it staged the first sit-down strike in the Fisher Body plant at Flint, Michigan, in 1936. Its hardest fight was the organization of the Ford Motor Company. Henry Ford paid relatively high wages, and he was determined to prevent unionization in his plants, but he eventually had to succumb to unionization.

Despite the labor-union activity, only about 10 per cent of the midwestern laborers were in unions in 1914, 20 per cent in 1920, 10 per cent in 1930, and 18 per cent in 1940.

—61—

Money and Banking

Overall, the Midwest had a period of prosperity that lasted through World War I. This was possible because of good crops, the discovery of gold in South Africa, Yukon, and Alaska, and the development of a new process to extract the precious metal from the ore.

In 1907 the United States again had a banker's panic caused by overexpansion and speculation. This resulted in a study of the banking system which revealed among other things poor banking practices and an inelasticity of credit. In 1908 Congress passed as a temporary measure the Aldrich-Vreeland Act, which allowed the issue of additional bank notes based upon approved securities owned by states, cities, and towns. A commission was also established to make further study. In 1913 the recommendations of this commission, known as the "Aldrich Plan," became the basis of the Federal Reserve System. This act divided the country up into twelve districts with a Federal Reserve bank located in the primary banking city of each district. The Midwest had five of these cities; Cleveland, Chicago, Minneapolis, Kansas City, and St. Louis. Every national bank was required (and other banks were encouraged) to join the system and subscribe six per cent of their capital stock to the capital stock of the Federal Reserve bank in their district. The whole system was directed by the Federal Reserve Board, and the district banks were administered by a board of nine members, chosen by the member banks and the Federal Reserve Board. The Federal Reserve banks were banker's banks and served the functions of rediscounting commercial paper for member banks, purchasing and selling bills of exchange, granting loans to member banks, and issuing Federal Reserve notes. Later amendments to the Federal Reserve Act of 1923 and 1933 allowed member banks, either national or state, to establish branches. The Intermediate Credit Act of 1923 also gave member banks the privilege of discounting short-term farm paper at the district banks and receiving Federal Reserve notes in return. Other banking agencies created between 1900 and 1940 that were especially beneficial to the Midwest included Postal Savings banks, established in 1910 to give more banking service to rural areas, and Federal Land banks, created in 1916 to loan farmers money at a low rate of interest.

After 1933 there was an attempt to create inflation and remedy some of the defects in the Federal Reserve System, pointed up by the depression. Inflation in 1933 was mainly stimulated by government spending, devaluating the dollar, and going off the gold standard. The main basis of increased regulation was the Glass-Steagall Act of 1933, which set up a Federal Deposit Insurance Corporation to insure deposits, restricted use of Federal Reserve bank credit for stock-market speculation, restrained national banks from dealing in foreign securities, forbade private banks that underwrote and promoted securities from acting as banks of deposit, and established a quick liquidating procedure for the benefit of depositors in banks that failed. Two years later the Banking Act of 1935 increased the authority of the Federal Reserve board. The board was given more supervision over credit policy, more power to vary reserve requirements of member banks, more voice in the selection of the president and vice-president of member banks, and other powers.

After 1900 the Midwest had little to distinguish its banking system from that of the rest of the United States. Fairly prosperous the Midwest had 43 per cent of the nation's 15,000 banks in 1940 and 23 per cent of the nation's deposits.

— 62 —

Transportation

Roads

In the 1890's interest in bicycling increased the demand for better roads. People courted, robbed, transacted business, and made trips on bicycles. Probably the most outstanding bicycle dealers at the turn of the century were the Wright brothers, Orville and Wilbur. At Dayton, Ohio, they sold the popular models, the Coventry Cross, Warwick, Reading, Envoy, and Fleetwing. They also sold models which they manufactured themselves; the Van Cleve, the St. Clair, and the Wright Special. The latter sold for eighteen dollars.

In 1900 a motor was added to the bicycle. In its first test run on Long Island this new vehicle attained a speed of 25 miles an hour. This was the origin of the motorcycle which also required better roads for comfortable and safe travel.

In 1900 automobiles were in the experimental and joke stage. There were less than 8,000 in the United States, and an owner had to be of necessity an automobile mechanic. The Bedford, Indiana, *Daily Mail* joked:

> Now ma, you know I'm anxious to make an impression on those New York people. Bring me the coal oil can; I want to perfume my clothes.'
>
> 'With coal oil! Mercy child, what do you mean?'
>
> 'Why I want 'em to think we own an automobile.'

But a revolution in transportation was in process. In 1901 the Haynes and Apperson automobile made a run from Kokomo,

Indiana, to New York City, 1,050 miles, in six days. The trip was completed in consecutive days of twelve hours each without a stop or accident. The mass producers of autos such as R. E. Olds, Henry Ford, Walter Chrysler, and Benjamin Briscoe began manufacturing large numbers of motor-powered vehicles. The number of registered motor vehicles in the United States jumped from 469,000 in 1910 to 32,025,365 in 1940. Of these the Midwest had 35 per cent.

To accomodate these new, faster automobiles, roads were rapidly improved. In the Midwest the number of miles of roads increased only about twenty-five per cent between 1904 and 1940, but the number of miles of surfaced roads increased almost four fold. From a low of 10 per cent in 1904, the percentage of paved roads had grown to about 40 per cent by 1940. There were a number of surfacing materials. Gravel and stone had been used since early times and were very popular. Brick and blocks were also used. The most popular surfacing materials, however, were asphalt, used in making black-top roads, and portland cement, a basic ingredient in the construction of the concrete highway. Asphalt came in about 1900. Cement was not used for road building until about the same time. One of the first rural strips of concrete pavement in the Midwest was built in Michigan in 1909. From these meager beginnings, highway building became one of the leading endeavors of all levels of government in the United States.

Waterways

Water travel in the Midwest after 1870 was significant but not colorful. The high point in river transportation for the lower Mississippi came in 1880, when over one-million tons were received and shipped at St. Louis. This figure dropped to 141,000 tons in 1905. Receipts and shipments at St. Louis to and from the upper Mississippi dropped from 340,000 tons in 1880 to less than 70,000 in 1905. The barge traffic on the Mississippi remained important, but it dropped in relative significance. The Ohio River held its own better due to the coal shipments there. In 1911 a federal appropriation of $10,000,000 was approved to improve navigation on the Ohio. Tonnage on the Ohio increased in more recent times to 29,549,000 tons in 1940. The Ohio, Mississippi, lower Missouri, and Illinois were all made navigable for barge traffic drawing up to nine feet of water through a series of dams, locks, and regulators. When this system was connected to the Great Lakes via the Illinois River in the 1930's by the Chicago Sanitary and Ship Canal, it became one of the largest inland waterways in the world. Vessels on the Great Lakes hauled a vast amount of iron ore, coal, grain, lumber, and limestone. For example in 1940, the vessels of the Great Lakes hauled around 89,858,000 tons of products through the canal at Sault Ste. Marie. In addition there were another 112,634,000 tons hauled on the Ohio, Allegheny, Monongahela, Kanawha, Illinois, Missouri, and upper-Mississippi rivers.

Railroads

Until around 1914 the federal government attempted to control the rail combines by breaking them up, but after that time the national government began to treat the railroads like public utilities and attempted to keep their rates and practices fair by governmental control rather than by competition. The first step in this direction was taken in 1887 with the creation of the Interstate Commerce Commission. It had the power to investigate procedures and rate policies of the railroads. The Elkins Act of 1903, the Hepburn Act of 1906, and the Mann-Elkins Act of 1910 gave more power to the I.C.C. and enlarged the scope of its authority. During World War I the United States' government took over complete operation of the railroads. In the Transportation Act of 1920, which returned the railroads to private ownership, the I.C.C. was to aid the railroads in consolidating for more efficiency in order to keep the weaker roads from going to the wall and to prevent the strong roads from obtaining more than six per cent profits. Boards of adjustment were also instituted to prevent strikes. Some of these provisions were repealed during the 1930's, but governmental control remained strong.

Despite this governmental assistance, railroad mileage was on the decline. Although midwestern railroad mileage was up to 89,574 in 1940, an increase of about 5,000 miles over 1900, it was still an overall drop from 1916 when other competing forms of transportation began to take their toll. Percentage-wise, the Midwest had dropped six points to 38 per cent of the nation's railroad mileage between 1900 and 1940.

Electric Railways

Electric railways, a variation of railroad transportation, were especially popular in the Middle West around 1900. More limited in size and distance of travel than trains, they were known as trolleys or electric cars. The first practical overhead trolley line was built in Kansas City in 1884. Although there were street railways before this time, most of them were powered by horses or steam. Their great period of popularity was 1900 to 1910. They were important for shuttling passengers between suburban and urban areas and between rural and urban areas.

They, too, were subject to accidents. In Chicago in September 1901, Michael Freedman, motorman of the Twelfth Street electric car struck a hayrack driven by Nicholas Liston. Five people on the streetcar were seriously injured. In Minneapolis in the same month, a bull charged the headlight of the Como interurban, half way between Lake Como and the state fairgrounds. In the collision the car was thrown from the tracks. Fortunately, the passengers escaped uninjured. The bull was killed by the impact.

Since these street railways could be lucrative, they often became objects of corruption in city governments. There were financiers who were willing to bribe and engage in ruthless practices in order to obtain street-railway franchises. Reform mayors like Samuel L. Jones of Toledo, Thomas L. Johnson of Cleveland, and Carter Harrison of Chicago were extremely interested in keeping street-railway rates low and the franchises honest.

After 1910 the electric railway declined in importance although it remained in use. In 1906 the mileage of street and electrical railways totaled 36,212 miles, of which 40 per cent was in the Midwest. As of 1920 this total United States' mileage had grown to 47,705 miles; by 1937 it had dropped back to 23,770 miles. The emergence of city buses was a chief factor in its decline.

Air Travel

Another form of transportation which had its start in the Midwest was the airplane. The Midwest's greatest contribution in this area were the Wright brothers, Wilbur and Orville. Originally merchants in Dayton, Ohio, they became interested in aerodynamics around 1896. Encouraged and aided by the work of Octave Chanute, a glider expert, and Samuel P. Langley, a scientist at the Smithsonian Institute, they began building and testing biplane kites and gliders around 1900. The first tests were in the sand dunes at the southern end of Lake Michigan. Later the Wright brothers moved their experimentation to Kitty Hawk, North Carolina. Finally in 1903, they constructed a "flying machine" with a 12 horse-power engine. It was a biplane with two rudders. The engine was mounted in the center of the lower wing and the chain-driven propellers were mounted just back of the wings. The initial flight occurred in December 1903 at Kitty Hawk. With Orville Wright at the controls, the kite-like vehicle raised itself into the air and flew 120 feet in 12 seconds before settling on the sand. In the fourth flight made by Wilbur Wright, the plane stayed airborne 59 seconds over a distance of 852 feet.

The Midwest also played a major role in at least two other major events in United States aeronautical history. The money for Charles Lindbergh's flight across the Atlantic in the "Spirit of St. Louis" in 1927 was provided by St. Louis backers. Three years later a record endurance flight by Dale Jackson and Forest O'Brien in a Curtiss-Robin monoplane was made at St. Louis. They flew 41,500 miles with 223 refueling contacts.

— 63 —

Religion

During World War I and after, the churches of the Midwest followed many of the traditional pursuits. The churches generally supported the war effort in World War I, although some sects like the Quakers, Mennonites, Amish, and Church of the Brethren maintained pacifist positions. Revivalists like Billy Sunday and Howard Paschal continued to exhort the sinner to be saved, although evangelists were becoming more organized and businesslike in their approach. The number of meetings and conferences in the churches increased. Some members and some sects as varied as Jehovah's Witnesses, Catholics, Baptists, and Methodists continued to think of themselves as the only ones assured of a ticket to heaven. Some midwestern Protestant leaders of the 1920's even joined the Ku Klux Klan so that they could more effectively, or so they thought, fight the Catholics.

In general, however, the trend in the churches of the Midwest, as elsewhere in the United States, was toward increased unity. In the early nineteenth century, many Protestant sects got together to support missions and the American Bible Society, both of which had as their purpose the carrying of Christianity to all peoples in the world. The Y.M.C.A., Y.W.C.A., and the Christian Endeavor lent themselves to interdenominational cooperation. The Gideon Society, or the Christian Commercial Travellers Association of America, originated in Wisconsin in 1898 by John H. Nicholson and Samuel E. Hill, had as its purpose the placing of a Bible in every hotel room, a project that had interdenominational backing. The attempts to cooperate among the churches resulted in 1908 in the creation of the Federal Council of Churches in America, which made it possible for American Protestantism to speak with more united voice. Although there were some fissions, church denominations also tended to unite. In 1905 a majority of the Cumberland Presbyterian church and the Presbyterian church of the U.S.A. reached an organic union. Thirteen years later the three English Lutheran bodies of the United States united in the United Lutheran church and in 1939 the Methodist Episcopal churches, North and South, were finally reunited.

In summing up the status of Christianity in the American Midwest in the 1930's, William A. White, in the *Changing West,* made the following comments. Heaven and hell as rewards and punishments, he said, have nearly disappeared except among the lower-income groups. When life becomes so hard that it does not justify itself, heaven is needed by the underprivileged and unfortunate to round out their ideals of justice and to punish those who have mistreated them. That the concepts of heaven and hell have largely disappeared in the West, concluded White, displays the fact that the West has done well materially.

— 64 —

Education

Problems Related to Elementary and Secondary Education

During the period 1890 to 1940, the school population increased even faster than the total population. The main reason for this was the fact that an ever larger percentage of the school-age population was attending school. Taking the 14 to 17 year old, high-school-age population as an example, seven per cent were enrolled in secondary schools in 1890 as compared to 73 per cent in 1940.

Although the number of public schools did increase after 1890, they still did not keep pace with the growing student body. Since people were loathe to pay taxes for schools, a lag in school facilities was inevitable. For example, the Chicago *Record Herald* reported in September 1901 that 15,000 Chicago children were limited to half-day sessions in rented buildings because of lack of funds. This situation was illustrative of the overcrowded conditions up to 1940.

There were a number of reasons why the Midwest experienced such a phenomenal increase in the percentage of school-age children in school. The most important reason for this development was the fact that the frontier was settled; as a result the standard of living was rising, and children could be spared for school. Along with this higher standard of living came a social awareness that all children must be required to go to school, because every illiterate person in a community lowered its economic prosperity and social climate. As a result of this feeling, the midwestern states began to pass compulsory school-attendance laws. Michigan was first in the Midwest and third in the nation to pass such a law in 1871. Missouri was the last state in the Midwest to pass a compulsory attendance law in 1905. Although many of the initial attendance laws passed in the Midwest were weak, by 1920 most of them were relatively strict and enforceable.

A corollary to the compulsory attendance laws were the child-labor laws which had the effect of cutting down the motives for missing school. Although child labor was spottily reduced by state child-labor laws, it was restricted much more by the Fair Labor Standards Act of 1938, a national law which prohibited child labor from producing goods for interstate commerce. The worst child-labor problem in the Midwest in 1940 was in rural areas where over 50 per cent of the children working for wages and many who were working without wages were employed. The use of child labor on farms contributed to absenteeism from school and at worst to no education at all.

Related to the inadequate funding and crowded schools were the low salaries for teachers. An example of low wages was demonstrated by Indiana in 1900. At that time the daily wages of teachers averaged $2.85 in cities, $2.42 in towns, and $2.04 in rural townships. This situation had improved some by 1940 when the average annual salary in Indiana was $1,433, a figure that was about $200 above the average for the Midwest as a whole.

Another problem were the biased groups in some communities who began witch hunts after teachers or schools that did not share their particular prejudices. During World War I, it was a hatred of anything German including the German language taught in the schools. After World War I it was the Ku Klux Klan and other agitation groups, which tried to ban private schools (especially Catholic) and other organizations because they did not fit into the Klan's peculiar definition of Americanism.

The private schools that were present also had other problems, primarily financial. Private funds for education were even harder to obtain than public funds. In the Midwest these schools consisted largely of parochial and military schools. As their names suggest, they stressed religion or militarism usually with discipline. Most of their instruction was similar to their public counterparts. Culver Military Academy in Indiana was a noted example of a military school. Although Catholic and Protestant schools, as well as other private schools, were numerous in the Midwest, they were less prevalent there than in the East and South, partly because of the Midwest's more democratic tradition.

Over the years after 1890, education in the Midwest generally improved. It was aided by more state taxes paid by people who had come to realize that education was a necessity for living a full and prosperous life. The federal government also contributed funds and assistance to public education. One of the most important acts to accomplish this purpose was the Smith-Hughes Act of 1917. Under its provisions around ten-million dollars were paid annually to states on a matching-funds basis to help pay the salaries of vocational subjects, to help pay for the preparation of teachers of vocational subjects, and to help pay for the study of problems related to the teaching of vocational subjects. In general the act was a secondary-school law because most Smith-Hughes teachers were at that level.

Out of the depression came the Civilian Conservation Corps and the National Youth Administration. With the C.C.C., education was an afterthought. It was organized primarily for the purpose of giving aid and work to needy young people. Some nine months after the C.C.C. began, education courses were introduced to provide young men with a worthwhile utilization of their spare time. Although classrooms and textbooks were inadequate, around 50 per cent of the young men in the conservation corps attended classes.

The National Youth Administration established in 1935 under the Works Progress Administration was created primarily to help students to attend school. To receive money under the plan, a student had to be unable to stay in school without financial help, be of good character, and have good academic ability. The amount to be earned was initially limited to fifteen dollars a month and the work done to earn this money could be clerical, bibliographical, research, or other as the instructor in charge might direct. Although N.Y.A. funds aided both high-school and college students, it did not provide enough aid for a student to stay in school without other help. There were some problems in its administration and some schools refused N.Y.A. money because they felt it would be an indorsement of New Deal extravagance. But overall the program greatly aided youth education during a trying time.

As a result of more money being available and increased emphasis on education, school facilities and instruction improved. In the Midwest, for example, revenue for public-elementary and secondary education increased from $165,033,000 in 1910 to $731,105,000 in 1940. The training of the teachers had similarly increased. In 1900 about one fifth of the teachers had graduated from a college or Normal school and about one fifth had only completed elementary school. Forty years later approximately one half had completed college and nearly all had completed some college work. Facilities had likewise improved. Buildings were more modern, libraries were larger, blackboards and other training aids were more plentiful, and sanitation, heating, and water were vastly improved. Many schools also instituted a system of renting textbooks so as to save students about 80 per cent on their books. The Goshen, Indiana, *Democrat* described this as an entirely new plan in 1901.

Innovations in Education

After 1890 a number of new educational philosophies and procedures were developed. Midwestern educators became aware of the views of the philosopher J. F. Herbart of Germany around 1890. Herbart believed in determinism in education; that is, one's environment is very important in determining the knowledge and attitudes of a person. He also stated that the mind was a unit, and a part of it could not be trained separately. His greatest contribution to educational philosophy was the concept that students learned faster when they were interested in a subject. The only thing he failed to explain was how to get students interested in the subjects that they should be interested in.

An American educator, associated with the Midwest who probably did most in this area of student motivation, was John Dewey. Dewey grew up on the edge of New England. In his last year of college, he was introduced to psychology, political science, and biology. These disciplines supplied the fuel which was ignited at John Hopkins and made Dewey a philosopher. His first book was *Psychology* (1886), which displayed the influence of the scientific psychologist, G. Stanley Hall. After teaching for a time at the Universities of Michigan and Minnesota, he went to the newly created University of Chicago. In 1896 the University elementary school at Chicago was opened and his book describing it, *The School and Society*, became the basis for a new type of education.

This book contained a number of fundamental principles for education. First, democracy provides the best way of living and it must be consciously promoted. Second, school must provide sharing, cooperation, and simple tasks such as weaving, spinning, and food processing, which have been placed beyond the ordinary experience of children by the industrial revolution. Third, school must provide cooperative and active occupations and activities based upon a simplified and organized version of life. Fourth, school must be child centered and be based on problem solving.

When put together, these concepts fitted into an educational philosophy which Dewey called Instrumentalism. Instrumentalism basically was an application to education of William James Pragmatism, which stated that a principle or value was measured by its utility. Combining this philosophy with child-centered education and his other principles, Dewey arrived at his system and goals of education. He felt that students should be directed to develop their own individual personalities for life in a democratic society. He wanted to develop thoughtful, self-disciplined students who would be morally and vocationally effective social beings. Dewey believed that the attention of the teacher should be focused on the child's needs rather than on the demands of the subject matter. To create the best type of instruction, Dewey was willing to experiment with different pedagogical approaches. Basically, however, he felt a child should work at his desk rather than just listen. Moreover, he did not believe that education should be conceived as a process which strove to habituate the young to a fixed system of social, economic, and political institutions. On the contrary he maintained that a democratic society aimed at its own social improvement and that school should play a large role in accomplishing this social regeneration.

Naturally not all of Dewey's ideas were accepted, but enough of them were to modify the educational process. Some university schools like the one at Chicago founded by Dewey and the one at the University of Missouri founded by J. L. Meriam went a long way toward this type of education, and some private schools went even further. As a whole, however, few Midwestern school systems followed Dewey's ideas completely, but on the other hand, many of them were influenced a little. In Indiana, for example, Gary's school system, inaugurated by Dr. William Wirt, boasted that it was built around John Dewey's philosophy of educating the whole child.

A number of other innovations in teaching and administration were also introduced into the Midwest after 1890. Statistical surveys to determine the quality of a school system became extremely popular after 1910. The surveyors had few tools with which to work at first and often met grim opposition from school officials who felt their systems would be discredited.

The supervised-study movement was popular for about a decade in the early 1900's. In this movement schools used a double period for each class. The first period was devoted to aiding students in their preparation and the second to reports, discussions, and tests on the work accomplished.

Another approach was the individual study plan in which each pupil worked by himself and at his own speed. Preston W. Search first began the plan in teaching bookkeeping at West Liberty, Ohio, in 1877. The Winnetka plan in Illinois, developed by Carleton Washburne, was an offshoot of Search's thinking. Under the Winnetka system group instruction was restricted to such areas as music and physical education, while individual instruction was used in many of the other academic studies.

Unit teaching had some appeal. In it, subject matter was put together so as to have logical, historical, psychological, geographical, or some other kind of unity. It especially applied to loosely connected materials such as the problems of democracy, housing, freedom, or nature which have no definite organization and can be arranged to suit the purpose of the class or the student. The unit in a sense capitalized upon a pupil's desire to work out a problem for himself. The unit method was a favorite of Henry C. Morrison, director of the University of Chicago High School. He believed that assimilation of material was not enough; that education must be an adjustment process. To obtain this adjustment, the student had to go through the five steps of exploration, presentation, assimilation, organization, and adjustment. Even though Morrison may have made this process appear to be too much like a magical formula, the emphasis on mastery and thoroughness embodied in this system had merit.

An innovation in curriculum involved increased emphasis on vocational and trade education at the secondary-school level. There were many students who did not have the ability, money, or desire to go to college; and subjects more closely related to their possible vocations were of more value to them. In 1901 the Bedford, Indiana, *Daily Mail* had an editorial to the effect that young men needed more industrial training. The editor felt that it was less important that a person know how to read in Latin how Caesar built a bridge than to know how to build a bridge himself. The editor believed that mechanical courses should be grafted upon the public-school system.

In Illinois Edwin S. Cooley, former superintendent of schools in Chicago, persuaded the Illinois legislature to petition Congress for federal aid to establish a separate, vocational-school system. Chancellor Samuel Avery of the University of Nebraska, John Dewey, and other leading educators opposed Cooley's separate, vocational-school plan. These latter educators generally carried the day and vocational training was largely placed in the high schools.

The senior high school at Springfield, Missouri, was an example. It had a dozen shop courses including machine shop, mechanical drawing, printing, radio, ceramics, and housecraft. In addition, it had a complete list of standard high-school courses. The Boy's Trade and Technical High School of Milwaukee was broken down into technical, trade, and tech-trade divisions. In all of these, varying stress was put on English, social studies, mathematics, and science. Arsenal Technical High School in Indianapolis even prepared musical performers. Although there were a large number of high schools that offered only vocational and trade courses, a far larger number offered some vocational and a lot of academic high-school subjects.

Probably one of the most interesting of the later administrative changes in public schools was the creation of the junior high school and the switch from the 8-4 to the 6-3-3 plan. Originally, a separate junior high was not planned. In one of the elementary schools in Richmond, Indiana, where it was first tried in 1896, the seventh and eighth grades were merely formed into a departmentalized organization with some elective subjects and a homeroom. It was not long, however, before the 6-3-3 system grew out of this experiment. The junior high-school system spread especially rapidly after World War I.

The junior high was created to bridge the gap between elementary and high school and to make the transition easier. It was to keep pupils from dropping out of school by offering a new school environment and work that was more interesting. The junior-high plan was based largely on a concept, emphasized by G. Stanley Hall, that children at age twelve become adolesent, individualistic, and independent and should no longer be treated as children. Although the reasoning for a separate junior high seemed sound, the results have been inconclusive as to their benefits. There has been no significant difference in the marks made by children under the 6-3-3 system and 8-4 system and there has been no appreciable difference in the number of children leaving school at age 14.

In reviewing the innovations in educational methods, philosophy, and administration after 1900, some skeptics were not especially impressed. The editor of the Bedford *Daily Mail* remarked that a new fad in education was "organized play." He said that the idea of teaching a "kid" how to play was a lot like teaching your grandmother how to fry potatoes. Finley P. Dunne also took a sly dig at the educational system through his medium, Mr. Dooley, in commenting on the Pan American exhibit in 1901. Dooley noted that:

> Martin Casey's daughter, th' school-teacher, th' wan that wears th' specs wint th' nex' day. 'Tis a great iddyca-

tional exhibit,' says she. 'I'm inthrested in th' study iv pidigoogy. I'm takin' along me notebook an' I will pick up what bets Petzalootzi, th' great leader iv our profission has overlooked,' she says. 'Well,' says I, 'I hope 'twill make a better third-grade teacher iv ye,' I says. 'But if ye miss Petzalootzi an wandher into the Indyan village be chanst,' says I, 'don't be worrid,' I says. 'A little knowledge in the Soos an' th' Arrypahoos an' their habits,' I says, 'is not a bad thing f'r anny wan that has to larn Chicago childher,' I says.

Growth in Higher Education

Like the public schools, the number of colleges and the people attending them greatly increased between 1890 and 1940. Over 70 new colleges which survived to the present were added. Of these in the Midwest, 24 were Normal schools (since renamed teachers colleges or universities) which were especially popular up to 1930 or 1940. They, with the other colleges and universities, did much to improve the training of the public elementary and secondary teachers.

There was also a great increase in the number of junior colleges in the period after 1890. About 15 per cent of the junior colleges in existance developed before 1890 and about 85 per cent between 1890 and 1940. The Midwest had around 125 of these institutions which was over one fourth of the nation's total. Some developed from high schools, some sprung full-blown as junior colleges, and some were decapitated senior colleges. Junior colleges developed to meet the needs of ever-increasing college populations, especially in large populated areas. These local institutions saved the students money and also relieved the colleges and universities of the lower-division load, considered by some educators to be a part of secondary education. This latter argument was used by William R. Harper, first president of the University of Chicago and sometimes referred to as "the father of the junior college." He with other promoters of the junior college like Henry P. Tappan of the University of Michigan and W. W. Folwell of the University of Minnesota believed that schooling up to the age of twenty should be considered secondary and university work should begin at that point.

Problems in Higher Education

The colleges experienced a number of problems in the period 1890-1940, many of which were perennial. Colleges were short on finances and the private institutions were even more hard-pressed than state institutions. Increasing enrollments made this problem increasingly difficult. In addition to being unable to provide adequate facilities, colleges were unable to pay reasonable salaries to their faculties.

A problem, especially in private-college education, that became somewhat less noticeable after 1900 was that of the "captive" college staff. If the professor did not teach the type of business and moral philosophy desired by the supporters of the college, he might find himself relieved of his duties and salary. Among those at the turn of the century who lost their educational berths because of unorthodox political economic views included J. Allen Smith, Edward W. Bemis, and Frank Parsons. Smith had been a professor of economics and sociology at Marietta College, Ohio, where he kept the campus churning with his vigorous criticism of high tariffs, the gold standard, and unregulated ownership of monopolies. When in 1896 he cast a protest vote for William J. Bryan, the trustees peremptorily fired him. Smith was soon offered a job by President Thomas E. Will at the populistic Kansas State Agricultural College. Smith was about to accept when he received an offer from the University of Washington where his views were also acceptable. Since President Will had only two openings available and since Will wanted to give jobs to Professors Edward W. Bemis and Frank Parsons, recently discharged from the University of Chicago for their economic views, Smith took the position in Washington state.

This type of removal by business interests was justified

by those who indulged in it. James H. Raymond, a trustee of Northwestern University, stated that professors in social and political science were not qualified to determine what should be taught concerning financial matters. Moreover, continued the big-business apologist, the professor was not a mere parrot to repeat and fairly explain to his students the diametrically opposed arguments of other writers and teachers. He must of necessity advocate, concluded Raymond, and his advocacy must be in harmony with the conclusion of the powers that operate and finance the university.

On the other hand, many educators were opposed to business control of higher education. Thomas E. Will of Kansas illustrated this point of view. Will said the business of college was to enlarge the intelligence, to quicken the conscience, to purify the ideals, and to consecrate life to its noblest ends. Instead, continued Will, business was forcing higher education into justifying business monopolies and corrupt politics. To keep his position the social-studies professor had to toe the trust line. Will concluded that wealth was using three methods to make American colleges their instruments. They either built their own colleges, helped a small, struggling institution, or else attempted to control state educational institutions. Whatever their method, Will believed their aim was a travesty on the name of education.

The position of football on the midwestern college campus was another problem that developed about the turn of the century. Abraham Flexner and Robert M. Hutchins agreed that "the social and athletic character that large numbers of students have given the universities had done more than most things to prevent them from being universities and to debase higher learning in America." In its report on higher education late in 1929, the Carnegie Foundation for the Advancement of Teaching did not go as far as Flexner and Hutchins in favoring abolition of intercollegiate football, but it did deplore the commercialism in football. Oftentimes, football was given undue attention on the college campus. Sometimes pressure was even brought to bear on instructors to lower their standards so a particular player or group of players might participate in a football game.

Nature of the Academic Program

Even though the students increased and the curriculum expanded and fluctuated, academic work at the college and university level plodded steadily onward. A description of graduate work at the turn of the century was virtually the same as in 1940. An example was Laurence M. Larson who did graduate work in history at the University of Wisconsin at the turn of the century.

The first year Larson took a course under Dr. Frederick J. Turner. He attended Turner's Seminar in American History which met two hours in the afternoon twice a week. This seminar began with the Constitutional Convention of 1787 and continued through the close of Washington's administration. To this decade the class devoted an entire year. Their labors were concerned largely with documentary materials. Occasionally, a recent writer was consulted if he had developed original views on the subject. It was a typical seminar on the John Hopkins model. There were seven or eight in the class. For his master's thesis Larson made a study of public opinion in 1787 and 1788 on the nature of the federal compact. He attacked the problem with the preconceived notion that the forming of a more perfect union was the result of a century of historical progress. Because there was not much recorded public opinion in those days, Larson's findings were inconclusive. Although Turner was not pleased with the emphasis of the study, he approved it and allowed Larson to receive his degree. After this the American-frontier historian lost interest in Larson's work, and so the Swedish student shifted his main interest to medieval history under Professor Charles H. Haskins. As a research topic for his Ph.D., Larson did research on the royal households of England in Anglo-Saxon times.

As a culmination of Larson's formal education career, he took his preliminary exams for the Ph.D. He also had to pass French and German proficiencies and a two-hour oral examination. After these were finished, he brought his research together in his doctoral dissertation. Larson observed that this thesis was supposed to make a contribution to the knowledge of a subject, which it usually did, although the contribution was often very small. In Larson's three-hour final examination, Turner asked him a lot of questions on colonial American history in which Larson said he was not prepared. Despite this the committee passed him and allowed him to be awarded the doctorate in history.

Adult Education

Adult education which cut across the lines of common and higher education was also on the increase in the period after 1890. One aspect of this, agricultural education for farmers, was greatly aided by the passage of the Smith-Lever Act in 1914. The purpose of the act was "to aid in diffusing among the people of the United States useful and practical information on subjects relating to agriculture and home economics and to encourage the application of the same." The county agent and the home-demonstration agent were key teachers in this extension program. The "Wisconsin idea" also developed in this period. In this program the University of Wisconsin took practical and technical assistance and training of many kinds to dairymen, gardeners, and other persons in the state.

Other forms of adult education were emphasized after 1890 in the Midwest. Near the end of the nineteenth century, the off-campus teaching of university classes was introduced from England. It was received in the Middle West with great acclaim. The universities which early initiated it included Wisconsin, Minnesota, and Chicago. In addition, correspondence courses were offered by universities and colleges. Some libraries even offered the public a reading advisor to aid them in pursuing an organized course of study.

As an aid to all forms of education, there was an ever-growing number of libraries, public and private. Libraries were extremely scarce until after 1850 when states began to pass laws permitting towns to establish public libraries. In 1876 the American Library Association was founded and it became a leader in library development. The period of most rapid library expansion, however, began about 1910. Great impetus to the movement was received from Andrew Carnegie and the Carnegie Corporation. In Michigan alone over 60 libraries were founded with the assistance of the Carnegie Fund. College, school, and public libraries were increased greatly after the turn of the century.

Although the growth of education was large in the Midwest, it was no greater than any other aspect of midwestern development. Education tended to reflect the growth of population and prosperity in the region. If any attributes were outstanding in midwestern education, they were the democratic spirit of the schools and the vision of the educational leaders.

—65—

Literature

The Midwest continued to pour out literature after World War I. During the period 1910 to 1940, Indiana, Missouri, Ohio, Michigan, and Minnesota ranked among the first ten in literary production in the United States. The older group of authors continued to write, and a new group also appeared on the scene to aid in the production of a diversified literature.

Among Ohio's literary set were Sherwood Anderson, Arthur M. Schlesinger, James Thurber, Louis Bromfield, and Harold H. Crane. Anderson was born in Camden, Ohio, in 1876 and received little education after age 14. Although he travelled a lot, he spent a large part of his life as a newspaper editor in Marion, Virginia. Anderson believed in freedom of realistic expression for all the emotions, and the emotion or drive that he emphasized most in his books was sex. His finest tales were *Winesburg, Ohio* (1919) and *The Triumph of the Egg* (1921); both of which were studies of thwarted personalities. His biggest seller, *Dark Laughter* (1925), was probably one of his poorest. His major works included some 23 books and plays.

One of Ohio's leading historians born at Xenia, Ohio, in 1888 was Arthur M. Schlesinger. After obtaining most of his education in Ohio, he moved to Massachusetts and taught at Harvard. His books covered American History from colonial times through the Franklin D. Roosevelt administration. Among his works were *Colonial Merchants and The American Revolution* (1918), *New Viewpoints in American History* (1922), and *The Rise of the City* (1933).

A somewhat different type of Ohio author was James Thurber, born in Columbus in 1894. He travelled widely but spent most of his life in the eastern United States where he worked as a newspaperman. Although he was a humorist and illustrator, he also had a grim note and a crusading fervor. Titles of some of his leading books and plays illustrated these tendencies: *Is Sex Necessary?* (1929); *The Owl in the Attic and Other Perplexities* (1931); *The Seal in the Bedroom and Other Predicaments* (1932); *The Male Animal* (1940); and *My World—and Welcome To It!* (1942).

The leading regionalist of this group of Ohio writers was Louis Bromfield. Born on a farm near Mansfield, Ohio, in 1896, he planned to go into agriculture. Sidetracked after a year in agriculture at Cornell, he went to Columbia University but soon left there to be an ambulance driver in World War I. He later became a newspaperman and travelled widely in Europe. In 1933 he bought a 1000-acre farm near his Ohio birthplace, where he lived and wrote. Most of his books were filled with disaster and sex. His first important work was *The Green Bay Tree* (1924). He won the Pulitzer Prize for *Early Autumn* (1926). His regionalism was best displayed in *The Farm* and *Pleasant Valley,* descriptions of Ohio rural life.

One of Ohio's leading poets was Harold H. Crane. The son of a broken home, he wandered aimlessly between his mother's and father's worlds. Undecided whether to be a poet or a businessman, he became a homosexual and an alcoholic. Winning a Guggenheim fellowship, he went to Mexico in 1931 to steep himself in the Latin American atmosphere in order to write an epic poem on Latin America similar to *The Bridge,* an interpretation of Anglo-Saxon America. Instead he steeped himself in alcohol and on his return trip to New York committed suicide at the age of 33 by jumping overboard. His principle volumes of verse were *White Buildings* (1926), *The Bridge* (1930), and *Collected Poems* (1933).

Neighboring Indiana displayed equal diversity in authors. Indiana had two prominent humorists, George Ade and Frank M. Hubbard. Both were newspapermen. Ade worked on the Chicago *Morning News,* later known as the *Record.* He said he meant to be serious, but people felt his writing was humorous and slangy. He quit newspaper work in 1900 and devoted himself full time to writing and travelling. He wrote more than 20 books. Many of them had fables in the title and most of the titles were catchy:

Pink March (1897); *The Girl Proposition* (1902); *Single Blessedness* (1922); and *Old Time Saloon* (1931).

Indiana's "Mr. Dooley" was "Abe Martin," the pseudonym of Frank M. Hubbard. Hubbard was born at Bellefontaine, Ohio, in 1868. His father was a newspaper publisher. After setting type in his father's printing shop, he proceeded to Indianapolis where he obtained a position on the *News*. His rural philosopher "Abe Martin" direct from the paw-paw belt of Indiana was born in 1904. Abe made remarks like: "Mrs. Tilford Moots is scarcely able t'do her housework an' th' doctor says she'll have to' have her' phone taken out"; and "The hardest thing t' stop is a temporary chairman." Hubbard had at least eight books published which were mostly reprints of his newspaper columns. They had titles like *Abe Martin's Almanak* (1907) and *Abe Martin: Hoss Sense and Nonsense* (1922).

One of Indiana's most popular authors was the nature writer Gene (Stratton) Porter. Born on an Indiana farm in 1868, she began writing seriously about 1900. She and her husband lived in a cabin on the edge of a large swamp (known as Limberlost) in northern Indiana, and this was the setting for many of her stories. A feather from a black vulture that fell at her feet helped motivate Mrs. Porter to conceive the plot for *Freckles*, published in 1904. Her sales were terrific, even though her writing has been described as trite and sentimental. Although she produced approximately 16 books, her best sellers were *Freckles*, which sold over two-million copies; and *A Girl of the Limberlost* (1909), *The Harvester* (1911), and *Laddie* (1913), each of which sold over a million-and-a-half copies.

Another somewhat sentimental Indiana writer was Newton B. Tarkington, born in Indianapolis in 1869. Although he spent a lot of time in Maine, he always claimed Indianapolis as home. Essentially a romantic and sentimental writer, he also had a touch of realism. He won two Pulitzer prizes, one for the *Magnificent Ambersons* (1918) and the other for *Alice Adams* (1921). The latter was by far his best work. An uneven writer, his output was tremendous. He produced over 60 major books of which many had their settings in Indiana.

Theodore Dreiser, born at Terre Haute in 1871, had far

more realism than Tarkington. Dreiser's primary vocation was journalism. Growing up on the wrong side of the tracks among coal miners and madames of sporting houses, he was concerned about the conditions that produced prostitutes, greedy financiers, and crime. *Sister Carrie* (1900)—the story of how a girl became a prostitute, *Jennie Gerhardt* (1911), and *The Financier* (1912) were among his best. With them he gave root to a different realism in America. He suggested that his leading characters were helpless victims of their environment. At first *Sister Carrie, The Genius* (1915), and *An American Tragedy* (1925) were not allowed on the market; Dreiser spent long years fighting this censorship. He became popular with a large audience when *An American Tragedy* was released in 1926.

Unlike Dreiser, Lloyd C. Douglas, born in Columbia City in 1877, stressed inspiration and morality. His characters were righteous and his conclusions generally happy. A Lutheran minister, who had formerly written inspirational books, he wrote his first novel, *Magnificent Obsession* (1929) after he was 50 . It was a great success. Among his other leading works were *Green Light* (1935), *White Banners* (1936), *Disputed Passage* (1939), and *The Robe* (1942).

Another Indiana author, Ross F. Lockridge, Jr., noted for his attempt to write the great regional novel, was born in Bloomington, Indiana, in 1914 and died in 1948. His book, *Raintree County*, which had its setting in Waycross, Raintree County, Indiana, took place in a single day (July 4, 1892), with a series of flashbacks to reveal the private and public lives of a group of the citizens of the town.

Among Indiana's historians were Charles A. Beard and Claude G. Bowers. Each was different in his approach and subject matter. Born at Knightstown, Indiana, in 1874, Beard became a college professor at Columbia University. He was best known for his economic interpretation of history. His first major work embodying his economic interpretation was *An Economic Interpretation of the Constitution* (1913), in which he tried to prove that the founders of the Constitution were primarily motivated by economic considerations. One of his most sweeping and readable books embodying the economic interpretation was the *Rise of*

William A. "Billy" Sunday (1862-1935)
Evangelist

Courtesy New York Historical Society. From *Dictionary of American Portraits* by Hayward and Blanche Cirker, Dover Publications, Inc., New York, 1967. *Reprinted through permission of the publisher.*

F. Scott Fitzgerald (1896-1940)
Novelist

Carl Sandburg (1878-1967)
Poet

Ernest Hemingway (1898-1961)
Novelist

American Civilization (1927). This was written in collaboration with his wife, Mary Beard, who was also a historian and sociologist in her own right. A most prolific writer, Charles A. Beard wrote over 30 books.

Claude G. Bowers, born in Westfield, Indiana, in 1879, was primarily a newspaperman and a politician and these facts influenced his writing. In *The Party Battles of the Jackson Period* (1925), he was pro-Jackson; in *The Tragic Era* (1929), he was extremely pro-Andrew Johnson; and in *Jefferson and Hamilton* (1925), he was pro-Jefferson. A devoted Democrat, he gave the key-note address at the Democratic convention at Houston in 1928. He wrote many books ranging from *Irish Orators* (1916) to the *Spanish Adventures of Washington Irving* (1940).

The outstanding triumverate of poets in Illinois were Edgar L. Masters, Carl Sandburg, and Nicholas V. Lindsay. They all wrote about Lincoln. Masters had a fall out with the other two, because he was critical of Lincoln. Masters was born in Kansas in 1868 but grew up in Petersburg and Lewistown, Illinois. He was a lawyer until 1920, when he gave up law for literature. His *Spoon River Anthology* (1915), a collection of apocryphal epitaphs from the graveyard of an Illinois town, was his masterpiece. Although much of his work was dull and opinionated, he did have flashes of genius. He wrote some 45 books, volumes of poetry, and plays.

Carl Sandburg, born at Galesburg, Illinois, began working at the age of 13. A veteran of the Spanish-American War, he returned to Lombard College at Galesburg but never graduated. He became a journalist and wrote for newspapers and magazines. His poetry was noted for its free verse and stark realism. Much of his poetry was set in the Midwest. The *American Songbag* (1927) was representative of his poetry. His monumental work was a biography of Lincoln in six volumes for which he received the Pulitzer Prize in history in 1940.

The third of the poets was Nicholas V. Lindsay, born in Springfield, Illinois, in 1879. He was for a time a lecturer for the Young Men's Christian Association and the Anti-Saloon League. Although he first won fame with *General Booth Enters Heaven,* his two most famous poems were *The Congo* and *The Chinese Nightingale. Abraham Lincoln Walks at Midnight* and *The*

Candle in the Cabin were also very popular. Although Lindsay always wrote with a warm faith in democracy, his personal disappointments drove him to suicide.

The Van Doren brothers, Carl C. and Mark, led very similar lives. Both were born at Hope, Illinois, both received their Ph.D. at Columbia University and spent most of their adult lives teaching there, and both wrote about literature and literary figures. In addition to literary criticism, Carl also wrote biographies of such persons as Thomas L. Peacock, James B. Cabell, Jonathan Swift, Sinclair Lewis, and Benjamin Franklin. Franklin's life, Carl Van Doren's only biography that was not a completely literary figure, won him the Pulitzer Prize and developed in him an interest in the American Revolution. He later wrote the *Secret History of the American Revolution* in 1941.

Although Mark Van Doren concentrated on poetry, he also wrote some biography and literary criticism. His first major volume of poems was *Spring Thunder and Other Poems* in 1924. He also wrote biographies of Henry D. Thoreau, John Dryden, and William Shakespeare. In all he wrote about 20 volumes.

Probably one of the most noted writers produced by Illinois was Ernest Hemingway. Born and educated in Oak Park, Illinois, he began his wanderings around the world at an early age. His service as an ambulance driver and infantryman in Italy during World War I was the basis for *Farewell to Arms. The Sun Also Rises* and *The Torrents of Spring* established his reputation. He went to Spain during the Spanish Civil War (1936) to write the commentary for the film, "The Spanish Earth." The following year he returned to Spain as a foreign correspondent. During these two trips, he obtained the background for *The Fifth Column* and *For Whom the Bells Toll.* Hemingway, a master of realism, description, and clipped speech, seized the feeling of the moment in his writing. Apparently belonging to the literary death cult, many of his heroes died.

A final Illinois author was John Dos Passos. Like Hemingway, he had been born in the Chicago area and had been an ambulance driver in World War I. A prolific writer, he was most noted for his trilogy, *U.S.A.*, composed of the novels *The 42nd Parallel* (1930), *1919* (1932), and *The Big Money* (1936). In this social criticism of America, he used the techniques of "newsreel," "the biographical prose poem," and the "camera eye." The result of his rambling, stream-of-consciousness prose tended to be a somewhat pessimistic, confused, and moody view of America.

Michigan had an array of novelists, short story writers, and historians. The short-story writer, Clarence B. Kelland, born in Portland, Michigan, in 1881, was primarily noted for the characters he created. They included Mark Tidd, Mr. Deeds, and most important, Scattergood Baines. Baines was supposed to represent the typical merchant. Kelland, a magazine editor and newspaperman, wrote over 40 books and innumerable short stories.

Another novelist and short-story writer, Ring Lardner, was born in Niles, Michigan, in 1885. He obtained his start as a short-story writer with a series of stories about Jack Keefe, a White Sox pitcher. From this beginning, Lardner went on to write all types of stories. Viewed as a humorist, he was actually a satirist of the Jonathan Swift type. He even wrote one book entitled *Gullible's Travels* (1917).

One of Wisconsin's leading literary figures was Edna Ferber. Born in Kalamazoo, Michigan, in 1887, she moved with her parents to Appleton, Wisconsin, while still a child. She became a reporter on the Milwaukee *Journal* and later on the Chicago *Tribune.* Although her books had the flavor of the locale, they were more noted for plot. Her first book was *Dawn O'Hara* in 1911. *So Big* in 1924 put her into the best-seller class, and it was followed by *Show Boat* and *Cimarron.* Although Ferber considered herself a social critic, most of her books had escapist themes.

Glenway Wescott, also from Wisconsin, was a more pessimistic version of an earlier Wisconsin product, Hamlin Garland. Although he was an expatriate in Paris during the thirties, Wescott seemed unable on the evidence of his stories and novels to escape from his native state. *Goodbye, Wisconsin* dealt with men and women who had made a physical escape from Wisconsin. In *The Apple of the Eye,* Wescott defined Wisconsin in terms of a repressive Puritanism. Although he viewed Puritanism as a disease, he did not underrate its appeal to the imagination. Hence in *The Grandmothers* he tried to come to terms with his puritanical

Wisconsin ancestors, an exercise that resulted in a bitter-sweet product.

Wisconsin's leading historian was Frederick J. Turner. Turner was born at Portage, Wisconsin, in 1861. His essay *The Frontier in American History* read at the American Historical Association meeting in 1893 made his reputation. He divided his teaching years between the University of Wisconsin and Harvard University. He disliked writing, but the books he did write were full of the thesis that the frontier had been extremely important in shaping the course of American history. His principal works included: *The Rise of the New West* (1906); *The Frontier in American History* (1920); *The Significance of Sections in American History* (1932), for which he won the Pulitzer Prize; and *The United States, 1830-50: The Nation and Its Sections* (1935).

Three of Minnesota's outstanding writers were Thorstein Veblen, Sinclair Lewis, and F. Scott Fitzgerald. Although Veblen was born in Wisconsin, he moved with his family to Minnesota when he was eight. A brilliant thinker and economist, he was a constant critic of the capitalist system. His most famous work, *The Theory of the Leisure Class* (1899), was followed by a dozen other books mainly on phases of economics. In his personal life, he was badly disordered. He was discharged from several university positions partly because of scandals involving women.

Sinclair Lewis was born in Sauk Center, Minnesota, in 1885. Although he was something of a failure as a newspaperman, he finally struck pay dirt with his novels. Some of his novels had regional settings in the Midwest. He was an uneven and prolific writer. Some of his novels were outstanding and others poor. He was an ordinary story teller until 1920 when he made his reputation as a satirist in *Main Street*. The setting for this novel was apparently his home town of Sauk Center. The setting for *Babbitt* was probably Minneapolis. Lewis wrote about persons and things as he saw them with a sprinkling of sex added. *Main Street* was a satire on small towns, *Babbitt* on business men, *Elmer Gantry* on ministers, and *Dodsworth* on reformers. *Arrowsmith* was a more sympathetic portrayal of a doctor. Although Lewis turned down a Pulitzer Prize for *Arrowsmith* in 1926, he accepted a Nobel Prize in 1930.

Unlike Lewis who had many of his novels set in the Middle West, F. Scott Fitzgerald, who was born in St. Paul, Minnesota, favored the eastern United States or even Europe for the settings of his novels. The nearest he came to using his midwestern background in his works was having some of his characters from that area. For example, in one of his best novels, *The Great Gatsby,* Jay Gatsby was from Minnesota, and the other main characters were also from the Middle West. Like Lewis, Fitzgerald was a generally unhappy person and this was reflected in his works.

Among Kansas' literary hall of fame was William A. White. White, primarily a newspaperman, was born in Emporia, Kansas, in 1868 and lived there most of his life. He was the owner and editor of the *Emporia Gazette.* He wrote a number of short stories and some novels, biographies, and essays. Among his best were *A Certain Rich Man; Woodrow Wilson: The Man, the Times and His Task; A Puritan in Babylon,* a biography of President Calvin Coolidge; and *The Changing West.*

Nebraska's best known author was Willa Cather. Although Cather was born in Virginia, she moved with her family to Nebraska at an early age. A journalist, she was managing editor of *McClure's Magazine* for six years. When her novels made her financially independent, she quit her editorial tasks. Among her best novels were those based on realistic accounts of foreign-born, farm families in Nebraska. These included *O, Pioneers, The Song of the Lark, My Antonia,* and *A Lost Lady.* In these she displayed her view that the pioneers were a race of giants.

Another regionalist of the Cather school was Ole E. Rolvaag. Born in Norway he reached America in 1896 at the age of 20. After going to college, he became professor of Norwegian at St. Olaf College in Minnesota. His great study of Norwegian immigrants and pioneers, who settled on the northern prairies, was *Giants in the Earth. Pedar Victorius* was the sequel to *Giants in the Earth.* They tell the realistic story of a Norwegian family and their part in developing a Dakota community. *The Boat of Longing,* a somewhat mystical novel, was about the Loengselens Boat, a vessel symbolic of the heartache caused by emigration.

The Midwest by 1940 had produced virtually hundreds of

authors and thousands of volumes of verse, novels, biography, essays, and history. But the authors and literature presented here are a representative sampling of the literature produced by the Midwest. Although some of this literary production was regional, it was, overall, as diversified as the people and the ideas of the world.

—66—

Music

Popular Music

The most famous name associated with the rise of ragtime was Scott Joplin, a Negro born in Texarkana, Texas. In 1885 at the age of 17, he arrived in St. Louis which became his headquarters. At the World's Columbian Exposition in 1893 at Chicago, he met some of the early Chicago ragtime players such as "Plunk" Henry and Johnny Seymour. In 1894 Joplin went to Sedalia, Missouri, where he wrote his first compositions which were sentimental songs rather than ragtime. Joplin, however, continued to play ragtime on his piano at the Maple Leaf Club in Sedalia. There in 1899 he was heard by John S. Stark, a music publisher, who became a central figure in the spread of ragtime. The first of the published ragtime numbers was "Maple Leaf Rag" in 1899. Others of Joplin's songs included "Peacherine Rag" (1901), "Palm Leaf Rag – A Slow Drag" (1903), "Rose Leaf Rag" (1907)), "Fig Leaf Rag" (1908), "Stoptime Rag" (1910), and "Scott Joplin's New Rag" (1912).

The number of ragtime composers was large and the number of their compositions even larger. A few composers and compositions selected at random in the period 1897 to 1916 include: Thomas M. Turpin of St. Louis who wrote "Harlem Rag," "St. Louis Rag," and "The Buffalo Rag"; James S. Scott of Neosho, Missouri, and Carthage, Kansas, who composed "Climax Rag," "Kansas City Rag," and "Sunburst Rag"; Louis Chauvin of St. Louis, who wrote "Heliotrope Bouquet"; Charles L. Johnson, who produced "Dill Pickles," "Swanee Rag," and "Blue Goose Rag"; and Percy Weinrich of Joplin, Missouri, who wrote "Peaches and Cream Rag," "Memphis Rag," and "Sunflower Rag." Weinrich also wrote many other popular tunes such as "Put on Your Old Grey Bonnet," and "When You Wore A Tulip and I Wore a Big Red Rose." The heydey of ragtime was from 1897 to 1910; and contrary to popular belief, Irving Berlin's "Alexander's Ragtime Band" did not usher in ragtime in 1911, but rather was a bubble in ragtime's decline.

The blues developed contemporaneously with ragtime. The blues were an aspect of Afro-American folk music in solo singing. When a lonely Negro man plowing in a hot, river bottom or a roustabout resting on the levee began to raise his voice in a wailing cornfield or river song, he was singing the birth of the blues with its three-line, twelve-bar pattern. Blues songs have a feeling of lament with an undertone of humor.

Among the musicians who made the blues a popular-type music, William C. Handy, born in Alabama in 1873, was very important. In 1905 he went to Memphis, Tennessee, where he formed a dance band. Handy's band was hired in 1909 to help elect E. H. Crump to office. Handy wrote a song for the campaign called "Mister Crump," which was published in 1912 as "Memphis Blues." Although known as the "Father of the Blues," Handy said he did not originate the blues, but merely popularized a musical medium which Negroes had long used to express their personal feelings. In his "St. Louis Blues" published in 1914, he used both three- and four-line verses. Others of his works included "Joe Turner Blues," "John Henry Blues," and "Blue Gummed Blues." After Memphis, Handy went to Chicago and then New York where he formed his own music publishing company. Handy stood about halfway between Negro folk music and tin-pan alley. Later, numerous composers began to write blues songs. Among them were Jerome Kern ("Left-All-Alone-Again Blues," 1920), George Gerschwin ("The Half of it, Dearie Blues," 1924), and Irving Berlin ("School-House Blues," 1921).

Jazz, which came into vogue about the end of World War I, originated in New Orleans. It was a combination of African music, Afro-American folk songs, Irish, Scottish, and British folk melodies, ragtime tunes, the blues, and Creole folk songs and dance tunes. Jazz apparently had its start in Negro street bands in New Orleans which played "hot music" for parades and funerals in the period 1870 to 1890. The most colorful figure associated with the beginnings of classic jazz in New Orleans was Charles Bolden (1868-1931). Leading with a cornet, his band consisted of a clarinet, trombone, guitar, bass, and drums. During its dozen years of existence, Bolden's band was composed of many of the pioneers of jazz. When "King" Bolden went insane in 1909, his place was taken by Freddie Keppard and his Olympia Band. Storyville, a red-light district in New Orleans during the period 1887 to 1917, gave great encouragement to jazz because cash was plentiful, prejudice rare, and liberty unrestrained. When Storyville was closed in 1917 because of pressure from the War and Navy departments, men like Joseph Oliver, new leader of the famous Olympia Band, went north. A great trumpeter and gifted leader, Oliver led his Creole jazz band in Chicago during most of the decade after 1918. The white imitation of jazz was referred to as Dixieland jazz. Its father was Jack Laine who led the Reliance Brass Band and Jack Laine's Ragtime Band. Laine played drums in his ragtime band. Other instruments in his band included cornet, clarinet, trombone, guitar, and string bass.

Louis Armstrong, brought to Chicago by Joseph Oliver, also helped bring jazz to the Midwest. Born in New Orleans in 1900, he learned to play a trumpet and joined Kis Ory's Brown Skinned Babies in 1918. The following year he played riverboats on the Mississippi. In 1922 he arrived in Chicago. There he married Lil Hardin, a pianist, and spent five years out of the next seven playing with his wife's Dreamland Syncopators and his own groups, the Hot Five and the Hot Seven. One of the most important white jazz bands in Chicago was the New Orleans Rhythm Kings, led by Paul Mares, which opened there in 1920. From 1920 to 1930, New Orleans jazz flourished in Chicago, played by both Negro and white musicians.

A variation of jazz was developed by a ragtime pianist named Bennie Moten of Kansas City. In place of the New Orleans two-beat rhythm, Moten developed a four-beat rhythm. Moten's style came to be known as the "Jump" or "Kansas City Style." William Basie, who continued to emphasize four heavy beats to the bar, took over Moten's band when the latter died.

However during the 1930's, the sweet orchestra trend featuring violins, saxophones, and sentimentality almost crowded jazz out. The peak of this sweet trend was Paul Whiteman's orchestra, which sweetened and orchestrated jazz and almost denatured it.

After 1936 came "swing" which Louis Armstrong characterized as jazz which had incorporated scored orchestrations and musicians who could read music. On the other hand Rudi Blesh said that swing was anti-jazz; they varied in spirit, form, and technique. But whatever their relationship, swing did become popular. One of the "kings" created by swing was Benny Goodman, born in Chicago in 1909 and later known as the "King of Swing." Playing a sensational clarinet from the age of 16, he played with Ben Pollack's Chicago Band from 1926 to 1931. He formed his own swing ensemble after 1934. Other names associated with swing music were Harry James, Gene Krupa, Tommy Dorsey, Woody Herman, Glenn Miller, and Artie Shaw.

Despite these periodical phases and crazes, a large number of people in the Midwest continued to be primarily interested in the old, the sentimental, and the melodious tunes. Many also continued to enjoy the marches of John P. Sousa, the "March King," and his successors. Sousa alone produced over 100 marches among which were the ever popular "Semper Fidelis," "Washington Post March," and "Stars and Stripes Forever."

Among the popular song writers in the Midwest during this period were Paul Dresser, Cole Porter, Hoagy Carmichael, and Egbert Van Alstyne. The first three of these were Indiana products and the fourth was from Iowa. Paul Dresser composed "On the Banks of the Wabash," "My Gal Sal," and "Just Tell Them That You Saw Me." Cole Porter, whose forte was spicy musical comedy, was born at Peru, Indiana, in 1892. His first complete musical-comedy score was *Fifty Million Frenchmen* produced in 1929. The titles of some of his productions demonstrated his fashionable spiciness: *The Gay Divorcee, Red Hot and Blue, DuBarry Was A Lady,* and *Something for the Boys.* His wide range of expression in songs was displayed by such numbers as "So in Love Am I," "Night and Day," and "Begin the Beguine." Hoagy Carmichael, also from Indiana, was noted for such numbers as *"Star Dust," "Rockin Chair,"* and *"Georgia on My Mind."* The

Iowa-born Egber Van Alstyne produced *"In the Shade of the Old Apple Tree,"* and the musical score for the *Thief of Bagdad.*

Classical Music

In addition to popular music, the Midwest also produced some classical music. Among the first of these classical composers was John A. Carpenter, born at Park Ridge, Illinois, in 1876. A businessman by profession, he was one of the earliest American composers to experiment with jazz inflections or "symphonic jazz." His most popular works were *Krazy Kat* (1921), a ballet inspired by the comic strip of that name; *Skyscrapers,* a ballet of modern American life, which appeared at the Metropolitan in 1926; and *Adventures in a Perambulator,* a descriptive suite for orchestra.

In contrast to Carpenter, David S. Smith, born in Toledo, Ohio, in 1877, was a conservative composer. A college professor, Smith studied with Horatio Parker at Yale and in 1920 succeeded his mentor as dean of the Yale School of Music. In addition to four symphonies and other orchestral works, Smith wrote a large quantity of chamber music and several choral works. Among his best choral works were *The Vision of Isaiah* and *Daybreak.* In two of his orchestral numbers, *1929,* a musical satire devoted to the year of the crash, and *Tomorrow,* an overture written in 1932 and 1933, he recorded his impressions of the world around him. Three of his symphonies were performed by the Chicago Symphony, the New York Philharmonic, and the Cleveland Symphony. His *Cathedral Prelude* was performed by the Detroit Symphony and his *1929* by the New York Philharmonic.

Another more progressive composer was Edwin J. Stringham born in Kenosha, Wisconsin, in 1890. After many teaching assignments, he eventually became a staff member at the Julliard School of Music in New York. In his music he liked rhythmic counterpoint and masses of orchestral color. He also used some jazz idiom. Among his orchestral works, *Visions, First Symphony,* and the *Ancient Mariner* were performed by the Chicago Symphony, the Rochester Philharmonic, the Minneapolis Symphony, and the New York Philharmonic.

Also on the Julliard faculty was Albert Stoessel, born in St. Louis in 1894. He succeeded Walter Damrosch as head of the New York Oratorio Society at the age of 26. Although Stoessel's music was charming, fluent, and graceful, it had no original idiom. Among his principal works were *Cyrano de Bergerac, Hispania,* and *Orchestral Suite in Ancient Style.*

Robert R. Bennett, born in Kansas City, Missouri, in 1894, was a most versatile composer. Although a major share of his works were in the jazz idiom, he gave the idiom a new dignity and beauty. Among his best orchestral works were *Sights and Sounds, Abraham Lincoln,* and *Six Variations on a Theme of Jerome Kern.* His *Abraham Lincoln* was introduced in 1931 by the Philadelphia Symphony with great success. Bennet, who also gave a part of his time to Tin Pan Alley, was a very successful orchestrator. Such song-composers as George Gerschwin, Jerome Kern, and Cole Porter brought their works to him for orchestration.

Another midwesterner of great versatility was Leo Sowerby of Grand Rapids, Michigan. He spent most of his adult life in Chicago as organist and choirmaster of St. James Episcopal Church. Two of his works that were regional in nature were *Prairie* and *From the Northland. Prairie* was a tone poem based on Carl Sandburg's poem of the same title. *From the Northland* was composed in Italy but its theme was the Canadian countryside near Lake Superior. A suite in four movements, it consisted of "Forest Voices," "Cascades," "Burnt Rock Pool," and "The Shining Big-sea Water." Among his best choral work was *The Vision of Sir Launfal.* One of the best writers of organ music in America, his compositions included *Canon, Chaconne,* and *Fugue.*

Howard H. Hanson, born at Wahoo, Nebraska, in 1896, was greatly influenced by his Swedish ancestry. The opening movement of his *First Symphony* displayed the influence of Sibelius in its "solemnity, austerity, and grandeur of the North." Referred to as a "conservative modern," his later works such as *Lament for Beowulf, Three Poems from Walt Whitman* (based on "Drum

Taps"), *Pan and the Priest,* and *Romantic Symphony* displayed a greater refinement and beauty and an expression which was uniquely his own. He also wrote an opera *Merry Mount* which was one of the few operas on an American theme. His major professional position was director of the Eastman School of Music at the University of Rochester.

Another American composer who also dabbled in opera was Virgil Thomson, born in Kansas City, Missouri, in 1896. The opera, *Four Saints in Three Acts,* was written by Gertrude Stein and set to music by Thomson. It concerned mainly the characters of St. Theresa of Avila and Ignatius Loyola. The music for it was simple, candid, and melodious. His symphonies were equally interesting. His *Symphony on a Hymn Tune* (1928) used "How Firm a Foundation Ye Saints of the Lord" as a main theme and "Yes, Jesus Loves Me" as a secondary theme. Thomson similarly drew on hymn tunes in his four sets of *Variations and Fugues* for organ, including "Come Ye Desolate," "There's Not a Friend Like the Lowly Jesus," "Will There be any Stars in My Crown," and "Shall we Gather At the River." Thomson's ballet, *Filling Station,* was a period piece that captured the popular tunes of the 1930's. In addition to his voluminous compositions, Thomson also wrote several books on music and was a music critic of the New York *Herald Tribune.*

Herbert Elwell, composer and music critic on the Cleveland *Plain Dealer,* was born in Minneapolis in 1898. To improve his style, he went to Paris where he studied with Nadia Boulanger. His best known work was the orchestral suite from a ballet entitled *The Happy Hypocrit* (1925). Among many others, he also wrote the cantata *Lincoln* and the chamber-music composition *Blue Symphony.* In addition to being a composer and a music critic, Elwell also taught at the Cleveland Institute of Music.

Harrison Kerr, also of Cleveland, Ohio, was born in 1899. Like Elwell he studied with Boulanger. An eclectic composer, he assimilated various elements of modern music in trying to evolve a personal style. Much of his music was characterized by chromaticism (superimposed fourths, dissonant counterpoint, and changing meters). His compositions included *Dance Suite, Symphony No. 1, Symphony No. 2 in E Minor,* and *Symphony No. 3 in D Minor.* He also wrote chamber and choral music.

Other midwestern composers included Burrill Phillips of Omaha, noted for *Selections from McGuffey's Reader* and *Tom Paine Overture;* Ray Green, of Cavendish, Missouri, who wrote *Three Inventories of Casey Jones, Holiday for Four,* and *Festival Fugues;* Don Gillis, also of Missouri, noted for *An American Symphony, Prairie Poem, Cowtown,* and *Symphony No. 7* ("Saga of a Prairie School") ; and Robert E. Ward of Cleveland, noted for *Jubilation, Night Music,* and *Hush'd Be the Camps Today.*

To bring classical music to the people of the Midwest, there were high school and college orchestras. In addition nearly every large midwestern city developed its own symphony orchestra. The St. Louis Symphony Orchestra was founded in 1880; the Chicago Symphony Orchestra in 1891; the Cincinnati Symphony Orchestra in 1895; the Minneapolis Symphony Orchestra in 1903; the Cleveland Orchestra in 1918; the Detroit Symphony Orchestra from 1872 to 1910 and again in 1919; the Indianapolis Symphonic Orchestra in 1930; and the Kansas City Philharmonic in 1933. Moreover, many of the smaller towns had community concert associations which provided choral, ballet, and instrumental music for their memberships.

—67—

Art, Sculpture, and Architecture

Art

Among the painters born after the Civil War, Ohio produced Robert Henri of Cincinnati and George W. Bellows of Columbus. Henri, who had French, English, and Irish ancestry, had seen the old masters first hand before he began to teach in Philadelphia. Henri believed in the orderliness of nature which should be revealed by the painter to rebuke the man-made chaos. In the book, *The Art Spirit,* Henri summed up his philosophy and insights gained from over 30 years of teaching. In Henri's landscapes such as "Far Rockaway" lay solid construction and in his "Mary" lay honesty and frankness. Henri's "verity" was also revealed in his "Martche in a White Dress" and his "Guide to Croaghan."

Among Henri's disciples was George Bellows, a fellow Ohioan, who attempted to keep Henri's truthfulness in painting. Bellows found the subjects for one of his first works, "Stag at Sharkey's," at Sharkey's Athletic Club across the street from Henri's Chase School of Art in New York City. Bellows, interested in the dynamics of picture making, showed his improved style in "Dempsey and Firpo" in 1923. Still later Bellows lost a bit of his dynamics in "Eleanor, Jean, and Anna," a triple portrait whose appearance suggested the stiffness of geometric calculations.

The outstanding painter in Kansas was John S. Curry. He with Grant Wood and Thomas H. Benton comprised the Midwest's outstanding triumverate of regional painters. Curry, whose father had been a stockman in Kansas, began his experiment in

"Mining"
Painting by Thomas H. Benton

"The Fountain of the Great Lakes"
Sculpture by Lorado Z. Taft

Frank L. Wright (1869-1959)
Architect
From *Dictionary of American Portraits* by Hayward and Blanche Cirker, Dover Publications, Inc., New York, 1967. *Reprinted through permission of the publisher.*

regionalism with "Baptism in Kansas." When Curry began this picture, he grouped some nudes around a circular pool, but within a few months the pool had become a wooden tank and the figures inside it had become a Baptist preacher and a farm girl. His great desire was to put on canvas the struggle of man with nature – storms, floods, and tornadoes. His concentration on these themes later stirred up a hornet's nest when in painting the Kansas statehouse rotunda he played up the tornado and depicted John Brown as a fanatic.

Grant Wood of Anamosa, Iowa, was more restrained in his portrayal of the countryside. His spongelike trees seemed to come from his mother's china plates, his faces looked stoney, and his rounded hills appeared monotonous. But despite this he captured the feeling of Iowa life in "Stone City," "American Gothic," and "Dinner for Threshers." The satire depicted in the "Daughters of Revolution" is effective because Wood was only mildly resentful.

The third of the triumverate, Thomas H. Benton of Missouri, had a style more similar to Curry's. Benton's preachers, racketeers, gamblers, cowboys, Indians, farmers, lumbermen, and stripteasers all writhed and pranced in similar fashion. The color oppositions, the pitting of one vortex of energy against another, and the bulging muscles were his forte. Benton's scenes were representative of the vibrancy of the Midwest.

Sculpture

The Midwest also had a noted group of sculptors. John Q. A. Ward of Urbana, Ohio, produced such pieces as the "Indian Hunter," "African Freedman," "George Washington," "Henry Ward Beecher," "Horace Greeley," and "General George H. Thomas." His "Indian Hunter," "Washington," and "Greeley" are all located in New York; "Beecher" is in Brooklyn.

Lorado Taft of Illinois had modeled a fountain for the Chicago Midway by the age of 33. He spent most of his adult life at the Chicago Art Institute where he instructed aspiring young sculptors. His works included "The Spirit of the Great Lakes" on the Chicago Art Institute building, the beardless "Lincoln" at Urbana, "Blackhawk" at Oregon, Illinois, and the Columbia Memorial Fountain in Washington, D.C. His writings on sculpture had the authority of experience behind them.

At Bloomfield Hills, Michigan, the Swedish born Carl Milles held forth. When Milles came to the United States in 1931, he already had a brilliant reputation for sculpture in Sweden. St. Louis commissioned him to design "The Marriage of the Rivers" which was a joy of nymphs and tritons. His St. Paul Peace Monument, his Orpheus fountain for Stockholm, as well as his "Astronomer," constructed for the New York World's Fair, all had clean solid lines. His flowing "Dancing Girls" grace the landscape at Bloomfield Hills. Like Taft, Miles communicated his own experience to his American students.

From St. Paul, Minnesota, came Paul Manship to work in New York with Solon Borglum before going on to Philadelphia and Rome. Manship developed his graceful curves in "Duck Girl," "A Dancer and Gazelles," "Moods of Time," "Centaur and Dryad," and "The Indian Hunter." His neat draperies, his precise beards and ringlets, and his clear-cut lines reminded one of Benvenuto Cellini.

One of Manship's mentors, Solon Borglum, made a lasting impression on Midwest sculpture by his creation of the four-president's heads (Theodore Roosevelt, George Washington, Abraham Lincoln, and Thomas Jefferson) on the face of Mt. Rushmore in South Dakota. A "sculptor with dynamite," he blasted the stone to within a few inches of the desired contour. When he completed the task, he signed himself, "sculptor and engineer."

Architecture

As has been noted earlier, there were many architects and many buildings in the nineteenth century but not very much originality. This had to wait for architects like Daniel H. Burnham, Cass Gilbert, Louis H. Sullivan, and Frank Lloyd Wright, all of whom were noted for originality and for the building of skyscrapers.

Burnham, born in New York in 1846, went to Chicago in 1873 where he and John W. Root founded an architectural firm. The Chicago fire in 1871 gave them a great opportunity and they made the most of it. The term "sky scraper" was allegedly first applied to their ten-story Montauk Building in Chicago. Their Masonic Temple, built in 1890, was the world's tallest building at that time, and they broke their own record in 1902 with the Flatiron Building in New York. Burnham and Root jointly planned a large portion of the Chicago World's Fair architecture. With Root's death in 1891, Burnham was left with the responsibility for it and with the honors when it succeeded. Among his other accomplishments were Union Station in Washington and civic improvements in San Francisco, Cleveland, and Baltimore.

Unlike Burnham, Cass Gilbert was born in the Midwest (Zanesville, Ohio) but went east to do most of his work. He did design the Minnesota State Capitol at St. Paul, before going to New York City where he designed the U.S. Custom House and the Woolworth tower of steel, 56 stories high, which was supported by flying buttresses and decorated with terra-cotta gargoyles. Gilbert is also remembered for the U. S. Supreme Court Building, with its huge Corinthian portico, and the Treasury Annex. As Oliver W. Larkin described his public buildings in *Art and Life in America,* they were as pompous as Gilbert himself.

Like Burnham, Louis Sullivan came from the East to form an architectural firm with Dankmar Adler. "Form follows function" was Sullivan's basic architectural philosophy. In office buildings he was the first to use masonry simply as a casing over a steel skeleton, rather than using it to build an artificial facade. Frank L. Wright referred to Sullivan Wainwright Building, completed in St. Louis in 1890, as "the master key to the skyscraper as architecture the world over." Sullivan's Transportation Building, designed for the Chicago World's Fair, set a new style in ornamentation. More in keeping with his philosophy, however, was his auditorium in Chicago, designed with Adler in 1895. It was noted for its wonderful acoustics. After his partner Adler died in 1900, Sullivan did no further work on a large scale. He was emotionally and temperamentally unsuited to deal with the public. Although he did design a number of small banks throughout the Midwest after this, his main contribution was in his writings and drawings which explained his philosophy on ornamentation and "form follows function."

Frank L. Wright, a former assistant of Sullivan, whose work has been referred to as the "New School of the Middle West" was born in Richland Center, Wisconsin, in 1869. Like Sullivan he believed in "form follows function," but he went further than his mentor in his belief in originality, utility, simplicity, and materials related to environment. All the private homes he designed were noted for their straight lines, their airiness, their originality, and their utility. Most outstanding and most indiginous of these were the "Taliesin," located on his 200 acres along the Wisconsin River, and the cantilevered "Falling Water" which he swung over a rocky stream at Bear Run, Pennsylvania. Of his larger works, some of the most outstanding were the Larkin Building in New York City, the Tokyo Imperial Hotel, built to withstand earthquakes, and the S. C. Johnson Company Administration Building at Racine, Wisconsin.

Other major architectural accomplishments in the Midwest included Henry H. Richardson's Glessner House and Marshall Field Store, and William Le Baron Jenny's Home Insurance Building all completed in Chicago in 1885. In 1890 the New York Life Insurance Building, designed by McKim, Mead, and White, was constructed in Kansas City. In the 1920's Raymond Hood's Tribune Building and Daily News Building were added to Chicago's skyline. Still later the Cranbrook buildings, designed by Eliel Saarinen, were built at Bloomfield Hills, Michigan.

—68—

Recreation in New Directions

In the years after World War I, recreation in the Midwest was greatly affected by automobiles and radio. Automobiles not only made it possible for people to travel widely and see every corner of the United States but also allowed rural people to participate in urban entertainments and city people to view the countryside and visit the beaches. The friendliness and sociability of the rural communities declined as people obtained automobiles and travelled to numerous places in search of commercial or individual amusement.

Although transportation and communication developments modified recreation, certain long-range trends continued into the twentieth century. Families obtained increased leisure time for recreation as the result of industrialization, modern home appliances, and shorter hours. Recreation also became more commercial, uniform, and vicarious. People continued to participate in individual and team activities like hunting, fishing, golfing, bowling, stamp and coin collecting, and parlor games, but much of their time was spent in listening and watching entertainment provided by large broadcasting companies, movie corporations, and professional athletic groups.

Dancing remained in vogue. By the time of World War I, the fox trot, the turkey trot, the bunny hug, the lame duck, and the grizzly bear were introduced to accompany the ragtime music. Following this came jazz in the 1920's built on the saxophone. Couples did the fox trot and Charleston to such tunes as "Kitten on the Keys," "Crazy Rhythm," "Tea for Two," and "You're the Cream in My Coffee." Although some felt the new jazz-dance craze was sensous and indecent, it continued. The most popular music for dancing in the 1930's was swing. The big apple, the shag, and the chestnut tree gave way to jitterbugging and the rhumba. But in 1930 all types of dances existed in the Middle West from the square dance to the waltz. Dancing continued popular, because how else could one obtain exercise, be sociable, and hug one's best girl all at the same time.

The overall result of the changes in midwestern recreation was toward uniformity and diversity. Although concentration of commercial entertainment in few corporations meant great uniformity of programming, the number of types of entertainment were infinitely greater. Movies tended to disrupt family life, while radios encouraged people to stay at home. Although motoring took people away from home recreation, it increased the possibilities of outdoor activities. Commercial entertainment led to the decline of the usual small-town and community recreation. Lodge night, the church social, the carnival, the county fair, the beer parlor, the burlesque show all lost part of their glamour. People often got tired of going and simply wanted to stay home and rest.

Overall, each individual could choose from a myriad of possible activities in 1940. Recreation had become big business, and the facilities available for entertainment were tremendous. For example, Detroit had an art institute, a public library, a symphony orchestra, a number of large parks, a baseball team, the Detroit-Windsor tunnel, an athletic club, an underground salt mine, hundreds of churches, and many other recreational facilities. Chicago had a symphony orchestra, 1,650 churches, a civic opera company, several legitimate theaters, the Field Museum of Natural History, the Museum of Science and Industry, a planetarium, an aquarium, an art instltute, a zoo, 136 parks, 12 large beaches, 400 movie houses, two professional baseball teams, and two professional football teams. When one added these to the nationwide entertainment, multiplied them by the hundreds of towns in the Midwest, and then listed the number of other individual activities that persons could engage in, one began to realize the varied entertainment that was available to every person in the Midwest.

PART VI

THE MIDDLE WEST, 1940 TO THE PRESENT: A SUMMARY

Goshen, Indiana (1970)

Cincinnati, Ohio (1970)

A Summary

In the period after 1940, the Midwest became increasingly an integral part of the United States. Although it remained distinctive in certain areas, even these became less noticeable. Probably the two factors that were most responsible for this were improved transportation and communication. Automobiles, especially, made it possible for people to travel widely and see every corner of the United States. Because of simultaneous communication, in which television played a leading role, people as a group began to play canasta, watch the same western, see the same news, hear the same tunes, and start the same fads at the same time.

Population trends remained essentially the same. The urban population increased from about 58 per cent to 72 per cent between 1940 and 1970. Only two midwestern states, North and South Dakota, remained predominantly rural. Although the total population of the Midwest continued to grow (57,000,000 in *1970*), its percentage of the United States population dropped slightly to a little over 28 per cent.

The restrictions on immigration were also reflected in the Midwest. The total number of foreign born had dropped in the North Central states; however, the nationalities with the largest numbers still remained German, Polish, Canadian, Italian, and Russian. Even though the Midwest continued to attract a large percentage of the immigrants because of its kindness to newcomers and its wealth and diversified economic structure which offered greater opportunities for securing a livlihood, the number coming to the Midwest declined because the total number arriving in the United States declined.

The midwesterners in 1970 enjoyed a relatively high standard of living. They had about 28 per cent of the total dwelling units in the United States and 68 per cent were owner occupied. These 12 states, which had 33 per cent of the nation's manufac-

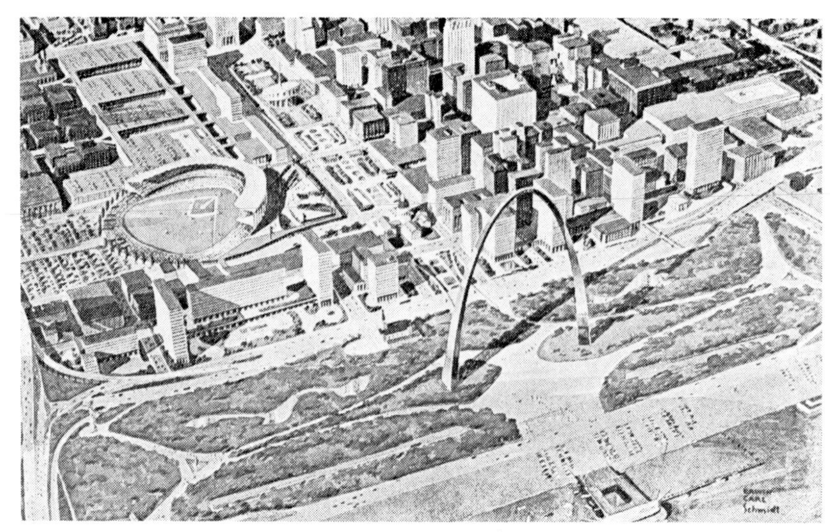

St. Louis, Missouri (1970)

Chicago, Illinois (1970)

turing and over 43 per cent of the agricultural output, paid 29 per cent of the United States' federal taxes. The average per capita in income in the Midwest was approximately $3,950, which was $40 above the national average. Both the western and northeastern states had a slightly higher average (but not modal) per capita income.

Although greater prosperity had come to the Midwest, it was not shared by the Indians. Even though their number in the Midwest had grown to 120,000 (about 20 per cent of the U. S. total) by 1970, the Indians were generally still eking out an existence on submarginal land in out-of-the-way reservations. Those who managed to overcome their cultural tradition and adopt white man's ways still often found themselves unacceptable as an integral part of the white community.

While the Negro was more accepted in the Midwest than the Indian, he was still lagging behind his white neighbor. By 1970 the blacks had increased to about eight per cent of the total midwestern population. Black urbanization had continued and about 96 per cent of the Negroes lived in the cities. Segregation was only slightly lower than in the South. On a 100-point scale the South had a mean rating of 90.9 compared to 87.7 for the North Central states. The midwestern black ghettos had about five times as many people per square mile as the white urban areas.

The black educational and employment level was still lower and the drug-addiction and crime rate still higher than that of the white. That race relations were still volatile in the Midwest was indicated by race riots in Cleveland in 1966 and Detroit in 1967. The Detroit riot resulted in 43 persons killed and $500,000,000 in damage. The most hopeful sign as to Negro progress in the Midwest in 1970 was the fact that they had elected three Negro congressmen, two from Detroit and one from Chicago, and also a few mayors.

In politics the Midwest also became more like the rest of the nation. The number of political positions at the national cabinet level held by midwesterners declined after 1940. In all the North Central states provided one president, three vice presidents, four secretaries of the treasury, four secretaries of defense,

Henry A. Wallace (1888-1965)
Vice-President of the United States,
Secretary of Agriculture,
Secretary of Commerce

Alfred M. Landon (1887-)
Governor of Kansas

Dwight D. Eisenhower (1890-1969)
President of the United States,
General of the Army

Courtesy Library of Congress. From *Dictionary of American Portraits* by Hayward and Blanche Cirker, Dover Publications, Inc., New York, 1967. *Reprinted through permission of the publisher.*

Adlai E. Stevenson (1900-1965)
Governor of Illinois,
Ambassador to the U. N.
Painting by Norman Rockwell.

two attorney generals, four postmaster generals, three secretaries of the interior, four secretaries of agriculture, four secretaries of labor, five secretaries of commerce, four secretaries of health, education, and welfare, one secretary of housing and urban development, two Speakers of the House of Representatives, and nine justices of the United States Supreme Court.

Although the Midwest continued its habit of voting Republican in presidential elections (seven Republican, two Democratic, and one tie), it was far less successful in electing its candidate to office. In ten presidential elections, five candidates supported by a majority of the Midwest won.

Although the Midwest did not elect many of its favorite sons to the presidency or vice presidency (only Harry S. Truman, Henry Wallace, and Hubert Humphrey were successful), it did provide a number of losing candidates. In 1936 the Republicans went to the Midwest for both of their candidates. For the presidential office, they chose Alfred M. Landon of Kansas, the only Republican governor to win in 1934. As his running mate, they selected Frank Knox of Illinois, publisher of the Chicago *Daily News* and a Theodore Roosevelt progressive. The Midwest also furnished Congressman William Lemke of North Dakota as a presidential candidate on the Union Party and Norman Thomas on the Socialist Party.

In 1940 the Republicans had several well-known midwestern politicians to choose from, but they passed over them in favor of a midwestern dark horse, Wendell Willkie of Indiana, President of Commonwealth and Southern (utilities company) and a violent opponent of the Tennessee Valley Authority. In 1948 the Republicans selected Senator John Bricker of Ohio as their vice-presidential candidate. In 1952 and 1956 the Democrats selected as their presidential candidate, ex-Governor Adlai E. Stevenson from Illinois; in 1968 they selected Hubert Humphrey from Minnesota.

In addition to its losing presidential contenders, the Midwest also provided some noted United States senators. Senator Robert A. Taft of Ohio was a leading contender for the Republican presidential nomination in every convention from 1940 through 1952. A leader of the Republicans in the Senate, his

Harry S. Truman (1884-)
President of the United States

Hubert H. Humphrey (1911-)
Vice President of the United States,
U. S. Senator

Courtesy Kurt Jafay. From *Dictionary of American Portraits* by Hayward and Blanche Cirker, Dover Publications, Inc., New York, 1967. *Reprinted through permission of the publisher.*

Missouri lead mine (1970)

name was attached to a labor law (Taft-Hartley) which was to make the labor leadership more responsible and eliminate labor abuses. It outlawed the closed shop, allowed federal injunctions in certain strikes, forbade certain type strikes, forced union officers to take a non-communist oath, and provided for joint management and labor administration of welfare funds.

Another midwestern senator, considered as Republican presidential timber, was Senator Arthur H. Vanderberg of Michigan. As chairman of the Foreign Relations Committee at the end of World War II, his wholehearted support of the United Nations made its quick passage a certainty.

Around 1950 internal Communism became a leading issue in politics. A leading figure in this Communist scare campaign was the Republican senator from Wisconsin, Joseph R. McCarthy. Large on reckless charges and short on proof, McCarthy moved in to flush out the Communists and anyone who disagreed with his methods or ideas. He created such a furor that this period of hysteria was labeled the McCarthy era. His colleagues in Congress finally got tired of his irresponsible antics and recorded their disapproval in a vote of censure. This hastened his decline into oblivion.

It is difficult to say what issues the midwesterners supported and opposed in the period after 1940. One of the best indices of their political views were the presidential elections and even these were far from conclusive. However, if these can be used as a guide, they indicated that the Midwest supported the Republican Party and its platforms. In the generation after 1932, the Republicans greatly opposed creeping socialism, the growing national debt, the growing strength of organized labor, and the increasing role of government in national affairs. On the other hand, the Republicans favored unemployment relief, collective bargaining, lower taxes, states' rights, congressional control of tariffs, and aid to businessmen.

On the economic scene, production in the Midwest increased, but its percentage of the total nation's production decreased slightly. In its production, the Midwest was at its best percentage-wise in the agricultural area in 1970. It produced 87 per cent of the nation's corn, 56 per cent of the wheat, 84 per cent of the oats, 51 per cent of the hay, and 71 per cent of the rye. In the animal line it contained 76 per cent of the nation's hogs, 47 per cent of the dairy cows, and 43 per cent of all cattle. In total value of all agricultural produts sold, the Midwest was still first among the regions with 43 per cent.

In the period after 1940, the trends and problems in agriculture remained the same even though the national government tried to help with subsidies in the form of agricultural adjustment acts, soil-bank plans, and the ever-normal granary. Average land values in the Midwest increased from $44 an acre in 1935 to about $122 an acre in 1970. This plus the higher cost of buildings, machinery, fertilizer, and stock made it increasingly difficult for the small farmer and/or the new farmer to begin or to maintain themselves.

Also increasing technology and larger machinery necessitated a larger farm unit. From 1925 to 1970, the average farm in the Midwest increased from about 74 to 300 acres. The basic cause of this was that the larger farm could produce at a lower cost per unit; the small farm needed the same basic machinery as the large farm and the large farm could spread relatively similar overhead costs over a larger production. Thus, despite all the efforts of the national government to save the small farmer, he was rapidly disappearing.

In mineral production in 1970, the Midwest produced 27 per cent of the nation's salt, 75 per cent of the lead, 24 per cent of the coal, 4 per cent of the copper, 35 per cent of the gold, and 80 per cent of the iron ore. Despite its high mineral production in certain areas such as lead and iron ore, the Midlands in 1970 still only produced 15 per cent of the nation's total value of minerals.

Lumber production in the Midwest had dropped off even more drastically. In 1970 the North Central states produced only five per cent of the nation's lumber.

Again even though the Midwest's manufacturing capability had greatly increased, its percentage of the nation's total production declined slightly. As of 1970 the Midwest's six leading industries continued to be farm machinery, meat packing, flour and meal processing, transportation equipment, fabricated metal products, and rubber and plastics. Although the Midwest produced a major share of the nation's industrial production in these areas, its industrial production was low enough in several other areas that in 1970 the Midwest had a respectable, but not outstanding, 33 per cent of the national factory production, of which 27 per cent was located in the five states east of the Mississippi, and six per cent in the seven states lying west of the Mississippi.

In transportation and communication, the Midwest continued to retain its proportionate share up to 1970. It had about 28 per cent of the nation's total vehicles, 40 percent of the nation's 207,005 miles of railroads, 29 percent of the civil aircraft, 30 per cent of the airports, 28 percent of the telephones, 25 percent of the AM and FM stations, and 29 per cent of the television stations. Two other indicators of the size of the circulation system in the Midwest in 1970 were the 1,327,456 miles of municipal and rural highway mileage (36 per cent of the U. S. total) and the 240-billion ton miles of products hauled on the Great Lakes and on the Ohio, Illinois, Missouri, and Mississippi rivers and their tributaries.

Finally, to support its industry, agriculture and transportation monetarily, the Midwest had 47 per cent of the nation's 13,511 banks in 1970, and 28 per cent of the nation's deposits of $482,506,000,000.

The Midwest's stand on foreign affairs after 1935 was difficult to determine. Governor Alfred Landon of Kansas worked with the American First Group to prevent America's entrance into the war until war was actually declared. At the same time, William A. White, also of Kansas, was chairman of the Committee to Defend America by Aiding the Allies, a group established to prepare America psychologically for war. The bombing of Pearl Harbor by the Japanese settled the issue and the Midwest joined the rest of the nation in defeating the Axis. The Midwest put its great industrial, agricultural, and population resources into the contest. In all the Midwest furnished around four-million troops, over 25 per cent of the total U. S. forces in World War II.

After World War II the Midwest still displayed some isolationistic and nationalistic tendencies. Senator Joseph R. McCarthy built his career out of hunting Communists and other alleged subversive foreign influences. In this he was aided by such men as Senators William E. Jenner of Indiana and Everett M. Dirksen of Illinois. Senator Robert A. Taft of Ohio suggested that American forces should be pulled back to American shores. He was supported in this by Robert R. McCormick of the Chicago *Tribune* who usually had an isolationistic approach. Senator John W. Bricker of Ohio wanted to reduce American participation in international affairs by limiting the president's powers in the making of military, political, or economic agreements with foreign nations. Similarly, Senator Homer E. Capehart of Indiana opposed a meeting between President Dwight D. Eisenhower and Nikita Kruschev of Russia in 1959 because he felt it was somehow a compromise of American nationalism and honor. Moreover, a study of the voting records of congressmen in the House of Representatives between 1933 and 1950 revealed that the Midwest had five of the six most isolationistic states in the Union. In the Senate the Midwest had the first four in isolationism; and in both the House and Senate, North Dakota was the most isolationist of all and Kansas was third.

Yet at the same time, the Midwest had leaders like William A. White and Senator Arthur H. Vandenberg of Michigan who favored internationalism.

Any statement of the Midwest position in international affairs after 1935 would have to be very indefinite. There were pockets of isolationism, nationalism, and nativism glossed over by a grudging internationalism. Although many midwesterners undoubtedly would have liked to forget the problems of the rest of the world, they felt it unsafe to do so. With improvements in transportation and communication, the world was becoming relatively smaller. And just as the United States no longer felt safe behind its oceans, the Midwest no longer felt safe in its interior position in the United States.

In midwestern education after 1935, the major trends continued to be increasing student bodies. Although increasing population was partially responsible for larger numbers of students, the fact that a larger percentage of the school-age population was attending school was also important. In 1970, for example, 94.8

per cent of the 14-17 year old population was enrolled in school. In this same year, the Midwest had 14,903,000 students in elementary and secondary schools (29 per cent of the U. S. total).

Also during the period, the problem of trying to apply the separation-of-church-and-state doctrine to schools became especially acute. In a few midwestern states, public funds could be used to transport students to parochial schools. A particularly knotty problem involved the teaching of religion in the schools. A bell-wether case in this area was the McCollum case (1949) in Champaign, Illinois. In this decision the United States Supreme Court ruled that students could not attend classes in religion in the public schools on released time. The Champaign county court interpreted this to mean that students could use released time for religious instruction if the classes did not meet in the public-school buildings. The Supreme Court later gave a ruling in line with the Champaign court interpretation in the *Zorach* v. *Clauson* case in New York in 1951.

Another educational problem that was of somewhat less importance in the Middle West than in the South was integration of Negroes and whites in the schools. In the areas where Negroes were concentrated in the Midwest, the school boards and city officials generally kept the races separated by property and school zoning. In most areas there were such a few Negroes that they were allowed to attend the predominantly white schools. It is interesting to note, however, that the Brown case of 1954 which was one of the cases cited in the reversal of the "separate but equal" doctine of 1895 concerned a family in Topeka, Kansas, on the southern edge of the Midwest.

In many respects, the average school today is much like its counterpart of a generation ago. Some educators believe that standards of education have risen and others feel they have declined. It is true that teachers now have more training and usually there are better facilities, libraries, and more compehensive course offerings. However, the simple fact of mass education may mean that standards have had to drop in order to get a larger number of students through twelve years of school. Although it is true that more people get a little education today and better means of technology and communication make more information available, the quality of the educated person today is not necessarily higher than formerly. The more thorough learning of less material fostered an exactness of knowledge which allowed a freedom and accuracy in expression. On written examinations the scholars of a generation earlier would have compared very favorably with those of the pesent day in preciseness of definition and in an ability to tell what they knew. The unintelligent students are no worse than they were. They just stay in school longer now and are more noticeable.

The quality and quantity of literature in the Midwest after 1935 probably declined. Although authors and playrights such as James Thurber, Louis Bromfield, Lloyd C. Douglass, Charles A. Beard, Claude G. Bower, Carl Sandburg, Carl Van Doren, Ernest Hemingway, James T. Farrell, Edna Ferber, McKinley Kantor, Sinclair Lewis, William Inge, and Willa Cather continued to produce after 1935, their production declined and few talented young authors arose on the literary horizon to replace them. Some of the leading works of Midwest authors after 1940 included James Thurber, *The Male Animal;* Louis Bromfield, *Wild is the River;* Lloyd C. Douglas, *The Big Fisherman;* Charles A. Beard,*Roosevelt and the Coming of the War 1941;* Carl Sandburg,*Abraham Lincoln;* Ernest Hemingway, *The Old Man and the Sea;* James T. Farrell, *Studs Lonigan;* Edna Ferber, *Saratoga Tunk;* MacKinley Kantor, *Andersonville;* Sinclair Lewis, *The Godseeker,* and William Inge, *Bus Stop* and *Picnic.*

In addition to books, the Midwest also had a large number of newspapers and periodicals. In 1970 the Midwest had 577 daily newspapers, 33 per cent of the United States total. The per centage of U. S. weekly newspapers in the Midwest was even higher. The Midwest had an equally large percentage of the nation's 9,573 periodicals.

Probably the most important development in recreation during the generation prior to 1970 was television. Television caused families to stay at home a bit more. It also made possible better entertainment for a much larger number of the American people. And as it was noted earlier, TV, more than any other one factor, has contributed to making the United States one nation culturally and reducing regional and local differences.

SELECTED BIBLIOGRAPHY*

*This bibliography is divided into three parts. There are General References which contain bibliography covering the whole book. Second, there are General References by Chronological Period which individually cover each of the six sections of the book. Third, there are Topical References which cover particular topics discussed throughout the whole book. Thus to determine the full bibliographical coverage for any particular topic, one should consult the General References, the General References by Chronological Period, and the Topical References.

General References

Alvord, Clarence W., ed., *The Centennial History of Illinois,* 5 vols., Springfield, Illinois, 1920.

Bald, Frederick C., *Michigan in Four Centuries,* New York, 1961.

Banta, Richard E., *The Ohio,* New York, 1949.

Barnhart, John D., and Carmony, Donald R., *Indiana: From Frontier to Industrial Commonwealth,* New York, 1954.

Beard, Charles A. and Mary R., *The Rise of American Civilization,* 3 vols., New York, 1939.

Bemis, Samuel F., *A Diplomatic History of the United States,* New York, 1965.

Billington, Ray A., *The American Frontier,* Washington, 1965.

———, *Westward Expansion: A History of the American Frontier,* New York, 1949.

Blegen, Theodore C., *Minnesota: A History of the State,* Minneapolis, 1963.

Bracke, William B., *Wheat Country,* New York, 1950.

Briggs, Harold E., *Frontiers of the Northwest: A History of the Upper Missouri Valley,* New York, 1940.

Brown, Ralph H., *Historical Geography of the United States,* New York, 1948.

Clark, Dan E., *The Middle West in American History,* New York, 1966.

Cole, Cyrenus, *Iowa Through the Years,* Iowa City, 1940.

Derleth, August, *The Wisconsin: River of a Thousand Isles,* New York, 1942.

De Voto, Bernard, *The Course of Empire,* Boston, 1952.

Dick, Everett N., *Tales of the Frontier; from Lewis and Clark to the Last Roundup,* Lincoln, 1963.

Dunbar, Willis F., *Michigan: A History of the Wolverine State,* Grand Rapids, 1965.

Dunn, James T., *The St. Croix,* New York, 1965.

Dwelle, Jessie M., *Iowa Beautiful Land: A History of Iowa,* Mason City, Iowa, 1954.

Ellet, Charles, *The Mississippi and Ohio Rivers,* New York, 1970.

Esarey, Logan, *A History of Indiana,* 2 vols., Ft. Wayne, 1924.

Fish, Herbert C., and Black, R. M., *Brief History of North Dakota,* New York, 1925.

Folwell, William W., *A History of Minnesota,* 2 vols., St. Paul, 1961.

Gabriel, Ralph H., *The Lure of the Frontier,* New Haven, 1929.

Gephart, William F., *Transportation and Industrial Development in the Middle West,* New York, 1909.

Gray, James, *The Illinois,* New York, 1940.

Greene, Francis V., *The Mississippi,* New York, 1885.

Hatcher, Harlan, *Lake Erie,* New York, 1945.

Havighurst, Walter, *The Heartland: Ohio, Indiana, Illinois,* New York, 1962.

———, *Upper Mississippi: A Wilderness Saga,* New York, 1944.

Heizer, Alta H., *West to Ohio,* Yellow Springs, Ohio, 1954.

Hutton, Graham, *Midwest at Noon,* Chicago, 1946.

Jones, Evan, *The Minnesota,* New York, 1962.

Kazeck, Melvin E., *North Dakota: A Human and Economic Geography,* Fargo, 1956.

Kraenzel, Carl F., *The Great Plains in Transition,* Norman, 1955.

Landon, Fred, *Lake Huron,* New York, 1944.

McReynolds, Edwin C., *Missouri: A History of the Crossroads State,* Norman, 1962.

Masters, Edgar L., *The Sangamon,* New York, 1942.

Murray, John J., ed., *The Heritage of the Middle West,* Norman, 1958.

Nash, Roderich, *Wilderness and the American Mind,* New Haven, 1967.

Nute, Grace L., *Lake Superior,* New York, 1944.

Olson, James C., *History of Nebraska,* Lincoln, 1955.

Paxson, Frederic L., *History of the American Frontier, 1763-1893,* Boston, 1924.

———, *Last American Frontier,* New York, 1910.

Pease, Theodore C., *The Story of Illinois,* Chicago, 1965.

Peterson, William J., *The Story of Iowa,* New York, 1952.

Pierce, Bessie L., *A History of Chicago,* 3 vols., New York, 1937-1957.

Quaife, Milo M., *Lake Michigan,* New York, 1944.

———, and Glazer, Sidney, *Michigan: From Primitive Wilderness to Industrial Commonwealth,* New York, 1948.

Rammelkamp, Charles H., *Centennial History of Illinois College,* New Haven, 1928.
Raney, William F., *Wisconsin: A Story of Progress,* New York, 1940.
Richman, Irving B., *Ioway to Iowa,* Iowa City, 1931.
Riegel, Robert E., *American Moves West,* New York, 1964.
Robinson, Elwyn B., *History of North Dakota,* Lincoln, 1966.
Roosevelt, Theodore, *The Winning of the West,* 6 vols., New York, 1889-1896.
Roseboom, Eugene H., and Weisenberger, Francis P., *A History of Ohio,* Columbus, 1953.
Scheiber, Harry N., ed., *The Old Northwest: Studies in Regional History, 1787-1910,* Lincoln, 1969.
Schell, Herbert S., *History of South Dakota,* Lincoln, 1961.
Statistical Abstract of the United States, Washington, 1909-1971.
Steckmesser, Kent L., *Westward Movement,* New York, 1969.
Turner, Frederick J., *The Frontier in American History,* New York, 1920.
------, *The Significance of Sections in American History,* New York, 1932.
Vestal, Stanley, *The Missouri,* New York, 1945.
Viles, Jonas, *A History of Missouri,* New York, 1935.
White, William A., *The Changing West,* New York, 1939.
------, *Selected Letters of William Allen White, 1899-1943,* New York, 1968.
Wilson, William E., *Indiana: A History,* Bloomington, Indiana, 1966.
------, *The Wabash,* New York, 1940.
Wish, Harvey, *Society and Thought in America,* 2 vols., New York, 1950-1962.
Wittke, Carl F., ed., *The History of the State of Ohio,* 6 vols., Columbus, 1941-1944.
Wyman, Walker D., ed., *The Frontier in Perspective,* Madison, 1956.
Zornow, William F., *Kansas: A History of the Jayhawk State,* Norman, 1957.

General References By Chronological Period

I—Setting, Exploration, and Settlement to 1801

Abernethy, Thomas P., *Western Lands and the American Revolution,* New York, 1937.

Alden, John R., *The American Revolution, 1775-1783,* New York, 1954.

Alvord, Clarence W., *The Illinois Country, 1673-1818,* Springfield, Illinois, 1920.

———, *The Mississippi Valley in British Politics,* 2 vols., Cleveland, 1917.

Bailey, Kenneth P., *The Ohio Company of Virginia and the Westward Movement, 1748-1792,* Glendale, California, 1939.

Bakeless, John E., *Background to Glory: The Life of George Rogers Clark,* New York, 1957.

———, *Daniel Boone, Wilderness Scout,* New York, 1939.

Barnhart, John D., "A New Evaluation of Henry Hamilton and George Rogers Clark," *Mississippi Valley Historical Review,* XXXVII, March, 1951.

———, *Valley of Democracy: The Frontier versus the Plantation in the Ohio Valley, 1775-1818,* Bloomington, Indiana, 1953.

Beer, George L., *British Colonial Policy, 1754-1765,* New York, 1920.

Belote, Theodore T., *The Scioto Speculation and the French Settlement at Gallipolis,* Cincinnati, 1907.

Billington, Ray A., "The Historians of the Northwest Ordinance," *Illinois State Historical Society Journal,* XL, 1947.

Black, Glenn A., *Angel Site: An Archaeological, Historical, and Ethnological Study,* 2 vols., Indianapolis, 1967.

Blegen, Theodore C., *The Kensington Rune Stone: New Light on an Old Riddle,* St. Paul, 1968.

Bolton, Herbert E., and Marshall, Thomas M., *The Colonization of North America,* New York, 1920.

Bond, Beverley W., Jr., "An American Experiment in Colonial Government," *Mississippi Valley Historical Review,* XV, September, 1928.

———, *The Civilization of the Old Northwest: A Study of Political, Social, and Economic Development, 1788-1812,* New York, 1934.

———, *The Correspondence of John Cleves Symmes, Founder of the Miami Purchase,* New York, 1926.

———, *The Foundations of Ohio,* Columbus, 1941.

Bourne, Edward G., *Spain in America,* New York, 1904.

Boyd, Thomas, *Simon Girty, The White Savage,* New York, 1928.

Brandes, George M. C., *Ferdinand La Salle,* Westport, Connecticut, 1970.

Brebner, John B., *The Explorers of North America,* New York, 1933.

Burnet, Jacob, *Notes on the Early Settlement of the Northwest Territory,* New York, 1847.

Bushnell, Geoffrey H. S., *The First Americans: The Pre-Columbian Civilizations,* New York, 1969.

Caldwell, Norman W., *The French in the Mississippi Valley, 1740-1750,* Urbana, 1941.

Campbell, Marjorie W., *The North West Company,* New York, 1957.

Carter, Clarence E., *Great Britain and the Illinois Country, 1763-1774,* Washington, 1910.

Caruso, John A., *The Great Lakes Frontier: An Epic of the Old Northwest,* Indianapolis, 1961.

———, *The Mississippi Valley Frontier: The Age of French Exploration and Settlement,* Indianapolis, 1966.

Cox, Issac J., ed., *The Journeys of La Salle,* 2 vols., New York, 1905.

Crevecoeur, St. John de, *Letters From an American Farmer,* London, 1782.

Darlington, William M., ed., *Christopher Gist's Journals,* Louisville, 1898.

Delanglez, Jean, *Life and Voyages of Louis Joliet, 1645-1700,* Chicago, 1948.

Downes, Randolph C., *Council Fires on the Upper Ohio,* Pittsburgh, 1940.

———, "Dunmore's War: An Interpretation," *Mississippi Valley Historical Review,* XXI, December, 1934.

——————, *Frontier Ohio, 1788-1803,* Columbus, 1935.
——————, "Indian War on the Upper Ohio, 1779-1782," *Western Pennsylvania Historical Magazine,* XVII, June, 1934.
Eccles, William J., *Frontenac, The Courtier Governor,* Toronto, 1959.
——————, *The Canadian Frontier, 1534-1760,* New York, 1969.
Every, Dale V., *A Company of Heroes: The American Frontier, 1775-1783,* New York, 1962.
Flexner, James T., *George Washington: The Forge of Experience, 1732-1775,* Boston, 1965.
Garland, John H., ed., *The North American Midwest: A Regional Geography,* New York, 1955.
Gibson, Charles, *Spain in America,* New York, 1966.
Gipson, Lawrence H., *The British Empire Before the American Revolution,* 12 vols., New York, 1956-1965.
——————, *The Coming of the Revolution, 1763-1775,* New York, 1954.
Greene, Evarts B., *The Revolutionary Generation, 1763-1790,* New York, 1943.
Haworth, Paul L., *Trailmakers of the Northwest,* New York, 1921.
Heagney, Anne, *De Tonti of the Iron Hand and the Exploration of the Mississippi,* New York, 1959.
Hulbert, Archer B., ed., *The Records of the Original Proceedings of the Ohio Company,* 2 vols., Marietta, Ohio, 1917.
Hunt, George T., *The Wars of the Iroquois,* Madison, 1940.
Hunter, William A., *Forts on the Pennsylvania Frontier, 1753-1758,* Harrisburg, 1960.
James, Alfred P., *The Ohio Company: Its Inner History,* Pittsburgh, 1959.
James, James A., *The Life of George Rogers Clark,* Chicago, 1928.
Jensen, Merrill, "The Cession of the Old Northwest," *Mississippi Valley Historical Review,* XXIII, June, 1936.
——————, *The New Nation,* New York, 1950.
Jones, Gwyn, *The Norse Atlantic Saga,* New York, 1964.
Kellogg, Louise P., ed., *The British Regime in Wisconsin and the Northwest,* Madison, 1935.
——————, "The Fox Indian Wars during the French Regime," *State Historical Society of Wisconsin, Proceedings,* 1907.
——————, ed., *Early Narratives of the Northwest, 1634-1699,* New York, 1946.
——————, *French Regime in Wisconsin and the Northwest,* Madison, 1925.
——————, "Indian Diplomacy During the Revolution in the West," *Illinois State Historical Society Transactions,* XXXVI, 1929.
Kennedy, John H., *Jesuit and Savage in New France,* New Haven, 1950.
Kenton, Edna, *Simon Kenton,* New York, 1930.
Kinnaird, Lawrence, "The Spanish Against Fort St. Joseph in 1781, A New Interpretation," *Mississippi Valley Historical Review,* XIX, September, 1932.
Koontz, Louis K., *Robert Dinwiddie,* Glendale, California, 1940.
Long, John C., *Lord Jeffrey Amherst,* New York, 1933.
McCardell, Lee, *Ill-Starred General: Braddock of the Coldstream Guards,* Pittsburg, 1958.
Mackesy, Piers, *The War for America, 1775-1783,* Cambridge, 1764.
McLaughlin, Robert, *The Heartland: Illinois, Indiana, Michigan, Ohio, Wisconsin,* New York, 1967.
Marquis, Thomas G., *The Jesuit Missions,* Toronto, 1916.
Miller, John C., *The Federalist Era, 1789-1801,* New York, 1960.
Morris, Richard B., *The Peacemakers: The Great Powers and American Independence,* New York, 1965.
Munro, William B., *Crusaders of New France: A Chronicle of the Fleur-de-Lis in the Wilderness,* New York, 1918.
——————, *The Seigneurs of Old Canada,* Cambridge, 1920.
Nasatir, Abraham P., ed., *Before Lewis and Clark: Documents Illustrating the History of the Missouri, 1785-1804,* 2 vols., St. Louis, 1952.
Nettels, Curtis P., *The Emergence of a National Economy, 1775-1815,* New York, 1962.
Notestein, Wallace, *The English People on the Eve of Colonization, 1603-1630,* New York, 1954.
Nute, Grace L., *Caesars of the Wilderness,* New York, 1943.
Nye, Russell B., *The Cultural Life of the New Nation, 1776-1830,* New York, 1960.

Ogg, Frederic A., *The Old Northwest,* New Haven, 1921.
Parkman, Francis, *Conspiracy of Pontiac,* 2 vols., Boston, 1910.
——————, *Frontenac and New France,* Boston, 1903.
——————, *A Half Century of Conflict,* 2 vols., Boston, 1894.
——————, *The Jesuits in North America,* Boston, 1963.
——————, *La Salle and the Discovery of the Great West,* Boston, 1926.
——————, *Montcalm and Wolfe,* 2 vols., Boston, 1898.
——————, *Pioneers of France in the New World,* 2 vols., Boston, 1865.
Pattison, William D., *The Beginnings of the American Rectangular Land Survey System, 1784-1800,* Chicago, 1957.
Pease, Theodore C., and Werner, Raymond C., *The French Foundations, 1680-1693,* Springfield, Illinois, 1934.
Pease, Theodore C., "The Ordinance of 1787," *Mississippi Valley Historical Review,* XXV, September, 1938.
Peckham, Howard R., *The Colonial Wars, 1689-1762,* Chicago, 1964.
——————, *Pontiac and the Indian Uprising,* Princeton, 1947.
——————, *The War for Independence,* Chicago, 1958.
Pennsylvania Historical Commission, *The Papers of Colonel Henry Bouquet,* 3 vols., Harrisburg, 1940.
Philbrick, Francis S., *The Rise of the New West, 1754-1830,* New York, 1965.
Power, Richard L., *Planting Corn Belt Culture: The Impress of the Upland Southerner and Yankee in the Old Northwest,* Indianapolis, 1953.
Priestly, Herbert I., *The Coming of the White Man, 1492-1848,* New York, 1929.
——————, *France Overseas through the Old Regime,* New York, 1939.
Quaife, Milo M., *The Capture of Old Vincennes,* Indianapolis, 1927.
Richman, Irving B., *The Spanish Conquerers,* Cambridge, 1919.
Russell, Nelson V., *The British Regime in Michigan and the Old Northwest, 1760-1796,* Northfield, Minnesota, 1939.
Sears, Alfred B., *Thomas Worthington: Father of Ohio Statehood,* Columbus, 1958.
Semple, Ellen C., *American History and Its Geographic Conditions,* Cambridge, 1933.
Silverberg, Robert, *Mound Builders of Ancient America: The Archaeology of a Myth,* New York, 1968.
Smith, Henry N., *Virgin Land: The American West as Symbol and Myth,* Cambridge, 1950.
Smith, William H., ed., *The St. Clair Papers: The Life and Public Services of Arthur St. Clair,* 2 vols., Cincinnati, 1882.
Sosin, Jack M., *Revolutionary Frontier, 1763-1783,* New York, 1967.
——————, *Whitehall and the Wilderness: The Middle West in British Colonial Policy, 1760-1775,* Lincoln, 1961.
Steck, Francis B., *The Joliet-Marquette Expedition, 1673,* Quincy, Illinois, 1928.
Terrell, John U., *LaSalle: The Life and Times of an Explorer,* New York, 1968.
Theirs, Adolphe, *The Mississippi Bubble,* New York, 1969.
Thwaites, Reuben G., *Daniel Boone,* New York, 1902.
——————, *Father Marquette,* New York, 1902.
——————, *France in America, 1497-1763,* New York, 1905.
——————, *Frontier Defense on the Upper Ohio, 1777-1778,* Madison, 1912.
——————, *Frontier Retreat on the Upper Ohio, 1779-1781,* Madison, 1917.
——————, *The Revolution on the Upper Ohio, 1775-1777,* Madison, 1908.
——————, and Kellogg, Louise P., *Documentary History of Lord Dunmore's War,* Madison, 1905.
——————, *Frontier Advance on the Upper Ohio, 1778-1779,* Madison, 1916.
Van Alstyne, Richard W., *Empire and Independence: the International History of the American Revolution,* New York, 1965.
Van Tyne, Claude H., *Causes of the War of Independence,* Cambridge, 1922.
Volwiler, Albert T., *George Croghan and the Westward Movement, 1741-1782,* Cleveland, 1926.
Wadsworth, Wallace C., *Paul Bunyan and His Great Blue Ox,* New York, 1926.
Wainwright, Nicholas B., *George Croghan, Wilderness Diplomat,* Chapel Hill, 1959.
Wallace, Joseph, *The History of Illinois and Louisiana Under the French Rule,* Cincinnati, 1893.
Weaver, John E., and Albertson, Frederick W., *Grasslands of the Great Plains: Their Nature and Use,* Lincoln, 1956.

Wedel, Waldo R., *Prehistoric Man on the Great Plains,* Norman, 1961.
Wertenbaker, Thomas J., *The First Americans, 1607-1690,* New York, 1929.
Whitaker, Arthur P., *The Spanish-American Frontier,* Gloucester, Massachusetts, 1962.
Wildes, Harry E., *Anthony Wayne,* Westport, Connecticut, 1970.
Wright, Louis B., *The Cultural Life of the American Colonies, 1607-1763,* New York, 1957.
Wrong, George M., *The Rise and Fall of New France,* 2 vols., New York, 1928.

II—The Young Midwest, 1801-1841

Athearn, Robert G., *Forts of the Upper Missouri,* Englewood Cliffs, 1967.
Babcock, Kendric B., *The Rise of American Nationality, 1811-1819,* New York, 1906.
Bakeless, John, *Lewis and Clark, Partners in Discovery,* New York, 1954.
Boorstin, Daniel J., *The Americans: The National Experience,* New York, 1965.
Briggs, Harold E., *Frontiers of the Northwest,* New York, 1950.
Buck, Solon J., *Illinois in 1818,* Springfield, Illinois, 1917.
Buley, R. Carlyle, *Old Northwest: Pioneer Period, 1815-1840,* 2 vols., Bloomington, Indiana, 1962.
Caruso, John A., *The Great Lakes Frontier,* Indianapolis, 1961.
Clarke, Charles G., The Men of the Lewis and Clark Expedition: *A Biographical Roster of the Fifty-one Members and a Composite Diary of their activities from all known sources,* Glendale, California, 1970.
Coues, Elliott, ed., *History of the Expedition under the Command of Lewis and Clark,* New York, 1965.
Dangerfield, George, *The Awakening of American Nationalism, 1815-1828,* New York, 1965.
DeVoto, Bernard, ed., *The Journals of Lewis and Clark,* Boston, 1953.
Dillon, Richard, *Meriwether Lewis: A Biography,* New York, 1965.
Dondore, Dorothy A., *The Prairie and the Making of Middle America,* Cedar Rapids, 1926.
Eide, Ingvard H., *American Odyssey: The Journeys of Lewis and Clark,* Chicago, 1969.
Fish, Carl R., *The Rise of the Common Man, 1830-1850,* New York, 1935.
Fuller, Harlin M., and Hafen, LeRoy R., eds., *The Journal of Captain John R. Bell, Official Journalist for the Stephen H. Long Expedition to the Rocky Mountains, 1820,* Glendale, California, 1957.
Gilbert, Edmund W., *The Exploration of Western America, 1800-1850,* Cambridge, England, 1933.
Goetzmann, William H., *Army Exploration in the American West, 1803-1863,* New Haven, 1965.
Goodrich, Carter, *The Government and the Economy, 1783-1861,* Indianapolis, 1967.
Handlin, Oscar, *Fire-Bell in the Night,* Boston, 1964.
Hawgood, John A., *America's Western Frontiers,* New York, 1967.
Hollon, W. Eugene, *The Lost Pathfinder: Zebulon Montgomery Pike,* Norman, 1949.
Horsman, Reginald, *The Frontier in the Formative Years, 1783-1815,* New York, 1970.
Jackson, Donald, ed., *The Journals of Zebulon Montgomery Pike: With Letters and Related Documents,* Norman, 1966.
———, *Letters of the Lewis and Clark Expedition, with Related Documents, 1783-1854,* Urbana, 1962.
Kohlmeier, Albert L., *The Old Northwest as the Keystone of the Arch of American Federal Union: A Study in Commerce and Politics,* Bloomington, Indiana, 1938.
Krout, John A., and Fox, Dixon R., *The Completion of Independence, 1790-1830,* New York, 1944.
McCarty, Dwight G., *The Territorial Governors of the Old Northwest,* Iowa City, 1910.
Mason, Philip P., ed., *Schoolcraft's Expedition to Lake Itasca,* East Lansing, 1958.
Merk, Frederick, *Manifest Destiny and Mission in American History,* New York, 1963.
Moore, Glover, *The Missouri Compromise, 1819-1821,* Lexington, 1953.
North, Douglas C., *The Economic Growth of the United States, 1790-1860,* Englewood Cliffs, 1961.

Pease, Theodore C., *The Frontier State, 1818-1848,* Springfield, Illinois, 1918.
Pessen, Edward, *Jacksonian America: Society, Personality, and Politics,* Homewood, Illinois, 1969.
Philbrick, Francis, ed., *The Laws of Indiana Territory, 1801-1809,* Springfield, Illinois, 1930.
———, *The Laws of the Illinois Territory, 1809-1818,* Springfield, Illinois, 1950.
———, *The Rise of the West, 1754-1830,* New York, 1965.
Pike, Zebulon M., *An Account of Expeditions to the Sources of the Mississippi, 1810,* Ann Arbor, 1966.
Primm, James N., *Economic Policy in the Development of a Western State, Missouri, 1820-1860,* Cambridge, 1954.
Rawling, Gerald, *The Pathfinders: The History of America's First Westerners,* New York, 1964.
Schlesinger, Arthur M., Jr., *The Age of Jackson,* Boston, 1945.
Schoolcraft, Henry R., *Travels through the Northwestern Regions of the United States,* Ann Arbor, 1966.
Smelser, Marshall, *The Democratic Republic, 1801-1815,* New York, 1968.
Terrell, John U., *Zebulon Pike,* New York, 1968.
Tocqueville, Alexis de, *Democracy in America,* 4 vols., London, 1835-1840.
Turner, Frederick J., *Rise of the New West, 1819-1828,* New York, 1961.
———, *The Frontier in American History,* New York, 1920.
———, *The United States, 1830-1850,* New York, 1958.
Utter, William T., *The Frontier State, 1803-1825,* Columbus, 1942.
Van Deusen, Glyndon G., *The Jacksonian Era, 1828-1848,* New York, 1959.
Weinberg, Albert K., *Manifest Destiny: A Study of Nationalist Expansion in American History,* Gloucester, Massachusetts, 1958.
Weisenburger, Francis P., *The Passing of the Frontier, 1825-1850,* Columbus, 1944.
Wood, Richard G., *Stephen Harriman Long, 1784-1864: Army Engineer, Explorer, Inventor,* Glendale, California, 1966.

III—The Disruptive Period in the Midwest, 1841-1877

Abels, Jules, *Man on Fire: John Brown and the Cause of Liberty,* New York, 1971.
Billington, Ray A., *The Protestant Crusade, 1830-1860,* New York, 1938.
Cole, Arthur C., *The Era of the Civil War, 1848-1870,* Chicago, 1920.
———, *The Irrepressible Conflict, 1850-1865,* New York, 1934.
De Voto, Bernard, *The Year of Decision, 1846,* Boston, 1943.
Dickens, Charles, *American Notes,* New York, 1842.
Ehrlich, Leonard, *God's Angry Man,* New York, 1941.
Filler, Louis, *The Crusade Against Slavery, 1830-1860,* New York, 1960.
Hubbart, Henry B., *The Older Middle West, 1840-1880: Its Social, Economic and Political Life,* New York, 1936.
Johnson, Samuel A., *The Battle Cry of Freedom: The New England Emigrant Aid Society in the Kansas Crusade,* Lawrence, 1954.
Lewis, Henry, *The Valley of the Mississippi Illustrated,* St. Paul, 1967.
Malin, James C., *John Brown and the Legend of Fifty-Six,* Philadelphia, 1942.
———, *The Nebraska Question, 1852-1854,* Lawrence, 1953.
Martineau, Harriet, *Retrospect of Western Travel,* New York, 1969.
Marryat, Frederick, *A Diary in America,* Bloomington, Indiana, 1960.
Nevins, Allan, *The Emergence of Modern America, 1865-1878,* New York, 1928.
———, *Fremont, Pathmarker of the West,* New York, 1939.
Nichols, Alice, *Bleeding Kansas,* New York, 1954.
Randall, James G., and David, Donald, *The Civil War and Reconstruction,* Boston, 1961.
Rawley, James A., *Race and Politics: Bleeding Kansas and the Coming of the Civil War,* New York, 1969.
Shoemaker, Floyd C., "Missouri's Pro-slavery Fight for Kansas, 1854-1855," *Missouri Historical Review,* XLVIII, April, 1954; XLIX, October, 1954.

Turner, Frederick J., *The Significance of Sections in American History,* Gloucester, Massachusetts, 1959.
Woodward, Comer V., *Reunion and Reaction: The Compromise of 1877 and the End of Reconstruction,* Garden City, 1956.

IV—The Midwest Comes of Age, 1864-1900

Athearn, Robert G., *High Country Empire: The High Plains and the Rockies,* New York, 1960.
Atherton, Lewis E., *Main Street on the Middle Border,* Bloomington, Indiana, 1954.
Bogart, Ernest L., and Thompson, Charles M., *The Industrial State, 1870-1893,* Springfield, Illinois, 1920.
Clugston, W. G., "Kansas and the Essence of Typical America," *Current History,* XXV, September, 1912.
Dick, Everett N., *The Story of the Frontier,* New York, 1941.
Faulkner, Harold U., *Politics, Reform, and Expansion, 1890-1900,* New York, 1959.
Garland, Hamlin, *A Son of the Middle Border,* New York, 1917.
Garraty, John A., *The New Commonwealth, 1877-1890,* New York, 1968.
Goff, John S., *Robert Todd Lincoln: A Man in His Own Right,* Norman, 1969.
Hafen, LeRoy R., and Rister, Carl C., *Western America,* Englewood Cliffs, 1950.
Hamilton, Holman, "Versatility and Variety: Hoosier Literary, Political, and Diplomatic Prominence, 1871-1901," *Indiana Magazine of History,* LXV, June, 1969.
Hirshson, Stanley P., *Grenville N. Dodge: Soldier, Politician, Railroad Pioneer,* Bloomington, Indiana, 1967.
Kirkland, Edward C., *Industry Comes of Age: Business, Labor, and Public Policy, 1860-1897,* New York, 1961.
Klement, Frank L., *Clement L. Vallandigham and the Civil War,* Lexington, 1970.
Leech, Margaret, *In the Days of McKinley,* New York, 1959.
Price, Robert, *Johnny Appleseed,* Gloucester, Massachusetts, 1954.
Schlesinger, Arthur M., *The Rise of the City, 1878-1898,* New York, 1933.
Tarbell, Ida M., *The Nationalizing of Business, 1878-1898,* New York, 1946.
Turner, Frederick J., *Frontier and Section,* Englewood Cliffs, 1961.
Vestal, Stanley, *The Old Santa Fe Trail,* Boston, 1939.
Webb, Walter P., *The Great Plains,* Boston, 1931.

V—Progressivism, Conservatism, and Pragmatism in the Midwest, 1900-1940

Adams, Samuel H., *Incredible Era: The Life and Times of Warren Gamaliel Harding,* Boston, 1964.
Allen, Frederick L., *Only Yesterday,* New York, 1931.
———, *Since Yesterday: The Nineteen Thirties in America,* New York, 1940.
Ellis, Elmer, *Mr. Dooley's America,* New York, 1941.
Faulkner, Harold U., *The Decline of Laissez Faire, 1897-1917,* New York, 1951.
———, *From Versailles to the New Deal,* New Haven, 1950.
———, *The Quest for Social Justice, 1898-1914,* New York, 1937.
Goldman, Eric F., *Rendezvous with Destiny: A History of Modern American Reform,* New York, 1952.
Harbaugh, William H., *Power and Responsibility: The Life and Times of Theodore Roosevelt,* New York, 1961.
Hicks, John D., *Republican Ascendancy, 1921-1933,* New York, 1960.
Hofstadter, Richard, *The Age of Reform: From Bryan to F.D.R.,* New York, 1955.
Leuchtenberg, William E., *Franklin D. Roosevelt and the New Deal, 1932-1940,* New York, 1963.
———, *The Perils of Prosperity, 1914-1932,* Chicago, 1958.
Link, Arthur S., *Woodrow Wilson and the Progressive Era,1910-1917,* New York, 1954.
Mitchell, Broadus, *Depression Decade: From New Era Through New Deal, 1929-1941,* New York, 1957.
Mowry, George E., *The Era of Theodore Roosevelt, 1900-1912,* New York, 1958.

———, *Theodore Roosevelt and the Progressive Movement,* Madison, 1946.
Murray, Robert K., *The Harding Era: Warren G. Harding and His Administration,* Minneapolis, 1969.
Nelli, Humbert S., *Italians in Chicago, 1880-1930: A Study in Ethnic Mobility,* New York, 1970.
Norris, George W., *Fighting Liberal: The Autobiography of George W. Norris,* New York, 1945.
Rollins, Alfred B., Jr., ed., *Depression, Recovery, and War, 1929-1945,* New York, 1966.
Slosson, Preston W., *The Great Crusade and After, 1914-1928,* New York, 1930.
Soule, George H., *Prosperity Decade: From War to Depression, 1917-1929,* New York, 1947.
Sullivan, Mark, *Our Times: The United States,* 7 vols., New York, 1927.
Wector, Dixon, *The Age of the Great Depression, 1929-1941,* New York, 1948.

VI—The Midwest, 1940-1970

Billington, Ray A., *America's Frontier Heritage,* New York, 1966.
Brooks, John N., *The Great Leap: The Past Twenty Five Years in America,* New York, 1966.
Buchanan, Albert R., *The United States and World War II,* 2 vols., New York, 1964.
Galbraith, John K., *The Affluent Society,* Boston, 1958.
Goldman, Eric F., *The Crucial Decade and After: America, 1945-1960,* New York, 1961.
Hollon, W. Eugene, *The Great American Desert, Then and Now,* New York, 1966.
Janeway, Eliot, *The Struggle for Survival: A Chronicle of Economic Mobilization in World War II,* New Haven, 1951.
Jensen, Merrill, ed., *Regionalism in America,* Madison, 1952.
Mowry, George E., *The Urban Nation, 1920-1960,* New York, 1965.
Quinn, Edward, and Dolan, Paul J., eds., *The Sense of the Sixties,* New York, 1968.
Rovere, Richard H., *The Eisenhower Years,* New York, 1956.
Steinberg, Alfred, *The Man From Missouri: The Life and Times of Harry S. Truman,* New York, 1961.
Vatter, Harold G., *The U.S. Economy in the 1950's,* New York, 1963.

Topical References

Agriculture

Atherton, Lewis E., *The Cattle Kings,* Bloomington, Indiana, 1961.

Benedict, Murray R., *Farm Policies of the United States, 1790-1950,* New York, 1953.

———, and Stine, Oscar, *The Agricultural Commodity Programs: Two Decades of Experience,* New York, 1955.

Benson, Ezra T., *Freedom to Farm,* Garden City, 1960.

Bidwell, Percy W., and Falconer, John I., *History of Agriculture in the Northern United States, 1820-1860,* Washington, 1925.

Bogue, Allen G., *From Prairie to Corn Belt: Farming on the Illinois and Iowa Prairies in the Nineteenth Century,* Chicago, 1968.

Clark, John G., "The Antibellum Grain Trade of New Orleans: Changing Patterns in the Relation of New Orleans with the Old Northwest," *Agricultural History,* XXXVIII, July, 1964.

———, *The Grain Trade in the Old Northwest,* Urbana, 1966.

Clark, William H., *Farms and Farmers: The Story of American Agriculture,* Freeport, New York, 1970.

Clawson, Marion, *The Western Range Livestock Industry,* New York, 1950.

Dale, Edward E., *Cow Country,* Norman, 1965.

———, *The Range Cattle Industry,* Norman, 1930.

Drache, Hiram M., *The Day of the Bonanza: A History of Bonanza Farming in the Red River Valley of the North,* Fargo, 1964.

Drago, Harry A., *Great American Cattle Trails,* New York, 1965.

Dykstra, Robert R., *The Cattle Towns,* New York, 1968.

Fite, Gilbert C., *American Agriculture and Farm Policy Since 1900,* New York, 1964.

———, *The Farmer's Frontier, 1865-1900,* New York, 1966.

———, *George N. Peek and the Fight for Farm Parity,* Norman, 1954.

Frantz, Joe B., and Choate, Julian E., Jr., *The American Cowboy: The Myth and the Reality,* Norman, 1955.

Gates, Paul W., *Agriculture and the Civil War,* New York, 1965.

———, *The Farmer's Age: Agriculture, 1815-1860,* New York, 1960.

Hargreaves, Mary W. M., *Dry Farming in the Northern Great Plains, 1900-1925,* Cambridge, 1957.

Henlein, Paul C., *The Cattle Kingdom in the Ohio Valley,* Lexington, 1959.

Highbee, Edward C., *Farms and Farmers in an Urban Age,* New York, 1963.

Johnson, Vance, *Heaven's Table Land: The Dust Bowl Story,* New York, 1947.

Kile, Orville M., *Farm Bureau Movement,* New York, 1921.

Knudtson, Arvid C., and Cox, Rex W., *Upper Midwest Agriculture: Structure and Problems,* Minneapolis, 1962.

Lampard, Eric E., *The Rise of the Dairy Industry in Wisconsin,* Madison, 1963.

Leavitt, Charles R., "Transportation and the Livestock Industry in the Middle West to 1860," *Agricultural History,* VIII, January, 1934.

McCormick, Cyrus, *The Century of the Reaper,* Boston, 1931.

Malin, James C., "The Adaptation of the Agricultural System to Subhumid Environment," *Agricultural History,* X, July, 1936.

Matusow, Allen J., *Farm Policies and Politics in the Truman Years,* Cambridge, 1967.

Miller, Nyle H., and Snell, Joseph W., *Great Gunfighters of the Kansas Cowtowns, 1867-1886,* Lincoln, 1967.

Osgood, Ernest S., *The Day of the Cattleman,* Minneapolis, 1929.

Pelzer, Louis, *The Cattleman's Frontier, 1850-1890,* Glendale, California, 1936.

Rogin, Leo, *The Introduction of Farm Machinery in Its Relationship to the Productivity of Labor during the Nineteenth Century,* Berkeley, 1931.

Saloutos, Theodore, "The Agricultural Problem and Nineteenth Century Industrialism," *Agricultural History,* XXII, July, 1948.

———, "The New Deal and Farm Policy in the Great Plains," *Agricultural History,* XLIII, July, 1969.

———, *Twentieth Century Populism: Agricultural Discontent in the Middle West, 1900-1939,* Lincoln, 1951.
———, and Hicks, John D., *Agriculture Discontent in the Middle West, 1900-1939,* Madison, 1951.
Schafer, Joseph, *The Social History of American Agriculture,* New York, 1936.
Shannon, Fred A., *The Farmer's Last Frontier: Agriculture, 1860-1897,* New York, 1945.
———, "The Status of the Midwestern Farmer in 1900," *Mississippi Valley Historical Review: Journal of American History,* XXXVII, December, 1950.
Shapsmeier, Edward L. and Frederick H., *Henry A. Wallace of Iowa: The Agrarian Years, 1910-1940,* Ames, 1968.
Steckmesser, Kent L., *The Western Hero in History and Legend,* Norman, 1965.
Streeter, Floyd B., *Prairie Trails and Cow Towns,* Boston, 1936.
Taylor, Carl C., *The Farmers Movement, 1620-1920,* New York, 1953.
Thompson, James W., *A History of Livestock Raising in the United States, 1607-1860,* Washington, 1942.
Towne, Charles W., and Wentworth, Edward N., *Shepherd's Empire,* Norman, 1945.
Vestal, Stanley, *Short Grass Country,* New York, 1941.
Wilcox, Walter W., *The Farmer in the Second World War,* Ames, 1947.
———, and Cochrane, Willard W., *Economics of American Agriculture,* Englewood Cliffs, 1960.
Winters, Donald L., *Henry Cantrell Wallace as Secretary of Agriculture,* Urbana, 1970.

Architecture

Burchard, John, and Brown-Bush, Albert, *The Architecture of America,* Boston, 1961.
Kimball, Fiske, *American Architecture,* Indianapolis, 1928.
Eaton, Leonard K., *Two Chicago Architects and Their Clients: Frank Lloyd Wright and Howard Van Doren Shaw,* Cambridge, 1969.
Hines, Thomas S., Jr., "Frank Lloyd Wright—The Madison Years: Records versus Recollections," *Wisconsin Magazine of History,* L, Winter, 1967.
McCallum, Ian R. M., *Architecture, U.S.A.,* New York, 1959.
Mumford, Lewis, *Sticks and Stones,* New York, 1924.
Newcomb, Rexford, *Architecture of the Old Northwest Territory,* Chicago, 1950.
Starrett, William A., *Skyscrapers and the Men Who Build Them,* New York, 1928.
Tallmadge, Thomas E., *The Story of American Architecture,* New York, 1927.

Art and Sculpture

Bloch, E. Maurice, *George Caleb Bingham,* 2 vols., Berkeley, 1967.
Flexner, James T., *A Short History of American Painting,* Boston, 1950.
Geldzahler, Henry, *American Painting in the Twentieth Century,* New York, 1965.
Isham, Samuel, *The History of American Painting,* New York, 1942.
La Fallette, Suzanne, *Art in America from Colonial Times to the Present Day,* New York, 1929.
Larkin, Oliver W., *Art and Life in America,* New York, 1960.
Miller, Lillian B., *Patrons and Patriotism: The Encouragement of the Fine Arts in the United States, 1790-1860,* Chicago, 1966.
Mumford, Lewis, *The Brown Decades: A Study of the Arts in America, 1865-1895,* New York, 1931.
Neuhaus, Eugene, *The History and Ideals of American Art,* Stanford, 1931.
Novak, Barbara, *American Painting of the Nineteenth Century,* New York, 1969.
Taft, Lorado, *History of American Sculpture,* New York, 1930.

Communal Societies

Arndt, Karl J. R., "The Indiana Decade of George Rapp's Harmony Society, 1814-1824," *Proceedings of the American Antiquarian Society,* 80, 1971.
Bester, Arthur E., Jr., *Backwoods Utopias,* Philadelphia, 1950.

Brodie, Fawn M., *No Man Knows My History: The Life Story of Joseph Smith,* New York, 1945.
Cole, George D. H., *The Life of Robert Owen,* London, 1930.
Fisher, Vardis, *Children of God,* New York, 1939.
Flanders, Robert B., *Nauvoo, Kingdom on the Mississippi,* Urbana, 1965.
Hirshson, Stanley P., *The Lion of the Lord: A Biography of Brigham Young,* New York, 1969.
Holloway, Mark, *Heavens on Earth,* New York, 1966.
Johnson, Oakley C., *Robert Owen in the United States,* New York, 1970.
Leopold, Richard W., *Robert Dale Owen, A Biography,* Cambridge, 1940.
Lockwood, George B., *The New Harmony Movement,* Marion, Indiana, 1902.
Mumford, Lewis, *The Story of Utopias,* Gloucester, Massachusetts, 1959.
O'Dea, Thomas F., *The Mormons,* Chicago, 1957.
Shambaugh, Bertha M. H., *Amana, The Community of True Inspiration,* Iowa City, 1908.
Shaw, Albert, *Icaria,* New York, 1884.
Werner, Morris R., *Brigham Young,* New York, 1925.
West, Ray B., Jr., *Kingdom of the Saints,* New York, 1957.

Culture and Life

Adams, James T., *Provincial Society, 1690-1763,* New York, 1936.
Baritz, Loren, *The Culture of the Twenties,* Indianapolis, 1970.
Berman, Ronald, *America in the 1960's: An Intellectual History,* New York, 1968.
Brown, Harriet, *Grandmother Brown's Hundred Years, 1827-1927,* Boston, 1929.
Calhoun, Arthur W., *A Social History of the American Family,* 3 vols., Cleveland, 1917-1919.
Cherrington, Ernest H., *The Evolution of Prohibition in the United States,* Westerville, Ohio, 1920.
Clapesattle, Helen B., *The Doctors Mayo,* Minneapolis, 1941.
Dick, Everett, *Vanguards of the Frontier,* New York, 1941.
Flexner, Eleanor, *Century of Struggle: The Women's Rights Movement in the United States,* Cambridge, 1959.
Flexner, James T., *Doctors on Horseback: Pioneers of American Medicine,* New York, 1937.
Fox, Dixon R., ed., *Sources of Culture in the Middle West,* New York, 1934.
Gabriel, Ralph H., *The Course of American Democratic Thought,* New York, 1956.
Gard, Wayne, *Frontier Justice,* Norman, 1949.
Hague, John A., ed., *American Character and Culture,* DeLand, Florida, 1964.
Hofstadter, Richard, and Wallace, Michael, eds., *American Violence: A Documentary History,* New York, 1970.
Hostetler, John A., *Amish Society,* Baltimore, 1963.
Kirkland, Caroline M., *A New Home: or, Life in the Clearings,* New York, 1953.
Lerner, Max, *America as a Civilization: Life and Thought in the United States Today,* 2 vols., New York, 1957.
Lynd, Robert S. and Helen M., *Middletown,* New York, 1929.
——————, *Middletown in Transition,* New York, 1937.
Main, Jackson T., *The Social Structure of Revolutionary America,* Princeton, 1965.
Martineau, Harriet, *Society in America,* 3 vols., London, 1837.
Mecklin, John M., *The Ku Klux Klan: A Study of the American Mind,* New York, 1963.
Merz, Charles, *The Dry Decade,* Seattle, 1931.
Miller, James M., *The Genesis of Western Culture: The Upper Ohio Valley, 1800-1825,* Columbus, 1938.
Moore, Arthur K., *The Frontier Mind,* Lexington, 1957.
Morris, Lloyd R., *Postscript to Yesterday: American Life and Thought, 1896-1946,* New York, 1947.
Nevins, Allan, ed., *American Social History as Recorded by British Travellers,* New York, 1931.
Nye, Russell B., *The Cultural Life of the New Nation, 1776-1830,* New York, 1960.

Odegard, Peter, *Pressure Politics: The Story of the Anti-Saloon League,* New York, 1928.
O'Neill, William L., *American Society Since 1945,* Chicago, 1969.
———, *Everyone was Brave: The Rise and Fall of Feminism in America,* Chicago, 1969.
Ossoli, Sarah M., *Woman in the Nineteenth Century,* New York, 1968.
Pickard, Madge E., and Buley, Roscoe C., *The Midwest Pioneer, His Ills, Cures, and Doctors,* Crawfordsville, Indiana, 1945.
Riegel, Robert E., *American Feminists,* Lawrence, 1963.
Riesman, David, and Others, *The Lonely Crowd: A Study of the Changing American Character,* Garden City, 1953.
Sigerist, Henry E., *American Medicine,* New York, 1934.
Sinclair, Andrew, *Era of Excess: A Social History of the Prohibition Movement,* Boston, 1962.
Thomson, Gladys S., *A Pioneer Family: Birdbecks in Illinois, 1818-1827,* London, 1953.
Tyler, Alice F., *Freedom's Ferment: Phases of American Social History to 1860,* New York, 1944.
Wade, Richard C., *The Urban Frontier: The Rise of Western Cities, 1790-1830,* Cambridge, 1959.
Wattenburg, Ben I., *This U.S.A.: An Unexpected Family Portrait of 194, 067, 296 Americans Drawn from the Census,* Garden City, 1965.
Wector, Dixon, *The Saga of American Society: A Record of Social Aspiration, 1607-1937,* New York, 1937.
White, Morton G., *Social Thought in America: The Revolt Against Formalism,* New York, 1949.
Wilson, Raymond J., *In Quest of Community: Social Philosophy in the United States, 1860-1920,* New York, 1968.
Wright, Louis B., *Culture on the Moving Frontier,* Bloomington, Indiana, 1955.

Education

Archer, Richard L., *Secondary Education in the Nineteenth Century,* New York, 1966.
Blanshard, Brand, ed., *Education in the Age of Science,* New York, 1959.
Boone, Richard G., *A History of Education in Indiana,* New York, 1892.
Brickman, William W., and Lehrer, Stanley, eds., *John Dewey,* New York, 1965.
Butts, Robert F., and Cremin, Lawrence A., *A History of Education in American Culture,* New York, 1953.
Cremin, Lawrence A., *The Transformation of the School: Progressivism in American Education, 1876-1957,* New York, 1961.
Cubberly, Elwood P., *Public Education in the United States,* Boston, 1934.
Edwards, Newton, and Rickey, Herman G., *The School in the American Social O der,* Boston, 1947.
Fletcher, Robert S., *A History of Oberlin College from its Foundation Through the Civil War,* Oberlin, 1943.
Frazier, Franklin E., *Negro Youth at the Crossways,* Washington, 1940.
Goldman, Eric F., "J. Allen Smith: The Reformer and his Dilemma," *Pacific Northwest Quarterly,* July, 1944.
Good, Harry G., *A History of American Education,* New York, 1962.
Goodspeed, Thomas W., *Story of the University of Chicago,* Chicago, 1925.
Hofstadter, Richard, ed., *American Higher Education, A Documentary History,* Chicago, 1961.
Kandel, Isaac L., ed., *Twenty-five years of American Education,* New York, 1924.
Larsen, Lawrence M., *The Log Book of a Young Immigrant,* Northfield, Minnesota, 1939.
Nevins, Archie P., "The Kalamazoo Case," *Michigan History,* XLIV, 1960.
Noble, Stuart G., *A History of American Education,* New York, 1938.
Putnam, Daniel, *A History of the Michigan State Normal School,* Ypsilanti, 1899.
Sagendorph, Kent, *Michigan: The Story of the University,* New York, 1948.
Woody, Thomas, *A History of Women's Education in the United States,* 2 vols., Lancaster, Pennsylvania, 1929.

Fur Trade

De Voto, Bernard, *Across the Wide Missouri,* Boston, 1947.
Gates, Charles M., *Five Fur Traders of the Northwest,* St. Paul, 1965.
Lavender, David, *The Fist in the Wilderness,* New York, 1964.
Lawson, Murray G., *Fur: A Study in English Mercantilism, 1700-1775,* Toronto, 1943.
Oglesby, Richard E., *Manuel Lisa and the Opening of the Missouri Fur Trade,* Norman, 1963.
Phillips, Paul C., *The Fur Trade,* 2 vols., Norman, 1961.
Porter, Kenneth W., *John Jacob Astor, Business Man,* 2 vols., Cambridge, 1931.
Rich, Edwin E., *The History of the Hudson's Bay Company, 1670-1870,* 2 vols., London, 1958-1959.
Saum, Lewis O., *The Fur Trader and the Indian,* Seattle, 1965.
Stevens, Wayne E., *The Northwest Fur Trade, 1763-1800,* Urbana, 1928.
Sunder, John E., *The Fur Trade on the Upper Missouri, 1840-1865,* Norman, 1965.
Vandiveer, Clarence A., *The Fur Trade and Early Western Exploration,* Cleveland, 1929.

Indians

Babcock, Willoughby M., "Minnesota's Indian War," *Minnesota History,* XXXVIII, September, 1962.
Blair, Emma H., *Indian Tribes of the Upper Mississippi and the Great Lakes Region,* Cleveland, 1911.
Brandon, William, *The American Heritage Book of Indians,* New York, 1961.
Burns, Robert I., *The Jesuits and the Indian Wars of the Northwest,* New Haven, 1966.
Cole, Cyrenus, *I Am A Man—The Indian Black Hawk,* Iowa City, 1938.
Cooke, David C., *Tecumseh, Destiny's Warrior,* New York, 1959.
Debo, Angie, *A History of the Indians of the United States,* Norman, 1970.
Driver, Harold E., *Indians of North America,* Chicago, 1961.
Farb, Peter, *Man's Rise to Civilization as Shown by the Indians of North America from Primeval Times to the Coming of the Industrial State,* New York, 1968.
Foreman, Grant, *Indian Removal,* Norman, 1932.
———, *The Last Trek of the Indians,* Chicago, 1946.
Fritz, Henry E., *The Movement for Indian Assimilation, 1860-1890,* Philadelphia, 1963.
Gard, Wayne, *The Great Buffalo Hunt,* New York, 1959.
Graham, William A., *The Story of the Little Big Horn,* New York, 1926.
Grant, Bruce, *American Indians, Yesterday and Today,* New York, 1958.
Hagan, William T., *American Indians,* Chicago, 1961.
Harmon, George D., *Sixty Years of Indian Affairs, 1789-1850,* Chapel Hill, 1941.
Horsman, Reginald, *Expansion and American Indian Policy, 1783-1812,* East Lansing, 1967.
Huntington, Ellsworth, *Red Man's Continent,* New Haven, 1919.
Hyde, George E., *Indians of the High Plains,* Norman, 1959.
———, *Indians of the Woodlands: From Prehistoric Times to 1725,* Norman, 1962.
Jackson, Donald, ed., *Ma-Ka-tai-me-she-kia-kiak-Black Hawk: An Autobiography,* Urbana, 1955.
Jackson, Helen H., *A Century of Dishonor,* New York, 1881.
James, Alfred P., and Stolz, Charles M., *Drums in the Forest,* Pittsburgh, 1958.
Jones, Douglas C., *The Treaty of Medicine Lodge,* Norman, 1966.
Josephy, Alvin M., Jr., *The Indian Heritage of America,* New York, 1968.
Kinietz, W. Vernon, *The Indians of the Western Great Lakes, 1615-1760,* Ann Arbor, 1965.
Kinney, Jay P., *A Continent Lost—A Civilization War: Indian Land Tenure in America,* Baltimore, 1937.
Klinck, Carl F., *Tecumseh,* Englewood Cliffs, 1961.
Kuhlman, Charles, *Legend into History: The Custer Mystery,* Harrisburg, 1952.
Lowie, Robert H., *Indians of the Plains,* New York, 1954.
MacLeod, William C., *The American Indian Frontier,* New York, 1928.

Meriam, Lewis, and Others, *The Problem of Indian Administration,* Baltimore, 1928.
Monaghan, Jay, *Custer: The Life of General George Armstrong Custer,* Boston, 1959.
Mooney, James, *The Ghost-Dance Religion and the Sioux Outbreak of 1890,* Chicago, 1965.
Moorehead, Warren K., *The American Indian in the United States,* Andover, Massachusetts, 1914.
Oehler, Chester M., *The Great Sioux Uprising,* New York, 1959.
Olsen, James C., *Red Cloud and the Sioux Problem,* Lincoln, 1965.
Parsons, Elsie, *American Indian Life,* Lincoln, 1967.
Peake, Ora B., *A History of the United States Indian Factory System, 1795-1822,* Denver, 1954.
Priest, Loring B., *Uncle Sam's Stepchildren: The Reformation of United States Indian Policy, 1865-1887,* New Brunswick, 1942.
Prucha, Francis P., *American Indian Policy in The Formative Years: The Indian Trade and Intercourse Acts, 1790-1835,* Cambridge, 1962.
———, "Indian Removal and the Great American Desert," *Indiana Magazine of History,* LIX, December, 1963.
Quimby, George I., *Indian Life in the Upper Great Lakes: 11,000 B.C. to A.D. 1800,* Chicago, 1960.
Raymond, Ethel, *Tecumseh,* Toronto, 1915.
Rister, Carl C., *Border Command: General Phil Sheridan in the West,* Norman, 1944.
Roddis, Louis H., *The Indian Wars of Minnesota,* Cedar Rapids, Iowa, 1956.
Roe, Frank G., *The Indian and the Horse,* Norman, 1955.
———, *The North American Buffalo: A Critical Study of the Species in Its Wild State,* Toronto, 1951.
Sandoz, Mari, *The Battle of the Little Big Horn,* Philadelphia, 1966.
Stewart, Edgar I., *Custer's Luck,* Norman, 1955.
Tucker, Glenn, *Tecumseh: Vision of Glory,* Indianapolis, 1956.
Underhill, Ruth M., *Red Man's America,* Chicago, 1953.
Utley, Robert M., *Frontiersmen in Blue: The United States Army and the Indian, 1848-1865,* New York, 1967.
Vestal, Stanley, *Sitting Bull: Champion of the Sioux,* Boston, 1932.
Wissler, Clark, *Indians of the United States: Four Centuries of Their History and Culture,* Garden City, 1953.

Labor

Berman, Edward, *Labor and the Sherman Act,* New York, 1931.
Berstein, Irving, *The Lean Years: A History of the American Workers, 1920-1933,* New York, 1960.
Commons, John R., and Others, *History of Labour in the United States,* 4 vols., New York, 1918-1935.
David, Henry, *The History of the Haymarket Affair,* New York, 1936.
Dayton, Eldorous, L., *Walter Reuther,* New York, 1958.
Dulles, Foster R., *Labor in America,* New York, 1949.
Jernegan, Marcus W., *Laboring and Dependent Classes in Colonial America, 1607-1783,* New York, 1960.
Johnson, Edward W., *Sinclair,* Macomb, Illinois, 1967.
Karson, Marc, *American Labor Unions and Politics, 1900-1918,* Carbondale, Illinois, 1958.
Kingdon, Frank, *An Uncommon Man: Henry Wallace and Sixty Million Jobs,* New York, 1945.
Lee, R. Alton, *Truman and Taft-Hartley,* Lexington, 1966.
Lens, Sidney, *The Crisis of American Labor,* New York, 1959.
Lindsey, Almont, *The Pullman Strike,* Chicago, 1942.
McMurray, Donald L., *Coxey's Army: A Study of the Industrial Army Movement of 1894,* Seattle, 1968.
Madison, Charles, *American Labor Leaders,* New York, 1962.
Ozanne, Robert, *A Century of Labor-Management Relations at McCormick and International Harvester,* Madison, 1967.
Perlman, Selig, *A History of Trade Unionism in the United States,* New York, 1922.
Rayback, Joseph G., *A History of American Labor,* New York, 1959.

Seidman, Joel I., *American Labor from Defense to Reconversion,* Chicago, 1953.
Sinclair, Upton, *The Jungle,* New York, 1906.
Taft, Philip, *Oragnized Labor in American History,* New York, 1964.
Ware, Norman J., *The Industrial Worker, 1840-1860,* Chicago, 1964.
———, *The Labor Movement in the United States, 1860-1895,* New York, 1929.
Wesley, Charles H., *Negro Labor in the United States, 1850-1925,* New York, 1927.

Literature

Anderson, David D., *Sherwood Anderson: An Introduction and Interpretation,* New York, 1967.
Baker, Sheridan W., *Ernest Hemingway: An Introduction and Interpretation,* New York, 1967.
Bowden, Edwin T., *James Thurber,* Columbus, 1968.
Brooks, Van Wyck, *The Confident Years, 1885-1915,* New York, 1952.
———, *Howells: His Life and World,* New York, 1959.
Carter, Everett, *Howells and the Age of Realism,* Hamden, Connecticut, 1954.
Cooke, Delmar G., *William Dean Howells: A Critical Study,* New York, 1967.
Curti, Merle E., *American Scholarship in the Twentieth Century,* Cambridge, 1953.
———, *The Growth of American Thought,* New York, 1964.
DeVoto, Bernard A., *Mark Twain's America,* Cambridge, 1951.
Dooley, David J., *The Art of Sinclair Lewis,* Lincoln, 1967.
Elias, Robert H., *Theodore Dreiser, Apostle of Nature,* New York, 1949.
Fussell, Edwin S., *Frontier: American Literature and the American West,* Princeton, 1965.
Hazard, Lucy L., *The Frontier in American Literature,* New York, 1961.
Holloway, Jean, *Hamlin Garland: A Biography,* Austin, 1960.
Hough, Robert L., *The Quiet Rebel: William Dean Howells as Social Commentator,* Lincoln, 1959.
Howe, Irving, *Sherwood Anderson,* Stanford, 1966.
Kenner, Hugh, ed., *T. S. Eliot,* Englewood Cliffs, 1962.
Kirkpatrick, John E., *Timothy Flint, Pioneer, Missionary, Author, Editor 1740-1840,* Cleveland, 1911.
Masters, Edgar Lee, *Mark Twain,* New York, 1966.
Moers, Ellen, *Two Dreisers,* New York, 1969.
Parrington, Vernon L., *Main Currents in American Thought,* New York, 1958.
Pattee, Fred L., *A History of American Literature Since 1870,* New York, 1915.
———, *The New American Literature, 1890-1930,* New York, 1930.
Randel, William P., *Edward Eggleston,* Gloucester, Massachusetts, 1962.
Rusk, Ralph L., *The Literature of the Middle Western Frontier,* 2 vols., New York, 1925.
Schorer, Mark, *Sinclair Lewis: An American Life,* Englewood Cliffs, 1962.
Spiller, Robert E., *The Cycle of American Literature,* New York, 1959.
———, and Others, ed., *Literary History of the United States,* New York, 1963.
Tyler, Moses C., *A History of American Literature, 1607-1783,* Chicago, 1967.
Wagenknecht, Edward, *Mark Twain: The Man and His Work,* Norman, 1967.
Wolford, Thorp L., "Edward Eggleston: Evolution of a Historian," *Indiana Magazine of History,* LXIII, 1967.
Woodress, James L., *Booth Tarkington,* New York, 1955.

Lumbering

Defebaugh, James E., *History of the Lumber Industry of America,* 4 vols., Chicago, 1906-1909.
Holbrook, Stewart H., *Yankee Loggers: A Recollection of Woodsmen, Cooks, and River Drivers,* New York, 1961.
Maybee, Rolland H., *Michigan's White Pine Era, 1840-1900,* Lansing, 1960.
Perry, Josephine, and Slauson, Celeste, *Forestry and Lumbering,* New York, 1939.

Manufacturing

Berglund, Abraham, *The United States Steel Corporation,* New York, 1907.
Bishop, John L., *A History of American Manufactures From 1608 to 1860,* 3 vols., Philadelphia, 1861-1868.
Bowden, Witt, *The Industrial History of the United States,* New York, 1930.
Buder, Stanley, *Pullman: An Experiment in Industrial Order and Community Planning, 1880-1930,* New York, 1967.
Clark, Victor S., *History of Manufacturers in the United States,* 2 vols., New York, 1929.
Clemen, Rudolf A., *The American Livestock and Meat Industry,* New York, 1923.
Cochran, Thomas C., and Miller, William, *The Age of Enterprise,* New York, 1942.
Cochran, Thomas C., *The American Business System: A Historical Perspective, 1900-1955,* Cambridge, 1957.
Commons, John R., ed., *Docurentary History of American Industrial Society,* 10 vols., Cleveland, 1909-1911.
Dorfman, Joseph, *Thorstein Veblen and His America,* New York, 1966.
Firestone, Harvey S., Jr., *Man on the Move,* New York, 1967.
Goff, John S., *Robert Todd Lincoln: A Man In His Own Right,* Norman, 1968.
Hendrick, Burton J., *The Age of Big Business,* New Haven, 1919.
Hidy, Ralph W. and Muriel E., *Pioneering in Big Business, 1882-1927: History of the Standard Oil Company,* 2 vols., New York, 1955-1956.
Holbrook, Stewart H., *Machines of Plenty,* New York, 1955.
Hutchinson, William T., *Cyrus Hall McCormick, 1809-84,* 2 vols., New York, 1930-1935.
Josephson, Matthew, *The Robber Barons, The Great American Capitalists, 1881-1901,* New York, 1934.
Kaempffert, Waldemar B., *A Popular History of American Invention,* 2 vols., New York, 1924.
Kuhlmann, Charles B., *Development of the Flour Milling Industry in the United States,* Boston, 1929.
Leech, Harper, and Carroll, John C., *Armour and His Times,* New York, 1938.
Lief, Alfred, *The Firestone Story: A History of the Firestone Tire and Rubber Company,* New York, 1951.
Lippincott, Isaac, *A History of Manufactures in the Ohio Valley to the Year 1860,* New York, 1914.
Nevins, Allan, *John D. Rockefeller,* 2 vols., New York, 1940.
Oliver, John W., *History of American Technology,* New York, 1956.
Smith, Joseph R., *The Story of Iron and Steel,* New York, 1918.
Tarbell, Ida M., *The History of the Standard Oil Company,* 2 vols., New York, 1904.
———, *The Life of Elbert H. Gary,* New York, 1925.
Walton, Francis, *Miracle of World War II: How American Industry Made Victory Possible,* New York, 1956.

Mining

Benedict, C. Harry, *Red Metal,* Ann Arbor, 1952.
Briggs, Harold E., "The Black Hills Gold Rush," *North Dakota Historical Quarterly,* V, January, 1931.
Greever, William S., *The Bonanza West: The Story of the Western Mining Rushes, 1848-1900,* Norman, 1963.
Holbrook, Stewart H., *Iron Brew: A Century of American Ore and Steel,* New York, 1939.
Parker, Watson, *Gold in the Black Hills,* Norman, 1966.
Rickard, Thomas A., *A History of American Mining,* New York, 1932.
Shinn, Charles H., *The Story of the Mine,* New York, 1901.

Money and Banking

Bogue, Allan G., *Money at Interest: The Farm Mortgage on the Middle Border,* Lincoln, 1969.

Dewey, Davis R., *Financial History of the United States,* New York, 1936.
Friedman, Milton, and Schwartz, Anna, *A Monetary History of the United States, 1867-1960,* Princeton, 1963.
Greer, Thomas H., "Economic and Social Effects of the Depression in the Old Northwest," *Indiana Magazine of History,* XLIV, September, 1948.
Hammond, Bray, *Banks and Politics in America from the Revolution to the Civil War,* Princeton, 1957.
Hepburn, Alonzo B., *A History of Currency in the United States,* New York, 1924.
Holmans, A. E., *United States Fiscal Policy, 1945-1959,* London, 1961.
Johnson, Gove G., Jr., *The Treasury and Monetary Policy, 1933-1938,* Cambridge, 1939.
McCrane, Reginald C., *The Panic of 1837,* Chicago, 1924.
Scott, William A., *The Repudiation of State Debts,* New York, 1893.
Scroggs, William O., *A Century of Banking Progress,* Garden City, 1924.
Studenski, Paul, and Krooss, Herman E., *Financial History of the United States,* New York, 1952.
Unger, Irwin, *The Greenback Era: A Social and Political History of American Finance, 1865-1879,* Princeton, 1964.
Van Fenstermaker, J. Van, *The Development of American Commercial Banking, 1782-1837,* Kent, Ohio, 1965.
Warburg, Paul M., *The Federal Reserve System,* 2 vols., New York, 1930.
Willis, Henry P., *The Federal Reserve System,* New York, 1923.

Music

Chase, Gilbert, *America's Music: From the Pilgrims to the Present,* New York, 1966.
Davis, Ronald L., *A History of Opera in the American West,* Englewood Cliffs, 1965.
Ewen, David, *American Popular Songs from the Revolutionary War to the Present,* New York, 1966.
———, *Popular American Composers, From Revolutionary Times to Present,* New York, 1962.
Field, James J., *American Popular Music, 1875-1950,* Philadelphia, 1955.
Hare, Maud C., *Negro Musicians and Their Music,* Washington, 1936.
Heaps, Willard A., *The Singing Sixties: The Spirit of Civil War Days Drawn from the Music of the Times,* Norman, 1960.
Howard, John T., *Our American Music: Three Hundred Years of It,* New York, 1931.
Lang, Paul H., *One Hundred Years of Music in America,* New York, 1961.
———, ed., *Problems of Modern Music,* New York, 1960.
Lewiton, Mina, *John Philip Sousa, The March King,* New York, 1944.
Marrocco, William T., *Music in America,* New York, 1964.
Oliver, Paul, *The Story of the Blues,* Philadelphia, 1969.
Sanders, Mary A., *Our Songs,* New York, 1942.
Schuller, Gunther, *The History of Jazz,* New York, 1968.
Stearns, Marshall W., *The Story of Jazz,* New York, 1956.
Williams, Martin T., *The Jazz Tradition,* New York, 1970.

Negro

Bennett, Lerone, Jr., *Before the Mayflower: A History of the Negro in America, 1619-1964,* Baltimore, 1966.
Frazier, Edward F., *The Negro in the United States,* New York, 1957.
Goldston, Robert, *The Negro Revolution,* New York, 1968.
Harris, Louis, *The Negro Revolution in America,* New York, 1964.
Hopkins, Vincent C., *Dred Scott's Case,* New York, 1951.
Ladenburg, Thomas J., *The Black Man in the Land of Equality,* New York, 1969.
Litwack, Leon F., *North of Slavery: The Negro in the Free States, 1790-1860,* Chicago, 1961.
Logan, Rayford W., *The Negro in American Life and Thought,* New York, 1954.
Meier, August, *From Plantation to Ghetto,* New York, 1966.

———, *Negro Thought in America, 1880-1915: Racial Ideologies in the Age of Booker T. Washington,* Ann Arbor, 1963.
Myrdal, Gunnar, *An American Dilemma: The Negro Problem and Modern Democracy,* 2 vols., New York, 1944.
Quarles, Benjamin, *Lincoln and the Negro,* New York, 1962.
———, *The Negro in the Making of America,* New York, 1964.
Sarratt, Reed, *The Ordeal of Desegregation: The First Decade,* New York, 1966.
Voegeli, V. Jacque, *Free but not Equal: The Midwest and the Negro during the Civil War,* Chicago, 1967.
Woodson, Carter G., *A Century of Negro Migration,* Washington, 1918.
———, *Negro Makers of History,* Washington, 1968.
———, and Wesley, Charles H., *The Negro in Our History,* Washington, 1966.

Politics and Political Figures

Abels, Jules, *Out of the Jaws of Victory,* New York, 1959.
Allswang, John M., *A House for all Peoples: Ethnic Politics in Chicago, 1890-1936,* Lexington, 1971.
Anderson, Jack, and May, Ronald W., *McCarthy,* Boston, 1952.
Angle, Paul M., *Created Equal? The Complete Lincoln-Douglas Debates of 1858,* Chicago, 1958.
Baringer, William E., *Lincoln's Vandalia: A Pioneer Portrait,* New Brunswick, 1949.
Barnard, Ellsworth, *Wendell Willkie: Fighter for Freedom,* Marquette, Michigan, 1966.
Barnard, Harry, *Eagle Forgotten: The Life of John Peter Altgeld,* Indianapolis, 1938.
———, *Rutherford B. Hayes and His America,* Indianapolis, 1954.
Barnes, Gilbert H., *The Anti-Slavery Impulse, 1830-1844,* New York, 1933.
Bartholomew, Paul C., *The Indiana Third Congressional District: A Political History,* South Bend, 1970.
Beale, Howard K., *The Critical Year,* New York, 1930.
Bennett, David H., *Demagogues in the Depression: American Radicals and the Union Party, 1932-1936,* New Brunswick, 1969.
Berwanger, Eugene H., *The Frontier Against Slavery: Anti-Negro Prejudice and the Slavery Extension Controversy,* Urbana, 1967.
Beveridge, Albert J., *Abraham Lincoln, 1809-1858,* 2 vols., Boston, 1928.
Blackorby, Edward C., *Prairie Rebel: The Public Life of William Lemke,* Lincoln, 1963.
Blake, I. George, *Paul V. McNutt: Portrait of a Hoosier Statesman,* Indianapolis, 1966.
Bloan, John P., ed., *The Territorial Papers of the United States,* vol. XXVII, Washington, 1969.
Bolles, Blair, *Tyrant from Illinois: Uncle Joe Cannon's Experiment with Personal Power,* New York, 1951.
Bonadio, Felice A., *North of Reconstruction: Ohio Politics, 1865-1870,* New York, 1970.
Boorstin, Daniel J., *The Genius of American Politics,* Chicago, 1953.
Bowers, Claude G., *Beveridge and the Progressive Era,* Boston, 1932.
Brant, Irving, *James Madison: Commander in Chief, 1812-1816,* Indianapolis, 1961.
———, *James Madison: The President 1809-1812,* Indianapolis, 1956.
Brown, Stuart G., *Conscience in Politics: Adlai E. Stevenson in the 1950's,* Syracuse, 1961.
Bryan, William J. and Mary B., *The Memoirs of William J. Bryan,* Chicago, 1925.
Buck, Solon J., *The Agrarian Crusade, New Haven,* 1920.
———, *The Granger Movement,* Cambridge, 1913.
Buckmaster, Henrieta, *Let My People Go: The Story of the Underground Railroad and the Growth of the Abolition Movement,* Boston, 1959.
Burton, Theodore, *John Sherman,* Boston, 1906.
Caldwell, Robert G., *James A. Garfield,* New York, 1931.
Capers, Gerald M., *Stephen A. Douglas, Defender of the Union,* Boston, 1959.
Carter, Clarence E., ed., *The Territorial Papers of the United States,* 26 vols., Washington, 1934-1965.

Catt, Carrie C., and Shuler, Nettie R., *Woman Suffrage and Politics,* New York, 1923.
Chalmers, David M., *The Social and Political Ideas of the Muckrakers,* New York, 1964.
Chambers, William N., *Old Bullion Benton: Senator from the New West,* New York, 1970.
Clanton, O. Gene, *Kansas Populism,* Lawrence, Kansas, 1969.
Clark, James B., *My Quarter Century in American Politics,* 2 vols., New York, 1920.
Cleaves, Freeman, *Old Tippecanoe: William Henry Harrison and His Times,* New York, 1939.
Coletta, Paola E., *William Jennings Bryan,* 3 vols., Lincoln, 1969.
Cox, James M., *Journey Through My Years,* New York, 1946.
Croly, Herbert, *Marcus Alonzo Hanna,* New York, 1912.
Crunden, Robert M., *A Hero in Spite of Himself: Brand Whitlock in Art, Politics, and War,* New York, 1969.
Cullom, Shelby M., *Fifty Years of Public Service,* Chicago, 1911.
Cunningham, Raymond J., *The Populists in Historical Perspective,* Boston, 1968.
Daniels, Jonathan, *The Man of Independence,* Philadelphia, 1950.
Darrow, Clarence, *Story of My Life,* New York, 1932.
Davis, Kenneth S., *A Prophet in His Own Country: The Triumphs and Defeats of Adlai Stevenson,* Garden City, 1957.
Dawes, Charles G., *A Journal of the McKinley Years,* Chicago, 1950.
Debs, Eugene V., *Debs: His Life, Writings, and Speeches,* Girard, Kansas, 1908.
Destler, Chester M., *American Radicalism, 1865-1901,* Chicago, 1946.
DeWitt, Benjamin P., *The Progressive Movement,* Seattle, 1968.
Dillon, Merton L., "The Antislavery Movement in Illinois, 1824-1835," *Illinois State Historical Society Journal,* XLVII, 1954.
———, *Benjamin Lundy and the Struggle for Negro Freedom,* Urbana, 1966.
Downes, Randolph C., *The Rise of Warren Gamaliel Harding, 1865-1920,* Columbus, 1970.
Dumond, Dwight L., *Antislavery: The Crusade for Freedom in America,* Ann Arbor, 1961.
Durden, Robert F., *The Climax of Populism,* Lexington, 1965.
Eckenrode, Hamilton J., *Rutherford B. Hayes: Statesman of Reunion,* Port Washington, New York, 1957.
Fehrenbacher, D. E., "Lincoln, Douglas, and the Freeport Question," *American Historical Review,* LXVI, April, 1961.
Filler, Louis, *Crusaders for American Liberalism,* Yellow Springs, Ohio, 1939.
Fine, Nathan, *Labor and Farmer Parties in the United States, 1828-1928,* New York, 1961.
Fite, Emerson D., *The Presidential Campaign of 1860,* New York, 1911.
Fleischman, Harry, *Norman Thomas,* New York, 1964.
Foraker, Joseph B., *Notes of a Busy Life,* 2 vols., Cincinnati, 1916.
Fowler, Dorothy G., *John Coit Spooner,* New York, 1961.
Fuess, Claude M., *Carl Schurz,* New York, 1932.
Gilbertson, Catherine, *Harriet Beecher Stowe,* New York, 1937.
Ginger, Ray, *The Bending Cross: A Biography of Eugene Victor Debs,* New Brunswick, 1949.
Glad, Paul W., *McKinley, Bryan, and the People,* New York, 1963.
———, *The Trumpet Soundeth: William Jennings Bryan and His Democracy, 1896-1912,* Lincoln, 1960.
Gottfried, Alex, *Boss Cermak of Chicago: A Study of Political Leadership,* Seattle, 1962.
Graebner, Norman A., ed., *Politics and the Crisis of 1860,* Urbana, 1961.
Griffith, Robert, *The Politics of Fear: Joseph R. McCarthy and the Senate,* Lexington, 1970.
Gunderson, Robert G., *The Log Cabin Campaign,* Lexington, 1957.
Gwinn, William R., *Uncle Joe Cannon,* New York, 1957.
Harrison, Carter H., *Stormy Years,* Indianapolis, 1935.
Hart, Albert B., *Salmon Portland Chase,* Boston, 1917.
Haynes, Fred E., *James Baird Weaver,* Iowa City, 1919.
———, *Third Party Movements Since the Civil War,* New York, 1966.

Heckman, Richard A., *Lincoln vs Douglas: The Great Debate Campaign,* Washington, 1967.
Hesseltine, William B., *Ulysses S. Grant: Politician,* New York, 1935.
Hicks, John D., *The Populist Revolt,* Minneapolis, 1931.
Hockett, Homer C., *Western Influences on Political Parties to 1825,* Columbus, 1917.
Holt, James, *Congressional Insurgents and the Party System, 1909-1916,* Cambridge, 1967.
Hoogenboom, Ari, *Outlawing the Spoils: A History of the Civil Service Reform Movement, 1865-1883,* Urbana, 1968.
Hopkins, Vincent C., *Dred Scott's Case, 1951,* New York, 1967.
Hutchinson, William T., *Lowden of Illinois: The Life of Governor Frank O. Lowden,* 2 vols., Chicago, 1957.
James, Marquis, *Andrew Jackson, Portrait of a President,* Indianapolis, 1937.
Johannsen, Robert W., *Frontier Politics on the Eve of the Civil War,* Seattle, 1966.
———, *The Letters of Stephen A. Douglas,* Urbana, 1961.
Johnpoll, Bernard K., *Pacifist's Progress: Norman Thomas and the Decline of American Socialism,* Chicago, 1970.
Johnson, Tom L., *My Story,* New York, 1911.
Johnson, Walter, "Politics in the Midwest," *Nebraska History,* XXXII, 1951.
Jones, Stanley L., *The Presidential Election of 1896,* Madison, 1964.
Josephson, Matthew, *The Politicos, 1865-1900,* New York, 1938.
King, Willard L., *Lincoln's Manager: David Davis,* Cambridge, 1960.
———, *Melville Weston Fuller,* Chicago, 1967.
Knoles, George H., *The Presidential Campaign and Election of 1892,* Stanford, California, 1942.
La Follette, Belle C. and Fola, *Robert M. LaFollette,* New York, 1953.
LaFollette, Robert M., *An Autobiography,* Madison, 1913.
Lamar, Howard R., *Dakota Territory, 1861-1889: A Study of Frontier Politics,* New Haven, 1956.
Lambert, Oscar D., *Stephen Benton Elkins,* Pittsburgh, 1955.
Lief, Alfred, *Democracy's Norris,* New York, 1939.
Lindsey, David, *"Sunset" Cox, Irrepressible Democrat,* Detroit, 1959.
Litwack, Leon F., *North of Slavery: The Negro in the Free States, 1790-1860,* Chicago, 1967.
Livingston, William, *A History of the Republican Party,* Detroit, 1900.
Lord, Russell, *The Wallaces of Iowa,* Boston, 1947.
Lowitt, Richard, *George W. Norris: The Making of a Progressive, 1861-1912,* Syracuse, 1963.
Lunt, Richard D., *High Ministry of Government: Political Career of Frank Murphy,* Detroit, 1965.
McCann, Kevin, *Man From Abilene,* Garden City, 1952.
McCarthy, Eugene J., *The Year of the People,* Garden City, 1969.
McCoy, Donald R., *Landon of Kansas,* Lincoln, 1966.
MacKay, Kenneth C., *The Progressive Movement of 1924,* New York, 1947.
McLean, Joseph E., *William Rufus Day,* Baltimore, 1946.
McLaughlin, Andrew C., *Lewis Cass,* Boston, 1891.
McMurry, Donald L., *Coxey's Army,* Boston, 1929.
McNaughton, Frank, and Hehmeyer, Walter, *This Man Truman,* New York, 1945.
Magrath, C. Peter, *Morrison R. Waite, The Triumph of Character,* New York, 1963.
Malin, James C., "The Motives of Stephen A. Douglas in the Organization of Nebraska Territory," *Kansas Historical Quarterly,* XIX, 1951.
———, *The Nebraska Question, 1852-1854,* Lawrence, Kansas, 1953.
Martin, John B., *Adlai Stevenson,* New York, 1952.
Mason, Alpheus T., *William Howard Taft: Chief Justice,* New York, 1965.
Matusow, Allen J., *Joseph R. McCarthy,* Englewood Cliffs, 1970.
Maxwell, Robert S., *La Follette and the Rise of the Progressives in Wisconsin,* Madison, 1956.
———, *La Follette,* Englewood Cliffs, 1969.
Mayer, George H., *The Republican Party, 1854-1964,* New York, 1964.
Meigs, William M., *The Life of Thomas Hart Benton,* New York, 1970.
Merrill, Horace S., *Bourbon Democracy of the Middle West, 1865-1896,* Baton Rouge, 1967.

Miller, Zane L., *Boss Cox's Cincinnati: Urban Politics in the Progressive Era,* New York, 1968.
Morgan, Howard W., *William McKinley and His America,* Syracuse, 1963.
Morlan, Robert L., *Political Prairie Fire: The Nonpartisan League, 1915-1922,* Minneapolis, 1955.
Muller, Herbert J., *Adlai Stevenson: A Study in Values,* New York, 1967.
Nash, Howard P., *Third Parties in American Politics,* Washington, 1959.
Nettles, Curtis, "The Mississippi Valley and the Constitution, 1815-1829," *Mississippi Valley Historical Review,* XI, December, 1924.
Nevins, Allan, *The Emergence of Lincoln,* 2 vols., New York, 1950.
Nichols, Roy F., *The Disruption of American Democracy,* New York, 1948.
———, "The Kansas Nebraska Act: A Century of Historiography," *Mississippi Valley Historical Review,* XLIII, September, 1956.
———, "The Territories: Seedbeds of Democracy," *Nebraska History,* XXXIV, 1954.
Nugent, Walter T., *The Tolerant Populists,* Chicago, 1963.
Nye, Russell B., *Midwestern Progressive Politics, 1870-1958,* East Lansing, 1959.
Olcott, Charles S., *The Life of William McKinley,* 2 vols., Boston, 1916.
Parrish, William E., *David Rice Atchison of Missouri: Border Politician,* Columbia, 1961.
Pollack, Norman, *The Populist Mind,* Indianapolis, 1967.
———, *The Populist Response to Industrial America,* New York, 1962.
Pomeroy, Earl S., *The Territories of the United States 1861-1890: Studies in Colonial Administration,* Philadelphia, 1947.
Porter, Kirk H., *A History of Suffrage in the United States,* New York, 1969.
Pringle, Henry F., *The Life and Times of William Howard Taft: A Biography,* 2 vols., New York, 1964.
———, *Theodore Roosevelt,* New York, 1931.
Randel, William P., *The Ku Klux Klan,* Philadelphia, 1965.
Randell, James G., and Current, Richard, *Lincoln: The President,* 4 vols., New York, 1945-1955.
Rice, Arnold S., *Ku Klux Klan in American Politics,* Washington, 1962.
Ridge, Martin, *Ignatius Donnelly: The Portrait of a Politician,* Chicago, 1962.
Roosevelt, Theodore, *Life of Thomas Hart Benton,* Boston, 1887.
Rosenberg, Morton M., "Iowa Politics and the Compromise of 1850," *Iowa Journal of History and Politics,* LVI, July, 1958.
Ross, Earle D., *The Liberal Republican Movement,* New York, 1919.
Rovere, Richard H., *Senator Joe McCarthy,* New York, 1959.
———, *Waist Deep in the Big Muddy: Personal on 1968,* Boston, 1968.
Russell, Francis, *The Shadow of Blooming Grove: Warren G. Harding and His Times,* New York, 1968.
Sage, Leland L., *William Boyd Allison: A Study in Practical Politics,* Iowa City, 1956.
Sageser, A. Bower, *Joseph L. Bristow: Kansas Progressive,* Lawrence, 1968.
Sandburg, Carl, *Abraham Lincoln,* 6 vols., New York, 1940.
Schapsmeier, Edward L. and Frederick H., *Henry A. Wallace,* 2 vols., Ames, 1970.
Scheele, Henry Z., *Charlie Halleck: A Political Biography,* New York, 1966.
Schlesinger, Arthur M., Jr., *The Age of Roosevelt,* 3 vols., Boston, 1957-1966.
Schmidt, Karl M., *Henry A. Wallace: Quixotic Crusade,* Syracuse, 1960.
Schruben, Francis W., *Kansas in Turmoil, 1930-1936,* Columbia, 1969.
Seidler, Murry B., *Norman Thomas: Respectable Rebel,* Syracuse, 1964.
Shannon, David A., *The Socialist Party of America: A History,* Chicago, 1967.
Sharkansky, Ira, *Regionalism in American Politics,* Indianapolis, 1969.
Siebert, Wilbur H., *The Mysteries of Ohio's Underground Railroads,* Columbus, 1951.
Sievers, Harry J., *Benjamin Harrison: Hoosier Statesman,* 2 vols., New York, 1962.
Simon, Paul, *Lincoln's Preparation for Greatness,* Norman, 1965.
Sinclair, Andrew, *The Available Man: Warren Gamaliel Harding,* New York, 1965.
Smith, Donald V., "The Influence of Foreign Born of the Northwest in the Election of 1860," *Mississippi Valley Historical Review,* XIX, September, 1932.
Smith, Elbert B., *Magnificent Missourian: The Life of Thomas Hart Benton,* Philadelphia, 1958.

Smith, Theodore C., *The Liberty and Free Soil Parties in the Northwest,* Cambridge, 1897.
———, *Life and Letters of James Abram Garfield,* 2 vols., New Haven, 1925.
Smith, Willard H., *Schuyler Colfax: The Changing Fortunes of a Political Idol,* Indianapolis, 1952.
Socolofsky, Homer E., *Arthur Capper: Publisher, Politician, Philanthropist,* Lawrence, 1962.
———, "Jacob Coxey: Ohio's Fairly Respectable Populist," *Kansas Quarterly,* I, Fall, 1969.
Stampp, Kenneth M., *Indiana Politics During the Civil War,* Indianapolis, 1949.
Steffens, Joseph L., *The Shame of the Cities,* New York, 1904.
Steiner, Gilbert Y., and Gove, Samuel K., *Legislative Politics in Illinois,* Urbana, 1960.
Stevens, Henry R., *The Early Jackson Party in Ohio,* Durham, North Carolina, 1957.
Thayer, William M., *From Log Cabin to the White House: The Life of James A. Garfield,* New York, 1908.
Thomas, Benjamin P., *Abraham Lincoln: A Biography,* New York, 1952.
Tocqueville, Alexis de, *Democracy in America,* 2 vols., New York, 1945.
Trefousse, Hans L., *Benjamin Franklin Wade, Radical Republican from Ohio,* New York, 1963.
Tull, Charles J., *Father Coughlin and the New Deal,* Syracuse, 1965.
Van Bolt, Roger H., "The Rise of the Republican Party in Indiana, 1855-1856," *Indiana Magazine of History,* LI, 1955.
Way, R. B., "The Mississippi Valley and Internal Improvements," *Mississippi Valley Historical Association Proceedings,* IV, 1910-1911.
Weisenburger, Francis P., *The Life of John McLean,* Columbus, 1937.
Werner, Morris R., *Bryan,* New York, 1929.
White, Horace, *The Life of Lyman Trumbull,* Boston, 1913.
White, William S., *The Taft Story,* New York, 1954.
Whitlock, Brand, *Forty Years of It,* New York, 1968.
Willard, Frances E., *Glimpses of Fifty Years,* Boston, 1889.
Williams, Charles R., *The Life of Rutherford Birchard Hayes,* 2 vols., Boston, 1914.
Williams, Thomas H., *Lincoln and the Radicals,* Madison, 1941.
Woodford, Frank B., *Lewis Cass: The Last Jeffersonian,* New Brunswick, 1950.

Population and Settlement

Adamic, Louis, *America and the Refugees,* New York, 1939.
Blegen, Theodore C., *Norwegian Migration to America,* 2 vols., Northfield, Minnesota, 1931-1940.
Clark, Dan E., "The Westward Movement in the Upper Mississippi Valley During the Fifties," *Mississippi Valley Historical Association Proceedings,* VII, 1913-1914.
Delano, Alonzo, *Life on the Plains and Among the Diggings,* Ann Arbor, 1966.
Dick, Everett, *The Lure of the Land: A Social History of the Public Lands from the Articles of Confederation to the New Deal,* Lincoln, 1970.
———, *Sod House Frontier, 1854-1890,* Lincoln, 1954.
Ellis, James F., *The Influence of Environment on the Settlement of Missouri,* St. Louis, 1929.
Faust, Albert B., *The German Element in the United States,* New York, 1927.
Fields, Harold, *The Refugee in the United States,* New York, 1938.
Gates, Paul W., *Fifty Million Acres: Conflicts over Kansas Land Policy, 1854-1890,* Ithica, 1954.
Hafen, Leroy R., and Others, *Western America: The Exploration, Settlement, and Development of the Region Beyond the Mississippi,* Englewood Cliffs, 1970.
Handlin, Oscar, *Imigration as a Factor in American History,* Englewood Cliffs, 1959.
———, *The Newcomers,* Cambridge, 1959.
———, *Race and Nationality in American Life,* Boston, 1957.
———, *The Uprooted: The Story (Epic) of the Great Migration That Made the American People,* Boston, 1951.
Hansen, Harry, *The Chicago,* New York, 1942.
Hansen, Marcus L., *The Atlantic Migration,* Cambridge, 1940.
———, *The Immigrant in American History,* Cambridge, 1940.

Havighurst, Walter, *Wilderness for Sale: The Story of the First Western Land Rush,* New York, 1956.
Hawgood, John A., *America's Western Frontiers, The Exploration and Settlement of the Trans-Mississippi West,* New York, 1967.
Hibbard, Benjamin H., *A History of the Public Land Policies,* Madison, 1965.
Higham, John, *Strangers in the Land: Patterns of American Nativism, 1860-1925,* New Brunswick, 1955.
Holbrook, Stewart H., *The Yankee Exodus: An Account of Migration from New England,* New York, 1950.
Hubbart, Henry C., "Pro-Southern Influences in the Free West, 1840-1865," *Mississippi Valley Historical Review,* XX, June, 1933.
Huebener, Theodore, *The Germans in America,* Philadelphia, 1962.
Lindquist, Emory, *Smoky Valley People: A History of Lindsborg, Kansas,* Lindsborg, 1953.
Robbins, Roy M., *Our Landed Heritage: The Public Domain,* Princeton, 1942.
———, "Preemption—A Frontier Triumph," *Mississippi Valley Historical Review,* XVIII, December, 1931.
Rohrbough, Malcolm J., *The Land Office Business: The Settlement and Administration of American Public Lands, 1789-1837,* New York, 1968.
Ruede, Howard, *Sod House Days: Letters from a Kansas Homesteader, 1877-1878,* New York, 1966.
Sakolski, Aaron M., *Land Tenure and Land Taxation in America,* New York, 1957.
Sandoz, Mari, *Old Jules,* New York, 1955.
Schermerhorn, Richard A., *These Our People: Minorities in American Culture,* Boston, 1949.
Smith, Charles H., *The Coming of the Russian Mennonites,* Chicago, 1927.
Spear, Allan H., *Black Chicago: The Making of a Negro Ghetto, 1890-1920,* Chicago, 1967.
Steen, Ivan D., "Cincinnati in the 1850's: As Described by British Travelers," *Bulletin of the Cincinnati Historical Society,* July, 1968.
Stephenson, George M., *A History of American Immigration,* Boston, 1926.
———, *The Political History of the Public Lands from 1840 to 1862,* Boston, 1917.
Treat, Payson J., *The National Land System, 1785-1820,* New York, 1920.
Warner, William L., and Srole, Leo, *The Social Systems of American Ethnic Groups,* New York, 1949.
Wittke, Carl F., *The Germans in America,* New York, 1967.
———, *Refugees of Revolution: The German Forty-Eighters in America,* Philadelphia, 1952.
———, *We Who Built America,* New York, 1939.

Press, Radio, and Television

Barnouw, Erik, *The Golden Web: A History of Broadcasting in the United States,* 2 vols., New York, 1968.
Bleyer, Willard G., *Main Currents in the History of American Journalism,* Boston, 1927.
Burlingame, Roger, *Don't Let Them Scare You: The Life and Times of Elmer Davis,* Philadelphia, 1961.
Evans, James F., *Prairie Farmer and WLS: The Burridge D. Butler Years,* Urbana, 1969.
Goldsmith, Alfred N., and Lescarboura, Austin C., *This Thing Called Broadcasting,* New York, 1930.
Jacobs, Norman, and Lazarsfeld, Paul, *Culture for the Millions: Mass Media in Modern Society,* Princeton, 1959.
Johnson, Walter, *William Allen White's America,* New York, 1947.
Miller, Lee G., *The Story of Ernie Pyle,* New York, 1950.
Mott, Frank H., *American Journalism,* New York, 1950.
Mott, Frank L., *A History of American Magazines, 1741-1850,* New York, 1930.
Rammelkamp, Julian S., *Pulitzer's Post-Dispatch, 1878-1883,* Princeton, 1967.
Rich, Everett, *William Allen White, The Man From Emporia,* New York, 1941.

Sevareid, Eric, *Not so Wild a Dream,* New York, 1946.
Walsh, Justin E., *To Print the News and Raise Hell! A Biography of Wilburn F. Storey,* Chapel Hill, 1968.

Recreation

Dulles, Foster R., *A History of Recreation: America Learns to Play,* New York, 1965.
Hampton, Benjamin B., *A History of the Movies,* New York, 1931.
Hornblow, Arthur, *A History of the Theatre in America From Its Beginnings To the Present Time,* New York, 1965.
Manchester, Herbert, *Four Centuries of Sport in America, 1490-1890,* New York, 1968.
Neely, Wayne C., *The Agricultural Fair,* New York, 1935.
Poggi, Jack, *Theater in America,* Ithaca, 1968.
Rosenberg, Bernard and White, David M., eds., *Mass Culture: The Popular Arts in America,* Glencoe, Illinois, 1957.
Seilhamer, George O., *History of the American Theatre,* New York, 1968.
Seldes, Gilbert V., *The Seven Lively Arts,* New York, 1924.
Towse, John R., *Sixty Years of the Theatre,* New York, 1916.
Weinberger, Julius, "Economic Aspects of Recreation," *Harvard Business Review,* Summer, 1937.
Werner, Morris R., *Barnum,* New York, 1927.

Religion and Reform

Addams, Jane, *Twenty Years at Hull House,* New York, 1910.
Bradford, Gamaliel, *Dwight L. Moody: A Worker in Souls,* New York, 1927.
Carter, Paul A., *The Decline and Revival of Social Gospel, 1920-1940,* Ithaca, 1956.
Cartwright, Peter, *Autobiography of Peter Cartwright: The Backwoods Preacher,* Cincinnati, 1856.
Chapman, J. Wilbur, *The Life and Work of Dwight L. Moody,* Boston, 1900.
Cleveland, Catharine C., *The Great Revival in the West, 1797-1805,* Chicago, 1916.
Cole, Charles C., Jr., *The Social Ideas of the Northern Evangelists, 1826-1860,* New York, 1966.
Cole, Stewart G., *The History of Fundamentalism,* New York, 1931.
Dillon, Merton L., *Elijah P. Lovejoy, Abolitionist Editor,* Urbana, 1961.
Dorn, Jacob H., *Washington Gladden: Prophet of the Social Gospel,* Columbus, 1967.
Farrell, John C., *Beloved Lady: A History of Jane Addam's Ideas on Reform and Peace,* Baltimore, 1967.
Findlay, James F., *Dwight L. Moody: American Evangelist, 1837-1899,* Chicago, 1969.
Fladeland, Betty L., "James G. Birney's Antislavery Activities in Cincinnati," *Historical and Philosophical Society of Ohio Bulletin,* IX, 1951.
———, *James Gillespie Birney: Slaveholder to Abolitionist,* Ithaca, 1955.
Gaustad, Edwin S., *A Religious History of America,* New York, 1966.
Greenbie, Sydney, *Hoof Beats to Heaven: A True Chronicle of the Life and Wild Times of Peter Cartwright, Circuit Rider,* Penobscot, Maine, 1962.
Handy, Robert T., ed., *The Social Gospel in America,* New York, 1966.
Hopkins, Charles H., *The Rise of the Social Gospel in American Protestantism, 1865-1915,* London, 1940.
Hudson, Winthrop S., *Religion in America,* New York, 1965.
Johnson, Charles A., *The Frontier Camp Meeting,* Dallas, 1955.
Linn, James W., *Jane Addams,* New York, 1935.
May, Henry F., *Protestant Churches and Industrial America,* New York, 1949.
Milburn, William H., *The Pioneers, Preachers and People of the Mississippi Valley,* New York, 1860.
———, *Rifle, Axe, and Saddlebags, and Other Lectures,* New York, 1857.
Nation, Carry A., *The Use and Need of the Life of Carry A. Nation,* Topeka, 1909.
Olmstead, Clifton E., *History of Religion in the United States,* Englewood Cliffs, 1960.
Schneider, Herbert W., *Religion in Twentieth Century America,* Cambridge, 1952.
Smith, Timothy L., *Revivalism and Social Reform in Mid-Nineteenth Century America,* New York, 1957.

Sperry, Willard L., *Religion in America,* Cambridge, England, 1948.
Stevens, Abe, *Compendious History of American Methodism,* New York, 1867.
Sweet, William W., *Religion on the American Frontier,* 4 vols., New York, 1931-1946.
———, *The Rise of Methodism in the West,* New York, 1920.
———, *The Story of Religion in America,* New York, 1939.
Thomas, Benjamin P., *Theodore Weld: Crusader for Freedom,* New Brunswick, 1950.
Thwaites, Reuben G., ed., *The Jesuit Relations, 1610-1729,* 73 vols., Cleveland, 1896-1901.
White, Edward A., *Science and Religion in American Thought,* Stanford, 1952.

Transportation

Ambler, Charles H., *A History of Transportation in the Ohio Valley,* Glendale, California, 1932.
Bald, Frederick C., *The Sault Canal Through 100 Years,* Ann Arbor, 1954.
Baldwin, Leland D., *The Keelboat Age on Western Waters,* Pittsburgh, 1941.
Barber, Herbert L., *The Story of the Automobile,* Chicago, 1927.
Blair, Walter, and Meine, Franklin J., *Mike Fink, King of the Mississippi Keelboatmen,* New York, 1933.
Chandler, Alfred D., *Giant Enterprise: Ford, General Motors, and the Automobile Industry,* New York, 1964.
Chrysler, Walter P., *Life of an American Workman,* New York, 1950.
Cochran, Thomas C., *Railroad Leaders, 1845-1890,* New York, 1966.
Conkling, Roscoe P. and Margaret B., *The Butterfield Overland Mail, 1857-1869,* 3 vols., Glendale, California, 1947.
Crawford, Jay B., *The Credit Mobilier of America,* New York, 1969.
Devol, George H., *Forty Years a Gambler on the Mississippi,* New York, 1968.
Dunbar, Seymour, *A History of Travel in America,* 4 vols., Indianapolis, 1915.
Earle, Alice M., *Stage Coach and Tavern Days,* New York, 1900.
Epstein, Ralph, *The Automobile Industry,* Chicago, 1928.
Esarey, Logan, "Internal Improvements in Early Indiana," *Indiana Historical Society Publications,* V, 1912.
Fowle, Otto, *Saulte Ste. Marie and Its Great Waterway,* New York, 1925.
Gates, Paul W., *The Illinois Central Railroad and its Colonization Work,* Cambridge, 1934.
Goodrich, Carter, *Government Promotion of American Canals and Railroads, 1800-1890,* New York, 1960.
———, and Others, *Canals and American Economic Development,* New York, 1961.
Grinling, Charles H., *The History of the Great Northern Railway, 1845-1922,* New York, 1966.
Haites, Eric F., and Mak, James, *"Ohio and Mississippi River Transportation 1810-1860," Explorations in Economic History,* VIII, Winter, 1970-1971.
Harlow, Alvin F., *Old Towpaths,* New York, 1926.
Hartsough, Mildred L., *From Canoe to Steel Barge,* Minneapolis, 1934.
Hatcher, Harlan, *A Century of Iron and Men,* Indianapolis, 1950.
Havighurst, Walter, *The Long Ships Passing: The Story of the Great Lakes,* New York, 1942.
Hedges, James B., *Henry Villard and the Railways of the Northwest,* New York, 1930.
Holbrook, Stewart H., *The Story of American Railroads,* New York, 1947.
Hulbert, Archer B., *The Cumberland Road,* Cleveland, 1904.
———, *The Great American Canals,* Cleveland, 1904.
———, *Historic Highways of America,* 12 vols., Cleveland, 1902.
———, *The Paths of Inland Commerce,* New Haven, 1920.
———, *Waterways of Western Expansion,* Cleveland, 1903.
Hunter, Louis C., *Steamboats on the Western Rivers,* Cambridge, 1949.
Jackson, William T., *Wagon Roads West,* New Haven, 1965.
Jordan, Philip D., *The National Road,* New York, 1948.
Kennan, George, *E. H. Harriman,* 2 vols., Boston, 1922.
Krenkel, John H., *Illinois Internal Improvements, 1818-1848,* Cedar Rapids, Iowa, 1958.

Lass, William E., *A History of Steamboating on the Upper Missouri River,* Lincoln, 1962.
Lewis, Oscar, *The Big Four: The Story of Huntington, Stanford, Hopkins, and Crocker, and of the Building of the Central Pacific,* New York, 1938.
McCague, James, *Moguls and Iron Men: The Story of the First Transcontinental Railroad,* New York, 1964.
McClelland, Cloys P., *History of the Ohio Canals, Their Construction, Cost, Use, and Partial Abandonment,* Columbus, 1905.
MacGill, Caroline E., and Others, *History of Transportation in the United States before 1860,* Washington, 1917.
MacDonald, Thomas H., *History and Development of Road Building in the United States,* Washington, 1926.
Meyer, Balthasar H., ed., *History of Transportation in the United States before 1860,* Washington, 1917.
Miller, George H., *Railroads and the Granger Laws,* Madison, 1970.
Moody, John, *The Railroad Builders,* New Haven, 1919.
Nevins, Allan, *Ford: The Times, The Man, The Company,* New York, 1954.
Ormsby, Waterman L., *The Butterfield Overland Mail,* San Marino, 1962.
Overton, Richard C., *Burlington Route: A History of the Burlington Lines,* New York, 1965.
Parsons, Coleman O., "Steamboating as Seen by Passengers and River Men: 1875-1884," *Mississippi Quarterly,* XXIV, Winter, 1970-1971.
Peterson, William J., *Steamboating on the Upper Mississippi,* Iowa City, 1968.
Pyle, Joseph G., *The Life of James J. Hill,* 2 vols., Garden City, 1917.
Rae, John B., *American Automobile Manufacturers,* Philadelphia, 1959.
———, *Henry Ford,* Cambridge, 1969.
Reizenstein, Milton, *The Baltimore and Ohio Railroad,* Baltimore, 1897.
Riegel, Robert E., *The Story of the Western Railroads,* New York, 1964.
Russell, Robert R., "A Revaluation of the Period Before the Civil War: Railroads," *Mississippi Valley Historical Review,* XV, December, 1928.
Settle, Raymond W. and Mary L., *Empire on Wheels,* Stanford, 1949.
———, *Saddles and Spurs: The Pony Express Saga,* Harrisburg, 1955.
———, *War Drums and Wagon Wheels,* San Francisco, 1961.
Smalley, Eugene V., *History of the Northern Pacific Railroad,* New York, 1883.
Starr, John W., *One Hundred Years of Railroading,* New York, 1928.
Stover, John F., *American Railroads,* Chicago, 1961.
Sward, Keith, *The Legend of Henry Ford,* New York, 1948.
Taylor, George R., *Transportation Revolution, 1815-1860,* New York, 1951.
Thompson, Slason, *A Short History of American Railways,* New York, 1925.
Thwaites, Reuben G., ed., *Early Western Travels, 1748-1846,* 32 vols., Cleveland, 1904-1907.
Van Orman, Richard A., *A Room for the Night: Hotels of the Old West,* Bloomington, Indiana, 1966.
Waggoner, Madeline S., *The Long Hand West: The Great Canal Era, 1817-1850,* New York, 1958.
Walker, Henry P., *The Wagonmasters: High Plains Freighting from the Earliest Days of the Santa Fe Trail to 1880,* Norman, 1966.
Weber, Thomas, *The Northern Railroads in the Civil War,* New York, 1952.
Wilcox, Frank N., *The Ohio Canals,* Kent, Ohio, 1969.
Winther, Oscar O., *The Transportation Frontier: Trans-Mississippi West, 1865-1890,* New York, 1964.
———, *Via Western Express and Stagecoach,* Lincoln, 1968.
Yoder, Paton, *Taverns and Travellers: Inns of the Early Midwest,* Bloomington, Indiana, 1969.

Wars and Foreign Affairs

Abzug, Robert H., "The Copperheads: Historical Approaches to Civil War Dissent in the Midwest," *Indiana Magazine of History,* LXVI, March, 1970.
Adler, Selig, *The Isolationist Impulse,* New York, 1957.
———, *The Uncertain Giant,* New York, 1966.
Bailey, Thomas A., *A Diplomatic History of the American People,* New York, 1964.

Bass, Herbert J., ed., *America's Entry into World War I: Submarines, Sentiment, or Security,* New York, 1964.
Beale, Howard K., *Theodore Roosevelt and the Rise of America to World Power,* Baltimore, 1956.
Beisner, Robert L., *Twelve Against Empire,* New York, 1968.
Bemis, Samuel F., *Jay's Treaty: A Study in Commerce and Diplomacy,* New York, 1962.
———, *Pinckney's Treaty: America's Advantage from Europe's Distress,* New Haven, 1960.
——— and Ferrell, Robert H., eds., *American Secretaries of State and Their Diplomacy,* 17 vols., New York, 1929-1967.
Bishop, Albert W., *Loyalty on the Frontier,* St. Louis, 1863.
Boyd, Thomas A., *Mad Anthony Wayne,* New York, 1929.
Brooks, Nathan C., *Complete History of the Mexican War,* Chicago, 1965.
Burt, Alfred L., *The United States, Great Britian, and British North America,* New York, 1940.
Carleton, William G., "Isolationism and the Middle West," *Mississippi Valley Historical Review,* XXXIII, December, 1946.
Castel, Albert, *William Clarke Quantrill: His Life and Times,* New York, 1962.
Catton, Bruce, *U. S. Grant and the American Military Tradition,* Boston, 1954.
Clarke, Dwight L., *Stephen Watts Kearny: Soldier of the West,* Norman, 1961.
Cole, Wayne S., *Senator Gerald P. Nye and American Foreign Relations,* Minneapolis, 1962.
Coles, Harry C., *The War of 1812,* Chicago, 1965.
Colton, Ray C., *The Civil War in the Western Territories,* Norman, 1959.
Commager, Henry S., *The Blue and the Gray: The Story of the Civil War as Told by Participants,* 2 vols., Indianapolis, 1950.
Coolidge, Louis A., *Ulysses S. Grant,* Boston, 1922.
Craven, Avery, *The Coming of the Civil War,* New York, 1942.
Cummins, Cedric C., *Indiana Public Opinion and the World War, 1914-1917,* Indianapolis, 1945.
Davis, Kenneth S., *Experience of War: The United States in World War II,* Garden City, 1965.
Dennett, Tyler, *John Hay: From Poetry to Politics,* New York, 1934.
Divine, Robert A., *The Illusion of Neutrality,* Chicago, 1962.
———, *The Reluctant Belligerent: American Entry into World War II,* New York, 1965.
Dulles, Foster R., *America's Rise to World Power, 1898-1954,* New York, 1954.
Ellis, Lewis E., *Frank B. Kellogg and American Foreign Relations, 1925-1929,* New Brunswick, 1961.
Gates, Charles M., "The West in American Diplomacy, 1812-1815," *Mississippi Valley Historical Review,* XXVI, March, 1940.
Gilpin, Alec R., *The War of 1812 in the Old Northwest,* East Lansing, 1958.
Goodman, Warren H., "The Origins of the War of 1812: A Survey of Changing Interpretations," *Mississippi Valley Historical Review,* XXVIII, September, 1941.
Graebner, Norman A., ed., *An Uncertain Tradition: American Secretaries of State in the Twentieth Century,* New York, 1961.
Hassler, Warren W., Jr., *General George B. McClellan: Shield of the Union,* Baton Rouge, 1957.
Hemphill, W. Edwin, "The Jeffersonian Background of the Louisiana Purchase," *Mississippi Valley Historical Review,* XXII, September, 1935.
Hilton, Ora A., *The Minnesota Commission of Public Safety in World War I, 1917-1918,* Stillwater, Oklahoma, 1951.
Hitsman, J. Mackay, *The Incredible War of 1812: A Military History,* Toronto, 1965.
Horsman, Reginald, *The Causes of the War of 1812,* Philadelphia, 1962.
Jones, Evan, *Citadel in the Wilderness: The Story of Fort Snelling and the Old Northwest Frontier,* New York, 1966.
Jones, James P., *"Black Jack" John A. Logan and Southern Illinois in the Civil War Era,* Tallahassee, 1967.
Jones, Robert H., *The Civil War in the Northwest: Nebraska, Wisconsin, Iowa, and the Dakotas,* Norman, 1960.
Klement, Frank L., *The Copperheads in the Middle West,* Chicago, 1960.

———, "Copperhead Secret Societies in Illinois During the Civil War," *Illinois State Historical Society Journal,* XLVIII, 1955.
Leopold, Richard W., "The Mississippi Valley and American Foreign Policy, 1890-1941: An Assessment and an Appeal," *Mississippi Valley Historical Review,* XXXVII, March, 1951.
Lewis, Lloyd, *Captain Sam Grant,* Boston, 1950.
———, *Sherman, Fighting Prophet,* New York, 1932.
Link, Arthur S., "The Middle West and the Coming of World War I," *Ohio Historical Quarterly,* LXII, 1953.
Lyon, Elijah W., *Louisiana in French Diplomacy, 1759-1804,* Norman, 1934.
Mahr, Walter H., *Federal Indian Relations, 1774-1788,* Philadelphia, 1933.
May, Ernest R., *Imperial Democracy: The Emergence of America as a Great Power,* New York, 1961.
———, *The World War and American Isolation, 1914-1917,* Cambridge, 1959.
Merk, Frederick, *Manifest Destiny and Mission in American History,* New York, 1963.
Milton, George F., *The Eve of Conflict: Stephen A. Douglas and the Needless War,* Boston, 1934.
Monaghan, Jay, *Civil War on the Western Border, 1854-1865,* Boston, 1955.
Morgan, Howard W., *America's Road to Empire,* New York, 1965.
Nevins, Allan, *Ordeal of the Union,* 2 vols., New York, 1947.
Nichols, Jeanette P., "The Middle West and the Coming of World War II," *Ohio Historical Quarterly,* LXII, 1953.
Ogg, Frederic A., *The Opening of the Mississippi,* New Haven, 1969.
Palmer, Frederick, *John J. Pershing: General of the Armies,* Harrisburg, 1948.
Perkins, Bradford, *The Causes of the War of 1812: National Honor or National Interest,* New York, 1962.
———, *Prologue to War: England and the United States, 1805-1812,* Berkeley, 1961.
Powell, Horace B., *The Original Has This Signature—W. K. Kellogg,* New York, 1956.
Pratt, Julius W., *Expansionists of 1812,* New York, 1926.
Prucha, Francis P., *Broadax and Bayonet: The Role of the United States Army in the Development of the Northwest, 1815-1860,* Madison, 1953.
———, *The Sword of the Republic: The United States Army on the Frontier, 1783-1846,* New York, 1969.
Sherman, William T., *The Sherman Letters,* New York, 1969.
Smith, Daniel M., ed., *American Intervention, 1917: Sentiment, Self-Interest, or Ideals,* Boston, 1966.
Smith, Justin H., *The War with Mexico,* 2 vols., New York, 1919.
Smith, William, *Expedition Against the Ohio Indians,* Ann Arbor, 1966.
Stanwood, Edward, *American Tariff Controversies in the Nineteenth Century,* 2 vols., Boston, 1903.
Tarbell, Ida M., *Owen D. Young,* New York, 1932.
Taussig, Frank W., *Tariff History of the United States,* New York, 1931.
Taylor, Foster J., *The United States and the Spanish Civil War, 1936-1939,* New York, 1956.
Tompkins, C. David, *Senator Arthur H. Vandenburg: The Evolution of a Modern Republican, 1884-1945,* East Lansing, 1970.
Updike, Frank A., *The Deplomacy of the War of 1812,* Baltimore, 1915.
Van Alstyne, Richard W., "The Significance of the Mississippi Valley in American Diplomatic History, 1686-1890," *Mississippi Valley Historical Review,* XXXVI, September, 1949.
Vandenberg, Arthur H., Jr., *The Private Papers of Senator Vandenberg,* Boston, 1952.
Vernant, Jacques, *The Refugees in the Post War World,* New Haven, 1953.
Weinberg, Albert K., *Manifest Destiny: A Study of Nationalist Expansionism in American History,* Gloucester, Massachusetts, 1958.
Werstein, Irving, *Kearny the Magnificent: The Story of General Phillip Kearny, 1815-1862,* New York, 1962.
West, Richard S., *Gideon Welles, Lincoln's Navy Department,* Indianapolis, 1943.
Wheeler, Kenneth W., *For the Union: Ohio Leaders in the Civil War,* Columbus, 1968.
Whitaker, Authur P., *The Mississippi Question, 1795-1803: A Study in Trade, Politics and Diplomacy,* New York, 1934.
White, Patrick C., *A Nation on Trial: America and the War of 1812,* New York, 1965.

Wildes, Harry E., *Anthony Wayne: Trouble Shooter of the American Revolution,* New York, 1941.
Wiley, Bell I., *Life of Billy Yank, Common Soldier of Union,* Indianapolis, 1952.
Williams, Kenneth P., *Lincoln Finds a General,* 5 vols., New York, 1949-1959.
Williams, Thomas H., *McClellan, Sherman, and Grant,* New Brunswick, 1962.
Wiltz, John E., *From Isolation to War, 1931-1941,* New York, 1968.

INDEX